THE WRITER'S DIGEST

# Dictionary
## OF
# Concise
# Writing

THE WRITER'S DIGEST

# Dictionary
## OF
# Concise
# Writing

ROBERT HARTWELL FISKE

**WRITER'S DIGEST BOOKS**
Cincinnati, Ohio

**The Writer's Digest Dictionary of Concise Writing.** Copyright © 1996 by Robert Hartwell Fiske. Printed and bound in the United States of America. All rights reserved. No part of this book may be reproduced in any form or by any electronic or mechanical means including information storage and retrieval systems without permission in writing from the publisher, except by a reviewer, who may quote brief passages in a review. Published by Writer's Digest Books, an imprint of F&W Publications, Inc., 1507 Dana Avenue, Cincinnati, Ohio 45207. (800) 289-0963. Second edition.

This hardcover edition of *The Writer's Digest Dictionary of Concise Writing* features a "self-jacket" that eliminates the need for a separate dust jacket. It provides sturdy protection for your book while it saves paper, trees and energy.

Other fine Writer's Digest Books are available from your local bookstore or direct from the publisher.

00   99   98   97   96      5   4   3   2   1

Library of Congress Cataloging-in-Publication Data

Fiske, Robert Hartwell.
  [Guide to concise writing]
  The Writer's Digest dictionary of concise writing / by Robert Hartwell Fiske
      p.     cm.
  Previously published as: Guide to concise writing—Webster's New World, 1990.
    ISBN 0-89879-755-1 (alk. paper)
    1. English language—Rhetoric—Dictionaries.   2. English language—Usage—Dictionaries.   I. Title.
PE1460.F47   1996
428'.003—dc20                                                96-6788
                                                              CIP

Edited by Jack Heffron and Roseann S. Biederman
Designed by Angela Lennert Wilcox

*POLONIUS: What do you read, my lord?*
*HAMLET: Words, words, words.*

William Shakespeare, *Hamlet,* act 2, scene 2

*A barren superfluity of words.*

Sir Samuel Garth, *The Dispensary*, canto II

# About This Book

This is a reference book and, like all such books, is meant to be referred to, not read through. Although I've long thought works of reference, dictionaries in particular, to be among the most spellbinding books, I cannot expect everyone to agree.

I do wish, as any writer would, that this were a work of creation instead of compilation; still, whether you refer to or read through the book, it will help you write and speak more clearly.

*The Writer's Digest Dictionary of Concise Writing* consists of two parts. In the first part, I suggest how to identify and correct wordiness. The second part of the book is a compilation of several thousand wordy phrases followed by concise alternative expressions and real-world examples. I show each sentence example in its original, wordy version and then in a revised, concise version.

In replacing a wordy phrase by one less wordy or by a single word or in deleting the phrase altogether, I have tried to show how wordiness can encumber clarity and that it can be corrected. The sentence examples have been edited only to remedy the wordiness diagnosed; rarely are they syntactically and stylistically indefectible.

I don't claim that the entries I've compiled are unfailingly inferior to the alternatives I suggest. All the alternatives are merely proposed; they are not inarguable. In your own writing, you may at times find that an alternative suggested here, though less wordy, does not work so well.

Finally, as sole author of this book, I am solely accountable for any errors or, if I may be so charitable, oversights that these pages may hold. Although I have tried to be as thorough as possible and to include as many entries, and alternatives to them, as time would allow, I don't doubt that I have overlooked some. Anyone who finds an error or omission is welcome to share his discovery with me, and in a revised edition, I will gladly include any correction.

Robert Hartwell Fiske
Vocabula Communications Company
P.O. Box 611
Andover, Massachusetts 01810

# Table of Contents

# Part I

# Chapter One

# The Perfectibility of Words

W ords are flawed, but they can easily be fixed. Words exist to be thought and then formed, to be written and then revised, and even to be said and then denied. They can be misused and neglected or cared for and corrected.

Inadequate though they may be, words distinguish us from all other living things. Only we humans can reflect on the past and plan for the future; it is language that allows us to do so. Indeed, our worth is partly in our words. Effective use of language—clear writing and speaking—is a measure of our humanness.

When they do their work best, words help people communicate; they promote understanding between people. And this, being well understood, is precisely the goal we should all aspire to when writing and speaking. As obvious as this seems, it is not a goal we commonly achieve.

Words often ill serve their purpose. When they do their work badly, words militate against us. Poor grammar, sloppy syntax, abused words, misspelled words, and other infelicities of style impede communication and advance only misunderstanding. But there is another, perhaps less well-known, obstacle to effective communication: too many words.

We often believe that many words are better than few. Perhaps we imagine that the more we say, the more we know or the more others will think we know, or that the more obscure our writing is, the more profound our thoughts are. Seldom, of course, is this so. Wordiness is arguably the biggest obstacle to clear writing and speaking. But it is also more than that.

- *Wordiness is an obstacle to success.* Almost all professional people know that success in business partly depends on good communications skills, on writing and speaking clearly and persuasively. Businesspeople who cannot express themselves well are often at a disadvantage in the corporate world.

- *Wordiness is an obstacle to companionship.* Few of us enjoy being with someone who speaks incessantly or incoherently. Wordiness in others may make us impatient; it may annoy us, and we may think it rude. Worse than that, when we have difficulty understanding someone, sooner or later we may not care what it is that he tries to convey. We lose interest in what a person says and, ultimately, in who a person is.

- *Wordiness is an obstacle to self-knowledge.* A superfluity of words conceals more than it reveals. We need time to be silent and still, time to reflect on the past and think about the future; without it, no one is knowable.

Wordiness is an obstacle to these goals and others. Whatever your profession, whatever your personality, wordiness is a condition for which we all should seek a cure.

## OF POLISH AND PANACHE

Usually, in reading someone's writing, we see more words than we need to, and in listening to someone speak, we hear more words than we care to. For example, how often have you heard someone say *at this juncture* or, worse still, *at this moment in the history of my life* when a simple *now* would serve? These two phrases are flawed; they are two and eight words longer than they need be. The extra words are not needed to convey the thought; in truth, they interfere with the conveyance of thought.

These are but two of the wordy phrases that we overindulge in when writing and speaking. Though it may be hard to fathom, the English language contains thousands of wordy phrases that dull our understanding of and interest in whatever is being expressed.

Wordiness is a flaw of style—in how we express our language. Today, the style is prevailingly shoddy. In almost everything we read and hear, there is complexity instead of simplicity and obscurity instead of clarity. This is particularly inexcusable in written material, where words can be reworked.

Few of us write well effortlessly. Typically, we have a thought, and then we write it down in whatever form it first occurred to us. Looking at our sentence further, though, we are usually able to improve on it. By reducing the number of words in a phrase, substituting a single word for a phrase, or deleting extraneous words or phrases, we are able to polish our sentence, to simplify and clarify our thought.

Reducing the number of words in a phrase

- The real test, however, lies in *the degree to which* the man's performance at his regular job improves.

  The real test, however, lies in *how much* the man's performance at his regular job improves.

- *Insofar as* the implementation of bank projects *is concerned,* the situation is going back to normal.

  *As for* the implementation of bank projects, the situation is going back to normal.

- There is no *evidence to support that* those new mortgages are any more likely to default than those insured by F.H.A. under current law.

  There is no *evidence that* those new mortgages are any more likely to default than those insured by F.H.A. under current law.

- The MWRA's decision will allow it to *concentrate its energies on* rebuilding the region's water and sewer systems.

  The MWRA's decision will allow it to *concentrate on* rebuilding the region's water and sewer systems.

Substituting a single word for a phrase

- The practice *is in violation of* perjury laws requiring candidates to attest that every signature was signed in person.

  The practice *violates* perjury laws requiring candidates to attest that every signature was signed in person.

- *Despite the fact that* Hanson PLC has revenues of over $12 billion, its corporate staff is exceedingly lean.

  *Although* Hanson PLC has revenues of over $12 billion, its corporate staff is exceedingly lean.

- I think *to a large extent* this kind of problem is a function of our society's inability to talk about sexuality in a reasonable way.

  I think this kind of problem is *largely* a function of our society's inability to talk about sexuality in a reasonable way.

- We're talking about a sport's anchor who stands to make *in the neighborhood of* a half million bucks a year.

  We're talking about a sport's anchor who stands to make *around* a half million bucks a year.

Deleting extraneous words or phrases

- The more sophisticated savings institutions were *located* in places like Boston, New York, and Los Angeles.

  The more sophisticated savings institutions were in places like Boston, New York, and Los Angeles.

- He or she must develop strategies to resolve potentially disruptive or dysfunctional conflict *situations*.

  He or she must develop strategies to resolve potentially disruptive or dysfunctional conflicts.

- The Japanese government is not supplying much *in the way of* guidance concerning comparative advantages involved in investments in particular countries.

  The Japanese government is not supplying much guidance concerning comparative advantages involved in investments in particular countries.

- *There are* a large number of applications *that* involve manipulating uncertain knowledge.

  A large number of applications involve manipulating uncertain knowledge.

A further benefit of applying some polish, of expressing ourselves more concisely, is that mistakes in grammar and word usage often are corrected as well. For example, we *compare* one person or thing *to* or *with* another, not *against* or *versus* another. The correct phrase is *compare to* or *compare with*, not *compare against* or *compare versus; to* and *with* both have one syllable fewer than *against* and *versus.* Fewer syllables count; life is short.

- The investigators will analyze the new data and *compare* them *against* computer models in an effort to link unequivocally the Arctic's perturbed chemistry to its ozone loss.

  The investigators will analyze the new data and *compare* them *with* computer models in an effort to link unequivocally the Arctic's perturbed chemistry to its ozone loss.

Likewise, the correct expression is *center on,* not *center around.*

- Much of their behavior *centers around* doing things to please others in an attempt to earn approval.

  Much of their behavior *centers on* doing things to please others in an attempt to earn approval.

And the analphabetic *that way there* and *this way here* are correct only without the *there* and *here.*

- *That way there,* I won't have to worry about someone hitting my car.

  *That way,* I won't have to worry about someone hitting my car.

But there are more telling examples.
Say *the reason is* or simply *because* instead of *the reason is because,* and you are at once concise and correct.

- A common *reason* people join groups *is because* they work near one another.

  A common *reason* people join groups *is* they work near one another.

- *The reason* you explore what-ifs sequentially *is because* few solutions to business problems can be achieved by making a single change.

  You explore what-ifs sequentially *because* few solutions to business problems can be achieved by making a single change.

The familiar *but rather* or *but instead* is also solecistic. Use *but* or *rather* or *instead,* for each alone does the job.

- It was not lack of sales that led to the downsizing of the project *but rather* the delays caused by a turnover of contractors.

  It was not lack of sales that led to the downsizing of the project *but* the delays caused by a turnover of contractors.

- Ericsson has not reduced its investments in the data processing field, *but* it has, *instead,* obtained greater resources with which to further develop and strengthen the advanced DP technology that constitutes its communications systems.

  Ericsson has not reduced its investments in the data processing field; *instead,* it has obtained greater resources with which to further develop and strengthen the advanced DP technology that constitutes its communications systems.

One final example is using *for example, for instance, like,* or *such as* along with *and others, and so forth, and so on, and such, and the like, et al.,* or *etc.* You don't need both sets of expressions to convey your meaning; use one or the other.

- These codes are used to change formats, *for example,* fonts, printer colors, *etc.*

  These codes are used to change formats, *for example,* fonts and printer colors.

- We have to give it the serious attention that we give illicit drugs *such as* heroin, cocaine, *and so on.*

We have to give it the serious attention that we give illicit drugs—heroin, cocaine, *and so on.*

I grumble about grammar because mistakes in it invariably vitiate one's style of writing and, like wordiness, often arrest the reader's flow of thought.

A good writing style starts with polish, but it does not stop with it. Style must also have presence and personality. Along with polish, then, a writing style would be a good deal improved by panache, which is as creative as polish is corrective. Panache means writing with variety as well as with balance, writing heedful of sound as well as of sense, and writing interestingly as well as enthusiastically. All this is panache, and it is far more than this.

With a dollop of polish and a dash of panache, our words will approach perfection.

## CLUES TO CONCISION

There are several clues to realizing a clear and concise writing style. By being vigilant, that is, by rereading and rewriting your material, you will become increasingly adept at identifying superfluous words.

Further, the more words you know and have at your command, the more concise you can be. You will repeatedly discover, in the definition of one word, two or three others that you may have faithfully relied on to express a thought. For example, *like* means *in the same way that, never* means *under no conditions, halve* means *cut in half, share* means *have in common, with* means *in the company of,* and *cynosure* means *center of attention.* By becoming well acquainted with the meanings of words, you will see that a single word often says as much as a string of words.

The key is to question. Ask yourself whether each word in every sentence that you write is needed. More than that, is it vital? Does it contribute to or interfere with the meaning of your sentence? Does it add anything to your meaning that another, perhaps adjacent, word does not?

Eventually, this constant questioning becomes second nature. Not only will you start writing better, you will start speaking better. As you question, be especially aware of phrases containing prepositions, verbs, and nouns and of extraneous adjectives and adverbs. Euphemisms, circumlocutions, clichés, idioms, and polysyllables are also frequent offenders.

### Preposition Phrases

All preposition phrases are suspect, particularly those longer than two words. A preposition phrase usually can be reduced to a single word or deleted altogether. We depend on these three- and four-word preposition phrases because we are unfamiliar with the meanings of so many one-word prepositions.

Consider a few examples.

> *Over the duration of* the project, we expect there will be some disruption due to noise, dirt, and dust.

*Over the duration of* is one of those four-word preposition phrases; it is an excrescence. *During* is all that is needed.

> As a result of last year's ONA process, a host of new network services will become available to providers of enhanced services *in the very near future.*

*In the very near future* is certainly a murky preposition phrase. Far better is the more clear *soon* or *shortly.*

> I think it is premature to relinquish our destiny to the hands of fate, for indeed much progress has been made *in the past,* and much more is still possible *in the future.*

*In the past,* like *in the future,* is often needlessly used. The context of the sentence usually makes the tense clear.

> We have used the MSE and the RMSE *for the purpose of* measuring how much fluctuation remains after a model has been built.

*For the purpose of -ing* is unpardonably wordy. Use the simpler *to.*

> *In the event that* you are not sure whether a particular problem is an emergency, we encourage you to call the Plan for advice.

*In the event that* usually can be reduced to *if* or *should.*

> We should be moving *in the direction of* finding psychotherapeutic measures to help correct this sexual disorder whenever the patient wishes it to be corrected.

*In the direction of* means *toward* in this sentence though the phrase also can mean a monosyllabic *on, to,* or *with.*

> You can even set these switches *in such a way that* the RAM area can be read from but not written to.

*In such a way that* is a long-winded way of saying *so* or *so that.*

> There are a number of theories *as to* how firm value is affected by a firm's capital structure design.

*As to,* like *as regards, in relation to, with reference to,* and other equally dull devices, usually means an unadorned *about, for, in, of,* or *on.*

### Verb Phrases

Many verb phrases are redundant. In these phrases, two words (generally, a verb followed by a noun) do the work of one (the noun made into a verb).

Consider the following examples.

*to arrive at, to come to,* and *to reach* phrases

- Space probers are reluctantly *reaching the conclusion* that there is little likelihood that intelligent life is out there in the empty spaces beyond our solar system.

  Space probers are reluctantly *concluding* that there is little likelihood that intelligent life is out there in the empty spaces beyond our solar system.

- Several economists predict that the expansion will *come to an end* in what is now its seventh year.

  Several economists predict that the expansion will *end* in what is now its seventh year.

*to be* phrases

- He *is lacking in* sensitivity.

  He *lacks* sensitivity.

- Unlike computers, which depended on the Cold War and the space race for the funds that drove their development, U.S. biotech *is dependent on* the flow of various health-care payment streams.

  Unlike computers, which depended on the Cold War and the space race for the funds that drove their development, U.S. biotech *depends on* the flow of various health-care payment streams.

*to express* and *to voice* phrases

- In one letter, dated June 15, 1892, Cather *expresses regret* that friendships between women are looked upon as unnatural.

  In one letter, dated June 15, 1892, Cather *regrets* that friendships between women are looked upon as unnatural.

- The government of Israel *voiced disapproval of* the decision.

  The government of Israel *disapproved of* the decision.

*to give* phrases

- The rest of the equation is to give people from diverse backgrounds a chance *to give expression to* their different views of the world.

  The rest of the equation is to give people from diverse backgrounds a chance *to express* their different views of the world.

- The continuing strong demand for our products and improving trends in component costs *give us encouragement* that this will be another year of significant growth in revenues and earnings.

  The continuing strong demand for our products and improving trends in component costs *encourage us* that this will be another year of significant growth in revenues and earnings.

*to have* phrases

- This measure *has the appearance of* reasonableness, but its application would have to be monitored to make sure it did not induce high turnovers by employers to cut labor costs.

This measure *appears* reasonable, but its application would have to be monitored to make sure it did not induce high turnovers by employers to cut labor costs.

- Any disruption of normal computer operations may *have a considerable impact on* the running of the business.

  Any disruption of normal computer operations may *considerably affect* the running of the business.

*to make* phrases

- The code is moved into place by *making use of* the system Monitor block move subroutine, MOVE.

  The code is moved into place by *using* the system Monitor block move subroutine, MOVE.

- The column does not *make a distinction* between having chronic pain as a symptom and being a "chronic pain patient," that is, having a chronic pain syndrome.

  The column does not *distinguish* between having chronic pain as a symptom and being a "chronic pain patient," that is, having a chronic pain syndrome.

*to place* and *to put* phrases

- As a result, the women's groups now *put heavy emphasis on* fielding candidates for open seats and on identifying incumbents who might be vulnerable.

  As a result, the women's groups now *heavily emphasize* fielding candidates for open seats and identifying incumbents who might be vulnerable.

- Excess supply within the next few years would *place pressure on* the cartel to maintain production restraint and keep average prices low.

Excess supply within the next few years would *pressure* the cartel to maintain production restraint and keep average prices low.

*to present, to provide,* and *to show* phrases

- The final section of the chapter *provides an explanation of* how to use most of MathCAD's more popular features.

  The final section of the chapter *explains* how to use most of Math-CAD's more popular features.

- The middle third of the screen *shows a listing of* the jobs waiting to be printed.

  The middle third of the screen *lists* the jobs waiting to be printed.

*to take* phrases

- I would like *to take this opportunity* to thank all of you who aided my candidacy.

  I would like to thank all of you who aided my candidacy.

- Their forecasts are best prepared when they *take* the functional area forecasts *into consideration.*

  Their forecasts are best prepared when they *consider* the functional area forecasts.

**Noun Phrases**

These are flaccid phrases that often begin with *a* or *the* followed by a noun and end with *of.* They can easily be made firm, as the following examples show.

*(a; the) -ance of* and *(a; the) -ence of* phrases

- *Maintenance of* this flow is assured by their willingness to rubber-stamp the decisions of their benefactor.

*Maintaining* this flow is assured by their willingness to rubber-stamp the decisions of their benefactor.

- When a number of investment proposals perform essentially the same function so that *the acceptance of* one proposal necessarily means rejecting the others, we are dealing with mutually exclusive investments.

  When a number of investment proposals perform essentially the same function so that *accepting* one proposal necessarily means rejecting the others, we are dealing with mutually exclusive investments.

*(a; the) -sion of* and *(a; the) -tion of* phrases

- *The inclusion of* families is crucial if nurses are to become a source of help rather than an addition to families' difficulties.

  *Including* families is crucial if nurses are to become a source of help rather than an addition to families' difficulties.

- *The installation* and testing *of* a new product, *the conversion of* user files, and training users are not small matters.

  *Installing* and testing a new product, *converting* user files, and training users are not small matters.

*(a; the) -ment of* phrases

- For more than a decade, Motorola invested in *the development* and marketing *of* cellular systems and phones around the world.

  For more than a decade, Motorola invested in *developing* and marketing cellular systems and phones around the world.

- To the masses, a good government is one that prevents the strong from exploiting the weak, which is best done by *the punishment of* transgression.

To the masses, a good government is one that prevents the strong from exploiting the weak, which is best done by *punishing* transgression.

*(a; the) -ing of* phrases

- Personal computers were meant to give people more flexibility in *the processing of* information.

  Personal computers were meant to give people more flexibility in *processing* information.

- Organizing at the middle level means *the making of* specific adjustments in the organizational structure and *the allocating of* the resources acquired by top management.

  Organizing at the middle level means *making* specific adjustments in the organizational structure and *allocating* the resources acquired by top management.

*(a; the) . . . of* phrases

- You have to deal with *the issues of* betrayal, anger, rejection—all these things.

  You have to deal with betrayal, anger, rejection—all these things.

- In other situations, *the practice of* rotating managers of work teams on a normal schedule can stimulate a group.

  In other situations, rotating managers of work teams on a normal schedule can stimulate a group.

### Adjectives and Adverbs

By coupling adjectives and adverbs to perfectly good nouns, verbs, or adjectives, we often diminish the force and effectiveness of our writing. Powerful writing is taut; it admits no weak word, no superfluous adjective or adverb.

Consider these examples.

*active; actively*

- Individual managers need to be *actively* involved in the human resource planning process.

  Individual managers need to be involved in the human resource planning process.

- Suicide attempts by hospitalized patients with "do not resuscitate" orders on their medical charts should be met by *active* resuscitation efforts unless recovery is unlikely.

  Suicide attempts by hospitalized patients with "do not resuscitate" orders on their medical charts should be met by resuscitation efforts unless recovery is unlikely.

*actual; actually; real; really*

- Ideas are exchanged, but there is no *real* closure or plan of action.

  Ideas are exchanged, but there is no closure or plan of action.

- My sense is that there is some interest, though it's too early to say how many companies will *actually* submit bids to set up demonstration projects.

  My sense is that there is some interest, though it's too early to say how many companies will submit bids to set up demonstration projects.

*total; totally; whole; wholly*

- I was *totally* overwhelmed by their generosity.

  I was overwhelmed by their generosity.

- The *whole* color-coding idea is perfect for marketing the books.

  The color-coding idea is perfect for marketing the books.

There are other examples: *full potential* says no more than *potential* does alone; *completely eliminate* no more than *eliminate*; *possibly may* no more than *may*; *close scrutiny* no more than *scrutiny*; *excruciatingly painful* no more than *excruciating*; *firm commitment* no more than *commitment*; and *exactly identical* no more than *identical*.

## Other Common Phrases to Watch For

*back* with *refer, repay, return, revert,* and the like

- The second section of the booklet, while occasionally *referring back* to ideas discussed in the first section, is more or less independent.

  The second section of the booklet, while occasionally *referring* to ideas discussed in the first section, is more or less independent.

- Type the new text, and then press Return to *return* the cursor *back* to the left margin.

  Type the new text, and then press Return to *return* the cursor to the left margin.

*mutual* with *and, between, both, two,* and the like

- I think this is *mutually* beneficial to *both* sides.

  I think this is beneficial to *both* sides.

- The receiver must share in these responsibilities if the *two* parties are to arrive at a *mutual* understanding.

  The receiver must share in these responsibilities if the *two* parties are to arrive at an understanding.

*old* with *adage, cliché, maxim, proverb, saying,* and the like

- Children, according to the *old adage,* are to be seen, not heard.

  Children, according to the *adage,* are to be seen, not heard.

- You may have heard the *old saying*, "the best laid plans of mice and men often go astray."

  You may have heard the *saying*, "the best laid plans of mice and men often go astray."

*past*, *previous*, or *prior* with *experience*, *history*, and the like

- From *previous experience*, we know that a compiler will find many typographical errors.

  From *experience*, we know that a compiler will find many typographical errors.

- *Past history* is full of people who didn't fit in and were left as outcasts.

  *History* is full of people who didn't fit in and were left as outcasts.

*record* with *all-time*, *high*, *new*, and the like

- "Knots Landing" has been on for nine years, the *all-time record* among prime-time soaps.

  "Knots Landing" has been on for nine years, the *record* among prime-time soaps.

- The number of days in the 90s in Boston and Washington may set a *record high*.

  The number of days in the 90s in Boston and Washington may set a *record*.

*separate* with *apart*, *distinct*, *entity*, *independent*, and the like

- The public permitting process was *separate and distinct* from the landlord's approval rights under the contract.

  The public permitting process was *separate* from the landlord's approval rights under the contract.

- In the biological world, there are many instances in which the same adaptation has evolved *separately and independently.*

  In the biological world, there are many instances in which the same adaptation has evolved *independently.*

*together* with *combine, group, join, link,* and the like

- Its many parts are *linked together* by computers and can respond to changing needs more quickly than their aging counterparts.

  Its many parts are *linked* by computers and can respond to changing needs more quickly than their aging counterparts.

- We're thousands of Americans who have *joined together* to lower our cost of living and live better on the money we earn.

  We're thousands of Americans who have *joined* to lower our cost of living and live better on the money we earn.

## Euphemisms

Euphemisms are inoffensive or tasteful words and phrases that we use in place of offensive or distasteful ones. Many well-known euphemisms deal with sex or death, topics long thought too delicate for candor. Other euphemisms, less well known, are expressions of politeness or deception. Euphemisms also mask disagreeable situations. It sounds better, for example, for a company to speak of *downsizing* or, even, *rightsizing* than it does for them to speak of *laying off* or *firing* employees. During wars or dubious governmental policies, euphemisms abound, like *pacification* for *killing, collateral damage* for *bombing,* and *forced landing* for *jet crash.* At other times, euphemisms are less recognizable, but only because we are less watchful.

Consider these euphemisms.

| Instead of | Use |
|---|---|
| advanced in years | old |
| comfort facilities | bathroom |
| correctional facility | prison |
| economic adjustments | price hikes |
| involuntary severance | layoff |

| | |
|---|---|
| loss prevention specialist | security guard |
| no longer with us | dead |
| put to sleep | destroy |
| revenue enhancements | taxes |
| seminal fluid | semen |
| succumb to injuries | die |
| unpleasant arousal | depression |

## Circumlocutions

Circumlocutions are roundabout words and phrases. Often they are simply indirect expressions that say in several words what one or two ably would. Occasionally, however, circumlocutions are used to evade an issue. When people do not want to commit themselves to a cause, or when they do not want to be held accountable for either supporting or not supporting a position, they hedge by using ambiguous words. Circumlocutions may mean something far different from what almost anyone would imagine.

Consider these circumlocutions.

| Instead of | Use |
|---|---|
| a limited number | one |
| an overwhelming majority of | most |
| a significant proportion of | some |
| a sizable percentage of | many |
| in the near future | soon |
| is at variance with | differs from |
| is of the opinion | believes |
| make a statement saying | say |
| on more than one occasion | twenty times |
| over the long term | ultimately |
| to a certain extent | in part |
| to a large degree | largely |

## Clichés

We should never become too attached to a term for fear that it be reduced to a cliché. Once people start using a word or phrase excessively, its meaning is blunted and its usefulness lost. Clichés are words or phrases that no longer effectively express thought or sentiment.

Consider these clichés.

| Instead of | Use |
| --- | --- |
| cautiously optimistic | optimistic |
| consensus of opinion | consensus |
| fear and trembling | dread |
| fly in the face of | defy |
| for all intents and purposes | virtually |
| goes to show | proves |
| in a timely fashion | promptly |
| it is imperative that | must |
| kinder and gentler | humane |
| par for the course | typical |
| sick and tired | annoyed |
| window of opportunity | opportunity |

## Idioms

An idiom is an expression that, on the surface, makes little, if any, sense. An idiom's literal meaning, even if decipherable, is frequently different from its actual meaning. Unlike euphemisms and clichés, which usually should be shunned, many popular idioms have their place in the language. Although idioms often say clearly and cleverly what other words cannot, many are wordy expressions that we can find a more economical phrase or particular word for.

Consider these idioms.

| Instead of | Use |
| --- | --- |
| as a matter of fact | in fact |
| before long | soon |
| day in and day out | every day |
| high and mighty | arrogant |
| in all probability | most likely |
| in a nutshell | briefly |
| in place of | for |
| on the part of | by |
| put on an act | pretend |
| take exception | object |
| take offense to | resent |
| the long and the short | the gist |

## Polysyllables

The more words you know and can correctly use, the wider your knowledge and understanding of the world and of yourself. Still, there are polysyllabic words that we can, without fear of unrefinement, do well without.

Consider these polysyllables.

| Instead of | Use |
| --- | --- |
| effectuate | effect |
| eventuality | event |
| indebtedness | debt |
| individuals | people |
| materialize | happen |
| methodology | method |
| multiplicity | many |
| necessitate | require |
| parameter | limit |
| remunerate | pay |
| stick-to-itiveness | resolve |
| terminate | end |

## Couples

A couple is two words, on either side of *and,* that have but one meaning. We often feel that two words do the job twice as well as one, that in a couple, the second word reinforces the first. In truth, the second word enfeebles the first. The English language contains scores of couples, and most of them should never have met.

Consider these couples.

| Instead of | Use |
| --- | --- |
| aid and abet | aid *or* abet |
| compare and contrast | compare *or* contrast |
| fair and equitable | fair *or* equitable |
| first and foremost | first *or* foremost |
| new and innovative | new *or* innovative |
| null and void | null *or* void |
| one and only | one *or* only |
| peace and quiet | peace *or* quiet |
| pick and choose | pick *or* choose |

plain and simple                plain *or* simple
rules and regulations           rules *or* regulations
various and sundry              various *or* sundry

## Embarrassments

Embarrassments are found more often in speech than in writing. Of course, these expressions are more embarrassing to the listener than the speaker, who were he embarrassed, wouldn't say them. Embarrassments are best abolished.

Consider these embarrassments.

| Instead of | Use |
| --- | --- |
| and everything | *delete* |
| and stuff like that | *delete* |
| anyway | *delete* |
| hopefully | I hope |
| how's it going? | hello |
| humongous | huge |
| I'll tell you | *delete* |
| I mean | *delete* |
| kind of thing | *delete* |
| most definitely | yes |
| or something | *delete* |
| you know? | *delete* |

*Chapter Two*
# The Imperfectibility of People

A s the several thousand entries in "The Dictionary of Concision" suggest, wordiness is a problem—an omnipresent problem. Though a contagion that nearly all of us suffer from, businesspeople, lawyers, politicians, journalists, and academics seem unusually afflicted with wordiness.

## BUSINESS JARGON

In a recent survey, 503 top executives at leading U.S. manufacturing and service firms reported that two-thirds of their entry-level managers and professionals wrote unclearly. Entry level or top level, it seems to matter not.

Consider this diffuse phrasing from the president and CEO of a bank, from whom we should expect a style more stately.

> We've enclosed an informative brochure that includes a map and information on the changes occurring February 17. As you will note, you can continue banking just as you have in the past. There is no action required on your part.

*Informative* and *information* are redundant, *in the past* is superfluous with *as you have,* and *There is no action required on your part* is much inferior to, for example, *You need do nothing.*

From a real-estate professional, we have this unwieldy wording.

> I'm under the impression, due to the fact that I've not heard from the main office, that your application has been accepted.

Had this person written *I believe* instead of *I'm under the impression that* and *since* instead of *due to the fact that,* we might have a bit more confidence in his abilities.

Here is an "explanation" from a credit card company.

The Minimum Payment Due each month shall be reduced by the amounts paid in excess of the Minimum Payment Due during the previous three months which have not already been so applied in determining the Minimum Payment Due in such earlier months, unless you have exceeded your line of credit or have paid the entire New Balance shown on your billing statement.

This language is so laborious to understand that many people simply wouldn't bother to try; they would disregard it. Of course, the purpose of a statement like this is less to lucidly convey a policy than to legally protect the company.

Consider this artful sentence from the chairman and CEO of a well-known consulting firm.

Management, with the participation and concurrence of key professional staff, has determined that we can best serve our shareowners and ourselves by resisting temptation to pursue all of the interesting challenges we are equipped to handle.

This is typical business bombast. It sounds fairly good, and it is meant to (coming as it does from an annual report). But as is often so in business, sound precedes sense. Though phrases like *participation* and *concurrence*, *key professional staff, resisting temptation,* and *all of the interesting challenges we are equipped to handle* may to shareholders sound sweet, the sentence means no more than

We will focus on only some areas of our expertise.

Among the verbose phrases valued by those in the business world are *a high level of, component part, course of action, from the standpoint of, game plan, have an impact on, in a timely fashion, in the not-too-distant future, is in receipt of, plan of action, please be advised that, prioritize, time frame, valuable asset,* and *window of opportunity.*

## LEGALESE

The language of the law is often complicated and unintelligible, but it could be made less so if lawyers would only choose to communicate with laymen in fewer words and syllables.

Neither party to this Agreement nor any persons to whom either party has disclosed the Proprietary Information pursuant to this paragraph shall disclose the Proprietary Information to any persons, or permit any person access to the Proprietary Information, or use the Proprietary Information or permit it to be used, directly or indirectly, for their own account, or for the account of another, or make any copy of the Proprietary Information without the express prior written consent in each instance of the party from whom it originated, with such consent being granted only by an individual with the capacity to authorize copying, except that each party may disclose and grant access to the Proprietary Information to those members of its staff who (a) need such access in order to effectuate the Arrangement and (b) have agreed not to further disclose or allow access to the Proprietary Information, and not to use it or permit it to be used, directly or indirectly, for their own account or for the account of another, but to safeguard the Proprietary Information and treat it as the highly confidential, proprietary and trade secret property of the other party and to use it only to effectuate the Arrangement and only so long as the Arrangement remains in effect.

And that's just one sentence. Here are several shorter, though no less bewildering, illustrations of lawyers' language.

To the best of my knowledge and belief, the above statements of fact are true and accurate.

If the statements are *of fact,* they are *true and accurate,* which itself is redundant.

This Agreement shall inure to the benefit of the Agent's successors and assigns, and it shall be binding upon Author's successors, assigns, executors, administrators, heirs, and legal representatives.

Boilerplate like this invariably contains the grandiloquent *inure to the benefit of;* in piecing together their contracts, lawyers should one day learn that *inure to* says no less.

The trust has agreed that in the event the advisory agreement between the investment adviser and the trust is terminated, or if the affiliation between the investment adviser and its parent company is terminated, the trust will eliminate the name "Allstate" from its name if the investment adviser or its parent company so request.

26

Legal phraseology frequently is exposed for what it truly is by those who write it. Here the phrase *in the event* on the first line means simply *if*, as the *if* on the second line makes plain.

Lawyers, too, have their preferred wording: *compensate, effectuate, expeditiously, in accordance with, in consideration of, in force and effect, in perpetuity, in the absence of, necessitate, notwithstanding, pursuant to, subsequent to*, and *until such time as*.

## POLITICAL CANT

In a poll of 1,513 adults, 70 percent of the respondents considered politicians "not so good" or "poor." The prevailing view was that most politicians make campaign promises they do not intend to fulfill, will lie if the truth would hurt them politically, and are mainly concerned with holding on to power.

Indeed, it is often in the interest of politicians and government officials to conceal their true thoughts from us. Consider this prize display of evasiveness by a political aide to a city mayor.

> I confirm that I said it, but I will neither confirm nor deny that I meant it.

Of saying as little as possible with as many words as possible, this phrasing by a high-ranking military official is paradigmatic.

> We will benefit from the experience that we've already had about how to implement that, and learning from the lessons of the past in terms of what we've already done.

Equally unsettling is how politicians are forever devising new expressions or redefining old ones to serve their own interests.

> "*I misspoke*," explained the politico when the committee asked about his stated opinion on abortion.

> **mis • speak**(mis spēk') *vt., vi. -spoke', -spok'en, -speak'ing* to speak or say incorrectly; *to lie.*

The danger here is that the euphemism will become synonymous with the word it is used for. When a word like *misspeak* is used euphemistically for a word like *lie*, we must all loudly complain. Lest euphemisms become synonyms, dictionaries become undone, and minds become mangled, we must all complain.

There are other illustrations of euphemism; for example, the wordy *it remains to be seen* and *that's an open question,* favored by politicians and their ilk, so often truly mean the inadmissible *I don't know.*

Allied to euphemism is circumlocution, another stratagem that politicians depend on.

> The senator, who once was seen as wavering, says he now "is supportive of the president's nominee" for secretary of defense.

The verb phrase *is supportive of* is less binding than the verb *supports* and nicely serves the senator his equivocal purpose. Verb phrases are more wordy than verbs, so it seems as though more is being said, but they are less direct and less meaningful. Deception requires more words than truthfulness.

Consider, too, this ineffectual phrasing by a government bureaucrat.

> It remains my hope and cautiously optimistic expectation that necessary legislation may be enacted prior to October 1.

The phrase *hope and expectation* is redundant, but to qualify *expectation* with *cautiously optimistic* is witless. Moreover, *cautiously optimistic*— one of officialdom's favorite phrases—is oxymoronic. But it is surely the incongruity of the words that so appeals to politicians; juxtaposed, they mean nothing, and politicians generally prefer saying nothing to saying something. Still uneasy with his pronouncement, the bureaucrat further tempers it with the *may* preceding *be enacted.* He might have written his words more capably had he used fewer of them.

> I expect legislation will be enacted before October 1.

## JOURNALESE

If politicians are attached to euphemism and circumlocution, journalists are surely attached to cliché and slang: *bear a striking resemblance to, despite the fact that, express concern, in connection with, in the meantime, in the midst of, in the wake of, on the condition that, on the part of, on the verge of, stand in sharp contrast to,* and *the vast majority of* are a few of their frightful phrases.

Moreover, despite the confines of their columns, newspaper and magazine writers have yet to learn much about using the shorter phrase or the single word.

Oftentimes, the Senate, as well as the White House, struggles with questions involving what is now being described as lifestyle. The problem is that, in effect, the Senate and the White House sometimes are being asked to put their stamp of approval on lifestyles that, while acceptable in Washington, are not acceptable by general standards elsewhere.

If we change *oftentimes* to *often, as well as* to *and, involving what is now being described as* to *of, the Senate and the White House* to *both, put their stamp of approval on* to *approve,* and *by general standards* to *generally* and delete *in effect* and *being,* we lose two lines of text but not a word of meaning.

Often, the Senate and the White House struggle with questions of lifestyle. The problem is that both sometimes are asked to approve lifestyles that, while acceptable in Washington, are not generally acceptable elsewhere.

Journalists furnish their newspapers and magazines with quantities of verbiage. Here, though, are just a few more examples.

Lack of experience on the part of the firm is also a source of delay and difficulty.

*Lack of experience* would be better phrased as *the inexperience,* and *on the part of* as, simply, *of.*

If sea levels rise to the extent that scientists predict, the Marshall Islands, which are composed of two chains of coral islands rising no more than 5 feet above the sea, would be submerged.

A more careful journalist might have written *as much as* instead of *to the extent that,* and *comprise* instead of *are composed of.*

In the course of the debate, legislators complained that the vote was futile, because the governor had the power to freeze spending regardless of what legislators did.

*In the course* of can be replaced by *during,* and *regardless of what* by *despite what.*

> The law created the Occupational Safety and Health Administration, a federal agency charged with the responsibility of ensuring the safety of workers.

The phrase *charged with the responsibility of* is repetitious; either *charged with* or *responsible for* is enough.

## ACADEMICSPEAK

Another area known for its reliance on jargon and gibberish is academia. Academics (especially social scientists, administrators, and self-important students) regularly try to give more prestige to their disciplines, and themselves, by breeding their own vocabularies. The author of a recent book on relationships identifies five levels of commitment.

1. dating—no commitment
2. steady dating—some commitment
3. monogamy—seeing yourselves as a couple
4. monogamy plus—you're a couple and everyone around you knows it
5. living together—you're making plans

*Monogamy plus* (which we might reasonably think a euphemism for bigamy) is one of their misbegotten idioms. Academics create terms like this so that they may explain the obvious to us. We need them to define their terminology. Of course, most of these words we can happily do without. More than just idioms, academics (and those who would have us think they are) tirelessly create their own spurious systems and subsystems. They categorize what the rest of us have long known and don't need to be reminded of.

From a college preparatory school catalog, here is an entertaining, some might say indecorous, description of a course in human sexuality.

> Human sexuality is a required skills course that teaches sexuality topics through the framework of values clarification activities.

I think most parents would like further explanation of *required skills course* and *values clarification activities,* but better yet would be a less ambiguous description.

Disturbingly often, the academics' language belies their intellectual standing. Consider this paragraph from the manuscript of a college text on finance.

> Mutual savings banks have grown steadily, but relatively slowly. A major reason for their relatively slow growth is that they are geographically limited. There are less than 500 of them operating in only 16 states. They primarily are located only in the Northeastern section of the country—with the sole exception of 6 states, and less than 20 mutual savings banks, that operate in the Far West and Midwest.

There's nothing inherently abstruse about the information in this paragraph. It is the wordiness of the writing, the fuzziness of the thinking, that interferes with our understanding.

> Mutual savings banks have grown steadily but slowly. Fewer than 500 of them operate in only 16 states. Except for some 20 mutual savings banks in the Far West and Midwest, they are all in the Northeast.

Finally, here are a few words from a recent college graduate's commencement address.

> I think back to freshman year when my parents called in those first couple of weeks, and in the course of the conversation they asked, "Well, what have you learned so far?" I think they were a little worried when I said I've learned to write a sentence—a short, simple, concise sentence that was to the point.

Well they worry.

# Part II

# The Dictionary of Concision

**about the fact that** *because; for; in that; since; that;* delete. • Management is also concerned about the fact that Walco has not developed brand identification within the market. *Management is also concerned that Walco has not developed brand identification within the market.*

**about (around) . . . to** *about (around); to.* • He works around 10 to 12 hours a day. *He works 10 to 12 hours a day.*

**above and beyond** *above; besides; beyond; more than; over.* • The officers were honored for actions that went above and beyond the call of duty. *The officers were honored for actions that went beyond the call of duty.*

**(after; for; in; over; within) a brief (limited; little; short) amount of time (length of time; period; period of time; span of time; time; while)** *before long; briefly; directly; presently; quickly; shortly; soon; straightaway.* • This anxiety will pass after a short time, and you will then be wondering why you felt it in the first place. *This anxiety will pass quickly, and you will then be wondering why you felt it in the first place.* • It snowed for a brief period of time. *It snowed briefly.* • In a short while, he will be making a speech before the convention delegates. *He will shortly be making a speech before the convention delegates.*

**a (the) broad (extensive; great; vast; wide) array of** *an array of; assorted; broad; countless; different; diverse; extensive; many; numerous; scores of; sundry; untold; varied; various; varying; vast;* delete. • In any domestic market, a wide array of official and unofficial sources provides information about the chosen market segments. *In any domestic market, numerous official and unofficial sources provide information about the chosen market segments.*

**a (the) broad (extensive; great; vast; wide) range of** *a range of; assorted; broad; countless; different; diverse; extensive; many; numerous; scores of; sundry; untold; varied; various; varying; vast;* delete. • A wide range of products is sold by NTIS as subscriptions or standing orders. *Various products are sold by NTIS as subscriptions or standing orders.*

**a (the) broad (extensive; great; vast; wide) spectrum of** *a spectrum of; assorted; broad; countless; different; diverse; extensive; many; numerous; scores of; sundry; untold; varied; various; varying; vast;* delete.

**a (the) broad (extensive; great; vast; wide) variety of** *a variety of; assorted; broad; countless; different; diverse; extensive; many; numerous; scores of; sundry; untold; varied; various; varying; vast;* delete. • A wide variety of templates are available for drawing nuts and bolts. *Various templates are available for drawing nuts and bolts.*

**(an; the) absence of** *dis-; having no; il-; im-; in-; ir-; lacking; -less(ness); mis-; missing; no; non-; not; not any; not having; scant; un-; with no; without.* • I wanted to communicate to young people the absence of purpose and how it felt so senseless and wasteful. *I wanted to communicate to young people the purposelessness and how it felt so senseless and wasteful.*

**absolutely** *at all;* delete. • Rarely am I dissatisfied with purchases of music I know absolutely nothing about. *Rarely am I dissatisfied with purchases of music I know nothing about.*

**absolutely** *yes.*

**absolutely essential (indispensable)** *essential (indispensable).* • I abhor government regulations except where absolutely indispensable. *I abhor government regulations except where indispensable.*

**absolutely not** *by no means; no; not at all.*

**absolutely positively** *absolutely; positively;* delete. • Descartes was an introspective man who probed his meditations for things he could be absolutely, positively sure of. *Descartes was an introspective man who probed his meditations for things he could be absolutely sure of.*

**a case in point** *an (one) example; for example; for instance.* • Teachers in the trades and industry program at Queen Anne's County High School are a case in point. *Teachers in the trades and industry program at Queen Anne's County High School are an example.*

**acclimatize** *acclimate.*

**accommodations** *rooms.*

**accompanied by** *along with; and; as well as; combined with; coupled with; joined with; paired with; together with; with.* • The behavioral implications of this emphasis are an increase in job satisfaction accompanied by a decrease in turnover and absenteeism. *The behavioral implications of this emphasis are an increase in job satisfaction coupled with a decrease in turnover and absenteeism.*

**accomplish** *achieve; do; perform.* • This can be accomplished by assigning consecutive numbers to consecutive periods. *This can be achieved by assigning consecutive numbers to consecutive periods.*

**accordingly** *hence; so; then; therefore; thus.* • Accordingly, the board of directors recommends a vote against this stockholder proposal. *Therefore, the board of directors recommends a vote against this stockholder proposal.*

**according to** *by; following; to; under.*

**according to** *affirm; allege; announce; assert; attest; aver; avow; claim; comment; contend; declare; maintain; note; say; state; suggest; vouch.* • According to various estimates, the measure would translate into a 10-percent trimming of insurance rates next year. *Various estimates suggest the measure would translate into a 10-percent trimming of insurance rates next year.*

**according to plan (projections)** *as planned (projected).* • If everything goes according to plan, five old-fashioned riverboat casinos should begin operating about a year from now on the Mississippi. *If everything goes as planned, five old-fashioned riverboat casinos should begin operating about a year from now on the Mississippi.*

**accumulative** *cumulative.* • The proportions reflect accumulative information as one reads the table from left to right. *The proportions reflect cumulative information as one reads the table from left to right.*

**accustomed to** *inured to; used to.* • I am accustomed to her sinful ways. *I am inured to her sinful ways.*

**a certain amount of** *much; some;* delete. • There's a certain amount of truth to what you say. *There's much truth to what you say.*

**a (the) consequence of** *because of; caused by; due to; owing to; resulting from.* • The increase is almost entirely the consequence of rising economic activity. *The increase is almost entirely caused by rising economic activity.*

**a couple of** *a few; two.*

**a couple three (two; two or three)** *a couple of; a few; two; two or three; three.* • I've known her for a couple two or three years, and never has she said anything like that to me before. *I've known her for a few years, and never has she said anything like that to me before.*

**(all) across (throughout) the country (nation)** *nationwide.*

**(all) across (throughout) the world** *worldwide.*

**act in accord (accordance) with** *act on; comply with; conform to; follow; obey.* • The bankers were responding to a Federal Reserve study that found that they were not acting in accordance with the federal Community Reinvestment Act. *The bankers were responding to a Federal Reserve study that found that they were not complying with the federal Community Reinvestment Act.*

**(a; the) . . . action** delete. • Jailing Danilov was retaliatory action against the seizure of a Soviet agent in the United States. *Jailing Danilov was retaliation against the seizure of a Soviet agent in the United States.* • We are taking steps to revoke the security clearances of individuals who have been involved in illegal actions. *We are taking steps to revoke the security clearances of individuals who have been involved in illegalities.*

**action (attack; battle; game) plan** *course; formula; method; plan; policy; procedure; scheme; strategy.* • The Democratic leadership's action plan is simple: Delay action as long as possible. *The Democratic leadership's strategy is simple: Delay action as long as possible.*

**active (actively)** delete. • They are learning to actively participate in their own decisions. *They are learning to participate in their own decisions.* • To counteract this, the change agent takes an active role in encouraging new solutions and approaches to problems. • *To counteract this, the change agent takes a role in encouraging new solutions and approaches to problems.* • Citibank is actively pursuing private banking in numerous domestic markets around the world. *Citibank is pursuing private banking in numerous domestic markets around the world.*

**. . . activity** delete. • There could be some thunderstorm activity as well. *There could be some thunderstorms as well.* • Unfortunately, countries where counterfeiting activity is widespread are generally not parties to such treaties. *Unfortunately, countries where counterfeiting is widespread are generally not parties to such treaties.*

**actual (actually)** delete.

**add . . . additional (further; more)** *add.* • If I can add any additional information, please do not hesitate to contact me. *If I can add any information, please do not hesitate to contact me.*

**(an) additional** *added; extra; further; more; other.* • It supports all Knowledge-Man/2 capabilities and integrates two additional components. *It supports all KnowledgeMan/2 capabilities and integrates two other components.*

**additionally** *also; and; as well; besides; beyond that (this); even; further; furthermore; moreover; more than that (this); still more; then; too; what is more.* • Additionally, he was an authority on butterflies. *He was also an authority on butterflies.*

**add together** *add.* • Add together the first 31 numbers in the sequence 6, 66, 666, 6666, . . . . *Add the first 31 numbers in the sequence 6, 66, 666, 6666, . . . .*

**a (a certain; some) degree (of)** *a certain; much (of); some (of); somewhat; delete.* • The best results will likely be obtained by firms that exercise some degree of restraint in their offshore activities. *The best results will likely be obtained by firms that exercise some restraint in their offshore activities.* • Each of us has a planning method that works with some degree of effectiveness. *Each of us has a planning method that works somewhat effectively.*

**adequate enough** *adequate; enough.* • As important as these rewards may be, no one would suggest that they are adequate enough to inspire the changes anticipated. *As important as these rewards may be, no one would suggest that they are enough to inspire the changes anticipated.*

**(an; the) adequate number (of)** *enough; five (ninety).* • Performance tasks appear quite feasible in large-scale assessments as well as in classroom use, provided an adequate number of good tasks are available. *Performance tasks appear quite feasible in large-scale assessments as well as in classroom use, provided enough good tasks are available.*

**a (the) diversity of different** *assorted; a variety of; broad; countless; different; diverse; extensive; many; numerous; scores of; sundry; varied; various; varying.* • The diversity of different types of music that the Society now offers would have been unheard of 20 years ago. *The diverse types of music that the Society now offers would have been unheard of 20 years ago.*

**adjacent to** *beside; close to; near; next to.*

**admit to** *admit.* • The General Accounting Office found 16 percent of the employers surveyed admitted to engaging in discriminatory hiring practices.

*The General Accounting Office found 16 percent of the employers surveyed admitted engaging in discriminatory hiring practices.*

**advance ahead (forward; on; onward)** *advance; continue; go on; move on; proceed; progress.*

**advanced (along) in years** *elderly; old; 82 (90).* • She's dating a man who's rather advanced in years. *She's dating a man who's rather old.*

**advance (prior) notice** *notice.* • Congress is in the thick of a new stage of the battle over my proposal to require businesses to give advance notice to workers before plants are closed or major layoffs are ordered. *Congress is in the thick of a new stage of the battle over my proposal to require businesses to give notice to workers before plants are closed or major layoffs are ordered.*

**advance planning (plans)** *planning (plans).* • The overhead projector is a powerful aid for demonstrations and is simple to use with a minimum of advance planning. *The overhead projector is a powerful aid for demonstrations and is simple to use with a minimum of planning.*

**advance preparation** *preparation.* • In a meeting designed to solve problems or make decisions, you should include in your advance preparations a statement of the problem and your recommended solution. *In a meeting designed to solve problems or make decisions, you should include in your preparations a statement of the problem and your recommended solution.*

**advance reservations** *reservations.*

**advance up** *advance.* • As the person's needs are met on one level, the person advances up to the next level of needs. *As the person's needs are met on one level, the person advances to the next level of needs.*

**advance warning** *warning.* • Seismologists generally concur that the science of earthquake prediction is such that a region about to be struck by a major quake would have, at best, only a few days' advance warning. *Seismologists generally concur that the science of earthquake prediction is such that a region about to be struck by a major quake would have, at best, only a few days' warning.*

**a (the) . . . experience** delete. • Just getting up in the morning is a painful experience for her. *Just getting up in the morning is painful for her.*

**a (the) . . . fact** delete. • This is an alarming fact, considering that these workers make up the foundation of our service-sector economy. *This is alarming,* *considering that these workers make up the foundation of our service-sector economy.*

**affiliated with** *belongs to; employed by; works for.*

**affirmative** *yes.* • If the answer is affirmative, selecting an optimal dividend policy is a valid concern. *If the answer is yes, selecting an optimal dividend policy is a valid concern.*

**afford (give; offer; present; provide) . . . (an; the) opportunity** *allow; give . . . (the) chance; let; permit.* • Winning the Boston Marathon provided me with an opportunity to make running my career. *Winning the Boston Marathon allowed me to make running my career.*

**afford with** *afford.*

**after all is said and done** *even so; finally; in the end; still; ultimately; yet;* delete.

**after . . . first** *after.* • Any model relying on deseasonalized data should be built after the modified Census II method of deseasonalization is first applied to the data. *Any model relying on deseasonalized data should be built after the modified Census II method of deseasonalization is applied to the data.*

**after . . . later (subsequently)** *after.* • After you have created and saved a file on the disk, you can retrieve it later for editing. *After you have created and saved a file on the disk, you can retrieve it for editing.*

**after the conclusion (end) of** *after; following.* • And 3.25 million women were pushed or persuaded to leave industrial jobs after the end of World War II. *And 3.25 million women were pushed or persuaded to leave industrial jobs after World War II.*

**after the event (incident; occurrence)** *after; afterward; later; next; then.*

**after . . . then** *after.* • After making changes, you can then use the transfer command to save the style sheet. *After making changes, you can use the transfer command to save the style sheet.*

**again and again** *frequently; often; recurrently; regularly; repeatedly.*

**again re-** *re-.* • It's an image that again reinforces my belief that we are more interested in pizzazz than performance. *It's an image that reinforces my belief that we are more interested in pizzazz than performance.*

**age (aged)** delete. • Women reach peak fertility at age 25 and then the ability to get pregnant naturally declines. *Women reach peak fertility at 25 and then the ability to get pregnant naturally declines.*

**a good (great) deal of** *great; much; vast.* • There is a great deal of disagreement about generations after the first three. *There is great disagreement about generations after the first three.*

**ahead of** *before.* • The ambassador departed five minutes ahead of the deadline imposed by the State Department. *The ambassador departed five minutes before the deadline imposed by the State Department.*

**ahead of schedule** *early; too soon.* • They arrived in the country two hours ahead of schedule. *They arrived in the country two hours early.*

**ahead of time** *before; beforehand; earlier; in advance; sooner.* • The production manager never knew what was in the pipeline, so he could never prepare the materials and staff ahead of time. *The production manager never knew what was in the pipeline, so he could never prepare the materials and staff beforehand.*

**a (whole) host of** *many; numerous.* • There are a whole host of reasons why these people resigned from their jobs. *There are many reasons why these people resigned from their jobs.*

**aid and abet** *abet; aid; help.* • The NRC, aided and abetted by the industry and most of the press, has chosen to wink at the law. *The NRC, aided by the industry and most of the press, has chosen to wink at the law.*

**aid in -ing** *help.* • In order to aid in recharging the groundwater, large spreading basins were constructed along the Santa Ana River. *In order to help recharge the groundwater, large spreading basins were constructed along the Santa Ana River.*

**a (the) . . . job of** delete. • When the banks offer the products of investment entities with a high market profile, the job of introducing the funds to bank customers is much easier. *When the banks offer the products of investment entities with a high market profile, introducing the funds to bank customers is much easier.*

**a . . . kind (sort; type) (of) thing** *like;* delete. • It became a competition type thing. *It became like a competition.*

**alas and alack** *regrettably; sadly; sorrowfully; unfortunately; unhappily.*

**albeit** *although; though.* • There appears to be enough fuel to propel stocks higher, albeit irregularly, even if the bond market is waylaid by fears of a too robust economy. *There appears to be enough fuel to propel stocks higher, although irregularly, even if the bond market is waylaid by fears of a too robust economy.*

**a little bit** *a bit; a little; fairly; rather; slightly; somewhat.* • They're a little bit hesitant. *They're a little hesitant.*

**all and sundry** *all; everybody; everyone; everything; one and all.* • He is cheered by all and sundry despite his confession. *He is cheered by everyone despite his confession.*

**all done (finished)** *complete; done; ended; finished; over; past.* • Are you all done with your homework? *Are you done with your homework?*

**alleged suspect** *suspect.*

**alleviate** *lessen; reduce.* • The proposal is designed to alleviate overcrowding at Framingham State Prison. *The proposal is designed to lessen overcrowding at Framingham State Prison.*

**all in all** *all told; in all; overall.* • All in all, it would be difficult to find a less suitable site. *All told, it would be difficult to find a less suitable site.*

**all . . . long** *all.* • The president, shop chairman, and entire shop committee of UAW Local 422 worked hard all winter long. *The president, shop chairman, and entire shop committee of UAW Local 422 worked hard all winter.*

**all of (the)** *all (the).* • Can you do all of them? *Can you do them all?*

**all of (us)** *(we) all.* • All of us practice a kind of inventory control. *We all practice a kind of inventory control.*

**all of a sudden** *suddenly.* • All of a sudden, I began getting memos from the corporate office criticizing my performance. *Suddenly, I began getting memos from the corporate office criticizing my performance.*

**all over with** *complete; done; ended; finished; over; past.*

**allow of** *allow; permit.*

**allow . . . to** *let.* • Do it in a way that allows you to look the consumer straight in the eye. *Do it in a way that lets you look the consumer straight in the eye.*

**all (just) the same** *anyhow; even so; still; yet.*

**all the time** *always; ceaselessly; constantly; endlessly; every day; forever.*

**all things considered** *all in all; all told; altogether; in all; on the whole; overall.*

**all-time record (high)** *record.* • International Falls, Minnesota, sometimes called the nation's icebox, tied its all-time record of 98 degrees. *International Falls, Minnesota, sometimes called the nation's icebox, tied its record of 98 degrees.*

**all-time record low** *record low.* • Temperatures in Alaska reached 78 degrees below zero, an all-time record low for the area. *Temperatures in Alaska reached 78 degrees below zero, a record low for the area.*

**almost without exception** *almost all; almost every; most; nearly all; nearly every.* • Almost without exception, those professionals stated that innovation was of major importance to the continued success of the company. *Almost all those professionals stated that innovation was of major importance to the continued success of the company.*

**alongside of** *alongside; among; beside; next to; with.* • You will work alongside of experienced workers and see what joys and frustrations they undergo. *You will work alongside experienced workers and see what joys and frustrations they undergo.*

**along that (this) line** *about (in; on) that (this).* • I don't know what the Twins' thinking was along that line. *I don't know what the Twins' thinking was on that.*

**along that (this) line** *like that (this).* • I can see using TrueScan for some work along that line but only if the documents aren't too complex in fonts or layout. *I can see using TrueScan for some work like that but only if the documents aren't too complex in fonts or layout.*

**along the line of** *in; with.*

**along the lines of** *akin to; close to; like; resembling; similar to; such as.* • They have no interest in publishing anything along the lines of Microsoft *Bookshelf*. *They have no interest in publishing anything similar to Microsoft Bookshelf.*

**along the same line** *alike; likewise; much the same; similar; similarly.* • Along the same line, increasing monetary benefits but not expanding opportunities for job variety would be a serious mistake. *Likewise, increasing monetary benefits but not expanding opportunities for job variety would be a serious mistake.*

**(for) a long time (while)** *long.* • She has wanted to travel to Europe for a long time. *She has long wanted to travel to Europe.*

**a long time (while) ago** *long ago.*

**along with (and; combined with; coupled with; plus; together with) the fact that** *and that.* • U.S. Labor Department figures show that most minimum-wage employees work part time coupled with the fact that 60 percent are between 16 and 24 years old. *U.S. Labor Department figures show that most minimum-wage employees work part time and that 60 percent are between 16 and 24 years old.*

**a lot** *much.* • It also makes assembly-language programs that use GS/OS a lot easier to read. *It also makes assembly-language programs that use GS/OS much easier to read.*

**a lot of** *many; much; numerous.* • In a lot of people's minds, there was no question of his guilt. *In many people's minds, there was no question of his guilt.*

**a lot of (the) time** *frequently; often.* • We went into the city a lot of times. *We went into the city often.*

**alphabetical** *alphabetic.*

**alphanumerical** *alphameric; alphanumeric.*

**also . . . as well** *also; as well.* • They also agreed to other demands as well. *They also agreed to other demands.*

**also . . . too** *also; too.* • We also know that Marilyn Monroe was one of his lovers, too. *We know that Marilyn Monroe was one of his lovers, too.*

**alternative choice** *alternative.*

**a matter of** *a;* delete. • The issue of automobile insurance has been a matter of concern to me since my early years as a legislator. *The issue of automobile insurance has been a concern to me since my early years as a legislator.*

**a matter of** *a few; some;* delete. • In a matter of seconds, SpinRite determines the interleave characteristics of the entire system. *In seconds, SpinRite determines the interleave characteristics of the entire system.*

**a (a certain; some) measure (of)** *a certain; much; some;* delete. • With the employer-employee relationship should come a certain measure of understanding. *With the employer-employee relationship should come a certain understanding.*

**ameliorate** *heal; help; improve; make better.* • As medical technology and surgical procedures increase in their ability to ameliorate, they unfortunately also increase in their ability to harm. *As medical technology and surgical procedures increase in their ability to heal, they unfortunately also increase in their ability to harm.*

**(8:00) A.M. . . . morning** *(8:00) A.M.; in the morning.* • I want the cost estimates by 9:00 A.M. tomorrow morning. *I want the cost estimates by 9:00 A.M. tomorrow.*

**(an; the) . . . amount of** delete. • If you have any amount of intelligence, you know what's right and what's wrong. *If you have any intelligence, you know what's right and what's wrong.* • In reality it takes a considerable amount of political skill and perseverance to get anything of significance through this process. *In reality it takes considerable political skill and perseverance to get anything of significance through this process.*

**amount (quantity; sum) of cash (money)** *sum.* • When the Soviets spent enormous amounts of money improving their antiaircraft systems, the United States responded not by giving up on its bomber program but rather by improving it with cruise missiles, electronic jammers, and so on. *When the Soviets spent enormous sums improving their antiaircraft systems, the United States responded not by giving up on its bomber program but rather by improving it with cruise missiles, electronic jammers, and so on.*

**(a; the) . . . amount of time (length of time; period of time; span of time)** *period; time; while;* delete. • They filmed our arguments over a three-month period of time. *They filmed our arguments over three months.* • You can get to know someone very well if you date him or her for a long enough period of time. *You can get to know someone very well if you date him or her for a long enough while.* • But over the same length of time, inflation averaged 3 percent a year. *But over the same period, inflation averaged 3 percent a year.*

**amounts to** *is; totals.* • The number of prisoners released amounts to less than one-third of those held. *The number of prisoners released is less than one-third of those held.*

**an (the) abundance of** *abundant; ample; copious; countless; legion; liberal; many; myriad; numerous; plentiful; plenty of; profuse.* • Among the educated, there is an abundance of people trained in these occupations. *Among the educated, there are plenty of people trained in these occupations.*

**an accomplished (established) fact** *accomplished (established); a fact;* delete.
• It is an established fact that reaction times and vision deteriorate with age. *It is established that reaction times and vision deteriorate with age.*

**an acknowledged (known) fact** *acknowledged (known); a fact;* delete. • It is an acknowledged fact that well-trained and highly skilled construction craftsmen are not willing to work for wages substandard to the prevailing wage rates. *It is acknowledged that well-trained and highly skilled construction craftsmen are not willing to work for wages substandard to the prevailing wage rates.*

**analytical** *analytic.*

**analyze in depth (in detail)** *analyze; detail.* • He analyzes in detail the three nativist eruptions that occurred during the era of mass immigration. *He details the three nativist eruptions that occurred during the era of mass immigration.*

**an array of** *assorted; countless; different; diverse; extensive; many; numerous; scores of; sundry; varied; various; varying;* delete. • Lately, however, an array of new troubles has surfaced—troubles like radon. *Lately, however, many new troubles have surfaced—troubles like radon.*

**(a; the) -ance (-ence) of** *-ing.* • With such asset and liability opportunities, the avoidance of large credit losses was a practical management consideration in ensuring attractive profitability. *With such asset and liability opportunities, avoiding large credit losses was a practical management consideration in ensuring attractive profitability.* • In the performance of their routines, they are acting as extensions of your position. *In performing their routines, they are acting as extensions of your position.*

**and ... also** *also; and.* • The Winters' models are more complex and also more potentially rewarding. *The Winters' models are more complex and more potentially rewarding.*

**and ... as well** *and; as well.* • It is being done by some of the women whose careers you chronicled and by a growing number of working women as well. *It is being done by some of the women whose careers you chronicled and by a growing number of working women.*

**and etc. (et cetera)** *and so forth; and so on; and the like; etc.*

**and everything** delete.

**and everything (stuff; things) like that** *and so forth; and so on; and the like; etc.;* delete.

**and . . . further (furthermore; in addition; moreover; what is more)** *also; and; as well; besides; beyond that (this); even; further; furthermore; moreover; more than that (this); still more; then; too; what is more.* • And furthermore, the company is seeking to cooperate with other companies with expertise for mutual advancement. *The company is also seeking to cooperate with other companies with expertise for mutual advancement.*

**and so** *and; so.* • Thank you for submitting your pieces to *Critical Inquiry;* however, they are inappropriate for our journal, and so we are returning them to you. *Thank you for submitting your pieces to* Critical Inquiry; *however, they are inappropriate for our journal, so we are returning them to you.*

**and so as a result** *as a result; consequently; hence; so; then; therefore; thus.*

**and so on and so forth** *and so forth; and so on; and the like; etc.* • We believe our neighbor started the conflict with propaganda, espionage, assassinations, bombings, and so on and so forth. *We believe our neighbor started the conflict with propaganda, espionage, assassinations, bombings, and so on.*

**and . . . too** *and; too.* • I have become acutely aware of the epidemic of abuse suffered by children in this country—and elsewhere, too. *I have become acutely aware of the epidemic of abuse suffered by children in this country— and elsewhere.*

**and yet** *and; yet.*

**an estimated** *about; around; close to; more or less; near; nearly; or so; roughly; some.* • An estimated 50,000 people lined up yesterday to register to vote. *Nearly 50,000 people lined up yesterday to register to vote.*

**(after; for; in; over; within) an extended (lengthy; long; prolonged; protracted) amount of time (length of time; period; period of time; span of time; time; while)** *at last; at length; eventually; finally; in due time; in time; over the months (years); over time; ultimately; with time.*

**an (a certain; some) extent of** *a certain; much; some; somewhat;* delete.

**an integral part of** *a part of; integral to.* • Keeping abreast of these developments is an integral part of successful EFT strategy development. *Keeping* *abreast of these developments is integral to successful EFT strategy development.*

**an (the) open question** *a (the) question; arguable; debatable; disputable; doubtful; dubious; in doubt; in question; moot; open; questionable; uncertain; unclear; undecided; unknown; unsettled; unsure.* • That remains an open question. *That remains questionable.*

**an order of magnitude** delete. • While the first CD-ROM copy costs an order of magnitude more than a WORM disk, subsequent copies cost much less, making CD-ROM practical for applications requiring many copies of document disks. *While the first CD-ROM copy costs more than a WORM disk, subsequent copies cost much less, making CD-ROM practical for applications requiring many copies of document disks.*

**anterior to** *before; earlier than.*

**a (a fair; any) number (of)** *a few; almost all; dozens (of); hundreds (of); many; most; nearly all; scores (of); several; sixty-seven (twenty); some;* delete. • A fair number of stores were either sited incorrectly or in the wrong markets and weren't producing the kind of profits they needed to. *Some stores were either sited incorrectly or in the wrong markets and weren't producing the kind of profits they needed to.*

**any and all** *any; all.* • This certificate replaces any and all insurance certificates that may have been issued previously to the Insured under the Group Policy and is subject to the terms of the Group Policy. *This certificate replaces all insurance certificates that may have been issued previously to the Insured under the Group Policy and is subject to the terms of the Group Policy.*

**anybody (anyone) and everybody (everyone)** *all; anybody (anyone); everybody (everyone).* • They told anyone and everyone that you are the one we want to use in our ads. *They told everyone that you are the one we want to use in our ads.*

**anyplace (anywhere) else** *elsewhere.* • This is an invaluable resource that you will not find anywhere else. *This is an invaluable resource that you will not find elsewhere.*

**anything and everything** *all; anything; anything at all; everything.* • These kids lie about anything and everything. *These kids lie about everything.*

**anything (something) in the way of** *any; some;* delete. • It has yet to accomplish anything in the way of practical benefits. *It has yet to accomplish any practical benefits.*

**anyway** delete.

**anywhere (somewhere) between ... and** *between ... and*. • Upjohn says Minoxidil's success rate ranges anywhere between 24 and 40 percent. *Upjohn says Minoxidil's success rate ranges between 24 and 40 percent.*

**anywhere (somewhere) in the range of ... to** *in the range of ... to.*

**anywhere near** *nearly.* • You are not anywhere near as dumb as some of this material will make you feel. *You are not nearly as dumb as some of this material will make you feel.*

**a (the) ... one** delete. • It remains to be seen, however, if this view will turn out to be the correct one. *It remains to be seen, however, if this view will turn out to be correct.*

**apart from** *besides; beyond.* • Apart from looking like the original, the counterfeit product often performs as well as the original. *Besides looking like the original, the counterfeit product often performs as well as the original.*

**apart from ... also (as well)** *apart from; besides; beyond.* • Apart from being expensive, the international development process is also very risky. *Besides being expensive, the international development process is very risky.*

**a (a certain; some) part (of)** *almost all (of); many (of); most (of); much (of); nearly all (of); (a) part (of); some (of).*

**a (a certain; some) percentage (of)** *almost all (of); many (of); most (of); much (of); nearly all (of); (a) part (of); (45) percent (of); some (of).* • I own a percentage of Caesar's Palace. *I own some of Caesar's Palace.*

**a (the) ... period (of)** delete. • The FBI conducted its investigation over a two-year period. *The FBI conducted its investigation over two years.*

**a (the) ... point** *a (the);* delete. • Identifying a need is the beginning point of the process. *Identifying a need is the beginning of the process.*

**a (the) point of (that)** *a (the);* delete. • Is this a point of concern for the rest of the pack? *Is this a concern for the rest of the pack?*

**a (a certain; some) portion (of)** *almost all (of); many (of); most (of); much (of); (a) part (of); nearly all (of); some (of).* • To print only a portion of the document, select the block. *To print only part of the document, select the block.*

**appear (arrive) on (upon) the scene** *appear (arrive).*

**appellation** *name; title.*

**appertain (appertaining) to** *pertain to; relate to.* • Moneys therefor having been deposited with the Trustee from and after June 12, 1989, interest thereon shall cease to accrue and coupons appertaining to said bonds payable after that date will be void. *Moneys therefor having been deposited with the Trustee from and after June 12, 1989, interest thereon shall cease to accrue and coupons pertaining to said bonds payable after that date will be void.*

**appoint as** *appoint.*

**appreciate** *admire; applaud; approve of; enjoy; (be) grateful (for); like; prize; (be) thankful (for); thank you (for); value; welcome.* • We appreciate it. *We are grateful.* • I appreciate your coming. *I thank you for coming.* • Your concern is very much appreciated. *Your concern is very much welcomed.*

**appreciate in value** *appreciate.* • Due to the overall rise of the stock market, many individuals have securities which have appreciated considerably in value. *Due to the overall rise of the stock market, many individuals have securities which have appreciated considerably.*

**appreciation** *gratefulness; gratitude; thankfulness; thanks.* • I would like to express my appreciation for Meals on Wheels. *I would like to express my thanks for Meals on Wheels.*

**apprehend** *arrest; capture; catch; seize.* • Daniel Mahoney, 30, was apprehended near Los Lunas shortly before 1:00 A.M. *Daniel Mahoney, 30, was captured near Los Lunas shortly before 1:00 A.M.*

**approbation** *approval; praise.*

**(for) approximately** *about; around; close to; more or less; near; nearly; or so; roughly; say; some.* • It will last for approximately two hours. *It will last about two hours.*

**a (the) preponderance (of)** *almost all (of); (nine) in (ten) (of); many (of); more (of); most (of); nearly all (of); (43) of (48) (of); (52) percent (of); delete.* • The preponderance of short selling is done by market professionals engaged in the day-to-day provision of liquidity to the market. *Almost all short selling is done by market professionals engaged in the day-to-day provision of liquidity to the market.*

**a (a certain; some) proportion (of)** *almost all (of); many (of); most (of); much (of); nearly all (of); (a) part (of); some (of).*

**a (a certain; some) quantity (of)** *almost all (of); many (of); most (of); much (of); nearly all (of); (a) part (of); some (of).*

**a range of** *assorted; countless; different; diverse; extensive; many; numerous; scores of; sundry; varied; various; varying;* delete. • It has been tested in a range of working situations in large manufacturing plants. *It has been tested in diverse working situations in large manufacturing plants.*

**a ratio (of)** delete. • When you add in those with subsyndromal SAD, the figure is closer to one in four, with women outnumbering men by a ratio of three or four to one. *When you add in those with subsyndromal SAD, the figure is closer to one in four, with women outnumbering men by three or four to one.*

**(an; the) area (locale; locality; location; place; point; position; region; site; spot)** *where; wherever.*

**(after; for; in; over; within) a reasonable amount of time (length of time; period; period of time; span of time; time; while)** *by next week (tomorrow); fast; in (within) a day (year); promptly; quickly; rapidly; shortly; soon; speedily; swiftly;* delete. • Unlike corporate sales, which can be tied up in a relatively reasonable period of time, government sales tend to be drawn out. *Unlike corporate sales, which can be tied up relatively quickly, government sales tend to be drawn out.*

**(an; the) area (locale; locality; location; place; point; position; region; site; spot) where** *where; wherever.* • The COMSPEC line will show the place where COMMAND.COM is expected. *The COMSPEC line will show where COMMAND.COM is expected.*

**argumentation** *argument; debate; dispute.* • Some members may take unyielding positions, leading to unproductive argumentation and bickering. *Some members may take unyielding positions, leading to unproductive arguments and bickering.*

**arithmetical** *arithmetic.*

**around about** *about; around.* • It was around about then that he left for East Africa. *It was around then that he left for East Africa.*

**arrive at (an; the) accord** *agree; compromise; concur; decide; resolve; settle.* • AT&T and unions representing about 160,000 employees arrived at an accord on a new three-year national contract. *AT&T and unions representing about 160,000 employees agreed on a new three-year national contract.*

**arrive at (an; the) agreement** *agree; compromise; concur; decide; resolve; settle.*

**arrive at (a; the) compromise** *agree; compromise; concur; decide; resolve; settle.*

**arrive at (a; the) conclusion** *conclude; decide; deduce; determine; infer; judge; reason; resolve; settle.* • I think they have arrived at the conclusion that he is now a neutralized force. *I think they have concluded that he is now a neutralized force.*

**arrive at (a; the) decision (on; upon)** *conclude; decide; deduce; determine; infer; judge; reason; resolve; settle.*

**arrive at (a; the) determination (on; upon)** *conclude; decide; deduce; determine; infer; judge; reason; resolve; settle.*

**arrive at (an; the) estimate (estimation) (of)** *approximate; assess; estimate; evaluate; rate.* • Since information from subsequent steps in an assessment is needed to arrive at an estimate of what the firm's actual marketing effort will be, the assessment from this point on is reitcrative. *Since information from subsequent steps in an assessment is needed to estimate what the firm's actual marketing effort will be, the assessment from this point on is reiterative.*

**arrive at (an; the) opinion** *conclude; decide; deduce; determine; infer; judge; reason; resolve; settle.*

**arrive at (a; the) resolution** *agree; conclude; decide; resolve; settle.*

**arrive at (a; the) settlement** *agree; conclude; decide; resolve; settle.*

**arrive at (an; the) understanding** *agree; compromise; concur; decide; resolve; settle.*

**as a consequence** *consequently; hence; so; then; therefore; thus.* • As a consequence, there are a lot of charlatans, zealots, and incompetents offering their services. *Thus, there are a lot of charlatans, zealots, and incompetents offering their services.*

**as a consequence of** *after; because of; by; due to; following; for; from; in; out of; owing to; through; with.* • As a consequence of the 43 million babies born in the years immediately following World War II, a middle-aged bulge is forming and eventually the 35- to 45-year-old age group will increase by 80 percent. *Because of the 43 million babies born in the years immediately* *following World War II, a middle-aged bulge is forming and eventually the 35- to 45-year-old age group will increase by 80 percent.*

**as a consequence of the fact that** *because; considering; for; in that; since.*

**as against** *against; to.* • Total investments in property, plant and equipment amounted to SEK 1,592 m. in 1987, as against SEK 1,643 m. in the preceding year. *Total investments in property, plant and equipment amounted to SEK 1,592 m. in 1987, against SEK 1,643 m. in the preceding year.*

**as a general rule** *almost all; as a rule; chiefly; commonly; customarily; generally; greatly; in general; largely; mainly; most; mostly; most often; much; nearly all; normally; overall; typically; usually.* • As a general rule, interest payments are made every six months. *Typically, interest payments are made every six months.*

**as a matter of course** *commonly; customarily; habitually; naturally; normally; ordinarily; regularly; routinely; typically; usually.* • Most veterinarians do it as a matter of course because it is a money-making procedure. *Most veterinarians do it routinely because it is a money-making procedure.*

**as a matter of fact** *actually; indeed; in fact; in faith; in reality; in truth; really; truly; delete.* • As a matter of fact, there are some rumors of discontent. *In fact, there are some rumors of discontent.*

**as a matter of fact** *also; and; as well; besides; beyond that (this); even; further; furthermore; moreover; more than that (this); still more; then; too; what is more.*

**as a means for (of; to) (-ing)** *for (-ing); so as to; to.* • I have found the spelling checker extremely useful as a means for proofreading text. *I have found the spelling checker extremely useful for proofreading text.*

**as and when** *as; when.* • At the same time, they have substantial outflows, ongoing expenses which cannot be shifted but must be paid as and when they become due. *At the same time, they have substantial outflows, ongoing expenses which cannot be shifted but must be paid as they become due.*

**as an example** *for example; for instance.*

**as . . . apply to** *about; as for; as to; concerning; for; in; of; on; over; regarding; respecting; to; toward; with; delete.* • I've always been intrigued by the concept of marketing as it applies to health care. *I've always been intrigued by the concept of health care marketing.*

**as a result** *consequently; hence; so; then; therefore; thus.* • The IDA was working to make jobs available to the graduates of these schools, and as a result, the educational climate in Ireland has changed dramatically. *The IDA was working to make jobs available to the graduates of these schools, and thus, the educational climate in Ireland has changed dramatically.*

**as a result of** *after; because of; by; due to; following; for; from; in; out of; owing to; through; with.* • More people die as a result of drinking alcohol than as a result of smoking marijuana. *More people die from drinking alcohol than from smoking marijuana.* • Much pain and resentment was rekindled as a result of recent political maneuverings between the Turkish and U.S. governments. *Much pain and resentment was rekindled following recent political maneuverings between the Turkish and U.S. governments.*

**as a result of the fact that** *because; considering; for; in that; since.* • This is clearly an area of growing importance to BOCs, particularly as a result of the fact that a recent court decision allows them to enter in certain segments of enhanced services. *This is clearly an area of growing importance to BOCs, particularly because a recent court decision allows them to enter in certain segments of enhanced services.*

**as a rule** *almost all; chiefly; commonly; generally; greatly; in general; largely; mainly; most; mostly; most often; much; nearly all; normally; overall; typically.* • As a rule, I wouldn't dream of doing something like this. *Normally, I wouldn't dream of doing something like this.*

**as a way for (of; to) (-ing)** *for (-ing); so as to; to.* • More and more professionals are using dating services as a way of meeting the perfect mate. *More and more professionals are using dating services to meet the perfect mate.*

**as a whole** *complete; entire; whole;* delete. • It's an embarrassment to the administration as a whole. *It's an embarrassment to the administration.*

**ascend up** *ascend.* • As you ascend up the status hierarchy, you get to select more expensive furnishings. *As you ascend the status hierarchy, you get to select more expensive furnishings.*

**as compared to (with)** *against; alongside; beside; compared to (with); -(i)er than; less; less than; more; more than; next to; over; than; to; versus; vis-à-vis.* • The governments of developing countries give low priority to these skills as compared to technological skills and knowledge. *The governments of developing countries give lower priority to these skills than to technological skills and knowledge.* • The Japanese can design and build a car in about

3½ years as compared to U.S. auto makers' average of 5 years. *The Japanese can design and build a car in about 3½ years against U.S. auto makers' average of 5 years.* • Data communications is not very familiar ground to the operating companies as compared to their expertise in voice. *Data communications is not very familiar ground to the operating companies compared to their expertise in voice.*

**as compared to (with) . . . relatively** *compared to (with).* • As compared to Western Europeans and the Japanese, Americans save a relatively small proportion of their disposable income. *Compared to Western Europeans and the Japanese, Americans save a small proportion of their disposable income.*

**as concerns** *about; as for; as to; concerning; for; in; of; on; over; regarding; respecting; to; toward; with.*

**as contrasted to (with)** *against; alongside; beside; compared to (with); -(i)er than; less; less than; more; more than; next to; over; than; to; unlike; versus; vis-à-vis.* • Epidemiologists find that people who eat a lot of fish have much lower rates of both cholesterol-caused heart disease and cholesterol gallstones as contrasted to people who don't. *Epidemiologists find that people who eat a lot of fish have much lower rates of both cholesterol-caused heart disease and cholesterol gallstones than people who don't.*

**a (the) score of** *delete.* • Sweden is on top by a score of 6 to 1. *Sweden is on top by 6 to 1.*

**ascribable to** *because of; caused by; due to; owing to; resulting from.*

**as (the) days (decades; months; weeks; years) go on** *at length; eventually; in time; later; one day; over the months (years); over time; someday; sometime; ultimately; with time; yet; delete.* • As the years go on, customers will look to NYNEX and others to give them more than just the transmission of information—they'll also need the software and the systems integration to run their businesses and homes more efficiently. *Over time, customers will look to NYNEX and others to give them more than just the transmission of information—they'll also need the software and the systems integration to run their businesses and homes more efficiently.*

**a second time** *again; once more.*

**as (so) far as . . . (goes; is concerned)** *about; as for; as to; concerning; for; in; of; on; over; regarding; respecting; to; toward; with; delete.* • The effect of lead is particularly traumatic as far as young children are concerned. *The effect of lead is particularly traumatic on young children.* • In fact, as far as the "secrets of entrepreneurial success" go, it's impossible to recognize that a little bit of luck helps and a lot of luck is even better. *In fact, concerning the "secrets of entrepreneurial success," it's impossible to recognize that a little bit of luck helps and a lot of luck is even better.* • The general view seems to be that infectious agents transmitted by rodents are not of particular relevance as far as public health goes. *The general view seems to be that infectious agents transmitted by rodents are not of particular relevance to public health.*

**as follows** delete. • The quote is as follows: "I never met a man who had better motives for all the trouble he's causing." *The quote is "I never met a man who had better motives for all the trouble he's causing."*

**as . . . for example (for instance)** *as; for example (for instance); like; say; such as.* • No such close match is necessary if the intent of the assessment is to monitor the general state of student knowledge and competence in science, as for example in past assessments conducted by NAEP. *No such close match is necessary if the intent of the assessment is to monitor the general state of student knowledge and competence in science, as in past assessments conducted by NAEP.*

**as for (in; with) the case of** *as for (in; with); like.* • Even when countries adopt state religions, as in the cases of the United Kingdom, Spain, and Italy, the religious context of the country is not necessarily monolithic. *Even when countries adopt state religions, as in the United Kingdom, Spain, and Italy, the religious context of the country is not necessarily monolithic.*

**as how** *that.* • He allowed as how he could further explore the idea. *He allowed that he could further explore the idea.*

**aside from** *besides; beyond.* • Aside from the lack of restraints, there are other differences a foreign investor must get used to. *Besides the lack of restraints, there are other differences a foreign investor must get used to.*

**aside from . . . also (as well)** *aside from; besides; beyond.*

**as, if, and when** *if; when.* • The Company will be deemed to have purchased tendered Shares as, if, and when it gives oral and written notice to the Depositary of its acceptance for payment of such Shares. *The Company will be deemed to have purchased tendered Shares when it gives oral and written notice to the Depositary of its acceptance for payment of such Shares.*

**a single one** *a single; one.* • Not a single one of the dire accusations or predictions made in that article has come true. *Not one of the dire accusations or predictions made in that article has come true.*

**a single solitary (one)** *a single; one.*

**(even) as I (we) speak** *(just; right) now;* delete. • As we speak, New York state is starting a drug education program. *New York state is now starting a drug education program.*

**as is the case** *as; like.* • As is the case with all of our new words, they sound terribly impressive at cocktail parties. *Like all of our new words, they sound terribly impressive at cocktail parties.*

**as it turned out** *by chance; luckily; unluckily.*

**ask (a; the) question** *ask.* • We need to ask ourselves the question if animals are necessary for medical training. *We need to ask ourselves if animals are necessary for medical training.*

**as long as (so long as) (that)** *if.* • This program, as well as others like it, will make a difference as long as we have strong public support for changing the plight of these children. *This program, as well as others like it, will make a difference if we have strong public support for changing the plight of these children.*

**as luck would have it** *by chance; luckily; unluckily.*

**as many (much) as** *up to.* • There are nearly 300 individual fund managers, ranging from those with a single fund to the very large mutual fund families that offer as many as 100 different funds. *There are nearly 300 individual fund managers, ranging from those with a single fund to the very large mutual fund families that offer up to 100 different funds.*

**as of** *on;* delete. • The plant will shut down as of November 1. *The plant will shut down November 1.*

**as often as not** *commonly; customarily; generally; normally; often; ordinarily; typically; usually.*

**as opposed to** *against; alongside; beside; compared to (with); -(i)er than; less; less than; more; more than; next to; over; than; to; unlike; versus; vis-à-vis.* • Thanks to the recent strength of the dollar, the U.S. markets remain attractive, as opposed to their foreign counterparts. *Thanks to the recent strength of the dollar, the U.S. markets remain more attractive than their* *foreign counterparts.* • You should experience better results with the cool white as opposed to the warm white because the cool white approximates natural sunlight. *You should experience better results with the cool white than the warm white because the cool white approximates natural sunlight.*

**as opposed to** *instead of; not; rather than; whereas.* • Why do customers choose one brand as opposed to another? *Why do customers choose one brand rather than another?*

**as opposed to . . . relatively** *compared to (with).* • As opposed to the organization and access rules of network and hierarchical data models, those of the relational model are relatively simple. *Compared to the organization and access rules of network and hierarchical data models, those of the relational model are simple.*

**a spectrum of** *assorted; countless; different; diverse; extensive; many; numerous; scores of; sundry; varied; various; varying;* delete.

**as regards** *about; as for; as to; concerning; for; in; of; on; over; regarding; respecting; to; toward; with.* • He promises to be less tightfisted in the future as regards training. *He promises to be less tightfisted in the future with training.*

**assemble together** *assemble.*

**assistance** *aid; help; succor.*

**assist in -ing** *help.* • This view assists you in visualizing the problem. *This view helps you visualize the problem.*

**associated with** *for; in; linked to; of; related to; -'s; with.* • The greater the required accuracy, the greater the cost associated with generating a plan. *The greater the required accuracy, the greater the cost of generating a plan.*

**associated with** *belongs to; employed by; works for.*

**association** *connection; link; relation; tie.* • The CDC study concluded there was no association between use of the pill and breast cancer. *The CDC study concluded there was no link between use of the pill and breast cancer.*

**as soon as** *once; when.* • I'll call you as soon as I can. *I'll call you when I can.*

**(most; very) assuredly** *yes.*

**assure (ensure; insure) . . . guarantee** *ensure; guarantee.* • There must be a way to ensure that their privacy is guaranteed. *There must be a way to ensure their privacy.*

**a (the) stage of** delete. • Other products take a long time to gain acceptance and may never reach a stage of widespread adoption. *Other products take a long time to gain acceptance and may never reach widespread adoption.*

**as the basis for (-ing)** *for (-ing); so as to; to.* • Data is any information used as the basis for discussing or deciding something. *Data is any information used for discussing or deciding something.*

**as the case (situation) may be** delete. • When both are used on the same drawing, the parts list is placed directly above and in contact with the title block or the title strip, as the case may be. *When both are used on the same drawing, the parts list is placed directly above and in contact with the title block or the title strip.*

**as the need arises (develops)** *as needed.* • Corrections and adjustments can be made as the need arises. *Corrections and adjustments can be made as needed.*

**as the saying goes** delete.

**as time goes on** *at length; in due time; in time; later; one day; over time; someday; sometime; ultimately; with time; yet;* delete. • As time goes on, maintenance revenues will rise for the average distributor. *Maintenance revenues will yet rise for the average distributor.*

**as time progresses (forward; on; onward)** *at length; eventually; in due time; in time; later; one day; over the months (years); over time; someday; sometime; ultimately; with time; yet;* delete. • As time progressed, she decided to divorce him. *At length, she decided to divorce him.*

**as to** *about; by; for; in; of; on; to; with;* delete. • I'm curious as to why you would choose to be in that situation. *I'm curious why you would choose to be in that situation.* • People have different ideas as to what is sexually acceptable to them. *People have different ideas on what is sexually acceptable to them.* • Once you know your skills, aptitudes, interests, and motivations, you will have a good idea as to what you have going for you and what you want. *Once you know your skills, aptitudes, interests, and motivations, you will have a good idea of what you have going for you and what you want.*

**as to whether** *whether.* • It's too early to speculate as to whether the two stabbings are connected. *It's too early to speculate whether the two stabbings are connected.*

**as well as** *and.* • Banks have added to their capital by retaining a higher share of current earnings, in some cases selling their undervalued real estate as well as business assets. *Banks have added to their capital by retaining a higher share of current earnings, in some cases selling their undervalued real estate and business assets.*

**as (of) yet** *yet.* • I haven't mastered the sport as of yet. *I haven't mastered the sport yet.*

**at about (around)** *about (around).* • We got there at about 7:00. *We got there about 7:00.*

**at a certain (any; one; some) point in my history (point in my life; point in the history of my life; point in time)** *at one time; ever; once; one day; someday; sometime;* delete. • At one point in the history of my life, I was a high school English teacher. *I was once a high school English teacher.*

**at a (some) future (later; subsequent) date (time)** *at length; eventually; in due time; in time; later; one day; over the months (years); over time; someday; sometime; ultimately; with time; yet.* • These guidelines also apply to other reading materials that you will need to reread and study at a later date. *These guidelines also apply to other reading materials that you will later need to reread and study.*

**at all** delete. • You're unwilling to make any sort of compromise at all. *You're unwilling to make any sort of compromise.*

**at a (the) juncture (juncture in time; moment; moment in time; period; period in time; point; point in time; stage; stage in time; time)** *when.* • At the point in time this book was published, several other titles were also available. *When this book was published, several other titles were also available.*

**at a (the) juncture (juncture in time; moment; moment in time; period; period in time; point; point in time; stage; stage in time; time) when** *when.* • On a computer, the design is created on the screen, and the scale can be decided, and changed, at the time when the final drawing is printed out on a printer or plotter. *On a computer, the design is created on the screen, and the scale can be decided, and changed, when the final drawing is printed out on a printer or plotter.*

**at an (some) earlier (former; past; previous) date (time)** *before; earlier; formerly; once.*

**at an end** *complete; done; ended; finished; over; past.* • Barring the unexpected, the 25-year search for a new arena is at an end. *Barring the unexpected, the 25-year search for a new arena is over.*

**at any date (hour; time)** *any time.*

**at any minute (moment)** *directly; momentarily; momently; presently; soon.*

**at any rate** *anyhow; even so; still; yet.*

**at (from; in; on; to) (a; the) area (locale; locality; location; place; point; position; region; site; spot)** *where; wherever.* • The program is temporarily interrupted, and can be restarted any time at the exact place it left off. *The program is temporarily interrupted, and can be restarted any time exactly where it left off.*

**at (from; in; on; to) (any; each; every; some) area (locale; locality; location; place; point; position; region; site; spot)** *anyplace; anywhere; ever; everyplace; everywhere; one day; someday; someplace; sometime; somewhere; where; wherever.* • If at any point I felt I was an embarrassment to the president, I would resign. *If I ever felt I was an embarrassment to the president, I would resign.*

**at (from; in; on; to) (a; the) area (locale; locality; location; place; point; position; region; site; spot) where** *where; wherever.* • The voodoo doctor told me to put them in a location where no one would ever find them. *The voodoo doctor told me to put them where no one would ever find them.*

**at (from; in; on; to) (any; each; every; some) area (locale; locality; location; place; point; position; region; site; spot) where** *anyplace; anywhere; ever; everyplace; everywhere; one day; someday; someplace; sometime; somewhere; where; wherever.* • At every place where food was available, people went hungry for lack of dry fuel. *Wherever food was available, people went hungry for lack of dry fuel.*

**at (for) (a; the) cost (price; sum) of** *at (for).* • The Tower was built from 1970 to 1974 at a cost of more than $150 million. *The Tower was built from 1970 to 1974 for more than $150 million.*

**at every turn** *always; ceaselessly; consistently; constantly; endlessly; eternally; everyday; forever; unfailingly.*

**at frequent (periodic; regular) intervals (periods)** *frequently; periodically; regularly.* • At periodic intervals, the entries made in the journals are posted to the general ledger. *Periodically, the entries made in the journals are posted to the general ledger.*

**at (a; the) . . . level** *-(al)ly;* delete. • Prices at the wholesale level will go up 6 cents per gallon. *Wholesale prices will go up 6 cents per gallon.*

**at long last** *at last; finally.*

**at (for) no charge (cost)** *free.* • It will be available at no charge through Avatar dealers nationwide. *It will be available free through Avatar dealers nationwide.*

**at no time** *never.* • At no time was it this union's position to oppose the Emerson College proposal or deprive fellow workers of jobs made available by this project. *Never was it this union's position to oppose the Emerson College proposal or deprive fellow workers of jobs made available by this project.*

**at one time (in the past)** *once.*

**atop of** *atop.*

**a (the) total . . . (of)** delete. • The United States sent a total of 3.4 million men and women to serve in Southeast Asia during the period. *The United States sent 3.4 million men and women to serve in Southeast Asia during the period.* • The status line displays the total number of words that were checked. *The status line displays the number of words that were checked.*

**at (a; the) . . . pace (of)** *at; by; -(al)ly;* delete. • We've had fairly stable interest rates and an economy that continues to grow at a moderate pace. *We've had fairly stable interest rates and an economy that continues to grow moderately.*

**at (the) present** *(just; right) now; nowadays; these days; today; (just) yet;* delete. • At present, nothing indicates that South Africa is prepared to completely dismantle apartheid. *Nothing yet indicates that South Africa is prepared to completely dismantle apartheid.*

**at (a; the) . . . rate (of)** *at; by; -(al)ly;* delete. • Crime on college campuses is increasing at a geometric rate. *Crime on college campuses is increasing geometrically.*

**at some point (time) along the line (the way)** *at some point; at some time.*

**at specific (specified; timed) intervals (periods)** *periodically; regularly.*

**at (a; the) . . . speed (of)** *at; by; -(al)ly;* delete. • Loosened by rain or melting snow, ordinary soil on a steep hillside can suddenly turn into a lethal wave sweeping downward at speeds of more than 30 miles per hour. *Loosened by rain or melting snow, ordinary soil on a steep hillside can suddenly turn into a lethal wave sweeping downward at more than 30 miles per hour.*

**attach together** *attach.*

**attacked by assailants** *assailed; assaulted; attacked.* • They were departing a local discotheque and entering their vehicle when they were attacked by assailants. *They were departing a local discotheque and entering their vehicle when they were attacked.*

**attempt** *try.* • My ex-wife and I attempted to have a child for six years. *My ex-wife and I tried to have a child for six years.*

**attention . . . focused on (upon)** *attention on; focus on.* • In presidential politics, everyone's attention is now focused on the South. *In presidential politics, everyone is now focused on the South.*

**at that (this) juncture** *at present; at that (this) time; current; currently; (just; right) now; nowadays; present; presently; then; these days; today; (just) yet;* delete. • For nimble investors, a little buying may be appropriate at this juncture. *For nimble investors, a little buying may now be appropriate.*

**at that (this) juncture (juncture in time; moment; moment in time; period; period in time; point; point in time; stage; stage in time; time) in my history (in my life; in the history of my life)** *at present; at that (this) time; current; currently; (just; right) now; nowadays; present; presently; then; these days; today; (just) yet;* delete. • At that point in my life, death seemed vague and romantic. *Death seemed vague and romantic then.* • At this point in time in our history, that can be a subtle and tricky distinction. *Today, that can be a subtle and tricky distinction.*

**at that (this) juncture (moment; period; point; stage) in time** *at present; at that (this) time; current; currently; (just; right) now; nowadays; present; presently; then; these days; today; (just) yet;* delete. • At this moment in time, he must abide by the way I want things to be. *He now must abide by the way I want things to be.*

**at that (this) moment** *at present; at that (this) time; current; currently; (just; right) now; nowadays; present; presently; then; these days; today; (just) yet;*

65

delete. • Did you know at that moment that your father had killed the rest of the family? *Did you know then that your father had killed the rest of the family?*

**at that (this) point** *at present; current; currently; (just; right) now; nowadays; present; presently; then; these days; today; (just) yet;* delete. • At that point, we will discontinue our aid to them. *We will then discontinue our aid to them.*

**at that (this) stage** *at present; at that (this) time; current; currently; (just; right) now; nowadays; present; presently; then; these days; today; (just) yet;* delete. • It's hard to tell at this stage. *It's hard to tell now.*

**at that (this) time** *at present; current; currently; (just; right) now; nowadays; present; presently; then; these days; today; (just) yet;* delete. • The potential return on the investment is uncertain at this time. *The potential return on the investment is presently uncertain.*

**at (on) the brink of** *about to; approaching; close to; near; nearly; verging on.* • Some 10,000 Sudanese are on the brink of starving to death in a southern town under siege by armed guerrillas. *Some 10,000 Sudanese are close to starving to death in a southern town under siege by armed guerrillas.*

**at the corner (intersection) of** *at.* • The site is located at the intersection of Buffum and Blake Streets in the Central Square Historic District. *The site is located at Buffum and Blake Streets in the Central Square Historic District.*

**at the current (present) time** *at present; at this time; current; currently; (just; right) now; nowadays; present; presently; these days; today; (just) yet;* delete. • What is the value of Digital's stock at the present time? *What is the current value of Digital's stock?*

**at the hands of** *by; from; through.* • I am enraged by the second-class treatment we are receiving at the hands of those who legislate for and govern us. *I am enraged by the second-class treatment we are receiving from those who legislate for and govern us.*

**at the (very) minimum** *at least.*

**at the (current; present) moment** *at present; current; currently; (just; right) now; nowadays; present; presently; these days; today; (just) yet;* delete. • At the moment, this effort is being left largely to individual state colleges and universities to initiate. *This effort is now being left largely to individual state colleges and universities to initiate.*

**at (on) the point of** *about to; approaching; close to; near; nearly; verging on.*

**at the same time** *as one; at once; collectively; concurrently; jointly; together.*
• If too many things happened at the same time, data would be lost in the process. *If too many things happened at once, data would be lost in the process.*

**(and) at the same time (as; that)** *as; while.* • In many cases, Soviet interest in smoothing East-West relations has been complicated by conflicting diplomatic priorities, such as improving ties with China and maintaining relations with Vietnam at the same time. *In many cases, Soviet interest in smoothing East-West relations has been complicated by conflicting diplomatic priorities, such as improving ties with China while maintaining relations with Vietnam.* • A similar dilemma faces Cray Research Inc., which relies on Japanese-made chips at the same time it fends off Japanese challenges to its role as the world's leading maker of supercomputers. *A similar dilemma faces Cray Research Inc., which relies on Japanese-made chips as it fends off Japanese challenges to its role as the world's leading maker of supercomputers.*

**attired** *dressed.*

**(a; the) . . . attitude (of)** delete. • He had a very cavalier attitude about money. *He was very cavalier about money.*

**at (on) (the) top (of)** *atop; on.* • It removes the dead cells that accumulate on top of the skin. *It removes the dead cells that accumulate on the skin.*

**attributable to** *because of; caused by; due to; owing to; result from.* • These increases were primarily attributable to a variety of merchant banking activities. *These increases were primarily caused by a variety of merchant banking activities.*

**attributable to the fact that** *because; considering; for; in that; since.* • The differing performance of black and white incomes is primarily attributable to the fact that white-married-couple families did significantly better last year than black-married-couple families. *The differing performance of black and white incomes is primarily because white-married-couple families did significantly better last year than black-married-couple families.*

**at what (which) juncture (juncture in time; moment; moment in time; period; period in time; point; point in time; stage; stage in time; time)** *when.* • At what point will you know if the business is profitable? *When will you know if the business is profitable?*

**at your earliest convenience** *as soon as possible; at once; presently; quickly; right away; shortly; soon; without delay;* delete. • Please return the signed and completed application to this office at your earliest convenience. *Please return the signed and completed application to this office.*

**audible to the ear** *audible.*

**authentic replica** *replica.*

**author** *(v) write.*

**authoress** *author.*

**a variety of** *assorted; countless; different; diverse; extensive; many; numerous; scores of; sundry; varied; various; varying;* delete. • Today, a variety of pricing approaches are used. *Today, various pricing approaches are used.*

**a (the) variety of different** *assorted; a variety of; countless; different; diverse; extensive; many; numerous; scores of; sundry; varied; various; varying.* • The children's museum will have a variety of different events. *The children's museum will have a variety of events.*

# B

**background of experience** *background; experience.* • It is, then, from a background of experience in communication that I want to present two ideas. *It is, then, from a background in communication that I want to present two ideas.*

**back in** *in; last.* • My daughter disappeared back in January. *My daughter disappeared last January.*

**back (before) in the past** *before; earlier; formerly; in the past; once;* delete. • Dealing with irrational people is something my father has done well back in the past and is something he'll do well in the future. *Dealing with irrational people is something my father has done well in the past and is something he'll do well in the future.*

**backward and forward** *completely; entirely; fully; thoroughly; totally; utterly; wholly.*

**badge (mark; sign; symbol) of authenticity (distinction; honor; prestige; rank)** *cachet.* • Basler says the bumps, which appear on the foot and are regarded as a badge of distinction among serious surfers, result from long hours spent in contact with a surfboard. *Basler says the bumps, which appear on the foot and are regarded as a cachet among serious surfers, result from long hours spent in contact with a surfboard.*

**balance out** *balance.* • Because seasonal forces are relative, they balance each other out by the completion of a full year. *Because seasonal forces are relative, they balance each other by the completion of a full year.*

**bald-headed** *bald.*

**-based** *from; in; of; -'s;* delete. • Sharon Howard, an Atlanta-based attorney, has given a lot of thought to the way she is treated in the courtroom. *Sharon Howard, an Atlanta attorney, has given a lot of thought to the way she is treated in the courtroom.*

**based in** *from; in; of; -'s;* delete. • PCE is a privately held company based in Portland, Oregon. *PCE is a privately held company in Portland, Oregon.*

**based on (upon)** *after; by; for; from; in; on; through; with;* delete. • Based on what I hear, everyone thinks Fan Pier has lost its moment of opportunity. *From what I hear, everyone thinks Fan Pier has lost its moment of opportunity.*

**based on (upon) my personal judgment (opinion)** *I assert; I believe; I claim; I consider; I contend; I feel; I hold; I judge; I maintain; I regard; I say; I think; I view; to me;* delete. • Based on my personal judgment, I think tax revenues will grow by 8.3 percent. *I think tax revenues will grow by 8.3 percent.*

**based on the fact that** *because; considering; for; in that; since.* • I'm not in favor of it based on the fact that a lot of small businesses will suffer. *I'm not in favor of it because a lot of small businesses will suffer.*

**baseless (groundless; unfounded; unsubstantiated) rumor** *hearsay; rumor.* • A Foreign Ministry spokesman characterized the reports as unfounded rumors. *A Foreign Ministry spokesman characterized the reports as rumors.*

**basic** delete. • In this section, we introduce you to the basic procedures to control page breaks and page numbers. *In this section, we introduce you to the procedures to control page breaks and page numbers.*

**basically** *chiefly; largely; mainly; most; mostly;* delete. • Basically, the social service groups involved are either indifferent or corrupt. *The social service groups involved are either indifferent or corrupt.*

**basic (and) fundamental** *basic; fundamental.* • Our basic, fundamental values are the same. *Our fundamental values are the same.*

**basic principle** *principle.* • We feel there are two basic principles to successful advertising. *We feel there are two principles to successful advertising.*

**basis in fact (reality; truth)** *basis; fact; reason; truth.* • About the only statement in the article that has any basis in fact is "I want to build the biggest film group in the world." *About the only statement in the article that has any truth is "I want to build the biggest film group in the world."*

**bathroom facilities** *bathroom; toilet.*

**(please) be advised (informed) that** delete. • Please be advised that we must be notified at least two weeks prior to your closing date in order to issue your 6(d) certificate. *We must be notified at least two weeks prior to your closing date in order to issue your 6(d) certificate.*

**bear (have; hold) a grudge (against)** *dislike; resent.*

**(please) bear in mind** *consider; heed; note; realize.*

**bear (a; the) . . . resemblance (similarity) to** *be like; look like; resemble.* • The Lumina's body bears a similarity to Chevrolet's Corsica and Beretta. *The Lumina's body resembles Chevrolet's Corsica and Beretta.*

**bear witness to** *affirm; attest to; certify to; declare; testify to; verify.* • A splendid perennial garden surrounds the house and bears witness to the collaboration in the family. *A splendid perennial garden surrounds the house and attests to the collaboration in the family.*

**because of** *after; by; for; from; in; out of; through; with.* • Such a model would be inappropriate because of two reasons. *Such a model would be inappropriate for two reasons.*

**because of the fact that** *because; considering; for; in that; since.* • Because of the fact that they are still monopoly suppliers of local exchange, I also see a discouraging prospect for the operating companies in this area. *Since they are still monopoly suppliers of local exchange, I also see a discouraging prospect for the operating companies in this area.* • I discounted these things because of the fact that I cared so much for you. *I discounted these things because I cared so much for you.*

**because why** *why.* • You say you are a submissive wife, but you are that way because why? *You say you are a submissive wife, but why are you that way?*

**become known** *emerge; surface; transpire.*

**before (earlier; previously) -ed (-en)** *-ed (-en).* • As we previously noted, the high-cost load funds distributed through a salesperson have dominated the industry. *As we noted, the high-cost load funds distributed through a salesperson have dominated the industry.*

**before . . . first** *before.* • Before you use the delete option, first extract the records you are considering deleting. *Before you use the delete option, extract the records you are considering deleting.*

**before (very) long** *shortly; soon.*

**begin (start) at . . . and end (finish) at** *(be) between . . . and; range from . . . to.* • Price tags for the condos will start at $350,000 and end at $1.75 million. *Price tags for the condos will range from $350,000 to $1.75 million.*

**begin . . . first** *begin.* • You should begin by sketching the centerline and guide-lines first. *You should begin by sketching the centerline and guidelines.*

**behavior pattern** *behavior.*

**(a; the) . . . being** delete. • What sets teachers apart from other mortal beings is that they never have first names. *What sets teachers apart from other mortals is that they never have first names.*

**being (as; as how; that)** *because; considering; for; in that; since.* • They usually deliver by noontime, and being that you're local, it'll probably be before noon. *They usually deliver by noontime, and because you're local, it'll probably be before noon.*

**besides . . . also (as well)** *besides; beyond.* • Besides providing the high-end AI tools, they have shells for IBM PCs and compatibles as well. *Besides providing the high-end AI tools, they have shells for IBM PCs and compatibles.*

**beside the point** *immaterial; inapt; irrelevant; not pertinent.*

**best (biggest; greatest; largest; most) . . . single** *best (biggest; greatest; largest; most).* • Great Britain, where annual production capacity was increased to 700,000 lines a year, is the largest single market. *Great Britain, where annual production capacity was increased to 700,000 lines a year, is the largest market.*

**be that as it may** *all (just) the same; anyhow; even so; still; still and all; yet.*

**between you and me (us)** *between us.* • Enclosed is a basic proposal which should lay the groundwork for future discussions between you and us. *Enclosed is a basic proposal which should lay the groundwork for future discussions between us.*

**between the two of them (us)** *between them (us).*

**betwixt and between** *in between; undecided.*

**beverage** *drink.*

**beyond (out of) all reason** *unreasonable.*

**beyond a (the) shadow of a doubt** *assuredly; certainly; doubtless; indisputably; irrefutably; no doubt; surely; undoubtedly; unquestionably.*

**beyond number** *countless; endless; infinite; millions (of); myriad; numberless; untold.*

**beyond (outside) the realm of possibility** *impossible; inconceivable; undoable; unthinkable.* • So it's not beyond the realm of possibility that corporate performance could be improved if directors surveyed other areas of corporate activity, like manufacturing and marketing. *So it's not inconceivable that corporate performance could be improved if directors surveyed other areas of corporate activity, like manufacturing and marketing.*

**biased opinion** *bias; prejudice.*

**big, huge (large)** *big; huge; large.* • I packed a big, huge picnic lunch for us. *I packed a huge picnic lunch for us.*

**biographical** *biographic.*

**biological** *biologic.*

**biometrical** *biometric.*

**biophysiological** *biophysiologic.*

**bit by bit** *gradually; slowly.*

**bits and pieces** *bits; pieces.* • Bits and pieces of segregation have been jettisoned or have rotted away. *Bits of segregation have been jettisoned or have rotted away.*

**blatantly evident (obvious; plain)** *blatant; evident (obvious; plain).*

**blend of both** *blend.* • Management is a blend of both science and art. *Management is a blend of science and art.*

**blend together** *blend.* • Blend this WordStar expertise together in a book, and you have the definitive resource to the most widely used word processing software. *Blend this WordStar expertise in a book, and you have the definitive resource to the most widely used word processing software.*

**block out** *block.* • Other conversations, the sound of machinery, and traffic noises can block out messages from being received. *Other conversations, the sound of machinery, and traffic noises can block messages from being received.*

**bode (ill; well) for the future** *bode (ill; well).* • The fact that electric companies had to institute such emergency procedures does not bode well for the future. *The fact that electric companies had to institute such emergency procedures does not bode well.*

**botch up** *botch.* • In my first transplant session, the doctor botched up the job. *In my first transplant session, the doctor botched the job.*

**both . . . alike** *alike; both.* • The adherence of career-oriented women to the masculine prototype has led both men and women alike to undermine the value of female qualities and responsibilities. *The adherence of career-oriented women to the masculine prototype has led men and women alike to undermine the value of female qualities and responsibilities.*

**both . . . as well as** *as well as; both . . . and.* • Both the source .PAS file as well as the compiled .PEN file are available. *Both the source .PAS file and the compiled .PEN file are available.*

**both equally** *both; equally.*

**both . . . in combination** *both; in combination.* • Both analytic techniques and judgmental methods might be used in combination to verify each other. *Analytic techniques and judgmental methods might be used in combination to verify each other.*

**both of (the)** *both.* • Both of the boys suffer from Tourette Syndrome. *Both boys suffer from Tourette Syndrome.*

**both share** *both; share.* • We both share a deep commitment to the welfare of the American people. *We share a deep commitment to the welfare of the American people.*

**both together** *both; together.* • Both of the products together cost $117.95. *Together, the products cost $117.95.*

**bound and determined** *determined; resolute; resolved.* • We are still bound and determined that we are going to build a new arena. *We are still determined that we are going to build a new arena.*

**brand new** *new.* • With a brand new product, there is a significant educational need. *With a new product, there is a significant educational need.*

**breadth and depth** *ambit; area; breadth; compass; degree; extent; field; magnitude; range; reach; scope; sphere; sweep.*

**briefly in passing** *briefly; in passing.* • Let me say briefly in passing that I am opposed to women not having control of their own bodies. *Let me say briefly that I am opposed to women not having control of their own bodies.*

**brief (concise; short; succinct) summary** *summary.* • A concise summary of the scope of the international product manager's task has been provided by

Wind. *A summary of the scope of the international product manager's task has been provided by Wind.*

**brief (concise; short; succinct) synopsis** *synopsis.* • I just wondered if I could give you a brief synopsis of the long-distance services that MCI offers. *I just wondered if I could give you a synopsis of the long-distance services that MCI offers.*

**bring about** *begin; cause; effect; occasion; produce.* • Rather than bring about the death of Yellowstone, the fires triggered natural processes of change that are a normal part of the ecosystem. *Rather than cause the death of Yellowstone, the fires triggered natural processes of change that are a normal part of the ecosystem.*

**bring (to) a close (to)** *cease; close; complete; conclude; end; finish; halt; settle; stop.* • How would you bring this meeting to a close? *How would you close this meeting?*

**bring (to) a completion (to)** *cease; close; complete; conclude; end; finish; halt; settle; stop.*

**bring (to) a conclusion (to)** *cease; close; complete; conclude; end; finish; halt; settle; stop.*

**bring (to) a halt (to)** *cease; close; complete; conclude; end; finish; halt; settle; stop.* • The timber industry said the decision could bring logging to a halt throughout much of the Pacific Northwest within 30 days and cause the loss of as many as 160,000 jobs. *The timber industry said the decision could halt logging throughout much of the Pacific Northwest within 30 days and cause the loss of as many as 160,000 jobs.*

**bring (to) an end (to)** *cease; close; complete; conclude; end; finish; halt; settle; stop.* • That comment well describes the work that is yet to be done to bring an end to the pain and suffering. *That comment well describes the work that is yet to be done to end the pain and suffering.*

**bring attention to** *advertise; announce; blazon; broadcast; disclose; divulge; expose; herald; indicate; make known; make public; mention; point out; point to; present; proclaim; promote; publicize; reveal; show; tell; uncover; unveil.* • They were demonstrating at the bank branch in order to bring attention to community lending and banking service issues. *They were demonstrating at the bank branch in order to disclose community lending and banking service issues.*

**bring (give) forth** *bear; effect; produce; yield.*

**bring into being (existence)** *conceive; conjure; create; devise; fashion; forge; form; invent; make; mold; plan; produce; shape.* • He says that reason itself is a ladder that can now be dispensed with—and should be dispensed with—to help bring the liberal utopia into existence. *He says that reason itself is a ladder that can now be dispensed with—and should be dispensed with—to help fashion the liberal utopia.*

**bring into question** *challenge; contradict; dispute; doubt; question.* • The issue goes beyond sexual politics and brings into question how the orthodox verities of an ancient religion fit into the modern world. *The issue goes beyond sexual politics and challenges how the orthodox verities of an ancient religion fit into the modern world.*

**bring into the open** *advertise; announce; blazon; broadcast; disclose; divulge; expose; herald; indicate; make known; make public; mention; point out; point to; present; proclaim; promote; publicize; reveal; show; tell; uncover; unveil.*

**bring into the world** *bear; give birth to; produce.*

**bring pressure to bear on (upon)** *coerce; compel; force; press; pressure.* • No matter who is president, the international community must bring pressure to bear on the government to end apartheid. *No matter who is president, the international community must pressure the government to end apartheid.*

**bring to account** *admonish; censure; chide; rebuke; reprimand; scold.*

**bring to a standstill** *cease; close; complete; conclude; end; finish; halt; settle; stop.* • It should seek to bring to a standstill the international flow of arms to the various Khmer factions. *It should seek to halt the international flow of arms to the various Khmer factions.*

**bring to ... attention (of)** *advertise; announce; blazon; broadcast; disclose; divulge; expose; herald; indicate; make known; make public; mention; point out; point to; present; proclaim; promote; publicize; reveal; show; tell; uncover; unveil.* • He was determined to bring to the world's attention the devastation of the innocents. *He was determined to publicize the devastation of the innocents.*

**bring to bear (on; upon)** *apply; employ; exercise; exert; influence; use.* • Whether such influence can be brought to bear now is of vital importance to the bottom half in the schools. *Whether such influence can be applied now is of vital importance to the bottom half in the schools.*

**bring together** *amass; collect; gather.*

**bring to light** *advertise; announce; blazon; broadcast; disclose; divulge; expose; herald; indicate; make known; make public; mention; point out; point to; present; proclaim; promote; publicize; reveal; show; tell; uncover; unveil.*
• Many uncertainties are brought to light when a bank makes a number of changes. *Many uncertainties are revealed when a bank makes a number of changes.*

**bring (back) to mind** *recall; recollect.*

**bring to pass** *begin; cause; start.*

**build a bridge across (between)** *bridge.*

**(a; the) burgeoning (growing; increasing; rising) amount (degree; extent; number; part; percentage; portion; proportion; quantity) (of)** *increasingly; more; more and more.* • A growing number of attorneys are bringing this up of their own initiative in the course of estate planning reviews. *Increasingly, attorneys are bringing this up of their own initiative in the course of estate planning reviews.*

**but all (just) the same** *all (just) the same; but.*

**but however** *but; however.*

**but instead** *but; instead.* • A child's mind is not a tabula rasa, but instead is filled with ideas generated through continuous interaction with the environment. *A child's mind is not a tabula rasa but is filled with ideas generated through continuous interaction with the environment.*

**but nevertheless** *but; nevertheless.*

**but on the other hand** *but; on the other hand.*

**but rather** *but; rather.* • Behavior is not an isolated event, but rather it is influenced by the past, present, and future. *Behavior is not an isolated event; rather it is influenced by the past, present, and future.*

**but whereas** *but; whereas.*

**by (to) all accounts (appearances; indications)** *apparently; ostensibly; seemingly.* • By all indications, the T-group was a great success. *Apparently, the T-group was a great success.*

77

**by and large** *chiefly; commonly; generally; largely; mainly; most; mostly; normally; typically; usually.* • But members involved argue the furor is by and large a phony one. *But members involved argue the furor is largely a phony one.*

**by any means** *at all.*

**by (in) comparison** *but; however; whereas; yet;* delete. • In comparison, about one-third of the patients whose vessels remained partly blocked showed late potentials on their EKGs. *Whereas about one-third of the patients whose vessels remained partly blocked showed late potentials on their EKGs.*

**by comparison (to; with)** *against; alongside; beside; compared to (with); -(i)er than; less; less than; more; more than; next to; over; than; to; versus; vis-à-vis.* • By comparison with the electronic speed of computers, the postal service and the telephone are slow. *Compared with the electronic speed of computers, the postal service and the telephone are slow.*

**by consequence of** *after; because of; by; due to; following; for; from; in; out of; owing to; through; with.*

**by (a; the) considerable (good; great; huge; large; overwhelming; sizable; vast; wide) margin** *by far; far and away; much.* • The leader by a considerable margin was the deep-water lake trout. *The leader by far was the deep-water lake trout.*

**by (in) contrast** *but; however; whereas; yet;* delete. • Post-modernism, by contrast, is indifferent to consistency and continuity altogether. *Yet post-modernism is indifferent to consistency and continuity altogether.*

**by contrast to (with)** *against; alongside; beside; compared to (with); -(i)er than; less; less than; more; more than; next to; over; than; to; unlike; versus; vis-à-vis.* • And, by contrast with the governor and some younger politicians, Crane has always seen politics as an essential part of the job. *And, unlike the governor and some younger politicians, Crane has always seen politics as an essential part of the job.*

**by definition** delete. • Collaboration, by definition, is a two-way venture. *Collaboration is a two-way venture.*

**(all) by itself (themselves)** *alone.* • Each microcomputer has its own computational ability, so it can function either by itself or as a part of the network. *Each microcomputer has its own computational ability, so it can function either alone or as a part of the network.*

**by (a; the) little (narrow; nominal; slender; slight; slim; small; tiny) margin** *marginally; narrowly; nominally; slightly.* • Blue-chip stocks closed higher by a small margin in a listless session as many participants were absent because of the Jewish New Year holiday. *Blue-chip stocks closed marginally higher in a listless session as many participants were absent because of the Jewish New Year holiday.*

**by (a; the)... margin (of)** *by; -(al)ly;* delete. • Advancing issues outpaced losers by a margin of more than 2 to 1 among issues listed on the New York Stock Exchange. *Advancing issues outpaced losers by more than 2 to 1 among issues listed on the New York Stock Exchange.*

**by (the) means of** *by; from; in; on; over; through; with.* • It retains control over product decisions and generally markets a standardized product and attempts to influence local decisions by means of persuasion. *It retains control over product decisions and generally markets a standardized product and attempts to influence local decisions through persuasion.* • He was convicted of assault and battery by means of a dangerous weapon. *He was convicted of assault and battery with a dangerous weapon.*

**by (its; their) nature** delete. • The truth is that genuine debt crises are, by their nature, almost impossible to predict. *The truth is that genuine debt crises are almost impossible to predict.*

**by no means** *far from; hardly; scarcely.* • Though this advice is extremely helpful to many families, it is by no means the only thing they need to know. *Though this advice is extremely helpful to many families, it is far from the only thing they need to know.*

**by occupation** delete. • He's a day laborer by occupation. *He's a day laborer.*

**by one means or another** *anyhow; anyway; by some means; however; in any way; in some way; in whatever way; somehow; somehow or another; someway(s).*

**by reason of** *after; because of; by; due to; following; for; from; in; out of; owing to; through; with.* • Nomura, by reason of its size, capital, research abilities, and leading position in the largest creditor nation, should certainly be in the top group. *Nomura, because of its size, capital, research abilities, and leading position in the largest creditor nation, should certainly be in the top group.*

**by reason of the fact that** *because; considering; for; in that; since.* • Property the decedent had interest in includes dividends payable to the decedent by reason of the fact that, on or before the date of death, the decedent was a shareholder of record. *Property the decedent had interest in includes dividends payable to the decedent because, on or before the date of death, the decedent was a shareholder of record.*

**(all) by -self (-selves)** *alone.* • She lives all by herself. *She lives alone.*

**by . . . standards** *-(al)ly; delete.* • By historical standards, these relative prices for thrifts are extremely low. *Historically, these relative prices for thrifts are extremely low.*

**by the fact that** *because; considering; for; in that; since.* • By the fact that they are using state capital, there can be no free competition. *Considering they are using state capital, there can be no free competition.*

**by the result of** *after; based on; because of; by; due to; following; for; from; in; on; owing to; through; with.* • In the United States, policies are determined mainly by the result of discussion and debate, whereas in Europe they are determined on the basis of authority and position. *In the United States, policies are determined mainly from discussion and debate, whereas in Europe they are determined on the basis of authority and position.*

**by the same token** *also; and; as well; besides; beyond that (this); even; further; furthermore; likewise; moreover; more than that (this); similarly; still more; then; too; what is more; delete.* • By the same token, northeastern and southeastern banks, which have been the fastest growing, could witness slower loan growth. *Similarly, northeastern and southeastern banks, which have been the fastest growing, could witness slower loan growth.*

**by (in) virtue of** *after; because of; by; due to; following; for; from; in; out of; owing to; through; with.* • The U.S. hockey team is up by one by virtue of their win over Austria. *The U.S. hockey team is up by one following their win over Austria.*

**by (in) virtue of the fact that** *because; considering; for; in that; since.* • People who can be helpful to you are attracted to you by virtue of the fact that you're a person who is doing interesting things and initiating activity yourself. *People who can be helpful to you are attracted to you because you're a person who is doing interesting things and initiating activity yourself.*

**by (the) way of** *by; from; in; on; over; through; with; delete.* • By way of conclusion, here are four salient facts. *In conclusion, here are four salient facts.*

**by way of (-ing)** *for (-ing); so as to; to.* • All of this is by way of making a point. *All of this is to make a point.*

**by way of being** delete. • Today's column is by way of being a commentary on a column that appeared in this space a week ago. *Today's column is a commentary on a column that appeared in this space a week ago.*

**by way of comparison (contrast)** *but; however; whereas; yet.* • The volume directory for a ProDOS-formatted disk can hold up to 51 files, and by way of contrast, a DOS 3.3 directory can hold 105 files. *The volume directory for a ProDOS-formatted disk can hold up to 51 files, whereas a DOS 3.3 directory can hold 105 files.*

**by way of example (illustration)** *for example; to illustrate.* • By way of illustration, here are the main points of a speech about Thailand given by a Thai student. *To illustrate, here are the main points of a speech about Thailand given by a Thai student.*

**by whatever (whichever) manner (means)** *despite how; however.* • By whatever means they have been brought to our attention, they have been corrected. *However they have been brought to our attention, they have been corrected.*

**by what (which) means (mechanism)** *how.* • Still a mystery is by what mechanism insulin resistance might cause heart disease. *Still a mystery is how insulin resistance might cause heart disease.*

# C

**call a halt to** *cease; close; complete; conclude; end; finish; halt; settle; stop.*
• We asked them to call a halt to the violence and harassment. *We asked them to stop the violence and harassment.*

**call an end to** *cease; close; complete; conclude; end; finish; halt; settle; stop.*

**call a stop to** *cease; close; complete; conclude; end; finish; halt; settle; stop.*

**call . . . attention to** *advertise; announce; blazon; broadcast; disclose; divulge; expose; herald; indicate; make known; make public; mention; point out; point to; present; proclaim; promote; publicize; reveal; show; tell; uncover; unveil.* • She said the sole purpose of the program was to call attention to what happened in Mexico. *She said the sole purpose of the program was to disclose what happened in Mexico.*

**called** delete. • A set is a collection of objects, and the objects in the set are called the elements. *A set is a collection of objects, and the objects in the set are the elements.*

**call into being (existence)** *conceive; create; devise; fashion; forge; form; invent; make; mold; plan; produce; shape.*

**call into question** *challenge; contradict; dispute; doubt; question.* • Whether the magazine has accurately interpreted what those interests are is a point some former staffers call into question. *Whether the magazine has accurately interpreted what those interests are is a point some former staffers dispute.*

**call to . . . attention (of)** *advertise; announce; blazon; broadcast; disclose; divulge; expose; herald; indicate; make known; make public; mention; point out; point to; present; proclaim; promote; publicize; reveal; show; tell; uncover; unveil.* • The results were called to the attention of the town's building inspector, who forced the ferry service to shut down. *The results were shown to the town's building inspector, who forced the ferry service to shut down.*

**call to mind** *recall; recollect.*

**call up** *call.*

**calm, cool, and collected** *calm; collected; cool.* • She is calm, cool, and collected now, but you should have seen her Friday night. *She is calm now, but you should have seen her Friday night.*

**candor and frankness** *candor; frankness.*

**capability** *ability.* • No two managers are equal in their abilities, and their subordinates will have differing capabilities and levels of experience. *No two managers are equal in their abilities, and their subordinates will have differing abilities and levels of experience.*

**capacity** *job; position.*

**cast about for** *look for; search for; seek.* • Toymakers have been casting about for something exciting enough to pull parents and children back into the toy stores. *Toymakers have been searching for something exciting enough to pull parents and children back into the toy stores.*

**cast doubt on (upon)** *challenge; contradict; dispute; doubt; question.*

**catch by surprise** *startle; surprise.* • He says the association was caught by surprise by the House's action. *He says the association was surprised by the House's action.*

**cause . . . to be (become)** *make; render.* • Reading his performance appraisal caused him to become angry. *Reading his performance appraisal made him angry.*

**cause to happen (occur; take place)** *bring about; cause; effect; produce.* • Although policy cannot in and of itself cause improvement to happen in the classroom, it can impede or facilitate improvement. *Although policy cannot in and of itself cause improvement in the classroom, it can impede or facilitate improvement.*

**cease and desist** *cease; desist.*

**center around** *center on.* • All these fears center around the loss of control, which may result in being embarrassed or ridiculed by others. *All these fears center on the loss of control, which may result in being embarrassed or ridiculed by others.*

**center of attention (attraction)** *cynosure; focus.*

**(of) central (critical; vital) importance** *central; critical; important; vital.*
• Although these contextual factors are often ignored by domestic firms, they are of central importance to international firms. *Although these contextual factors are often ignored by domestic firms, they are central to international firms.* • This information will be critically important to researchers and to the quality of health care for all Americans well into the next century. *This information will be critical to researchers and to the quality of health care for all Americans well into the next century.*

**(a; the) central . . . in (of; to)** *central to.* • His experience is a central part of the resume on which he is running for office. *His experience is central to the resume on which he is running for office.* • As such, religion (or its traces) is a central element of a culture. *As such, religion (or its traces) is central to a culture.*

**characterize as** *call; name; term.*

**charge with the responsibility for (of)** *charge with; responsible for.* • The organization might have a management information system that is charged with the responsibility for gathering and processing data. *The organization might have a management information system that is responsible for gathering and processing data.*

**check to see** *check; examine; inspect; look; see.* • You should also check to see if the original warranty is still in effect. *You should also check if the original warranty is still in effect.*

**christen as** *christen.*

**climb up** *climb.* • Young Americans have become increasingly disillusioned with their ability to successfully climb up the corporate ladder. *Young Americans have become increasingly disillusioned with their ability to successfully climb the corporate ladder.*

**close (near; rough) approximation (estimate; estimation)** *approximation (estimate; estimation).* • Powers of two roughly approximate powers of ten. *Powers of two approximate powers of ten.*

**close (near) at hand** *close by; close to; near; nearby.*

**close down** *close.* • Both health plans will close down as of December 31 because of projected financial losses. *Both health plans will close as of December 31 because of projected financial losses.*

**close scrutiny** *scrutiny.* • The interest deduction is likely to receive close scrutiny when the chairman of the House Ways and Means Committee looks into the matter this month. *The interest deduction is likely to receive scrutiny when the chairman of the House Ways and Means Committee looks into the matter this month.*

**cluster together** *cluster.* • Groups of chapters in textbooks may be clustered together into units or parts. *Groups of chapters in textbooks may be clustered into units or parts.*

**cobble together** *cobble.* • This might scan articles on a computerized news service to cobble together a personalized daily news bulletin containing articles of interest to a particular individual. *This might scan articles on a computerized news service to cobble a personalized daily news bulletin containing articles of interest to a particular individual.*

**cohabit together** *cohabit.*

**collaborate together** *collaborate.*

**collect together** *collect.* • Collect together your word processing, desktop publishing, document conversion, and text search programs under one main menu entry. *Collect your word processing, desktop publishing, document conversion, and text search programs under one main menu entry.*

**(a; the) combination (of)** *both; delete.* • Architects use a combination of feet and inches, but the inch units are omitted (e.g., 7'2). *Architects use feet and inches, but the inch units are omitted (e.g., 7'2).*

**(a; the) combination of . . . along with (combined with; coupled with; joined with; paired with; together with)** *along with (combined with; coupled with; joined with; paired with; together with).* • The combination of the Relaxation Response coupled with the person's particular belief will work. *The Relaxation Response coupled with the person's particular belief will work.*

**(a; the) combination of both** *both (of them); combination.* • A combination of both whites and blacks are members of these groups. *Both whites and blacks are members of these groups.*

**(a; the) combination of the two** *both (of them); combination.* • You may use either technique or a combination of the two. *You may use either or both techniques.*

**combine both** *combine.* • The latest development is to combine both record and programming so the user can record and then edit macros. *The latest* *development is to combine record and programming so the user can record and then edit macros.*

**combine into one** *combine.* • The single justice noted that combining the two motions into one was a minor procedural discrepancy. *The single justice noted that combining the two motions was a minor procedural discrepancy.*

**combine together** *combine.* • The mixed chart allows you to combine different types of charts together. *The mixed chart allows you to combine different types of charts.*

**come about** *befall; happen; occur; result; take place.*

**come as a disappointment (to)** *disappoint.* • I know this may come as a disappointment to some of you, but my husband is not going to be running for office. *I know this may disappoint some of you, but my husband is not going to be running for office.*

**come as a relief (to)** *relieve.* • The pronunciation system of the former OED, a frequent source of criticism, has been replaced by the International Phonetic Alphabet, which should come as a relief to many. *The pronunciation system of the former OED, a frequent source of criticism, has been replaced by the International Phonetic Alphabet, which should relieve many.*

**come as a surprise (to)** *startle; surprise.* • It came as a surprise to all the women who work with the senator to learn that his wife left him. *It surprised all the women who work with the senator to learn that his wife left him.*

**come close (near) to** *approach; resemble.* • The results of a true national probability sample would most likely come close to these findings. *The results of a true national probability sample would most likely approach these findings.*

**come equipped (furnished) with** *come with; equipped (furnished) with.* • All computers come equipped with a keyboard. *All computers come with a keyboard.*

**come in contact (with)** *come across; contact; discover; encounter; find; locate; meet (with); spot; touch.* • If the part is designed to come in contact with another surface, the rough surface must be machined. *If the part is designed to touch another surface, the rough surface must be machined.*

**come into being** *appear; arise; evolve; exist.*

**come into existence** *appear; arise; evolve; exist.* • In the chain network, the possibility of screening by levels comes into existence. *In the chain network, the possibility of screening by levels arises.*

**come into play** *appear; arise; come about; develop; emerge; happen; occur; result; surface; take place; turn up; unfold.* • When they act out their depression, thoughts of suicide can come into play. *When they act out their depression, thoughts of suicide can surface.*

**come into (to) (a; the) . . . (of)** delete. • Eventually they came to the recognition that the supercomputer business is a high stakes poker game. *Eventually they recognized that the supercomputer business is a high stakes poker game.* • It neither glosses over the true historical picture nor attempts to come to the defense of any individuals. *It neither glosses over the true historical picture nor attempts to defend any individuals.*

**come to (an; the) accord** *agree; compromise; concur; decide; resolve; settle.*

**come to a close** *cease; close; complete; conclude; end; finish; halt; stop.*

**come to a (the) conclusion** *cease; close; complete; conclude; end; finish; halt; stop.* • In August, the first wave of exploration of the solar system came to a conclusion with Voyager 2's swoop past the present outermost planet, Neptune. *In August, the first wave of exploration of the solar system concluded with Voyager 2's swoop past the present outermost planet, Neptune.*

**come to (an; the) agreement** *agree; compromise; concur; decide; resolve; settle.* • The parents and the school board have not yet come to an agreement on whether the child should be in regular classes. *The parents and the school board have not yet agreed on whether the child should be in regular classes.*

**come to a halt** *cease; close; complete; conclude; end; finish; halt; stop.* • Suddenly, all activity came to a halt. *Suddenly, all activity stopped.*

**come to an end** *cease; close; complete; conclude; end; finish; halt; stop.* • He sees himself as the last survivor of the so-called Bengal Renaissance, the vital and creative cultural movement that was initiated by Ram Mohan Roy (c. 1774–1833) and that came to an end with the death of Rabindranath Tagore in 1941. *He sees himself as the last survivor of the so-called Bengal Renaissance, the vital and creative cultural movement that was initiated by Ram Mohan Roy (c. 1774–1833) and that ceased with the death of Rabindranath Tagore in 1941.*

**come to a standstill** *cease; close; complete; conclude; end; finish; halt; stop.* • A spokesman for the Export-Import Bank of Japan said talks with China have come to a standstill. *A spokesman for the Export-Import Bank of Japan said talks with China have ceased.*

**come to (a; the) compromise** *agree; compromise; concur; decide; resolve; settle.*

**come to (a; the) conclusion** *conclude; decide; deduce; determine; infer; judge; reason; resolve; settle.* • We came to the conclusion that she should start with antibiotics. *We decided that she should start with antibiotics.*

**come to (a; the) decision (on; upon)** *conclude; decide; deduce; determine; infer; judge; reason; resolve; settle.* • It was during the counseling session that we came to the decision to let Allison move in with us. *It was during the counseling session that we decided to let Allison move in with us.*

**come to (a; the) determination (on; upon)** *conclude; decide; deduce; determine; infer; judge; reason; resolve; settle.*

**come to discover (find; find out)** *discover; find; learn.*

**come to (an; the) estimate (estimation) (of)** *approximate; assess; estimate; evaluate; rate.*

**come to find out** *discern; discover; find out.*

**come together** *assemble; congregate; converge; gather.* • In the days before mass immunizations when compulsory education began, disease could spread quickly as large numbers of children came together in unsanitary, poorly heated, poorly ventilated buildings. *In the days before mass immunizations when compulsory education began, disease could spread quickly as large numbers of children gathered in unsanitary, poorly heated, poorly ventilated buildings.*

**come to grips with** *accept; comprehend; cope with; deal with; face; struggle with; understand.* • The systems software maker is now coming to grips with a period of rapid growth. *The systems software maker is now struggling with a period of rapid growth.*

**come to light** *emerge; surface; transpire.* • In the past year, a few new clues have come to light. *In the past year, a few new clues have transpired.*

**come to (an; the) opinion** *conclude; decide; deduce; determine; infer; judge; reason; resolve; settle.* • I came to the opinion that it was an electrical fire, not arson. *I deduced that it was an electrical fire, not arson.*

**come to pass** *befall; happen; occur; result; take place.* • If this should come to pass, it would benefit everybody. *If this should happen, it would benefit everybody.*

**come to (a; the) resolution (about; on)** *agree; conclude; decide; determine; resolve; settle.* • I don't understand why they did what they did, and I hope we can come to a resolution about it. *I don't understand why they did what they did, and I hope we can resolve it.*

**come to (a; the) settlement** *agree; conclude; decide; resolve; settle.*

**come to terms (on; upon)** *agree; arbitrate; compromise; concur; decide; settle.* • What they can't come to terms on is whether selling the profitable Eastern Shuttle will cure the airline or kill it. *What they can't agree on is whether selling the profitable Eastern Shuttle will cure the airline or kill it.*

**come to terms with** *accept; comprehend; cope with; deal with; face; struggle with; understand.* • Fitzwater said the president has come to terms with the constant press attention. *Fitzwater said the president has accepted the constant press attention.*

**come to (an; the) understanding** *agree; compromise; concur; decide; resolve; settle.*

**come up with** *craft; create; design; devise; draft; fashion; find; form; make; map (out); mold; plan; plot; prepare; produce; propose; shape; sketch; suggest.* • The NRC has given the nuclear plant a month to come up with a workable plan. *The NRC has given the nuclear plant a month to devise a workable plan.*

**comfortably ensconced** *ensconced.* • He is comfortably ensconced as head of the national guard of Panama. *He is ensconced as head of the national guard of Panama.*

**comfort facilities** *bathroom; toilet.* • It seems to me that the required visitor-information services, tour departments, and comfort facilities could be provided in a leased ground-floor space in an existing nearby building. *It seems to me that the required visitor-information services, tour departments, and bathrooms could be provided in a leased ground-floor space in an existing nearby building.*

**comical** *comic.*

**commence** *begin; start.* • If the candidate accepts the employment offer, the next phase commences. *If the candidate accepts the employment offer, the next phase begins.*

**commencement** *start.* • Investment of the net proceeds will take place during a period which will not exceed six months from the commencement of operations. *Investment of the net proceeds will take place during a period which will not exceed six months from the start of operations.*

**commit (a; the) . . . (of)** delete. • You could not give it to your spouse without committing a violation of federal law. *You could not give it to your spouse without violating federal law.*

**common (and) everyday** *common; everyday.*

**communicate (with)** *call; call or write; phone; speak (with); talk (to); write (to).* • Please communicate with us at your first opportunity. *Please call us at your first opportunity.*

**communicate in writing** *write.*

**communication** *dialogue; letter; message; note; report; speech; talk; text; words.* • Nurses frequently make the assumption that their communication has been listened to and understood by patients. *Nurses frequently make the assumption that their words have been listened to and understood by patients.*

**comparatively** *-(i)er; less; more.* • Computing what happens to stars and gas in a galactic cube, 100 cells on a side, turns out to be comparatively straightforward. *Computing what happens to stars and gas in a galactic cube, 100 cells on a side, turns out to be more straightforward.*

**comparatively . . . compared (contrasted) to (with)** *compared (contrasted) to (with).* • The muscle mass is comparatively small compared to other ruminants. *The muscle mass is small compared to other ruminants.*

**comparatively -(i)er than (less than; more than)** *-(i)er than (less than; more than).* • U.S. experts say the Soviet budget deficit that Moscow has finally acknowledged is comparatively larger than that of America. *U.S. experts say the Soviet budget deficit that Moscow has finally acknowledged is larger than that of America.*

**compare against (versus)** *compare to (with).* • Compare the printout carefully against Figure 50. *Compare the printout carefully with Figure 50.*

**compare and contrast (versus)** *compare (to); contrast (to).* • Perhaps it should have appeared in the Living section, where lifestyles of women from other Arab populations could be compared and contrasted to those living in the occupied territories under Israeli control. *Perhaps it should have appeared* *in the Living section, where lifestyles of women from other Arab populations could be contrasted to those living in the occupied territories under Israeli control.* • Compare and contrast logical versus physical organization. *Compare logical to physical organization.*

**compared to (with)** *against; alongside; beside; -(i)er than; less; less than; more; more than; next to; over; than; to; versus.* • Smoking prevalence has declined across all educational groups, but the decline has occurred five times faster among the higher educated compared with the less educated. *Smoking prevalence has declined across all educational groups, but the decline has occurred five times faster among the higher educated than the less educated.* • Volume on the Big Board averaged 153.57 million shares a day compared to 153.39 million in the first week of 1989. *Volume on the Big Board averaged 153.57 million shares a day against 153.39 million in the first week of 1989.* • Heavy buying of dollars by traders, or governments, on exchange markets drives up its price, making it strong compared to other currencies. *Heavy buying of dollars by traders, or governments, on exchange markets drives up its price, making it stronger than other currencies.*

**compared (contrasted) to (with) . . . relatively** *compared (contrasted) to (with).* • Compared to the advantages, there are relatively few disadvantages for a sole proprietorship. *Compared to the advantages, there are few disadvantages for a sole proprietorship.*

**compartmentalize** *compartment.*

**compensate** *pay.*

**compensation** *cash; fee; money; pay; payment; reward; wage.*

**competency** *competence.* • I feel this would be a good way of assessing his competency. *I feel this would be a good way of assessing his competence.*

**compile together** *compile.* • A database is a compilation of data, such as PsychLit, which compiles all psychological journal abstracts together. *A database is a compilation of data, such as PsychLit, which compiles all psychological journal abstracts.*

**complete and utter** *complete; utter.* • It is going to be a complete and utter mess for people to figure out. *It is going to be an utter mess for people to figure out.*

**completely** delete. • The car was completely destroyed in the fire. *The car was destroyed in the fire.*

**completely (entirely; exclusively; fully; solely; thoroughly; totally; utterly; wholly) dedicated to** *dedicated to.* • SDS recently moved into a new facility exclusively dedicated to EWSD development for the U.S. market. *SDS recently moved into a new facility dedicated to EWSD development for the U.S. market.*

**completely (entirely; exclusively; fully; solely; thoroughly; totally; utterly; wholly) devoted to** *devoted to.* • The store was devoted entirely to consumer-oriented systems of racks, shelves, bins and hooks, largely of European manufacture, all designed to make a small space more serviceable. *The store was devoted to consumer-oriented systems of racks, shelves, bins and hooks, largely of European manufacture, all designed to make a small space more serviceable.*

**completely (entirely; fully; thoroughly; totally; utterly; wholly) eliminate** *eliminate.* • Computer specialists at MIT said it would take several more days to entirely eliminate the virus. *Computer specialists at MIT said it would take several more days to eliminate the virus.*

**completely (entirely; fully; thoroughly; totally; utterly; wholly) eradicate** *eradicate.* • Dr. Carlos said he expects the trend to continue, although completely eradicating the decay is probably not possible. *Dr. Carlos said he expects the trend to continue, although eradicating the decay is probably not possible.*

**completely (entirely; fully; thoroughly; totally; utterly; wholly) unanimous** *unanimous.*

**complete monopoly** *monopoly.*

**component** *part.* • Two-tier coverage was cited as an important component of successful marketing. *Two-tier coverage was cited as an important part of successful marketing.*

**component (and) part (piece)** *component; part; piece.* • The plants manufacture electrical appliances or component parts for the appliances. *The plants manufacture electrical appliances or parts for the appliances.*

**conceive (of) an (the) idea (for)** *conceive (of).* • While a student at Cambridge University, he conceived an idea for a calculator that would calculate and print logarithmic tables. *While a student at Cambridge University, he conceived of a calculator that would calculate and print logarithmic tables.*

**concentrate ... attention on (upon)** *concentrate on; focus on.* • Eastern has decided to concentrate most of its attention on keeping its shuttle going. *Eastern has decided to concentrate on keeping its shuttle going.*

**concentrate (media; people's; public) attention on (upon)** *advertise; announce; blazon; broadcast; disclose; divulge; expose; herald; indicate; make known; make public; mention; point out; point to; present; proclaim; promote; publicize; reveal; show; tell; uncover; unveil.* • She never became president of the American Economics Association—perhaps because of her relentless work concentrating attention on the low status of women in the profession. *She never became president of the American Economics Association—perhaps because of her relentless work exposing the low status of women in the profession.*

**concentrate . . . effort on (upon)** *concentrate on; focus on.* • If we concentrate our effort on the areas of most need, we might be able to make a difference. *If we concentrate on the areas of most need, we might be able to make a difference.*

**concentrate . . . energy on (upon)** *concentrate on; focus on.* • Students need to concentrate their energies on their studies, extracurricular activities, and work. *Students need to focus on their studies, extracurricular activities, and work.*

**concentrate . . . time and energy on (upon)** *concentrate on; focus on.* • We still have 10 million gallons of oil in the water, and we ought to be concentrating our time and energy on minimizing the damage that that does. *We still have 10 million gallons of oil in the water, and we ought to be concentrating on minimizing the damage that that does.*

**concerning** *about; as for; as to; for; in; of; on; over; to; toward; with;* delete. • The Federal Reserve Board makes available various indexes, including one concerning industrial production. *The Federal Reserve Board makes available various indexes, including one about industrial production.*

**conclusive end** *conclusion; end.*

**concurrently** *as one; at once; jointly; together.*

**concurrently . . . while** *while.* • Schools need better tools to help them concurrently diagnose their level of functioning while establishing developmental plans for improvement. *Schools need better tools to help them diagnose their level of functioning while establishing developmental plans for improvement.*

**concurrent (concurrently) with** *while; with.* • Concurrent with rejecting the tender offer, Prime's directors approved a series of defensive measures.

*While rejecting the tender offer, Prime's directors approved a series of defensive measures.*

**(a; the) . . . condition** delete. • Congruency is a necessary condition for clients to develop trust in nurses. *Congruency is necessary for clients to develop trust in nurses.*

**conduct (a; the) . . . (into; of; on; to; with)** delete. • We conducted interviews with EFT industry experts early in the study. *We interviewed EFT industry experts early in the study.* • Another method of collecting information is to conduct research on hunters' opinions about the merits of introducing a hunting seat on the market. *Another method of collecting information is to research hunters' opinions about the merits of introducing a hunting seat on the market.* • They should conduct an investigation into how these scholarships were awarded with no set criteria for selection, and explain why linguistic minorities are seemingly underrepresented. *They should investigate how these scholarships were awarded with no set criteria for selection, and explain why linguistic minorities are seemingly underrepresented.*

**congregate together** *congregate*. • We feel that the five baby dinosaurs were congregating together behind a sand dune in a sandstorm. *We feel that the five baby dinosaurs were congregating behind a sand dune in a sandstorm.*

**connected with** *for; in; linked to; of; -'s; with*. • Obviously, the most profitable method of investing would be to buy low and sell high; however, there are several problems connected with this method. *Obviously, the most profitable method of investing would be to buy low and sell high; however, there are several problems with this method.*

**connect together** *connect; link*. • A network is two or more computers connected together with cables so that they can exchange files and share resources. *A network is two or more computers connected with cables so that they can exchange files and share resources.*

**consecutive** *straight*.

**consensus (of) opinion** *consensus*. • There is a consensus of opinion in this country against executing our young. *There is a consensus in this country against executing our young.*

**consequence** *import; moment*.

**consequence** *effect; outcome; result*.

**consequence (effect; outcome) resulting from** *consequence (effect; outcome) of; result of.* • The potential long-term outcomes resulting from their reactions are destroyed creativity and stifled initiative. *The potential long-term outcomes of their reactions are destroyed creativity and stifled initiative.*

**consequently** *hence; so; then; therefore; thus.* • They were victims of misfortune or of circumstances beyond their control, and consequently, they live in shelters or on the streets. *They were victims of misfortune or of circumstances beyond their control, and thus, they live in shelters or on the streets.*

**(a; the) considerable (good; great; huge; large; sizable; vast) amount (of)** *a good (great) deal (of); a good (great) many (of); almost all (of); considerable; many (of); most (of); much (of); nearly all (of); vast; delete.* • It's operationally complex and requires a large amount of resources. *It's operationally complex and requires vast resources.*

**(a; the) considerable (good; great; huge; large; sizable; vast) degree (of)** *a good (great) deal (of); considerable; great; much (of); vast; delete.* • They now realize they showed a considerable degree of insensitivity toward small businesses. *They now realize they showed great insensitivity toward small businesses.*

**(a; the) considerable (good; great; huge; large; sizable; vast) element (of)** *a good (great) deal (of); considerable; great; much (of); vast; delete.* • True to the spirit of covert operations, there was a large element of deception and dissembling in this struggle. *True to the spirit of covert operations, there was much deception and dissembling in this struggle.*

**(a; the) considerable (good; great; huge; large; overwhelming; vast; sizable; wide) majority (of)** *a good (great) deal (of); a good (great) many (of); almost all (of); (nine) in (ten) (of); many (of); most (of); much (of); nearly all (of); (43) of (48) (of); ... percent (of); three-fourths (two-thirds) (of); delete.* • The two own the vast majority of the stock. *The two own almost all the stock.*

**(a; the) considerable (good; great; huge; large; overwhelming; sizable; vast) number (of)** *a good (great) many (of); almost all (of); countless; dozens (of); hundreds (of); many (of); millions (of); most (of); nearly all (of); numerous; scores (of); six hundred (twelve hundred); thousands (of).* • The language provides a large number of primitive data types. *The language provides dozens of primitive data types.*

**(a; the) considerable (good; great; huge; large; sizable; vast) part (of)** *a good (great) deal (of); a good (great) many (of); almost all (of); (nine) in (ten)* *(of); many (of); most (of); much (of); nearly all (of); (43) of (48) (of); (67) percent (of); three-fourths (two-thirds) (of);* delete. • What may surprise you, however, is that a large part of this analysis is within your reach at little or no cost. *What may surprise you, however, is that much of this analysis is within your reach at little or no cost.*

**(a; the) considerable (good; great; huge; large; overwhelming; sizable; vast) percentage (of)** *a good (great) deal (of); a good (great) many (of); almost all (of); (nine) in (ten) (of); many (of); most (of); much (of); nearly all (of); (43) of (48) (of); (67) percent (of); three-fourths (two-thirds) (of);* delete. • We know that a large percentage of IRA contributors had been saving very little before IRAs were created. *We know that one-third of IRA contributors had been saving very little before IRAs were created.*

**(a; the) considerable (good; great; huge; large; sizable; vast) portion (of)** *a good (great) deal (of); a good (great) many (of); almost all (of); (nine) in (ten) (of); many (of); most (of); much (of); nearly all (of); (43) of (48) (of); (67) percent (of); three-fourths (two-thirds) (of);* delete. • It will be unseasonably cool over a considerable portion of the United States today. *It will be unseasonably cool over much of the United States today.*

**(a; the) considerable (good; great; huge; large; sizable; vast) proportion (of)** *a good (great) deal (of); a good (great) many (of); almost all (of); (nine) in (ten) (of); many (of); most (of); much (of); nearly all (of); (43) of (48) (of); (67) percent (of); three-fourths (two-thirds) (of);* delete. • They may squander huge proportions of their purchasing power by paying high instead of low prices on each purchase. *They may squander much of their purchasing power by paying high instead of low prices on each purchase.*

**(a; the) considerable (good; great; huge; large; sizable; vast) quantity (of)** *a good (great) deal (of); a good (great) many (of); almost all (of); dozens (of); hundreds (of); many (of); millions (of); most (of); much (of); nearly all (of); scores (of); six hundred (twelve hundred) (of); thousands (of).* • Students often fail to remember or understand large quantities of their elementary calculus. *Students often fail to remember or understand much of their elementary calculus.*

**considerably** *a good (great) deal; amply; far; greatly; largely; mostly; much; vastly.* • This is considerably different from the past, when information was printed and approved before being passed up the hierarchy. *This is far different from the past, when information was printed and approved before being passed up the hierarchy.*

**consider as** *consider.* • It could be considered as false advertising. *It could be considered false advertising.*

**consider as being** *consider.* • In many ways, software engineering may be considered as being similar to various other sciences and branches of engineering. *In many ways, software engineering may be considered similar to various other sciences and branches of engineering.*

**considering the fact that** *because; considering; for; in that; since; when.* • Considering the fact that the average person uses 77 gallons of water a day, we can estimate that each person uses close to 26 gallons of water every day simply by flushing the toilet. *Since the average person uses 77 gallons of water a day, we can estimate that each person uses close to 26 gallons of water every day simply by flushing the toilet.*

**consolidate together** *consolidate.* • Cooperatives are independent firms that have consolidated parts of their operations together into one organization. *Cooperatives are independent firms that have consolidated parts of their operations into one organization.*

**constitute** *be; compose; form; make up.* • Corporate debt issues constitute the largest segment, totaling more than $341 billion in 1986. *Corporate debt issues make up the largest segment, totaling more than $341 billion in 1986.*

**contact** *call; phone; reach; write (to).* • She contacted the state agency that helps welfare recipients. *She called the state agency that helps welfare recipients.*

**contagious disease** *contagion.*

**contain (a; the) . . . of** delete. • Chapter 15 contains a formal discussion of the theoretical underpinnings of these formulas. *Chapter 15 formally discusses the theoretical underpinnings of these formulas.* • Table 4-3 contains a list of all 26 ProDOS commands and command numbers. *Table 4-3 lists all 26 ProDOS commands and command numbers.*

**continue in existence (to exist)** *continue; endure; exist; last; persevere; persist; prevail; remain; survive.* • The possibility of becoming an independent company continues to exist. *The possibility of becoming an independent company persists.*

**continue into the future** *continue.* • The rate of growth in the market is expected to continue into the future. *The rate of growth in the market is expected to continue.*

**continue on** *continue.* • If he doesn't raise enough money, he won't be able to continue on. *If he doesn't raise enough money, he won't be able to continue.*

**continue to be** *be still; remain; stay.* • This was the case before the New York state law and continues to be the case after the New York state law. *This was the case before the New York state law and remains the case after the New York state law.*

**continue to remain** *be still; remain; stay.* • Sex stereotypes continue to remain a problem in the military. *Sex stereotypes remain a problem in the military.*

**contractual agreement** *agreement; contract.* • Contractual agreements with independent distributors in Indonesia are required by law to be for a minimum of three years. *Contracts with independent distributors in Indonesia are required by law to be for a minimum of three years.*

**contrariwise** *but; conversely; however; instead; not so; rather; still; whereas; yet.*

**contrary to** *after all; apart (from); aside (from); despite; even with; for all; with all.* • Contrary to some of the things you've heard, I am the same man I was when I came to Washington. *Despite some of the things you've heard, I am the same man I was when I came to Washington.*

**contrasted to (with)** *against; alongside; beside; compared to (with); -(i)er than; less; less than; more; more than; next to; over; than; to; unlike; versus; vis-à-vis.*

**contribute to** *add to.*

**converge together** *converge.*

**(in) conversation** *talk.*

**converse** *speak; talk.* • She has multiple personalities, and I was able to converse with all of them. *She has multiple personalities, and I was able to talk with all of them.*

**convicted felon** *felon.* • There are concerns over the fact that the bank loaned money to convicted felons. *There are concerns over the fact that the bank loaned money to felons.*

**cooperate together** *cooperate.*

**core essence** *core; crux; essence; gist; pith; substance.* • Issues are supposed to be the core essence of a political convention. *Issues are supposed to be the core of a political convention.*

**correctional (prison) facility** *jail; prison.* • Opponents complained that a prison facility for 500 inmates and several hundred staff members would overwhelm the town of barely 800 people. *Opponents complained that a prison for 500 inmates and several hundred staff members would overwhelm the town of barely 800 people.*

**correspondence** *letter; memo; note; report.*

**(a; the) countless number (of)** *countless; endless; infinite; millions (of); myriad; numberless; untold.* • The congestion has resulted in interminable delays and countless numbers of accidents for motorists. *The congestion has resulted in interminable delays and countless accidents for motorists.*

**couple together** *couple.*

**course of action** *action; course; direction; intention; method; move; plan; policy; procedure; route; scheme; strategy.* • The coalition has urged a boycott of tuna, but strengthening existing laws—and enforcing them—would be a better course of action. *The coalition has urged a boycott of tuna, but strengthening existing laws—and enforcing them—would be a better course.*

**cover over** *cover.*

**criminal act** *crime.* • Certainly if a public official commits a criminal act, he or she must face full consequences. *Certainly if a public official commits a crime, he or she must face full consequences.*

**criminal offense** *crime; offense.* • Mr. Hurd said he had misgivings about making drinking on the streets a criminal offense. *Mr. Hurd said he had misgivings about making drinking on the streets an offense.*

**criminal record** *record.*

**criminal wrongdoing** *crime; wrongdoing.* • He may not be guilty of any criminal wrongdoing, but he is a terrible U.S. attorney. *He may not be guilty of any crime, but he is a terrible U.S. attorney.*

**(a; the) critical . . . in (of; to)** *critical to.* • A critical ingredient in a manager's philosophy of change is how much emphasis is placed on trust in the work environment. *Critical to a manager's philosophy of change is how much emphasis is placed on trust in the work environment.* • Active cooperation between all industry groups is a critical factor to the success of EFT and POS. *Active cooperation between all industry groups is critical to the success of EFT and POS.*

**(a; the) crucial . . . in (of; to)** *crucial to.* • He believes hostility is a crucial component of the Type A personality and a potent predictor of heart trouble. *He believes hostility is crucial to the Type A personality and a potent predictor of heart trouble.*

**currently** *(just; right) now; today; (just) yet;* delete. • It's the only spreadsheet currently on the market that has the look and feel of WordPerfect. *It's the only spreadsheet now on the market that has the look and feel of WordPerfect.*

**current (present) status** *status.* • Nothing material to date can be reported on the current status of these negotiations. *Nothing material to date can be reported on the status of these negotiations.*

**custom-built** *custom; tailored.* • At least one vendor uses a custom-built database system in addition to a commercial one to speed up operations. *At least one vendor uses a custom database system in addition to a commercial one to speed up operations.*

**custom-made** *custom; tailored.* • Our courses are custom-made to meet the training needs of each client. *Our courses are tailored to meet the training needs of each client.*

**custom-tailored** *custom; customized; tailored.* • Customers today demand custom-tailored solutions to communications problems. *Customers today demand customized solutions to communications problems.*

**cut by (in) half** *halve.* • A cooperative agreement was announced that could cut by half the amount of ozone-destroying chemicals released in the service and repair of auto air conditioners. *A cooperative agreement was announced that could halve the amount of ozone-destroying chemicals released in the service and repair of auto air conditioners.*

**cyclical** *cyclic.* • The lengths of time within cyclical periods tend to vary. *The lengths of time within cyclic periods tend to vary.*

# D

**date back to** *date from; date to.* • Rogation Days date back at least to the 13th century and probably to the days before the Norman Conquest. *Rogation Days date to at least the 13th century and probably to the days before the Norman Conquest.*

**day in (and) day out** *always; ceaselessly; consistently; constantly; daily; endlessly; eternally; everlastingly; every day; forever; invariably; never ending; perpetually; routinely; unfailingly.* • I was doing portraits day in and day out. *I was doing portraits every day.*

**day-to-day routine** *routine.* • I am greatly tired of the day-to-day routine. *I am greatly tired of the routine.*

**dead body** *body.* • They found a dead body in the river. *They found a body in the river.*

**(a) decade's (year's) history of** *(a) decade (year) of.* • In spite of over a year's history of unusual trading in "Inside Wall Street" highlighted stocks, BW amazingly did not alert the New York Stock Exchange or the Securities & Exchange Commission. *In spite of over a year of unusual trading in "Inside Wall Street" highlighted stocks, BW amazingly did not alert the New York Stock Exchange or the Securities & Exchange Commission.*

**decapitate (the) head (of)** *behead; decapitate.* • I never could watch my father decapitate the heads of our chickens. *I never could watch my father decapitate our chickens.*

**(a; the) declining (decreasing; diminishing; dwindling) amount (degree; extent; part; percentage; portion; proportion) (of)** *decreasingly; less; less and less.*

**(a; the) declining (decreasing; diminishing; dwindling) number (quantity) (of)** *decreasingly; few; fewer and fewer.*

**decrease down** *decrease.*

**decreasing in** *decreasingly.*

**deductive reasoning** *deduction.*

**deem as** *deem.*

**(most; very) definitely** *yes.*

**(a; the) . . . degree of** delete. • He provides a healthy and thoughtful degree of skepticism about prospects for positive change at the national level. *He provides a healthy and thoughtful skepticism about prospects for positive change at the national level.* • Competitor reaction cannot be predicted with any degree of accuracy. *Competitor reaction cannot be predicted with any accuracy.*

**demise** *death; end.* • That access is hastening the demise of many U.S. industries. *That access is hastening the end of many U.S. industries.*

**depart** *leave.* • The president departs for Moscow this morning. *The president leaves for Moscow this morning.*

**dependency** *dependence.* • It may also be difficult for these people to make the decision to marry because of the dependency and commitment required in an intimate relationship. *It may also be difficult for these people to make the decision to marry because of the dependence and commitment required in an intimate relationship.*

**depreciate in value** *depreciate.* • He was carrying several hundred condos which depreciated between 10 and 30 percent in value. *He was carrying several hundred condos which depreciated between 10 and 30 percent.*

**derive benefit (from)** *benefit.* • This suggests that many people would derive benefit from "stand-up and stretch" workbreaks. *This suggests that many people would benefit from "stand-up and stretch" workbreaks.*

**derive enjoyment from** *admire; delight in; enjoy; rejoice in; relish; savor.*

**derive pleasure from** *admire; appreciate; delight in; enjoy; rejoice in; relish; savor.* • We derived great pleasure from their performance. *We delighted in their performance.*

**derive satisfaction from** *admire; appreciate; delight in; enjoy; rejoice in; relish; savor.* • If you derive genuine satisfaction from being in a leadership role, you will obviously bring that attitude to your role as a meeting leader. *If you genuinely enjoy being in a leadership role, you will obviously bring that attitude to your role as a meeting leader.*

**descend down** *descend.* • The summer months of December through February hit the mid-80s and descend down to the mid-60s at night. *The summer months of December through February hit the mid-80s and descend to the mid-60s at night.*

**describe (explain) in . . . detail** *detail.* • The proposal should describe in detail the procedure to be used to obtain data. *The proposal should detail the procedure to be used to obtain data.*

**desideratum** *need.*

**designate as** *designate.* • Designating schools as failed or unsatisfactory could do more damage than the label of success would do good. *Designating schools failed or unsatisfactory could do more damage than the label of success would do good.*

**despite the fact that** *although; but; even though; still; though; yet.* • Despite the fact that all the charts are on paper rather than on-line, the bank reports that departments competed to improve their performance. *Although all the charts are on paper rather than on-line, the bank reports that departments competed to improve their performance.*

**detailed (in-depth) analysis** *analysis; detail.* • Apparently there are some who would discourage any detailed analysis of these weaknesses. *Apparently there are some who would discourage any analysis of these weaknesses.*

**determine the truth (truthfulness; validity; veracity) of** *verify.*

**devoid of** *dis-; il-; im-; in-; ir-; lack; -less(ness); mis-; no; non-; not; un-; want; with no; without.* • Your editorial makes the term censorship somewhat devoid of meaning. *Your editorial makes the term censorship somewhat meaningless.*

**diametrical** *diametral.* • The diametrical pitch is the number of teeth about the circumference divided by the diameter. *The diametral pitch is the number of teeth about the circumference divided by the diameter.*

**(five; many; several) different** *(five; many; several); different.* • My parents own five different homes. *My parents own five homes.*

**(a; the) difficult task** *difficult; task.* • The difficult task of obtaining information for marketing decision-making presents two overriding challenges. *The task of obtaining information for marketing decision-making presents two overriding challenges.*

**difficulty in (of) -ing** *difficulty -ing.* • She has great difficulty in falling asleep. *She has great difficulty falling asleep.*

**diminish down** *diminish.*

**direct . . . attention to** *advertise; announce; blazon; broadcast; disclose; divulge; expose; herald; indicate; make known; make public; mention; point out; point to; present; proclaim; promote; publicize; reveal; show; tell; uncover; unveil.* • The Draper award is seen by some engineering leaders as a way of directing attention to the profession and making sure engineers share the spotlight with scientists. *The Draper award is seen by some engineering leaders as a way of promoting the profession and making sure engineers share the spotlight with scientists.*

**disassociate** *dissociate.* • It set off calls by the faculty for nationally known conservatives to disassociate themselves from alleged Jew-baiting by the *Review,* which in the past has been accused of race-baiting and unfair characterization of women and homosexuals. *It set off calls by the faculty for nationally known conservatives to dissociate themselves from alleged Jew-baiting by the* Review, *which in the past has been accused of race-baiting and unfair characterization of women and homosexuals.*

**discomfiture** *discomfit; discomfort.*

**(in) discussion** *speaking; talking.* • At Honda, managers spend up to 50 percent of their time in discussions with dealers and distributors. *At Honda, managers spend up to 50 percent of their time talking with dealers and distributors.*

**display (a; the) . . . (of; to)** delete. • The Task Manager displays a list of the programs that are currently running. *The Task Manager lists the programs that are currently running.*

**distinct difference (distinctly different)** *different; distinct; distinction.* • We wanted to do something distinctly different. *We wanted to do something distinct.*

**divide in half** *halve.*

**divide up** *divide.* • He suggested we divide up the money between us. *He suggested we divide the money between us.*

**do (a; the) . . . (about; in; of; on; to)** *-(al)ly;* delete. • We did a thorough search of the area and found nothing. *We thoroughly searched the area and found nothing.* • They'd rather build a roadway than provide a program that prevents someone from doing harm to someone else. *They'd rather build a roadway than provide a program that prevents someone from harming someone else.* • Are we supposed to be doing the underlining of the title twice? *Are we supposed to be underlining the title twice?*

**do away with** *cancel; destroy; end; kill; stop.*

**does not ... any** *no; none; nothing.* • I do not understand any of this. *I understand none of this.*

**does not have to** *needs not.* • You do not have to specify extensions when you save or load files. *You need not specify extensions when you save or load files.*

**does not necessarily** *needs not.* • A long waiting time does not necessarily mean that your doctor is smart, successful, busy, dedicated, or involved in saving lives. *A long waiting time need not mean that your doctor is smart, successful, busy, dedicated, or involved in saving lives.*

**does not pay attention to** *ignores.*

**does not remember** *forgets.*

**$ ... dollar** *$. . . .* • A single day of downtime for one of these huge generators can cost up to $1 million dollars. *A single day of downtime for one of these huge generators can cost up to $1 million.*

**dollar amount** delete. • The daily maximum price change is 50 basis points, which is equivalent to a dollar amount of $1,250. *The daily maximum price change is 50 basis points, which is equivalent to $1,250.*

**dollar value** *value.*

**domicile** *(n) home; house.*

**domicile** *(v) dwell; live; reside.*

**done (finished; over) with** *done (finished; over).*

**doomed to fail (failure)** *doomed.* • The governor said the president's strategy is doomed to fail. *The governor said the president's strategy is doomed.*

**dosage** *dose.* • If the recommended dosage does not provide relief of symptoms or symptoms become worse, seek immediate medical attention. *If the recommended dose does not provide relief of symptoms or symptoms become worse, seek immediate medical attention.*

**doubt but that** *doubt that.*

**down the line (pike; road; way)** *at length; from now; in time; later.* • Ten years down the line where are you going to be? *Ten years from now where are you going to be?*

**down to a minimum of** *down to.*

**dramatical** *dramatic.*

**draw attention to** *advertise; announce; blazon; broadcast; disclose; divulge; expose; herald; indicate; make known; make public; mention; point out; point to; present; proclaim; promote; publicize; reveal; show; tell; uncover; unveil.* • Our goal is to draw attention to what has been accomplished in improving the world food situation. *Our goal is to point out what has been accomplished in improving the world food situation.*

**draw (a; the) conclusion** *conclude; deduce; draw; infer; reason.* • What conclusions were you able to draw from your experience? *What were you able to conclude from your experience?*

**draw (an; the) inference** *conclude; deduce; draw; infer; reason.*

**draw to a close (end)** *cease; close; complete; conclude; end; finish; halt; stop.* • Scientists expect to feel in the next few days a real sense of letdown as the first phase of humanity's exploration of the Earth's neighborhood draws to a close. *Scientists expect to feel in the next few days a real sense of letdown as the first phase of humanity's exploration of the Earth's neighborhood concludes.*

**draw to a conclusion** *cease; close; complete; conclude; end; finish; halt; stop.*

**driving force** *drive; energy; force; impetus; motivation; power.* • He is especially concerned about young people and is the driving force behind Catholic Schools United. *He is especially concerned about young people and is the impetus behind Catholic Schools United.*

**drop down** *down; drop.*

**dualistic** *dual.* • They have dualistic meanings. *They have dual meanings.*

**due to the fact that** *because; considering; for; in that; since.* • This procedure is impractical due to the fact that the game tree for any interesting games is extremely large. *This procedure is impractical because the game tree for any interesting games is extremely large.*

**duplicate copy** *copy; duplicate.* • When you want a duplicate copy of one or more files, you use the COPY command. *When you want a copy of one or more files, you use the COPY command.*

**during a (the) juncture (juncture in time; moment; moment in time; period; period in time; point; point in time; stage; stage in time; time) when** *when.* • He had supported my friends and I during the time when we retrieved the abusive pictures from the Marine in Mississippi. *He had supported my friends and I when we retrieved the abusive pictures from the Marine in Mississippi.*

**during the course (length) of** *during; for; in; over; throughout; when; while; with.* • During the course of the analysis, we suppose the array or list contains *n* elements. *Throughout the analysis, we suppose the array or list contains n elements.*

**during (for; over) the decade (period; period of time; span of time; time; years) (from) . . . through (till; to; until)** *between . . . and; from . . . through (to).* • The fees and expenses of the non-interested Trustees for the period November 26, 1986 to October 31, 1987 amounted to $3,731. *The fees and expenses of the non-interested Trustees from November 26, 1986 to October 31, 1987 amounted to $3,731.*

**during the period (period of time; span of time; time; years) (that)** *while.*

**during the rule of** *under.*

**dwindle down** *dwindle.* • A $10,000 gross bonus can dwindle down to a surprisingly small amount with income tax deductions. *A $10,000 gross bonus can dwindle to a surprisingly small amount with income tax deductions.*

**dynamical** *dynamic.*

# E

**each and every (one)** *all; each; every (one).* • Each and every one of these crimes was committed by a pathological killer. *Each of these crimes was committed by a pathological killer.*

**each one** *each.* • My method is to introduce the key elements of office automation and explain each one in concrete terms. *My method is to introduce the key elements of office automation and explain each in concrete terms.*

**(from) each other** delete. • The two dates on the printout differ from each other because the first was entered as text and the second as a code. *The two dates on the printout differ because the first was entered as text and the second as a code.*

**early beginnings** *beginnings.*

**-ed (-en) before (earlier; previously)** *-ed (-en).* • Actually the term was used previously by Thomas Edison. *Actually the term was used by Thomas Edison.*

**edifice** *building.*

**educational institution** *college; school; university.* • Locate and identify a newsgroup available at your educational institution related to marketing. *Locate and identify a newsgroup available at your school related to marketing.*

**effectuate** *bring about; carry out; effect; execute.* • In order to effectuate this policy, the legislature imposed strict liability for all damages resulting from a failure to remove such materials on the owners of residential premises. *In order to effect this policy, the legislature imposed strict liability for all damages resulting from a failure to remove such materials on the owners of residential premises.*

**e.g. . . . and others (and so forth; and so on; and such; and the like; et al.; etc.)** *and others (and so forth; and so on; and such; and the like; et al.; etc.); e.g.; for example; for instance.* • They typically have unpredictable ranges of occurrences, and they usually have related attributes (e.g., skill category, detailed skill description, etc.) that are of interest to the organization. *They* *typically have unpredictable ranges of occurrences, and they usually have related attributes (skill category, detailed skill description, etc.) that are of interest to the organization.*

**egoistical (egotistical)** *egoistic; egotistic.*

**either one** *either.* • The vice president doesn't like either one of them. *The vice president doesn't like either of them.*

**elect as** *elect.*

**electrical** *electric.*

**(a; the) . . . element (in; of; to)** *some;* delete. • There will always be an element of doubt. *There will always be some doubt.* • The florid phrases and poor editing suggest some element of haste in the booklet's concoction. *The florid phrases and poor editing suggest some haste in the booklet's concoction.* • A common element to any system is the need for continuous involvement by top management. *Common to any system is the need for continuous involvement by top management.*

**elliptical** *elliptic.*

**emblematical** *emblematic.*

**emerge out** *emerge.* • Part (d) corresponds to a time when the reflected shock waves have emerged out from the dust cloud. *Part (d) corresponds to a time when the reflected shock waves have emerged from the dust cloud.*

**employ** *use.* • Fewer than one-tenth of the small business prospects worldwide employ computers today. *Fewer than one-tenth of the small business prospects worldwide use computers today.*

**employment** *use.* • The consistent employment of particular defenses leads to the development of personality traits. *The consistent use of particular defenses leads to the development of personality traits.*

**enable . . . to** *let.* • This enables analysts to sense the need for changes in methods. *This lets analysts sense the need for changes in methods.*

**encapsulate** *encapsule.* • The responses provide a snapshot view of current U.S. efforts to use Japanese information and encapsulate some of the challenges faced by both providers and users. *The responses provide a snapshot view of current U.S. efforts to use Japanese information and encapsule some of the challenges faced by both providers and users.*

**encircle** *circle.*

**enclosed herein (herewith) is (please find)** *enclosed is; here is.* • Enclosed herewith please find a letter from our client, Mr. Edward Price, which is self-explanatory. *Here is a letter from our client, Mr. Edward Price, which is self-explanatory.*

**enclosed is** *here is.*

**encounter** *find; have; meet;* delete. • This support usually consists of a technical representative you can call if you encounter a problem. *This support usually consists of a technical representative you can call if you have a problem.*

**endeavor** *try.*

**end product** *product.* • Each writer has his or her own process because there are different ways to make the end product. *Each writer has his or her own process because there are different ways to make the product.*

**end (final; net; ultimate) result** *result.* • The end result was a series of consolidations that lasted until a single company was left to serve the market. *The result was a series of consolidations that lasted until a single company was left to serve the market.*

**engage in . . . (a; the)** delete. • I appreciate the straightforward way in which you've engaged in this discussion. *I appreciate the straightforward way in which you've discussed this.* • Known as an active force in the labor movement, the unions at the Gillette France plant are engaged in a nationwide campaign to shape public opinion. *Known as an active force in the labor movement, the unions at the Gillette France plant are campaigning nationwide to shape public opinion.*

**enter into a contract** *agree; contract.*

**enter into an agreement** *agree; contract.* • Courier Dispatch Group Inc. said it has entered into an agreement in principle to acquire the assets of J. A. Finn Inc. *Courier Dispatch Group Inc. said it has agreed in principle to acquire the assets of J. A. Finn Inc.*

**entirely** delete. • Our competition introduced an entirely new product. *Our competition introduced a new product.*

**entitle** *title.* • The report is entitled "Outlook for EFTPOS: An Executive Summary." *The report is titled "Outlook for EFTPOS: An Executive Summary."*

**enumerate** *count; list; name; numerate.*

**epidemical** *epidemic.*

**epidemiological** *epidemiologic.*

**epigrammatical** *epigrammatic.*

**epigraphical** *epigraphic.*

**equally as** *equally; as.* • It was equally as difficult for me. *It was equally difficult for me.*

**equitable** *fair.*

**(the) -(i)er . . . of the two** *(the) -(i)er; (the) more.* • Sunday will probably be the better of the two days. *Sunday will probably be the better day.*

**-(i)er . . . rather than** *-(i)er . . . than.* • It is quicker to multiply both sides by the reciprocal of the fraction rather than by the common denominator. *It is quicker to multiply both sides by the reciprocal of the fraction than by the common denominator.*

**essential core** *core; crux; essence; gist; pith; substance.* • The reviewer let himself be diverted by the book's feminist frame and missed its essential core. *The reviewer let himself be diverted by the book's feminist frame and missed its essence.*

**(an; the) essential . . . for (in; of; to)** *essential to.* • Homeownership is an essential part of the American dream. *Homeownership is essential to the American dream.* • His point is that physical contact is an essential element in everyone's life, and most people don't get enough. *His point is that physical contact is essential to everyone's life, and most people don't get enough.* • Toughness is not an essential ingredient for getting ahead, and it isn't the same as resolve. *Toughness is not essential to getting ahead, and it isn't the same as resolve.*

**essential prerequisite** *essential; prerequisite.* • Categorizing a given product is an essential prerequisite for a successful marketing effort. *Categorizing a given product is essential for a successful marketing effort.*

**establish** *set up.*

**establish conclusive evidence (proof) of** *prove.*

**established standard** *standard.* • Over the past few years, a number of spreadsheet, database, and word processing programs have become established

111

standards in their areas of application. *Over the past few years, a number of spreadsheet, database, and word processing programs have become standards in their areas of application.*

**established tradition** *tradition.* • IBM broke established traditions and set up a special group at Boca Raton, Florida, to develop their own microcomputer. *IBM broke traditions and set up a special group at Boca Raton, Florida, to develop their own microcomputer.*

**establishment** *business; club; company; firm; shop; store.* • The state supreme court will decide whether to allow nude dancing to continue at that establishment. *The state supreme court will decide whether to allow nude dancing to continue at that club.*

**-est ever** *-est.* • That amount is the largest ever paid by the city in a civil right's action. *That amount is the largest paid by the city in a civil right's action.*

**et cetera, et cetera, et cetera** *and so forth; and so on; and the like; etc.*

**eventuality** *event; occurrence; outcome;* delete. • Kodak should have prepared for this eventuality. *Kodak should have prepared for this outcome.*

**eventuate** *befall; come about; happen; occur; result; take place.*

**ever and anon** *at times; now and again; now and then; occasionally; once in a while; on occasion; sometimes.*

**every day (month; week; year)** *daily (monthly; weekly; yearly).*

**every now and then** *at times; from time to time; now and again; now and then; occasionally; once in a while; on occasion; sometimes.*

**every once in a while** *at times; from time to time; now and again; now and then; occasionally; once in a while; on occasion; sometimes.* • Every once in a while, I was struck by how hot it was. *Now and then, I was struck by how hot it was.*

**every single (solitary)** *all; every.* • Every single solitary juvenile in these four states was examined. *Every juvenile in these four states was examined.*

**evidence in (to) support of (that)** *evidence for (of; that).* • The great pay-raise debate is on, and the spectator sees very little evidence to support that higher salaries will attract and keep higher-quality candidates. *The great pay-raise debate is on, and the spectator sees very little evidence that higher salaries will attract and keep higher-quality candidates.*

**exact (exactly) duplicate** *duplicate; exact; identical; match; (the) same.*
• Nothing could exactly duplicate what we just heard. *Nothing could match what we just heard.*

**exact (exactly) equivalent** *duplicate; equivalent; exact; identical; match; (the) same.* • This situation is exactly equivalent to our usual neglect of the Earth's rotation when we do experiments in laboratories. *This situation is equivalent to our usual neglect of the Earth's rotation when we do experiments in laboratories.*

**exact (exactly) identical** *duplicate; exact; identical; match; (the) same.* • This pattern, though not exactly identical, tends to recur every year. *This pattern, though not identical, tends to recur every year.*

**exactly sure** *sure.* • I'm not exactly sure of her name. *I'm not sure of her name.*

**exact (exactly) match** *duplicate; exact; identical; match; (the) same.* • When you enter a value that doesn't exactly match one of those listed on the lookup table, the function will find the value equal to or less than the value being looked up. *When you enter a value that doesn't match one of those listed on the lookup table, the function will find the value equal to or less than the value being looked up.*

**exact (exactly) (the) same** *duplicate; exact; identical; just; match; (the) same.* • He used those exact same words. *He used those exact words.*

**examination** *exam.*

**(an) example that illustrates (to illustrate)** *example (of); (to) illustrate.* • Here are some examples to illustrate the benefits of word processing on a network. *Here are some examples of the benefits of word processing on a network.*

**excerption** *excerpt.*

**(an; the) excessive amount (of)** *excessive; too much.*

**(an; the) excessive number (of)** *excessive; too many.* • If your failure to detect errors in the proofing stage results in a published text that contains an excessive number of errors, the costs of making these corrections in a subsequent printing will be charged against your royalties. *If your failure to detect errors in the proofing stage results in a published text that contains excessive errors, the costs of making these corrections in a subsequent printing will be charged against your royalties.*

**excess verbiage** *verbiage.*

**excruciatingly painful** *excruciating; painful.* • It has been an excruciatingly painful experience for the town's 8,000 residents. *It has been an excruciating experience for the town's 8,000 residents.*

**(that) exist** delete. • Ample evidence exists to support the differences in investment tax shields across industries. *Ample evidence supports the differences in investment tax shields across industries.*

**expect (expectation) and hope** *expect (expectation); hope; trust.* • We're pleased with our progress and expect and hope that it will continue as our initiatives take hold. *We're pleased with our progress and expect that it will continue as our initiatives take hold.*

**expediency** *expedience.*

**expeditiously** *apace; fast; promptly; quickly; rapidly; speedily; straightaway.* • This problem must be dealt with expeditiously. *This problem must be dealt with quickly.*

**expenditure (of money)** *cost; expense.* • He deplored the long electoral campaigns that involved heavy expenditures of money and brought the country to a virtual standstill for months. *He deplored the long electoral campaigns that involved heavy costs and brought the country to a virtual standstill for months.*

**experience** *feel; find; go through; have; know; see.* • According to this book, many people have experienced boredom and alienation. *According to this book, many people have known boredom and alienation.*

**experience** delete. • This magazine has experienced tremendous growth in the past two years. *This magazine has grown tremendously in the past two years.*

**express . . . (about; for; of; to)** delete. • He expressed doubt whether the issue would be much of a headache on the campaign trail this fall. *He doubted whether the issue would be much of a headache on the campaign trail this fall.* • Most top executives seem to believe strongly in the need for better human relations, but they often express distrust of the training program itself. *Most top executives seem to believe strongly in the need for better human relations, but they often distrust the training program itself.* • We wish to express our sincere thanks to our special representative for her responsiveness. *We wish to sincerely thank our special representative for her responsiveness.*

**express concern (about)** *agonize (over; about); brood (on; over); dread; fear; fret (about; over); regret; stew (about; over); worry (about; over).* • Some scientists express concern about the implications of splicing the genes for certain insecticides into plants. *Some scientists worry about the implications of splicing the genes for certain insecticides into plants.*

**express opposition to** *contest; criticize; disagree with; disapprove of; dispute; object to; oppose; protest.*

**express skepticism (about)** *disbelieve; distrust; doubt; mistrust; question.* • But others express skepticism about those results, with some scientists' questions verging upon accusations of exaggeration. *But others distrust those results, with some scientists' questions verging upon accusations of exaggeration.*

**express sorrow (about)** *bemoan; deplore; grieve; lament; moan; mourn; regret.* • At a press conference earlier in the day, he had expressed sorrow that American writers and American politics seem to occupy two different worlds. *At a press conference earlier in the day, he had bemoaned that American writers and American politics seem to occupy two different worlds.*

**extend (issue) an invitation to** *invite.* • The Open Software Foundation would like to extend an invitation to you to explore the OSF/Motif user environment. *The Open Software Foundation would like to invite you to explore the OSF/Motif user environment.*

**extend out** *extend.* • Press the right arrow until the highlight extends out to cell F4, and then press Return. *Press the right arrow until the highlight extends to cell F4, and then press Return.*

**extensively throughout** *all through; extensively in (through); throughout.* • Our reporter has traveled extensively throughout South America. *Our reporter has traveled throughout South America.*

**(a; the) . . . extent of** delete.

# F

**face up to** *face.*

**facilitate** *ease; help.*

**facility** *bathroom; building; factory; hospital; jail; office; place; plant; prison; school;* delete. • In 1986, hospital executives estimated that 21 percent of their facilities might close. *In 1986, hospital executives estimated that 21 percent of their hospitals might close.*

**(a; the) . . . factor (in; of; to)** delete. • The fact that we could not have children was a contributing factor to our divorce. *The fact that we could not have children contributed to our divorce.* • Knowing the consequences of obesity should be a motivating factor in losing weight. *Knowing the consequences of obesity should be a motivation in losing weight.* • Researchers indicate, however, that after age 50 lifestyle becomes a less influential factor in physiological change than aging itself. *Researchers indicate, however, that after age 50 lifestyle becomes less influential in physiological change than aging itself.*

**facts and information** *facts; information.* • Request a full disclosure statement highlighting all the pertinent facts and information about the franchisor. *Request a full disclosure statement highlighting all the pertinent facts about the franchisor.*

**factual basis** *basis; fact; reason; truth.* • People who know me know there's no factual basis to the story. *People who know me know there's no truth to the story.*

**fair (just) and equitable** *fair; just; equitable.* • I support fair and equitable taxes to ensure human services are funded. *I support equitable taxes to ensure human services are funded.*

**fair and square** *fair; honest; just; square.*

**false and misleading** *deceptive; false; misleading.*

**false illusion** *illusion.*

**false pretense** *pretense.*

**far and away** *by far; much.* • The judgment was for $10.3 billion, far and away the biggest ever in American commerce. *The judgment was for $10.3 billion, by far the biggest ever in American commerce.*

**far and wide** *broadly; widely.*

**far away from** *far from.* • These blocks are usually physically located far away from the file's data blocks. *These blocks are usually physically located far from the file's data blocks.*

**fasten together** *fasten.* • Screw threads provide a fast and easy method of fastening two parts together and of exerting a force that can be used for adjustment of movable parts. *Screw threads provide a fast and easy method of fastening two parts and of exerting a force that can be used for adjustment of movable parts.*

**favor . . . as opposed to (instead of; rather than)** *favor . . . over; favor . . . to.* • Lager is a pale, American-style beer favored by the young as opposed to the dark, traditional "bitter" English beer. *Lager is a pale, American-style beer favored by the young over the dark, traditional "bitter" English beer.*

**fear and trembling** *anxiety; dismay; dread; fear; foreboding; horror; terror; trembling.*

**(a; the) . . . feeling(s) (of)** delete. • We describe the intensity of the feeling of anger along a four-point scale. *We describe the intensity of anger along a four-point scale.* • Neither of us has any guilt feelings about it. *Neither of us has any guilt about it.*

**feel inside** *feel.* • What's most important is how you feel inside about it. *What's most important is how you feel about it.*

**fervency** *fervor.*

**few and far between** *exiguous; few; infrequent; meager; rare; scant; scanty; scarce; scattered; seldom; sparse; uncommon; unusual.* • Since then the shooting stars have been few and far between. *Since then the shooting stars have been infrequent.*

**few (small) in number** *exiguous; few; infrequent; limited; meager; not many; rare; scant; scanty; scarce; sparse; uncommon.* • Although the clinical trials are few in number and have small patient populations, the response rates are higher than those reported with intravenous chemotherapy. *Although the clinical trials are few and have small patient populations, the response rates are higher than those reported with intravenous chemotherapy.*

**fifty (50) percent (of)** *half (of); one-half (of).* • Nearly fifty percent of the town's population is associated with the university. *Nearly half the town's population is associated with the university.*

**figuratively speaking** *as it were; in a sense; in a way; so to speak.*

**(a; the) . . . figure** delete. • Alan Paton has become something of a legendary figure. *Alan Paton has become something of a legend.*

**figure in** *add; include.*

**figure on (upon)** *expect; plan on.*

**figure out** *decide; determine; discern; discover; think.* • Now, at the age of 50, I have to figure out what I'm going to do with the rest of my life. *Now, at the age of 50, I have to decide what I'm going to do with the rest of my life.*

**figure up** *add; total.*

**fill up** *fill.* • Fill up the tank when you're in town. *Fill the tank when you're in town.*

**fill to capacity** *fill.* • The auditorium was filled to capacity with the singer's adoring fans. *The auditorium was filled with the singer's adoring fans.*

**filter out** *filter.* • It's very hard to filter out fact from fiction. *It's very hard to filter fact from fiction.*

**filthy dirty** *dirty; filthy.*

**final and irrevocable** *final; irrevocable.* • His decision not to seek a fourth term as governor is final and irrevocable. *His decision not to seek a fourth term as governor is final.*

**final (ultimate) completion** *completion.* • Because the order, timing, and costs of the individual tasks are interrelated, they all affect the total cost of the project and its final completion date. *Because the order, timing, and costs of the individual tasks are interrelated, they all affect the total cost of the project and its completion date.*

**final (ultimate) conclusion** *conclusion.* • I haven't yet come to a final conclusion about what we should do. *I haven't yet come to a conclusion about what we should do.*

**final (ultimate) culmination** *culmination.*

**finalize** *complete; conclude; finish.* • After five or ten successful projects, you should review guidelines and begin to finalize the procedure. *After five or ten successful projects, you should review guidelines and begin to complete the procedure.*

**final (ultimate) outcome** *outcome.* • We were saddened by the final outcome. *We were saddened by the outcome.*

**final (ultimate) resolution** *resolution.* • The outcome of these matters is not presently determinable, but the ultimate resolution of such matters will not have a material adverse impact on NYNEX's financial position. *The outcome of these matters is not presently determinable, but the resolution of such matters will not have a material adverse impact on NYNEX's financial position.*

**final (ultimate) settlement** *settlement.*

**financial (monetary) resources** *assets; capital; money; resources.*

**financial wherewithal** *assets; cash; funds; means; money; wherewithal.* • The commission also is considering whether owners have the financial wherewithal to operate the plant. *The commission also is considering whether owners have the money to operate the plant.*

**find out** *find; learn.* • We found out that today's teenagers are very anxious about the future. *We learned that today's teenagers are very anxious about the future.*

**(all) fine (good) and well** *all right; fine; good; great; nice; pleasant; pleasing; welcome; well.*

**finish up** *finish.*

**firm (strong) commitment** *commitment.* • Voters are not firmly committed to any of the candidates. *Voters are not committed to any of the candidates.*

**firm (strong) conviction** *conviction.* • This participative process has enabled us to develop a strong conviction throughout the Company that our strategy is the right one. *This participative process has enabled us to develop a conviction throughout the Company that our strategy is the right one.*

**firmly establish** *establish; firm.* • We should have resolved them earlier in the implementation of the reorganization, before structure and behavior patterns became firmly established. *We should have resolved them earlier* *in the implementation of the reorganization, before structure and behavior patterns became firm.*

**firm (strong) resolution** *resolution.*

**first and foremost** *chief; chiefly; first; foremost; main; mainly; mostly; primarily; primary; principal; principally;* delete. • Football is first and foremost a running game. *Football is primarily a running game.*

**first and last** *only; sole.*

**first and only** *only; sole.* • Was he the first and only person to have superheated ice, yet whose work has fallen into obscurity? *Was he the only person to have superheated ice, yet whose work has fallen into obscurity?*

**first ... before** *before.* • You cannot print a document on the disk that has been fast-saved unless you first positioned the cursor at the end of the document before you saved it. *You cannot print a document on the disk that has been fast-saved unless you positioned the cursor at the end of the document before you saved it.*

**first begin** *begin; start.* • If you note the appropriate framework when you first begin your assignment, you will be able to relate what you know from these broader areas to the text at hand. *If you note the appropriate framework when you begin your assignment, you will be able to relate what you know from these broader areas to the text at hand.*

**first (initially) coined** *coined.* • The term *psychic distance* was initially coined by Swedish researchers at the University of Uppsala. *The term* psychic distance *was coined by Swedish researchers at the University of Uppsala.*

**first come into being** *arise; begin; start.* • When Social Security first came into being, relatively few people lived to the retirement age of 65, so the many were supporting the few. *When Social Security began, relatively few people lived to the retirement age of 65, so the many were supporting the few.*

**first created** *created.*

**first ever** *first.* • This was the first-ever congressional review of the condition of wilderness areas protected from development under a landmark 1964 law. *This was the first congressional review of the condition of wilderness areas protected from development under a landmark 1964 law.*

**first initially** *first; initially.* • When he first initially got the complaint, he wrote a letter to the Human Rights Commission admitting his guilt. *When he* *first got the complaint, he wrote a letter to the Human Rights Commission admitting his guilt.*

**first introduced** *introduced.* • He built on some ideas first introduced by Leibniz almost 200 years earlier. *He built on some ideas introduced by Leibniz almost 200 years earlier.*

**first invented** *invented.*

**firstly** *first.* • Firstly, Brookside Estates is a privately managed and maintained housing complex. *First, Brookside Estates is a privately managed and maintained housing complex.*

**first of all** *first.* • I would first of all ask how many of you are going to help us. *I would first ask how many of you are going to help us.*

**first off** *first.* • First off, these price and yield figures are for multimillion-dollar dealer-to-dealer negotiated transactions at any given hour or day. *First, these price and yield figures are for multimillion-dollar dealer-to-dealer negotiated transactions at any given hour or day.*

**first start** *begin; start.* • The market share of Searle's Calan was fairly low when we first started. *The market share of Searle's Calan was fairly low when we began.*

**first time ever** *first time.* • It's the first time ever that disabled skiers were represented at the Olympics. *It's the first time that disabled skiers were represented at the Olympics.*

**flood over** *flood.*

**fly in the face of** *challenge; contradict; defy; dispute; disregard; go against; ignore; neglect; overlook.* • Although it may be morally reassuring, this tale flies in the face of historical fact. *Although it may be morally reassuring, this tale defies historical fact.*

**focal point** *center; focus.* • The U.S.-Canada trade agreement has been the focal point of the campaign. *The U.S.-Canada trade agreement has been the focus of the campaign.*

**focus . . . attention on (upon)** *concentrate on; focus on.* • It's time we focus our attention on the plight of the poor. *It's time we focus on the plight of the poor.* • I was too wrapped up in my own concerns to be able to focus my attention on him. *I was too wrapped up in my own concerns to be able to concentrate on him.*

**focus (media; people's; public) attention on (upon)** *advertise; announce; blazon; broadcast; disclose; divulge; expose; herald; indicate; make known; make public; mention; point out; point to; present; proclaim; promote; publicize; reveal; show; tell; uncover; unveil.* • All this has helped us focus attention on the problem. *All this has helped us publicize the problem.*

**focus . . . effort on (upon)** *concentrate on; focus on.* • He said the crew would focus efforts on saving baby penguins. *He said the crew would concentrate on saving baby penguins.*

**focus . . . energy on (upon)** *concentrate on; focus on.* • If production focuses its energies on manufacturing a product at the lowest possible cost, but the sales department is willing to accept unprofitable orders, conflict will arise. *If production focuses on manufacturing a product at the lowest possible cost, but the sales department is willing to accept unprofitable orders, conflict will arise.*

**focus in** *focus.* • We're focusing in on what we have to do to achieve this. *We're focusing on what we have to do to achieve this.*

**focus of attention** *cynosure; focus.*

**focus . . . time and energy on (upon)** *concentrate on; focus on.*

**fold up** *fold.* • The commission folded up because the voters implicitly voted to have it fold up. *The commission folded because the voters implicitly voted to have it fold.*

**follow after** *follow.*

**follow along the lines of** *duplicate; imitate; match; resemble.* • There might be a settlement on rates by the end of this year; however, we doubt it will follow along the lines of the New York rate case moratorium. *There might be a settlement on rates by the end of this year; however, we doubt it will resemble the New York rate case moratorium.*

**for all intents and purposes** *effectively; essentially; in effect; in essence; practically; virtually.* • Following treatment with interleukin-2, the nodule for all intents and purposes disappeared. *Following treatment with interleukin-2, the nodule virtually disappeared.*

**for all practical purposes** *effectively; essentially; in effect; in essence; practically; virtually.* • For all practical purposes, there will be no expansion in existing programs. *There will be virtually no expansion in existing programs.*

**for an extended (prolonged; protracted) amount of time (length of time; period; period of time; span of time; time; while)** *awhile; for a long time (while); for a time (while); for days (hours; weeks; years); for six months (three years); long.* • We had observed this family for a prolonged period of time. *We had long observed this family.*

**for another (thing)** *second.* • For another thing, there is still ample legal precedent for highly effective affirmative action programs that stop short of specific quotas. *Second, there is still ample legal precedent for highly effective affirmative action programs that stop short of specific quotas.*

**forasmuch as** *because; considering; for; in that; since.*

**for a while** *awhile.* • After this program executes for a while, procedure B is called. *After this program executes awhile, procedure B is called.*

**for awhile** *awhile.* • If the program continues to run for awhile, the answer may not be so clear. *If the program continues to run awhile, the answer may not be so clear.*

**forebearer** *forebear.* • Episodic reform movements were separated by long periods when many citizens, much like their Colonial forebearers, fantasized that Americans had created a near-utopian society. *Episodic reform movements were separated by long periods when many citizens, much like their Colonial forebears, fantasized that Americans had created a near-utopian society.*

**forecast . . . future** *forecast; foretell; predict.* • After a model is identified as being a good predictor, it is used to forecast future sales. *After a model is identified as being a good predictor, it is used to forecast sales.*

**foretell . . . future** *forecast; foretell; predict.*

**for ever and a day** *always; ceaselessly; consistently; constantly; endlessly; eternally; everlastingly; every day; forever; invariably; never ending; perpetually; routinely; unfailingly.*

**forevermore** *always; evermore; forever.* • I am not naive enough to think that we will forevermore walk hand in hand with the business community to clean the environment. *I am not naive enough to think that we will forever walk hand in hand with the business community to clean the environment.*

**forewarn** *warn.*

**for example (for instance)** *say.* • When the scanner reads the bar code on, for example, a can of beans, the computer looks up the product number the bar code represents and returns its name and price to the register. *When the scanner reads the bar code on, say, a can of beans, the computer looks up the product number the bar code represents and returns its name and price to the register.*

**for example . . . and others (and so forth; and so on; and such; and the like; et al.; etc.; or whatever)** *and others (and so forth; and so on; and such; and the like; et al.; etc.; or whatever); e.g.; for example; for instance.* • Many other examples of the influence religion has on buyer behavior—for example, on values and norms, time, sense of self, and so forth—will be found in the following sections. *Many other examples of the influence religion has on buyer behavior—on values and norms, time, sense of self, and so forth— will be found in the following sections.* • For example, you may create one directory to hold word processing documents, another to hold Applesoft programs, etc. *For example, you may create one directory to hold word processing documents and another to hold Applesoft programs.*

**for fear (that; of) . . . can (could; may; might; shall; should; will; would)** *lest.* • Few of us know what to say to friends who are mourning, so we may avoid them for fear we'll say the wrong thing. *Few of us know what to say to friends who are mourning, so we may avoid them lest we say the wrong thing.*

**for free** *free.* • Purchasers of 1.0 versions will receive 1.1 upgrades for free from IBM. *Purchasers of 1.0 versions will receive free 1.1 upgrades from IBM.*

**for (in; to) (the) furtherance of** *for; to advance; to further; to promote.* • Neither the conspiracy itself nor the overt acts allegedly done in furtherance of it were directed toward Boisjoly. *Neither the conspiracy itself nor the overt acts allegedly done to further it were directed toward Boisjoly.*

**for (an) indefinite (indeterminate) amount of time (length of time; period; period of time; span of time; time; while)** *briefly; for a time; for a while; indefinitely; temporarily.* • We are freezing prices and wages for an indefinite period. *We are freezing prices and wages temporarily.*

**for instance . . . and others (and so forth; and so on; and such; and the like; et al.; etc.; or whatever)** *and others (and so forth; and so on; and such; and the like; et al.; etc.; or whatever); e.g.; for example; for instance.* • Use one of these labels to assign a number and perhaps a descriptive title to each disk, for instance, Disk 1: Letters, Disk 2: Spreadsheet Files, Disk 3: Reports, and so on. *Use one of these labels to assign a number and perhaps a descrip-*

*tive title to each disk, for instance, Disk 1: Letters, Disk 2: Spreadsheet Files, and Disk 3: Reports.*

**for long** *long.* • If top executives cannot control their responsibilities, they usually do not remain in their positions for long. *If top executives cannot control their responsibilities, they usually do not remain long in their positions.*

**form (a; the) judgment** *conclude; decide; deduce; determine; infer; judge; reason; resolve; settle.*

**form (an; the) opinion** *conclude; decide; deduce; determine; infer; judge; reason; resolve; settle.*

**form (a; the) resolution** *conclude; decide; determine; resolve; settle.*

**formulate** *devise; form; make.* • Have you formulated no opinion about her? *Have you formed no opinion about her?*

**for obvious reasons** *obviously.* • For obvious reasons, he wants to announce his choice at the convention. *Obviously, he wants to announce his choice at the convention.*

**for one . . . (be) an example (an instance)** *(be) an example (an instance); for one; one example (one instance).* • The Massachusetts Industrial Services Program, for one, is an example of the kind of broad industrial extension service we think is needed to retool manufacturing facilities. *The Massachusetts Industrial Services Program is one example of the kind of broad industrial extension service we think is needed to retool manufacturing facilities.*

**for one (thing)** *first.* • For one thing, a national program would have to be tailored to each state because the delivery of health care services can differ significantly. *First, a national program would have to be tailored to each state because the delivery of health care services can differ significantly.*

**for . . . purposes (of)** *for; so as to; to.* • The money we receive from licensing John Wayne's image is used entirely for charitable purposes. *The money we receive from licensing John Wayne's image is used entirely for charity.*

**for reasons of** *after; because of; by; for; from; in; out of; through.* • When airlines have replaced older planes, they have done so primarily for reasons of economics—newer aircraft cost less to inspect and repair. *When airlines have replaced older planes, they have done so primarily because of economics—newer aircraft cost less to inspect and repair.*

125

**for some time (now)** *long.* • I have enjoyed reading your articles for some time now. *I have long enjoyed reading your articles.*

**for that matter** *also; and; as well; besides; beyond that (this); even; further; furthermore; moreover; more than that (this); still more; then; too; what is more;* delete. • How can they speak up and tell the South Africans what they should do with their people or, for that matter, what the Soviet Union should do with its Jewish population? *How can they speak up and tell the South Africans what they should do with their people, or even what the Soviet Union should do with its Jewish population?*

**for that (this) reason** *consequently; hence; so; then; therefore; thus.* • For that reason, I wouldn't do it again. *I therefore wouldn't do it again.*

**for the duration (length) of** *during; throughout.* • The company intends to maintain silence for the duration of the sale process. *The company intends to maintain silence during the sale process.*

**for the first (last) time** *first (last).* • The series of studies were presented for the first time at the three-day conference. *The series of studies were first presented at the three-day conference.*

**for the foreseeable future** *for a time; for a while; for now; for many (several) months (years); for six (two) months (years); for some time; for the present; for the time being; temporarily.* • He is one of those who believes that a recession can be avoided for the foreseeable future. *He is one of those who believes that a recession can be avoided for now.*

**for the immediate future** *for a time; for a while; for now; for many (several) months (years); for six (two) months (years); for some time; for the present; for the time being; temporarily.* • Several said they were canceling planned business trips for the immediate future. *Several said they were canceling planned business trips for the present.*

**for the most part** *almost all; chiefly; commonly; generally; greatly; in general; largely; mainly; most; mostly; most often; much; nearly all; normally; overall; typically; usually.* • Those problems for the most part have been overcome. *Those problems have been largely overcome.*

**for the (very) near future** *for a time; for a while; for now; for many (several) months (years); for six (two) months (years); for some time; for the present; for the time being; temporarily.* • While the analysts expected Kraft and General Foods to exist as separate entities for the near future, they said they did not expect the honeymoon to last forever. *While the analysts expected*

*Kraft and General Foods to exist as separate entities for now, they said they did not expect the honeymoon to last forever.*

**for the not-so-distant (not-too-distant) future** *for a time; for a while; for now; for many (several) months (years); for six (two) months (years); for some time; for the present; for the time being; temporarily.*

**for the present** *for now;* delete. • Perhaps one day we shall find an Etruscan library, buried deep in the Italian countryside, but for the present, we have to make do with what we have, which is precious little. *Perhaps one day we shall find an Etruscan library, buried deep in the Italian countryside, but for now, we have to make do with what we have, which is precious little.*

**for the purpose of (-ing)** *for (-ing); so as to; to.* • All deposited items are received for the purpose of collection, and all credits for deposited items are provisional. *All deposited items are received for collection, and all credits for deposited items are provisional.*

**for the (simple) reason that** *because; considering; for; in that; since.* • Normally, short-term Treasuries yield less than longer-term Treasuries, for the simple reason that investors demand to be rewarded for tying up their money in longer-term instruments. *Normally, short-term Treasuries yield less than longer-term Treasuries because investors demand to be rewarded for tying up their money in longer-term instruments.*

**for the sake of** *for; so as to; to.* • I have never found it necessary to practice "defensive medicine," if that means doing that which would not otherwise be done solely for the sake of protecting oneself against possible legal action. *I have never found it necessary to practice "defensive medicine," if that means doing that which would not otherwise be done solely to protect oneself against possible legal action.*

**for the time (while) being** *for now; for the moment; for the present;* delete. • For the time being, look at the current PLOT ORIGIN and the SCALE. *For the moment, look at the current PLOT ORIGIN and the SCALE.*

**for . . . to come** *for.* • This can go on for generations to come. *This can go on for generations.*

**forward in (into) the future** *in (into) the future; later.*

**for (many; several) years (now)** *long.* • The few policies I was able to get from SBLI have, for many years now, paid me an annual dividend, with no payment of any premium. *The few policies I was able to get from SBLI have long paid me an annual dividend, with no payment of any premium.*

**for your information** delete.

**fourthly** *fourth.*

**frame of mind** *attitude; belief; opinion; position; posture; stand; standpoint; vantage; view; viewpoint;* delete.

**fraught with meaning (significance)** *meaningful (significant).* • If nothing else, the question is fraught with significance for Democrats trying to figure out whether to mount a campaign today that will peak three years from now. *If nothing else, the question is significant for Democrats trying to figure out whether to mount a campaign today that will peak three years from now.*

**free and gratis** *free.*

**free gift** *gift.* • For your free gift, fill out this form today. *For your gift, fill out this form today.*

**free of charge** *free.* • All meetings are free of charge and open to the public. *All meetings are free and open to the public.*

**free pass** *pass.*

**free up** *free.* • On some programs, rows and columns can be deleted to free up memory for new data on a model. *On some programs, rows and columns can be deleted to free memory for new data on a model.*

**freezing cold** *cold; freezing.* • It's freezing cold outside. *It's freezing outside.*

**from (a; the) . . . aspect (of)** *as (does); as for; as to; for; from; in; in that; -(al)ly; since; to;* delete. • From a legal aspect, the joint venture falls under local company or corporation law when participation is in the form of equity. *Legally, the joint venture falls under local company or corporation law when participation is in the form of equity.*

**from beginning to end** *all through; completely; entirely; thoroughly; throughout; totally; wholly.*

**from (a; the) . . . distance of** *from; from . . . away.* • Most of the spectators watched from a distance of 1,300 feet, while the Soviet observers viewed the firings from a concrete bunker. *Most of the spectators watched from 1,300 feet away, while the Soviet observers viewed the firings from a concrete bunker.*

**from hence** *hence.*

**from minute (moment) to minute (moment)** *directly; momentarily; momently; presently; soon.* • I expect them from moment to moment. *I expect them momently.*

**from now (on)** *hence.*

**from . . . on (onward)** *since.* • Other researchers had already confirmed that from A.D. 200 onward there had been human sacrifices of varying kinds. *Other researchers had already confirmed that since A.D. 200 there had been human sacrifices of varying kinds.*

**from one . . . to another** *between.* • Moving your funds from one institution to another is easy to do, and there is no tax liability or IRS penalty at all, if you follow the correct procedures. *Moving your funds between institutions is easy to do, and there is no tax liability or IRS penalty at all, if you follow the correct procedures.*

**from (a; the) . . . perspective (of)** *as (does); as for; as to; for; from; in; in that; -(al)ly; since; to; delete.* • From my perspective, trashing my system makes a lot of sense. *Trashing my system makes a lot of sense to me.*

**from (a; the) . . . point of view (of)** *as (does); as for; as to; for; from; in; in that; -(al)ly; since; to; delete.* • You've got to look at it from an optimistic point of view. *You've got to look at it optimistically.* • I try to see things from the customer's point of view. *I try to see things as the customer does.*

**from (a; the) . . . standpoint (of)** *as (does); as for; as to; for; from; in; in that; -(al)ly; since; to; delete.* • From a statistical standpoint, who is most vulnerable to colon-rectal cancer? *Statistically, who is most vulnerable to colon-rectal cancer?* • I have had some experience with grief from a personal standpoint. *I have had some personal experience with grief.* • The proposed purchase price is indeed a good value from the city's standpoint. *The proposed purchase price is indeed a good value for the city.* • A move to Jacksonville will be highly profitable for the club and would be smart from a business standpoint. *A move to Jacksonville will be highly profitable for the club and would be smart business.* • From a medical standpoint, we don't have any evidence that the senator abuses alcohol. *We don't have any medical evidence that the senator abuses alcohol.*

**from start to finish** *all through; completely; entirely; thoroughly; throughout; totally; wholly.*

**from that day (moment; point; time) (forward; on; onward)** *from then (on); since; since then;* delete. • From that point on, she hasn't said a word to me. *Since then, she hasn't said a word to me.*

**from the beginning (start)** *always.* • From the start, it has been a haven for those whose religions or political beliefs were not tolerated in their homelands. *It has always been a haven for those whose religions or political beliefs were not tolerated in their homelands.*

**from the fact that** *because; considering; for; in that; since.*

**from (in) the following year** *from (in) (1991).*

**from (in) the preceding year** *from (in) (1989).* • At year-end 1987, 70,893 persons were employed within Ericsson, a decrease of 1,682 from the preceding year. *At year-end 1987, 70,893 persons were employed within Ericsson, a decrease of 1,682 from 1986.*

**from the time of** *since.*

**from this day (moment; point; time) (forward; on; onward)** *from now (on); hence; henceforth; henceforward;* delete. • From this point on, elected students and faculty will be running the affairs of the school. *Henceforth, elected students and faculty will be running the affairs of the school.*

**from . . . until** *from . . . to.* • This book is intriguing because it also concerns the role of that on-again, off-again colonial revival in popular culture from 1876 until the present. *This book is intriguing because it also concerns the role of that on-again, off-again colonial revival in popular culture from 1876 to the present.*

**from (a; the) . . . viewpoint (of)** *as (does); as for; as to; for; from; in; in that; -(al)ly; since; to;* delete. • From a business viewpoint, it makes good sense to free brain power from the drudgery of processing data and to engage it in finding new ways to apply that data. *It makes good sense for business to free brain power from the drudgery of processing data and to engage it in finding new ways to apply that data.*

**from whence** *whence.* • From whence did he draw his strength? *Whence did he draw his strength?*

**full capacity** *capacity.* • Demand for petroleum products was so strong that refineries were operating at or near full capacity. *Demand for petroleum products was so strong that refineries were operating at or near capacity.*

**full (maximum) potential (potentiality)** *potential (potentiality).* • If we are to achieve our full potential, we must see beyond the routine. *If we are to achieve our potential, we must see beyond the routine.*

**full satisfaction** *satisfaction.*

**fundamental** *basic;* delete.

**fundamental (and) basic** *basic; fundamental.* • These are fundamental and basic rights. *These are basic rights.*

**fundamental basis** *basis.* • The fundamental basis of any relationship is truth. *The basis of any relationship is truth.*

**fundamental principle** *principle.*

**furiously angry** *angry; furious.* • She's furiously angry. *She's furious.*

**further** *more.* • For further information, or free form samples, contact Deluxe at their toll-free number. *For more information, or free form samples, contact Deluxe at their toll-free number.*

**furthermore** *also; and; as well; besides; even; further; still more; then; too.* • Furthermore, some of the changes may reduce the extent to which issuers may issue tax-exempt bonds. *Further, some of the changes may reduce the extent to which issuers may issue tax-exempt bonds.*

**fuse together** *fuse.* • Most metals, except for low- and medium-carbon steels, require fluxes to aid in the process of melting and fusing the metals together. *Most metals, except for low- and medium-carbon steels, require fluxes to aid in the process of melting and fusing the metals.*

**future developments** *developments.*

**future plans** *plans.* • He said future plans call for the introduction of 2-Mbs service in the switched network by 1992, which would mean videoconferences could be switched like normal phone calls. *He said plans call for the introduction of 2-Mbs service in the switched network by 1992, which would mean videoconferences could be switched like normal phone calls.*

**future projections** *projections.*

**future prospects** *prospects.* • Proponents of the information center concept, Atre Consultants are not overly romantic about its future prospects. *Proponents of the information center concept, Atre Consultants are not overly romantic about its prospects.*

131

# G

**gather together** *gather.* • In Dubai, about 400 relatives of the dead and their supporters gathered together for a memorial service at a large Shiite mosque. *In Dubai, about 400 relatives of the dead and their supporters gathered for a memorial service at a large Shiite mosque.*

**general consensus** *consensus.* • The general consensus among corporations is to be cautious about 1989. *The consensus among corporations is to be cautious about 1989.*

**general public** *public.*

**general vicinity** *vicinity; area.*

**gentleman** *man.* • Nothing would give me greater pleasure than to see these gentlemen put out of business. *Nothing would give me greater pleasure than to see these men put out of business.*

**geographical** *geographic.* • Several large commercial banks provide economic data and forecasts for the geographical area they serve. *Several large commercial banks provide economic data and forecasts for the geographic area they serve.*

**geological** *geologic.* • On-site geological studies would be needed to confirm an impact origin. *On-site geologic studies would be needed to confirm an impact origin.*

**geometrical** *geometric.*

**get -ed** delete. • We plan to get married in the fall. *We plan to marry in the fall.*

**get across** *convey; explain.* • There's an important element here that we need to get across. *There's an important element here that we need to convey.*

**get in touch with** *call; contact; phone; reach; visit; write (to).* • Agency representatives with reports to enter can get in touch with him at that number. *Agency representatives with reports to enter can reach him at that number.*

**give (a; the) . . . (for; of; to)** delete. • Give an estimate on the amount of time it will take and the number of people you will need. *Estimate the amount of time it will take and the number of people you will need.* • The Book of Leviticus gives a list of the women who are not available to marry certain men. *The Book of Leviticus lists the women who are not available to marry certain men.* • The main purpose of choosing an outside auditor is to guarantee to insiders and interested outsiders that the financial data presented in financial documents give an accurate representation of events. *The main purpose of choosing an outside auditor is to guarantee to insiders and interested outsiders that the financial data presented in financial documents accurately represent events.* • They work hard; they deserve to be given compensation. *They work hard; they deserve to be compensated.* • Did he give any indication of what he plans to do? *Did he indicate what he plans to do?* • I'll give you a call at the end of the week. *I'll call you at the end of the week.* • I hope you will give me consideration for diverse projects. *I hope you will consider me for diverse projects.*

**give birth to** *bear.*

**give . . . consideration (thought; weight) to** *consider; examine; ponder; reflect on; study; weigh.* • Many small businesses and private individuals are giving serious consideration to their energy and resource needs for the year ahead. *Many small businesses and private individuals are seriously considering their energy and resource needs for the year ahead.*

**given at (in)** *at (in).* • Since all limits are given in thousandths, the values can be converted by moving the decimal point three places to the left. *Since all limits are in thousandths, the values can be converted by moving the decimal point three places to the left.*

**given the fact that** *because; considering; for; in that; since; when.* • Given the fact that she only read 400 pages of the book, she didn't do too badly. *Considering she only read 400 pages of the book, she didn't do too badly.*

**give offense to** *offend.* • Ask them to develop a set of labels that does not give offense to any group of countries. *Ask them to develop a set of labels that does not offend any group of countries.*

**give rise to** *bear; cause.* • The researchers concluded that abnormalities in the neurotransmitter system may give rise to the depression in demented patients. *The researchers concluded that abnormalities in the neurotransmitter system may cause the depression in demented patients.*

**go along with** *agree with; back; endorse; favor; support.* • He was unwilling to say whether he would go along with such a recommendation. *He was unwilling to say whether he would support such a recommendation.*

**(just) goes to show** *attests; proves; reveals; shows; supports; verifies;* delete. • It just goes to show that safety in driving is most important. *It shows that safety in driving is most important.*

**(it) goes without saying (that)** *clearly; naturally; obviously; of course; plainly;* delete. • This may go without saying, but I also look at a person's motivation, commitment, and energy. *Naturally, I also look at a person's motivation, commitment, and energy.*

**go forward** *advance; continue; go on; move on; proceed; progress.* • We want the project to go forward as soon as possible, and we are confident that these issues can be addressed. *We want the project to proceed as soon as possible, and we are confident that these issues can be addressed.*

**good and sufficient** *adequate; good; sufficient.* • We think that the safety of present plants is good and sufficient. *We think that the safety of present plants is adequate.*

**go through . . . experience** *experience; go through.* • I think I'm a much better person for having gone through that experience. *I think I'm a much better person for having experienced that.*

**grateful thanks** *gratitude; thanks.*

**(a; the) greater (larger) number (of)** *more.* • Usually the greater number of services offered, the larger the margin needed on each side to maintain profitability. *Usually the more services offered, the larger the margin needed on each side to maintain profitability.*

**(a; the) great (large) fraction (of)** *a good (great) deal (of); a good (great) many (of); almost all (of); (nine) in (ten) (of); many (of); most (of); much (of); nearly all (of); (43) of (48) (of); . . . percent (of); three-fourths (two-thirds) (of).* • Of the numerous complete fossils discovered in this quarry, a large fraction are either babies or mothers carrying young. *Of the numerous complete fossils discovered in this quarry, most are either babies or mothers carrying young.*

**group together** *group.* • The Chapter command divides your Notepad pages into chapters and groups together related information. *The Chapter command divides your Notepad pages into chapters and groups related information.*

# H

**had . . . then** *had.* • Had he exhibited the kind of behavior that would have warranted such a recommendation, then it would have been made. *Had he exhibited the kind of behavior that would have warranted such a recommendation, it would have been made.*

**hale and hearty** *hale; healthy; hearty; well.*

**half (a) dozen** *six.*

**half of** *half.* • The menus occupy almost half of the screen display. *The menus occupy almost half the screen display.*

**harbinger of the future (of things to come)** *harbinger; omen; sign.* • I hope it is a harbinger of the future. *I hope it is an omen.*

**hard and fast** *firm; fixed; steadfast; strict.*

**has (a; the) . . . (about; for; of; on; over)** delete. • If you have intentions of going, you should make your reservations now. *If you intend to go, you should make your reservations now.* • He has control over the entire program. *He controls the entire program.* • Boston has the need for a new harbor tunnel. *Boston needs a new harbor tunnel.* • The strategic partnering lawyer must have a firm grasp of the fundamentals of the legal principles in Europe and in the Far East. *The strategic partnering lawyer must firmly grasp the fundamentals of the legal principles in Europe and in the Far East.*

**has a bearing on (upon)** *acts on; affects; bears on; influences.* • What we are learning about primates and other social species has a direct bearing on our own species. *What we are learning about primates and other social species directly bears on our own species.*

**has a (the) capability to** *can; is able to.*

**has a difference of opinion with** *differs; disagrees with; disputes; objects to; opposes.* • We have a difference of opinion with the decision the judge made. *We disagree with the decision the judge made.*

**has a (the) habit of (-ing)** *tends to; will.* • He has a habit of biting his nails. *He tends to bite his nails.*

**has an (the) ability to** *can; is able to.* • Eighty percent of the retail deposit accounts have the ability to be accessed by a debit card even though actual usage is much less. *Eighty percent of the retail deposit accounts can be accessed by a debit card even though actual usage is much less.*

**has an (the) appreciation for** *appreciates; approves of; cherishes; enjoys; esteems; likes; prizes; treasures; understands; values.* • Most people don't have an appreciation for esoteric beliefs. *Most people don't appreciate esoteric beliefs.*

**has a (the) preference for** *favors; prefers.* • By now, you will have gathered that I have a strong preference for organization along functional lines. *By now, you will have gathered that I strongly prefer organization along functional lines.*

**has a (the) tendency (to)** *tends to; will.* • As a community, the Basques have a tendency to be healthy and long-lived. *As a community, the Basques tend to be healthy and long-lived.*

**has (a) . . . effect on (upon)** *acts on; affects; bears on; influences;* delete. • Over the past twenty years, the U.S. economy has had a significant effect on the Amish way of life. *Over the past twenty years, the U.S. economy has significantly influenced the Amish way of life.* • Human activity is changing the composition of the atmosphere in ways that could have profound effects upon life on the Earth. *Human activity is changing the composition of the atmosphere in ways that could profoundly affect life on the Earth.*

**has got** *has.*

**has (a) . . . impact (on; upon)** *acts on; affects; bears on; influences;* delete. • It has a direct impact on the majority of the American people. *It directly affects the majority of the American people.* • Your tone of voice, expression, and apparent receptiveness to others' responses all have a tremendous impact upon those you wish to reach. *Your tone of voice, expression, and apparent receptiveness to others' responses all tremendously influence those you wish to reach.*

**has (a) . . . influence on (upon)** *acts on; affects; bears on; influences;* delete. • Management was alerted to the fact that the social environment of employees had a great influence on productivity. *Management was alerted to the fact that the social environment of employees greatly affected productivity.*

**has only to** *need only.* • To view any of the channels available, you have only to switch between channels. *To view any of the channels available, you need only switch between channels.*

**has reference to** *concerns; deals with; is about; pertains to; regards; relates to.*

**has the effect of -ing** delete. • Such a slowdown would have the effect of easing inflationary fears. *Such a slowdown would ease inflationary fears.*

**has (got) to** *must.* • I have to be going. *I must be going.*

**(that) has to do with** *concerns; deals with; is about; pertains to; regards; relates to.* • The first has to do with the relative merits of CD versus analog. *The first pertains to the relative merits of CD versus analog.*

**have (possess) . . . in common** *share.* • We have no interests in common. *We share no interests.*

**have . . . in (my) possession** *have; possess.* • We now have in our possession a class of machines that are right around energy breakeven. *We now possess a class of machines that are right around energy breakeven.*

**head up** *direct; head; lead.* • Bush headed up the committee that eliminated those regulations. *Bush headed the committee that eliminated those regulations.*

**heat up** *heat.* • I just threw it all together and then heated it up. *I just threw it all together and then heated it.*

**(a; the) height of** delete. • The stratosphere is one of the middle layers of the atmosphere that starts some 15 kilometers above Earth's surface and extends to a height of about 50 kilometers. *The stratosphere is one of the middle layers of the atmosphere that starts some 15 kilometers above Earth's surface and extends to about 50 kilometers.*

**help in (of) -ing** *help -ing.* • Those who have no diversions or hobbies may need help in selecting appropriate activities. *Those who have no diversions or hobbies may need help selecting appropriate activities.* • The work may also help in tracking down inherited influences in mental diseases. *The work may also help track down inherited influences in mental diseases.*

**help out** *help.* • They're very eager to help out. *They're very eager to help.*

**help . . . to** *help.* • Following these guidelines may help to cut down on the amount of aspirin you need. *Following these guidelines may help cut down on the amount of aspirin you need.*

**henceforth (henceforward)** *hence.*

**hereafter** *hence.*

**(the) here and now** *(just; right) now; presently; the present.*

**high and dry** *alone; helpless; powerless.*

**high and low** *everywhere.*

**high and mighty** *arrogant; dogmatic; domineering; haughty.*

**(a; the) high degree (of)** *abundant; a good (great) deal (of); a good (great) many (of); ample; great; high; many (of); marked; most (of); much (of); salient; striking; vast;* delete. • One of the distinguishing characteristics of the Eurobond market is its high degree of competitiveness. *One of the distinguishing characteristics of the Eurobond market is its marked competitiveness.*

**(a; the) high level (of)** *abundant; a good (great) deal (of); a good (great) many (of); ample; great; high; many (of); marked; most (of); much (of); salient; striking; vast;* delete. • The London merchant banks have a very high level of expertise. *The London merchant banks have vast expertise.*

**(a; the) high number (of)** *a good (great) many (of); almost all; countless; dozens (of); hundreds (of); many (of); millions (of); most (of); nearly all (of); numerous; scores (of); six hundred (twelve hundred) (of); thousands (of).* • Hampton's high number of published recordings further supports the idea that he has spent several decades sharing his vibe playing with those who would listen. *Hampton's numerous published recordings further supports the idea that he has spent several decades sharing his vibe playing with those who would listen.*

**(a; the) high percentage (of)** *a good (great) deal (of); a good (great) many (of); almost all (of); (nine) in (ten) (of); many (of); most (of); much (of); nearly all (of); (43) of (48) (of); (67) percent (of); three-fourths (two-thirds) (of).* • That probably is excellent advice, if these bonds represent a high percentage of your total investments. *That probably is excellent advice, if these bonds represent much of your total investments.*

**(a; the) high proportion (of)** *a good (great) deal (of); a good (great) many (of); almost all (of); (nine) in (ten) (of); many (of); most (of); much (of); nearly all (of); (43) of (48) (of); (67) percent (of); three-fourths (two-thirds) (of).* • In the pharmaceutical industry, most companies devote a high proportion of their budgets to R&D expenditures. *In the pharmaceutical industry, most companies devote much of their budgets to R&D expenditures.*

**hired mercenary** *mercenary.*

**historical experience** *experience; history.* • The quote could be misconstrued to leave the impression that we made an explicit assumption that was at odds with recent historical experience. *The quote could be misconstrued to leave the impression that we made an explicit assumption that was at odds with recent experience.*

**historical precedent** *history; precedent.* • We are unaware of any historical precedent that has seen a nation indefinitely borrow and consume its way to prosperity. *We are unaware of any precedent that has seen a nation indefinitely borrow and consume its way to prosperity.*

**historical record** *history; record.* • Mr. Macdonald is too young to have known this, but neither youth nor filial piety justifies distorting the historical record. *Mr. Macdonald is too young to have known this, but neither youth nor filial piety justifies distorting the record.*

**hoist up** *hoist.*

**hold a meeting** *meet.*

**hold (to) the view (that)** *assert; believe; claim; consider; contend; feel; hold; judge; maintain; regard; say; think; to; view.* • Most utility regulators and economists hold to the view that electric utilities are "natural monopolies." *Most utility regulators and economists hold that electric utilities are "natural monopolies."*

**hold (to) the opinion (that)** *assert; believe; claim; consider; contend; feel; hold; judge; maintain; regard; say; think; to; view.*

**hold true** *hold.* • As we age, our muscles become weaker and more easily tired, and the same holds true for polio victims. *As we age, our muscles become weaker and more easily tired, and the same holds for polio victims.*

**hollow tube** *tube.*

**honestly and truly (truthfully)** *honestly; truly; truthfully;* delete. • I tell people what I honestly and truthfully believe. *I tell people what I honestly believe.*

**(the) honest truth** *honestly; truly; (the) truth; truthfully.* • The person you're interviewing doesn't want you to discover the honest truth. *The person you're interviewing doesn't want you to discover the truth.*

**hope and expect (expectation)** *expect (expectation); hope; trust.* • It is my hope and expectation that these cuts won't take effect. *It is my hope that these cuts won't take effect.*

**hopefully** *(I; we) hope; let's hope;* delete. • Today, hopefully, we have some answers to these problems. *Today, I hope, we have some answers to these problems.*

**how do (you) go about (-ing)** *how do (you).* • How do you go about getting an income tax extension? *How do you get an income tax extension?*

**how in God's (heaven's) name** *however; how ever.*

**how in the world (on earth)** *however; how ever.* • How in the world did you manage that? *However did you manage that?*

**how is it (that)** *how come; why.*

**howsoever** *however.*

**hue and cry** *clamor; hubbub; outcry.* • He moved to stem the hue and cry by saying that the House would vote next week on trimming the raise to 30 percent. *He moved to stem the outcry by saying that the House would vote next week on trimming the raise to 30 percent.*

**huge (large) throng** *throng.* • At the hotel, Sitting Bull welcomed large throngs of people who simply wanted to see him. *At the hotel, Sitting Bull welcomed throngs of people who simply wanted to see him.*

**human being** *being; female; human; male; man; person; woman.* • Such a statement is beneath the dignity of any civilized human being. *Such a statement is beneath the dignity of any civilized person.*

**human resources** *employees; people; persons; workers.* • If the company does not have enough human resources to meet future needs, it must begin hiring them. *If the company does not have enough employees to meet future needs, it must begin hiring them.*

**humongous** *big; giant; grand; great; huge; immense; large; mammoth; mighty; monstrous.* • It's a humongous amount, oceans and oceans of material. *It's a huge amount, oceans and oceans of material.*

**hurry up** *hurry.*

# I

**identical (identically) match** *duplicate; exact; identical; match; (the) same.*

**identical (identically) (the) same** *duplicate; exact; identical; match; (the) same.*
• The operating system assumes they are the same file because the first eight characters are identically the same. *The operating system assumes they are the same file because the first eight characters are identical.*

**I do not think so** *I think not.*

**I don't think** *I doubt; I think;* delete. • If Dole doesn't act more civilized, he's not going to make it, I don't think. *If Dole doesn't act more civilized, he's not going to make it.* • Technology is not now being taxed, and I don't think it will ever be taxed in the supply of these services. *Technology is not now being taxed, and I doubt it will ever be taxed in the supply of these services.*

**if and only if** *if; only if.* • It is agreed that the premiums stated in the Coverage Selections page are subject to recomputation if, and only if, the rates fixed and established are found not to meet the requirements of state law. *It is agreed that the premiums stated in the Coverage Selections page are subject to recomputation only if the rates fixed and established are found not to meet the requirements of state law.*

**if and (or) when** *if; when.* • To use a program, it is not necessary for you to know all the commands because many of them are for advanced features that you learn if and when you need them. *To use a program, it is not necessary for you to know all the commands because many of them are for advanced features that you learn if you need them.*

**if by way of hypothesis (supposition)** *assuming (that); supposing (that).*

**if . . . had** *had.* • If you had run a large number of trials, the results would be very similar. *Had you run a large number of trials, the results would be very similar.*

**if in return** *if.* • I will ask him if you in return will stop talking about him. *I will ask him if you will stop talking about him.*

**if it were not for** *but for; except for.* • The loss would have been $261 million if it were not for an accounting change related to the treatment of income taxes. *The loss would have been $261 million but for an accounting change related to the treatment of income taxes.*

**ifs, ands, or buts** *conditions.*

**if . . . should** *should.* • We will be alert to other opportunities if this one should collapse. *We will be alert to other opportunities should this one collapse.*

**if . . . then** *if.* • If he tells you he doesn't ever want to have children, then you will have to make a decision. *If he tells you he doesn't ever want to have children, you will have to make a decision.*

**if that (this) is the case (situation)** *if so.*

**if that (this) is true** *if so.*

**if . . . were** *should; were.* • If that were the only penalty, I would settle for keeping 22 cents on the dollar. *Were that the only penalty, I would settle for keeping 22 cents on the dollar.*

**I'll (let me) tell you (something)** *delete.*

**illustrative example** *example; illustration.* • From the Software Library, you can download illustrative code examples and the latest technical specifications. *From the Software Library, you can download code examples and the latest technical specifications.*

**I'm curious why** *why (do).* • I'm curious why you want to see him. *Why do you want to see him?*

**I mean** *delete.*

**immunological** *immunologic.*

**impact (on; upon)** *(v) act on; affect; bear on; influence.* • It's the numbers that impact on all of us. *It's the numbers that influence all of us.*

**implement** *achieve; complete; effect; fulfill; make; perform; produce; realize; set.*

**importance** *import; moment.*

**important essentials** *essentials.*

**(an; the) important . . . for (in; of; to)** *important for (to).* • Because decision making is an important element of a manager's job, we need to discover anything that can improve the quality of decision making. *Because decision making is important to a manager's job, we need to discover anything that can improve the quality of decision making.* • Their willingness to commit capital was an important factor for success. *Their willingness to commit capital was important for success.* • Certainly, overall physical health is an important component in any society. *Certainly, overall physical health is important to any society.*

**important significance** *consequence; importance; significance.*

**in (on; with) (a; the) . . . (of; that)** *-ing (that).* • In the 1980s, many people made plans on the assumption that oil prices would exceed $75 per barrel by 1990. *In the 1980s, many people made plans assuming that oil prices would exceed $75 per barrel by 1990.* • These same people are making significant international dispositions on the expectation that Japan will continue to be the world's largest creditor. *These same people are making significant international dispositions expecting that Japan will continue to be the world's largest creditor.*

**in a bad mood** *angry; dejected; depressed; displeased; downcast; glum; grouchy; sad; unhappy; vexed.*

**in accord (accordance) with** *according to; by; following; in keeping with; in line with; in step with; to; under.* • This document shall be governed and construed in accordance with the laws of the State of Utah. *This document shall be governed and construed under the laws of the State of Utah.*

**in a class by itself** *matchless; novel; peerless; singular; special; unequaled; unique; unmatched; unrivaled.*

**in a (the) . . . condition** delete. • The Tenant must keep the Apartment in a clean and sanitary condition, free of garbage, rubbish, and other filth. *The Tenant must keep the Apartment clean and sanitary, free of garbage, rubbish, and other filth.*

**in actual fact** *actually; indeed; in fact; in faith; in reality; in truth; really; truly;* delete. • And, in actual fact, the copywriter who created the spots and several other people who worked on it are also Catholic. *And, in fact, the copywriter who created the spots and several other people who worked on it are also Catholic.*

**in actuality** *actually; indeed; in fact; in faith; in truth; really; truly;* delete. • In actuality, such a situation seldom occurs. *In fact, such a situation seldom occurs.*

**in addition** *also; and; as well; besides; beyond that (this); even; further; furthermore; moreover; more than that (this); still more; then; too; what is more.* • In addition, we reviewed several net present value models. *We even reviewed several net present value models.*

**in addition to** *besides; beyond.* • In addition to using words to communicate, all of us talk with our body poses and facial expressions. *Besides using words to communicate, all of us talk with our body poses and facial expressions.*

**in addition to ... also (as well; too)** *besides; beyond; in addition to.* • In addition to measuring a computer in terms óf its memory and processing speed, we must also analyze the computer's ability to handle list processing. *In addition to measuring a computer in terms of its memory and processing speed, we must analyze the computer's ability to handle list processing.*

**in a (the) ... direction** delete. • Vertical lines are drawn along the left side of a triangle in an upward direction. *Vertical lines are drawn upward along the left side of a triangle.*

**in advance** *before; beforehand; earlier; sooner;* delete. • If I'd known in advance that out of every 100 books published, only one becomes a best seller, I wouldn't have started a book. *If I'd known sooner that out of every 100 books published, only one becomes a best seller, I wouldn't have started a book.*

**in advance of** *ahead of; before.* • In advance of our first break, let me introduce Thomas Armstrong, Ph.D., a learning and education specialist. *Before our first break, let me introduce Thomas Armstrong, Ph.D., a learning and education specialist.*

**inadvertent (unintended; unintentional) oversight** *oversight.*

**in a (the) fashion (manner; way) (in which; that)** *as; like.* • Zeus allows you to work intuitively in the way that you think best. *Zeus allows you to work intuitively as you think best.* • But such a scientific inquiry already took place years ago, in the manner provided for by law. *But such a scientific inquiry already took place years ago, as provided for by law.*

**in a (the) fashion (manner; way) characteristic of** *as; like.*

**in a (the) fashion (manner; way) similar to** *alike; as; like; much as; much like; much the same (as); rather like; resembling; similar to; similarly to.* • In a manner similar to modern-day whales, ichthyosaurs seem to have frequented breeding or birthing areas. *Like modern-day whales, ichthyosaurs seem to have frequented breeding or birthing areas.*

**in a few minutes (moments)** *briefly; directly; momently; presently; quickly; shortly; soon; straightaway.* • Press any key, and in a few moments, the Lotus 1-2-3 spreadsheet will appear on the screen. *Press any key, and the Lotus 1-2-3 spreadsheet will directly appear on the screen.*

**in a good mood** *cheerful; glad; gleeful; happy; joyful; joyous; merry; pleased.*

**in agreement with** *according to; by; following; in keeping with; in line with; in step with; to; under.*

**in (almost) all (every) cases (circumstances; instances; situations)** *all; almost all; almost always; always; consistently; constantly; invariably; nearly all; nearly always; unfailingly.* • The actual percentage should be given in all cases. *The actual percentage should always be given.*

**in all likelihood** *likely; most (very) likely; probably; most (very) probably.* • In all likelihood, it will get extended until there is a determination of the ESOP litigation. *Most likely, it will get extended until there is a determination of the ESOP litigation.*

**in all probability** *likely; most (very) likely; probably; most (very) probably.* • A telephone call to the coordinator keeps the bank from stepping on its own toes by duplicating efforts and, in all probability, makes the call more effective. *A telephone call to the coordinator keeps the bank from stepping on its own toes by duplicating efforts and, most probably, makes the call more effective.*

**in a lot of cases (circumstances; instances; situations)** *frequently; most often; often; sometimes; usually.* • In a lot of cases, serial killers seek power over others. *Often, serial killers seek power over others.*

**in a (the) majority of cases (circumstances; instances; situations)** *frequently; most often; often; usually.*

**in a manner of speaking** *as it were; in a sense; in a way; so to speak.*

**in a (some) measure** *partially; partly; somewhat.*

**in a minute (moment)** *briefly; directly; momently; presently; quickly; shortly; soon; straightaway.*

**in an attempt (effort; endeavor) to** *in trying to; to try to.* • In an attempt to satisfy the informal group, the employee may come in conflict with the formal organization. *In trying to satisfy the informal group, the employee may come in conflict with the formal organization.*

**in an attempt (effort; endeavor) to try to** *in trying to; to try to.* • In an effort to try to contain the spiraling cost of automobile insurance, a number of legislative changes have been proposed. *In trying to contain the spiraling cost of automobile insurance, a number of legislative changes have been proposed.*

**in and of itself (themselves)** *as such; in itself (in themselves).* • The mere claim of protection asserted by a witness of his constitutional rights does not in and of itself constitute the admission of a crime. *The mere claim of protection asserted by a witness of his constitutional rights does not in itself constitute the admission of a crime.*

**in a nutshell** *briefly; concisely; succinctly; tersely.* • That, in a nutshell, explains the financial community's attitude toward the crash. *That briefly explains the financial community's attitude toward the crash.*

**in any case (event)** *all (just) the same; anyhow; even so; still; still and all; yet.*

**in any fashion (manner; way)** *at all; in the least; delete.* • And he personally is not obligated in any way to stand behind the $675 million bond offering, or any other debt of the project. *And he personally is not at all obligated to stand behind the $675 million bond offering, or any other debt of the project.*

**in any way, shape, or form** *at all; in any way; in the least; in the slightest; delete.* • Can that evidence be used in any way, shape, or form? *Can that evidence be used in any way?*

**in a position to** *able to; ready to.* • By the end of the year, we will be in a position to hire another person. *By the end of the year, we will be ready to hire another person.*

**in appearance** *delete.* • They may look different in appearance, but each is built essentially with the same type of components that perform the same functions. *They may look different, but each is built essentially with the same type of components that perform the same functions.*

**in a row** *straight.* • Whether the bill dies on Beacon Hill for the third year in a row or becomes law in some form, the advocates of acupuncture are pressing their case with a gentle insistence. *Whether the bill dies on Beacon*

*Hill for the third straight year or becomes law in some form, the advocates of acupuncture are pressing their case with a gentle insistence.*

**in arrears** *late; overdue.*

**in a (the) . . . sense** *-(al)ly;* delete. • In a broad sense, office automation is the incorporation of technology to help people manage information. *Broadly, office automation is the incorporation of technology to help people manage information.* • Although there is a significant relationship in a statistical sense, the association is not strong. *Although there is a significant statistical relationship, the association is not strong.* • I don't mean this in a pejorative sense. *I don't mean this pejoratively.* • There was really nothing which could be called communication in any genuine sense. *There was really nothing which could be called genuine communication.*

**in a similar fashion (manner; way) (to)** *alike; as; like; much as; much like; much the same (as); rather like; resembling; similar (to); similarly (to).* • My guess is 99 percent of the customers will behave in a similar manner. *My guess is 99 percent of the customers will behave similarly.*

**inasmuch (insomuch) as** *as far as; as much as; so far as; so much as.*

**inasmuch (insomuch) as** *because; considering; for; in that; since.* • All seemed to share the conviction that the American educational system is far superior inasmuch as it focuses on the individual student. *All seemed to share the conviction that the American educational system is far superior because it focuses on the individual student.*

**in association with** *along with; and; as well as; combined with; coupled with; joined with; paired with; together with; with.*

**in a (the). . . state (of) . . .** *in;* delete. • I'm in a state of uncertainty about how to travel. *I'm uncertain about how to travel.* • But while men's wear has been doing pretty well, women's wear storeowners are in a state of shock. *But while men's wear has been doing pretty well, women's wear storeowners are in shock.*

**in a timely fashion (manner; way)** *by next week (tomorrow); fast; in (within) a day (year); in (on) time; promptly; quickly; rapidly; right away; shortly; soon; speedily; swiftly; timely.* • Please give me your response in a timely manner. *Please give me your response by tomorrow.*

**in attendance** *present.* • Also in attendance were key attorneys and representatives on both sides of the lawsuit. *Also present were key attorneys and representatives on both sides of the lawsuit.*

**in a way** *rather; somehow; someway(s); somewhat.* • In a way, I find it intimidating. *I somehow find it intimidating.*

**in back of** *after; behind.*

**in . . . behalf (of)** *by; for.*

**(something; somewhere) in between** *between; in; within.* • The bonds are selling at $2 bid, $4 offered for a $100 face value bond, which means that the selling price would probably fall somewhere in between that range. *The bonds are selling at $2 bid, $4 offered for a $100 face value bond, which means that the selling price would probably fall in that range.*

**in (a; the) bigger (greater; higher; larger) amount (degree; number; quantity)** *more; more often; more so.* • Apple must wait until high-quality flat-panel screens are available in greater numbers before it can release a laptop Macintosh. *Apple must wait until more high-quality flat-panel screens are available before it can release a laptop Macintosh.*

**in big (great; high; huge; large; overwhelming; sizable; vast) numbers** *a good (great) many; almost all; dozens (of); hundreds (of); many; millions (of); most; nearly all; scores (of); six hundred (twelve hundred); thousands (of).* • Riot police in large numbers were called in to stop the protestors. *Scores of riot police were called in to stop the protestors.*

**in both cases (circumstances; instances; situations)** *both; for (in) both; delete.* • In both cases, about 10 percent of the sales force accounted for about 90 percent of the revenues. *For both, about 10 percent of the sales force accounted for about 90 percent of the revenues.*

**in brief (concise; succinct) summary** *briefly (concisely; succinctly); in brief; in fine; in short; in sum.* • In brief summary, those are some of the reasons why original intention cannot be a neat solution to the problem of expounding our Constitution—and living under it. *In sum, those are some of the reasons why original intention cannot be a neat solution to the problem of expounding our Constitution—and living under it.*

**in (a; the) . . . capacity (function; position; role) (as; of)** *as (a; the).* • In my capacity as chairman of the Arab group, I would like to express our deep regret for the steps taken by the United States in this regard. *As chairman of the Arab group, I would like to express our deep regret for the steps taken by the United States in this regard.*

**incarcerate** *jail.*

**in case** *if; lest; should.* • In case you've just joined us, we're talking about men's perception of the Women's Movement. *If you've just joined us, we're talking about men's perception of the Women's Movement.*

**in (a; the) . . . case (circumstance; instance; situation)** *-(al)ly.* • In a typical situation, the MLI command will have stored important information in an MLI data area that is used by all MLI commands. *Typically, the MLI command will have stored important information in an MLI data area that is used by all MLI commands.*

**in (the) . . . case (of)** *about; as for; as to; concerning; for; in; of; on; over; regarding; respecting; to; toward; with;* delete. • In the case of the airport, that role is performed by the air traffic controller and each airline's operations center. *As to the airport, that role is performed by the air traffic controller and each airline's operations center.*

**in cases (circumstances; instances; situations) in which** *if; when; where.* • In cases in which improperly tested blood products had been released, Dr. Sandler said the donors were contacted for retesting to assure that no tainted blood had been transmitted. *Where improperly tested blood products had been released, Dr. Sandler said the donors were contacted for retesting to assure that no tainted blood had been transmitted.*

**in cases when (where)** *if; when; where.* • In cases where one topic requires knowledge of another, the required topic is cross-referenced. *Where one topic requires knowledge of another, the required topic is cross-referenced.*

**in certain (some) cases** *at times; now and then; occasionally; on occasion; some; sometimes;* delete. • In some cases, smoking does affect mental acuity. *Smoking sometimes does affect mental acuity.*

**in certain (some) circumstances** *at times; every so often; now and again; now and then; occasionally; on occasion; some; sometimes;* delete. • In some circumstances, the computer can augment or replace many of the engineer's other tools. *Now and then, the computer can augment or replace many of the engineer's other tools.*

**in certain (some) instances** *at times; every so often; now and again; now and then; occasionally; on occasion; some; sometimes;* delete. • In some instances, we lost the customer to the competition. *We lost some customers to the competition.*

**in certain (some) regards** *rather; somehow; someway(s); somewhat.*

**in certain (some) respects** *rather; somehow; someway(s); somewhat.* • The finding is somewhat surprising since auditory information processing seems in some respects quite different from the operations required to sense visual patterns. *The finding is somewhat surprising since auditory information processing seems somehow quite different from the operations required to sense visual patterns.*

**in certain (some) situations** *at times; every so often; now and again; now and then; occasionally; on occasion; some; sometimes;* delete. • In some situations, change threatens security. *Sometimes change threatens security.*

**in character** delete. • As the market becomes more institutional in character, it will be easier for foreign companies to enter the U.S. market. *As the market becomes more institutional, it will be easier for foreign companies to enter the U.S. market.*

**in . . . circumstances (conditions)** *-(al)ly;* delete. • The attack was a carefully planned military operation that ended in tragic circumstances. *The attack was a carefully planned military operation that ended tragically.*

**in circumstances when (where)** *if; when; where.* • Independent counsel might well be required prior to accepting a defendant's waiver of important constitutional rights in circumstances where there is reason to believe that independent legal advice is necessary in order to permit the defendant to decide whether to waive or to exercise his rights. *Independent counsel might well be required prior to accepting a defendant's waiver of important constitutional rights where there is reason to believe that independent legal advice is necessary in order to permit the defendant to decide whether to waive or to exercise his rights.*

**in close proximity (to)** *close by; close to; in proximity; near; nearby.* • Some who have worked in close proximity to the Oval Office in recent years support his major propositions. *Some who have worked close to the Oval Office in recent years support his major propositions.*

**including everything** *in all; overall.*

**in color** delete. • Chalkboards are commonly black or green in color. *Chalkboards are commonly black or green.*

**in combination with** *along with; and; as well as; combined with; coupled with; joined with; paired with; together with; with.* • This risk is now avoided by using estrogen in combination with progesterone. *This risk is now avoided by using estrogen along with progesterone.*

**in (over) (the) coming days (decades; months; weeks; years)** *at length; before long; eventually; in time; later; one day; over time; presently; quickly; shortly; someday; sometime; soon; ultimately; with time; yet;* delcte. • Other schemes could emerge in coming months. *Other schemes could emerge before long.*

**in common with** *like.* • You are quite right in pointing out that I, in common with other cultural historians, have singled out but one out of several possible Adams lines. *You are quite right in pointing out that I, like other cultural historians, have singled out but one out of several possible Adams lines.*

**in company with** *along with; and; as well as; together with; with.* • If anything, the Reagan administration, in company with the Kremlin and the other big powers, has waited too long to denounce the use of chemical weapons. *If anything, the Reagan administration, as well as the Kremlin and the other big powers, has waited too long to denounce the use of chemical weapons.*

**in comparison to (with)** *against; alongside; beside; compared to (with); -(i)er than; less; less than; more; more than; next to; over; than; to; versus; vis-à-vis.* • The reunion's turnout was large in comparison to other reunions. *The reunion's turnout was larger than other reunions.* • U.S. students are inferior in their spelling ability in comparison to the other nations' students. *U.S. students are inferior in their spelling ability to the other nations' students.* • Dutch auction issues experience less price volatility in comparison to ARPS. *Dutch auction issues experience less price volatility compared to ARPS.*

**in comparison (in contrast) to (with) . . . relatively** *compared (contrasted) to (with).* • In comparison to earlier years, inflation has been relatively moderate over the last half decade. *Compared to earlier years, inflation has been moderate over the last half decade.*

**incompetency** *incompetence.* • Hospitalization often makes clients vulnerable to thoughts of inadequacy and incompetency. *Hospitalization often makes clients vulnerable to thoughts of inadequacy and incompetence.*

**in compliance with** *according to; by; following; in keeping with; in line with; in step with; to; under.* • In compliance with the new order, participants now receive a 2 percent discount from market prices on shares made available directly from the company. *Under the new order, participants now receive a 2 percent discount from market prices on shares made available directly from the company.*

**in conclusion** *finally; in closing; lastly.*

**in conformance to (with)** *according to; by; following; in keeping with; in line with; in step with; to; under.* • Certain terms of the Agreement shall be completed in conformance to the terms of the successful proposal. *Certain terms of the Agreement shall be completed according to the terms of the successful proposal.*

**in conformity to (with)** *according to; by; following; in keeping with; in line with; in step with; to; under.* • The law says a product is presumed to be free of defects when it is produced in conformity to government standards. *The law says a product is presumed to be free of defects when it is produced to government standards.*

**in conjunction** *combined; together.* • The primary evidence with which the Warren Report failed to deal consists of the ballistics report, the Zapruder film, and the autopsy report, taken in conjunction. *The primary evidence with which the Warren Report failed to deal consists of the ballistics report, the Zapruder film, and the autopsy report, taken together.*

**in conjunction with** *along with; and; as well as; combined with; coupled with; joined with; paired with; together with; with.* • The results of the interviews in conjunction with other supporting data are contained in the report. *The results of the interviews and other supporting data are contained in the report.*

**in connection with** *along with; and; as well as; combined with; coupled with; joined with; paired with; together with; with.*

**in connection with** *about; as for; as to; concerning; for; in; of; on; over; regarding; respecting; to; toward; with;* delete. • The bank with sufficient presence and skills may be asked to work with the client's own local advisors in connection with purely domestic transactions. *The bank with sufficient presence and skills may be asked to work with the client's own local advisors on purely domestic transactions.*

**in consequence** *consequently; hence; so; then; therefore; thus.*

**in consequence of** *after; because of; by; due to; following; for; from; in; out of; owing to; through; with.* • The defendants cannot claim to have suffered damage in consequence of the plaintiffs' early entry onto premises they had already vacated pursuant to a notice to quit for nonpayment of rent. *The defendants cannot claim to have suffered damage from the plaintiffs' early* *entry onto premises they had already vacated pursuant to a notice to quit for nonpayment of rent.*

**in consequence of the fact that** *because; considering; for; in that; since.*

**in consideration of (payment of; sum of)** *because of; due to; for; in return for; in view of; on account of; owing to; through.* • In consideration of the foregoing and of the mutual promises contained herein, the parties mutually agree as follows. *In view of the foregoing and the mutual promises contained herein, the parties mutually agree as follows.*

**in consideration of the fact that** *because; considering; for; in that; since.* • In consideration of the fact that Medicare payments are already deducted from my Social Security checks, am I entitled to a credit for this further deduction? *Since Medicare payments are already deducted from my Social Security checks, am I entitled to a credit for this further deduction?*

**in consonance to (with)** *according to; by; following; in keeping with; in line with; in step with; to; under.*

**in contempt of** *despite.*

**in contrast to (with)** *against; alongside; beside; compared to (with); -(i)er than; less; less than; more; more than; next to; over; than; to; unlike; versus; vis-à-vis.* • In contrast to last month, September sales of government debt are expected to be light. *Compared to last month, September sales of government debt are expected to be light.*

**in conversation with** *conversing with; speaking to (with); talking to (with).* • I don't know what happened; I was in conversation with my friend. *I don't know what happened; I was talking with my friend.*

**in copious profusion** *copiously; in profusion.* • As naturally and spontaneously as the notes that issue from the throat of a thrush, the melodies poured forth from Schubert's pen in copious profusion. *As naturally and spontaneously as the notes that issue from the throat of a thrush, the melodies poured forth from Schubert's pen in profusion.*

**incorporate in(to)** *add; contain; have; include.*

**in correspondence to (with)** *according to; by; following; in keeping with; in line with; in step with; to; under.*

**(a) . . . increase over** *more than.* • That's a 33-percent increase over last year. *That's 33 percent more than last year.*

**increasing in** *increasingly.* • The seaweed treatments are increasing in popularity with both men and women. *The seaweed treatments are increasingly popular with both men and women.*

**increasingly more** *increasingly; more and more.* • Information processing is becoming increasingly more automated through the use of machines. *Information processing is becoming increasingly automated through the use of machines.*

**in (over) (the) days (decades; months; weeks; years) ahead** *at length; before long; eventually; in time; later; one day; over time; presently; quickly; shortly; someday; sometime; soon; ultimately; with time; yet;* delete. • We expect prospects will improve over the years ahead. *We expect prospects will improve in time.*

**in (the) days (decades; months; weeks; years) gone by** *before; earlier; formerly; once; over the (years); over time;* delete. • In years gone by, much has been written about perceived gains in the powers of the presidency compared with the powers of the Congress and vice versa. *Much has been written about perceived gains in the powers of the presidency compared with the powers of the Congress and vice versa.*

**in (the) days (decades; months; weeks; years) of old** *before; earlier; formerly; once; over the (years); over time;* delete. • The world must have seemed a larger place in days of old. *The world must have once seemed a larger place.*

**in (the) days (decades; months; weeks; years) past** *before; earlier; formerly; once; over the (years); over time;* delete. • Police academy training is more extensive for new officers, providing extensive computer training, whereas in years past only a few officers would have had any experience with computers. *Police academy training is more extensive for new officers, providing extensive computer training, whereas before only a few officers would have had any experience with computers.*

**in (the) days (decades; months; weeks; years) since** *since; since then.* • However, in the years since 1970, the same continent has experienced precipitation levels above the mean measurements for the reference period. *However, since 1970, the same continent has experienced precipitation levels above the mean measurements for the reference period.*

**in (over) . . . days (decades; hours; minutes; months; weeks; years) time** *in (over) . . . days (decades; hours; minutes; months; weeks; years).* • I'm going to be visiting some Navy bases in a few months time. *I'm going to be visiting some Navy bases in a few months.*

**in (over) (the) days (decades; months; weeks; years) to come** *at length; before long; eventually; in time; later; one day; over time; presently; quickly; shortly; someday; sometime; soon; ultimately; with time; yet;* delete. • We are deadly serious about making changes that will allow us to remain a viable competitor in the years to come. *We are deadly serious about making changes that will allow us to remain a viable competitor.*

**indebtedness** *debt(s).* • Sales tax revenues are down because people are spending less, paying off their indebtedness, and saving more. *Sales tax revenues are down because people are spending less, paying off their debts, and saving more.*

**in defense of** *for; with.* • May I please put in a word in defense of poor Livia Budai, who has been lambasted out of all proportion in your articles? *May I please put in a word for poor Livia Budai, who has been lambasted out of all proportion in your articles?*

**in defiance of** *against; despite.* • Responsibility for the tragedy rests exclusively on the war criminals in the Iranian government who have elected, in defiance of the rules of warfare established for many centuries, to make regular murderous attacks on neutral merchant ships on the high seas. *Responsibility for the tragedy rests exclusively on the war criminals in the Iranian government who have elected, despite the rules of warfare established for many centuries, to make regular murderous attacks on neutral merchant ships on the high seas.*

**in depth** *deep.*

**in despite of** *after all; apart; aside; despite; even with; for all; with all.* • In despite of his good looks, he has never married. *For all his good looks, he has never married.*

**indicate** *feel; hint; mention; say; show; suggest; tell.* • He indicated that he would be fine. *He said that he would be fine.*

**indication** *clue; cue; hint; inkling; sign.* • There are indications that Iran may have its own chemical weapons. *There are clues that Iran may have its own chemical weapons.*

**individual** *(adj)* delete. • I think there are individual exceptions. *I think there are exceptions.*

**individual(s)** *(n) anybody; anyone; everybody; everyone; man; men; people; person; somebody; someone; those; woman; women; you;* delete. • The dominant behavioral characteristic of phobic individuals is avoidance. *The dominant behavioral characteristic of phobic persons is avoidance.*

**individuals (men; people; persons; women) who are** delete. • People who are obsessive-compulsive have difficulty making decisions. *Obsessive-compulsives have difficulty making decisions.*

**inductive reasoning** *induction.*

**in due course (time)** *at length; in time; later; one day; over time; someday; sometime; with time; yet.* • We will consider your statement in due time. *We will yet consider your statement.*

**in duration** *last; long;* delete. • Girls are at far greater risk for sexual abuse than boys, and their sexual abuse apparently is more common and longer in duration than the abuse boys are likely to experience. *Girls are at far greater risk for sexual abuse than boys, and their sexual abuse apparently is more common and lasts longer than the abuse boys are likely to experience.*

**in each (every) case (circumstance; instance; situation)** *all; always; consistently; constantly; each; each time; for (in) each; for (in) every; every one; every time; invariably; unfailingly;* delete. • In every instance, the acquirer selected is the one with the best bid. *The acquirer selected is always the one with the best bid.*

**in earlier (former; prior) times** *before; earlier; formerly; once.* • There was plenty of weekend ticketing in prior times. *There once was plenty of weekend ticketing.*

**in either (neither) case (circumstance; instance; situation)** *either (neither) way;* delete. • In either case, a veto would have provided Democratic opponents with powerful rhetorical ammunition in light of the 80 percent approval for the legislation in public opinion polls. *Either way, a veto would have provided Democratic opponents with powerful rhetorical ammunition in light of the 80 percent approval for the legislation in public opinion polls.*

**in either (neither) event** *either (neither) way;* delete. • In either event, you have a few options. *Either way, you have a few options.*

**in error** *wrong.* • He will not listen, nor will he back down even when he knows he is in error. *He will not listen, nor will he back down even when he knows he is wrong.*

**in (the) event (of; that)** *if (there were); if . . . should; in case (of); should (there); were (there; . . . to); when;* delete. • In the event that any liquid or solid object falls into the cabinet, unplug the unit and have it checked by qualified personnel. *Should any liquid or solid object fall into the cabinet, unplug the unit and have it checked by qualified personnel.* • Such information would be vital in the event they choose to have children. *Such information would be vital if they choose to have children.*

**in evidence** *apparent; conspicuous; evident; obvious; plain.* • Little of that has been in evidence among the thrifts. *Little of that has been evident among the thrifts.*

**in excess of** *above; better than; beyond; faster than; greater than; larger than; more than; over; stronger than.* • Annually, retailers lose in excess of $1.5 billion, and only about 30 percent of those losses are to shoplifters and other outsiders. *Annually, retailers lose more than $1.5 billion, and only about 30 percent of those losses are to shoplifters and other outsiders.*

**in exchange (for)** *for.* • The deal would involve his gaining credibility with the administration in exchange for his helping Nicaraguan Contras in their fight against the Sandinistas. *The deal would involve his gaining credibility with the administration for his helping Nicaraguan Contras in their fight against the Sandinistas.*

**in (the) face of** *after all; apart; aside; despite; even with; for all; with all.* • He persevered in the face of strong pressure within his agency. *He persevered despite strong pressure within his agency.*

**in fact** delete. • Women not able to have power in the external world have in fact developed a secondary power. *Women not able to have power in the external world have developed a secondary power.*

**in (a; the) . . . fashion** *-(al)ly;* delete. • It is true that the records are stored in a sequential fashion. *It is true that the records are stored sequentially.* • I don't think I was treated in a loyal fashion by the president. *I don't think I was treated loyally by the president.* • Your story quotes antismokers 11 times and tobacco industry representatives only twice—and then in a disdainful fashion. *Your story quotes antismokers 11 times and tobacco industry representatives only twice—and then disdainfully.*

**in favor (of)** *for; with.* • Five circuit courts of appeal have ruled in favor of testing without individualized suspicion. *Five circuit courts of appeal have ruled for testing without individualized suspicion.*

**(an; the) infinite number (of)** *countless; endless; infinite; millions (of); myriad; numberless; untold.* • The voice is capable of an infinite number of sounds and pitches. *The voice is capable of countless sounds and pitches.*

**inflammable** *flammable.*

**in force and effect** *active; at work; effective; in action; in effect; in force; in play; working.* • Tenant agrees to pay Landlord at the rate of $1200 per month on the first day of each and every month in advance so long as this lease is in force and effect. *Tenant agrees to pay Landlord at the rate of $1200 per month on the first day of each and every month in advance so long as this lease is in effect.*

**inform** *tell; write.* • She informed me that she wants a divorce. *She told me that she wants a divorce.*

**in (a; the) . . . form** *in; -(al)ly; delete.* • An analyst must be able to state the assumption in explicit form. *An analyst must be able to explicitly state the assumption.* • Specifications of a patent must be attached to the application in written form describing the invention in detail so that a person skilled in the field can produce the item. *Written specifications of a patent must be attached to the application describing the invention in detail so that a person skilled in the field can produce the item.*

**in . . . from now** *from now; in.* • In about six to seven years from now, OPEC will once again be able to capture 50 percent of the world market. *In about six to seven years, OPEC will once again be able to capture 50 percent of the world market.*

**in front of** *before.* • We have tough challenges in front of us. *We have tough challenges before us.*

**in fulfillment of** *to complete; to finish; to fulfill; to satisfy.* • In fulfillment of its open-ended agreement, Saatchi & Saatchi will also advise the Soviets on how much they should charge for TV spots that could reach some 180 million Soviet citizens and another 30 million viewers in Eastern Europe. *To fulfill its open-ended agreement, Saatchi & Saatchi will also advise the Soviets on how much they should charge for TV spots that could reach some 180 million Soviet citizens and another 30 million viewers in Eastern Europe.*

**in general** *delete.* • Women in general have a responsibility to one another. *Women have a responsibility to one another.*

**(a; the) -ing of** *-ing.* • The taking of drugs is bad for people. *Taking drugs is bad for people.* • Often the initial development of a program focuses on the obtaining of some correct solution to the given problem. *Often the initial development of a program focuses on obtaining some correct solution to the given problem.* • It has several verification problems that can only be appreciated by a careful reading of the treaty. *It has several verification problems that can only be appreciated by carefully reading the treaty.*

**in good time** *at length; in time; later; one day; over time; someday; sometime; with time; yet.*

**in great (large) measure** *almost all; chiefly; commonly; generally; greatly; in general; largely; mainly; most; mostly; most often; much; nearly all; normally; overall; typically; usually.* • Your today is in large measure a result of your yesterdays. *Your today is largely a result of your yesterdays.*

**in great (large) part** *almost all; chiefly; commonly; generally; greatly; in general; largely; mainly; most; mostly; most often; much; nearly all; normally; overall; typically; usually.* • The lower cost of U.S. labor was due in large part to the drop in value of the dollar compared with most other currencies. *The lower cost of U.S. labor was largely due to the drop in value of the dollar compared with most other currencies.*

**in great (large) quantities** *a good (great) deal (of); a good (great) many (of); almost all; dozens (of); hundreds (of); many; millions (of); most; nearly all; scores (of); six hundred (twelve hundred); thousands (of).* • The $2 bills are not being ordered by area banks even though the Federal Reserve has them in large quantities. *The $2 bills are not being ordered by area banks even though the Federal Reserve has millions of them.*

**in height** *high;* delete. • They should be at least ⅛ inch in height, not encircled, and placed close to the parts they apply to. *They should be at least ⅛ inch high, not encircled, and placed close to the parts they apply to.*

**in (the) history (of the world)** *ever.* • Original plans called for a fleet of 132 bombers with the cost of each plane estimated at $500 million, making it the most expensive plane in history. *Original plans called for a fleet of 132 bombers with the cost of each plane estimated at $500 million, making it the most expensive plane ever.*

**in honor of** *after; for; to.*

**in imitation of** *after; follow.*

**in instances when (where)** *if; when; where.* • In instances where the products and services being traded within the firm are unique, the cost-plus method seems appropriate. *When the products and services being traded within the firm are unique, the cost-plus method seems appropriate.*

**in isolation (from)** *alone; apart (from); by itself; separate (from).* • It makes no sense to discuss one issue in isolation from the other. *It makes no sense to discuss one issue separate from the other.*

**initial (initially)** *at first; first.* • Initially, the key was successfully marketing the fund to commercial banks. *At first, the key was successfully marketing the fund to commercial banks.*

**initially . . . begin (start)** *begin (start).* • I believe he initially started as a stand-up comic. *I believe he started as a stand-up comic.*

**in its (their) entirety** *all (the); (the) complete; completely; (the) entire; entirely; every; (the) full; fully; (the) whole; wholly;* delete. • When you read the book in its entirety, you will understand my position. *When you read the entire book, you will understand my position.*

**(be) in jeopardy** *endangered; imperiled; jeopardized.* • None of us can avoid the responsibility of working in all ways open to us to shore up the democracy that is so clearly in jeopardy. *None of us can avoid the responsibility of working in all ways open to us to shore up the democracy that is so clearly jeopardized.*

**in length** *last; long;* delete. • The panel discussion itself will be two hours in length. *The panel discussion itself will last two hours.*

**in (the) light of the fact that** *because; considering; for; in that; since; when.* • This is clumsy by comparison to the Macintosh file system's embedded information about files, especially in light of the fact that you might have MultiMate, Word, and DisplayWrite on the same disk—and they all use .DOC extensions on their files. *This is clumsy by comparison to the Macintosh file system's embedded information about files, especially since you might have MultiMate, Word, and DisplayWrite on the same disk—and they all use .DOC extensions on their files.*

**in like fashion (manner)** *likewise; similarly.* • In like fashion, managers need to know how they are doing from the viewpoints of those they are paid to serve. *Likewise, managers need to know how they are doing from the viewpoints of those they are paid to serve.*

**in (a; the) . . . manner** -*(al)ly*; delete. • I hope future stories dealing with sensitive issues such as this will be handled in a more responsible and accurate manner. *I hope future stories dealing with sensitive issues such as this will be handled more responsibly and accurately.*

**in many (most) cases** *almost all; almost always; commonly; frequently; many; many times; most; most often; much; nearly all; nearly always; normally; often; typically; usually.* • In most cases, the pitch can be approximated or laid off with a scale or dividers. *Usually, the pitch can be approximated or laid off with a scale or dividers.*

**in many (most) circumstances** *almost all; almost always; commonly; frequently; many; many times; most; most often; much; nearly all; nearly always; normally; often; ordinarily; typically; usually.* • RISC microprocessors operate faster than CISC microprocessors in many circumstances. *RISC microprocessors often operate faster than CISC microprocessors.*

**in many (most) instances** *almost all; almost always; commonly; frequently; many; many times; most; most often; much; nearly all; nearly always; normally; often; ordinarily; typically; usually.* • In many instances, the family is in a state of dysfunction and disrepair. *Often, the family is in a state of dysfunction and disrepair.*

**in many (most) regards** *almost always; largely; many; most; mostly; most often; nearly always; often; usually.*

**in many (most) respects** *almost always; largely; many; most; mostly; most often; nearly always; often; usually.* • In most respects, competition among banks has been polite. *Competition among banks has been largely polite.*

**in many (most) situations** *almost all; almost always; commonly; frequently; many; many times; most; most often; much; nearly all; nearly always; normally; often; ordinarily; typically; usually.* • The speed with which a modem can transmit and receive data is important in many situations. *The speed with which a modem can transmit and receive data is usually important.*

**in (our) midst** *among (us).*

**in much the same fashion (manner; way) (as; that)** *much as; much like.* • Though similar in size, material, and color and fabricated in much the same way as their plainer cousins, the new tokens bore various kinds of surface markings and showed a greater variety of shapes. *Though similar in size, material, and color and fabricated much like their plainer cousins,* *the new tokens bore various kinds of surface markings and showed a greater variety of shapes.*

**in my assessment** *I assert; I believe; I claim; I consider; I contend; I feel; I hold; I judge; I maintain; I regard; I say; I think; I view; to me;* delete.
• In my assessment, the most desirable changes for commercial banks to incorporate are as follows. *To me, the most desirable changes for commercial banks to incorporate are as follows.*

**in my estimation** *I assert; I believe; I claim; I consider; I contend; I feel; I hold; I judge; I maintain; I regard; I say; I think; I view; to me;* delete. • In my estimation, the treatment is suitable to Mr. Ross's case. *I feel the treatment is suitable to Mr. Ross's case.*

**in my judgment** *I assert; I believe; I claim; I consider; I contend; I feel; I hold; I judge; I maintain; I regard; I say; I think; I view; to me;* delete. • The most critical issue confronting America, in my judgment, is how we match educational accessibility and opportunity to the demographic change. *The most critical issue confronting America, I contend, is how we match educational accessibility and opportunity to the demographic change.*

**in my (own) mind(s)** *for myself;* delete. • I had to find out in my own mind if quiet diplomacy would work. *I had to find out for myself if quiet diplomacy would work.*

**(to) . . . in my (own) mind's eye** *envisage; envision; imagine; visualize;* delete.
• Once you get to the gate, you need to review in your mind's eye where the engines are. *Once you get to the gate, you need to visualize where the engines are.*

**in my opinion** *I assert; I believe; I claim; I consider; I contend; I feel; I hold; I judge; I maintain; I regard; I say; I think; I view; to me;* delete. • In my opinion, the cruelest aggression is nonverbal, passive aggression. *To me, the cruelest aggression is nonverbal, passive aggression.*

**in my view** *I assert; I believe; I claim; I consider; I contend; I feel; I hold; I judge; I maintain; I regard; I say; I think; I view; to me;* delete. • In my view, most of these principles were narrow in scope. *I believe most of these principles were narrow in scope.*

**in nature** delete. • Christianity is theistic and revelatory in nature; the New Age is humanistic and generally solipsistic in nature. *Christianity is theistic and revelatory; the New Age is humanistic and generally solipsistic.*

**in no case** *never; not; not ever; not once.* • In no case would I recommend anything that could lead to the situation at Agawam. *Never would I recommend anything that could lead to the situation at Agawam.*

**in normal (ordinary; typical; usual) practice** *commonly; customarily; normally; ordinarily; typically; usually.* • In normal practice, the party chairman is nominated, and the voting delegation then stands in unison to express its support. *Normally, the party chairman is nominated, and the voting delegation then stands in unison to express its support.*

**in no small measure** *almost all; chiefly; commonly; generally; greatly; in general; largely; mainly; most; mostly; most often; much; nearly all; normally; overall; typically; usually.* • Our continued success is due in no small measure to their contribution on a daily basis. *Our continued success is greatly due to their contribution on a daily basis.*

**in no small part** *almost all; chiefly; commonly; generally; greatly; in general; largely; mainly; most; mostly; most often; much; nearly all; normally; overall; typically; usually.* • And I continue to feel that his lifelong feelings of inadequacy and frustration stemmed in no small part from the limitations that he imposed upon his work. *And I continue to feel that his lifelong feelings of inadequacy and frustration stemmed largely from the limitations that he imposed upon his work.*

**in no time (at all)** *promptly; quickly; rapidly; right away; shortly; soon; speedily; swiftly.*

**innovative new** *innovative; new.* • An innovative new product combining the latest in communications technology is being installed in courthouses and recording offices throughout the country for public use. *A new product combining the latest in communications technology is being installed in courthouses and recording offices throughout the country for public use.*

**in no way** *never; not; not ever; not once.* • In no way are they meant to represent the official position of NYNEX. *They are not meant to represent the official position of NYNEX.*

**in no way, shape, or form** *in no way; never; not; not ever; not once.* • In no way, shape, or form did we aid anyone or offer incentives to anyone to go to the town meeting. *Never did we aid anyone or offer incentives to anyone to go to the town meeting.*

**in number** *delete.* • Nineteenth-century sweatshops are once again increasing in number. *Nineteenth-century sweatshops are once again increasing.*

**innumerable** *countless; endless; infinite; millions (of); myriad; numberless; untold.*

**in March (July) of 1992 (1957)** *in March (July) 1992 (1957).* • The second moving year begins in February of 1984 and extends through January *of 1985. The second moving year begins in February 1984 and extends through January 1985.*

**in (the) olden days** *before; earlier; formerly; once.*

**in operation** *active; functioning; in place; running; set up; working;* delete. • A large midwestern bank has had a performance monitoring program in operation since 1981. *A large midwestern bank has had a performance monitoring program since 1981.*

**in opposition to** *against; opposed to; with.* • Lenin set himself in opposition to the blundering, indecisive czar; Khomeini against the blundering, indecisive shah. *Lenin set himself against the blundering, indecisive czar; Khomeini against the blundering, indecisive shah.*

**in . . . order** *-(al)ly;* delete. • We examine, in alphabetical order, all the MLI commands that make up GS/OS and ProDOS 8. *We examine, alphabetically, all the MLI commands that make up GS/OS and ProDOS 8.*

**in order for** *for.* • Is it necessary that animals die in order for humans to live? *Is it necessary that animals die for humans to live?*

**in order that** *for; so; so that; that.* • The overall dimension and the radii are given in order that their centers may be located. *The overall dimension and the radii are given so that their centers may be located.*

**in order to** *so as to; to.* • In order to qualify for a heart transplant, certain criteria must be met, one of which is having less than a year to live. *To qualify for a heart transplant, certain criteria must be met, one of which is having less than a year to live.*

**in other cases (circumstances; instances; situations)** *at times; other; (at) other times; some; sometimes;* delete. • In other cases, the application may be more mundane, like helping users set up newly delivered microcomputers. *Other applications may be more mundane, like helping users set up newly delivered microcomputers.*

**in other words** *namely; that is; to wit.* • The directory names in the chain must define a continuous path; in other words, each directory specified must be contained within the preceding directory. *The directory names in the* *chain must define a continuous path; that is, each directory specified must be contained within the preceding directory.*

**in partial fulfillment of** *toward.*

**in (over) (the) past days (decades; months; weeks; years)** *before; earlier; formerly; once.*

**in payment for (of)** *for.* • Connoisseurs of the region cannot help wondering what Assad could offer Washington in payment for such a favor. *Connoisseurs of the region cannot help wondering what Assad could offer Washington for such a favor.*

**in perpetuity** *always; ceaselessly; constantly; endlessly; eternally; everlastingly; forever; never ending; perpetually.* • It promised to preserve the rest of the farm in perpetuity as farm or forest. *It promised to preserve the rest of the farm forever as farm or forest.*

**in place of** *for.* • No reasonably literate person of my acquaintance says "sunk" in place of "sank." *No reasonably literate person of my acquaintance says "sunk" for "sank."*

**in point of** *about; as for; as to; concerning; for; in; of; on; over; regarding; respecting; to; toward; with;* delete.

**in point of fact** *actually; indeed; in fact; in faith; in reality; in truth; really; truly;* delete. • The U.S. government said he wasn't working for them, but in point of fact, he was a military attache. *The U.S. government said he wasn't working for them, but in truth he was a military attache.*

**in preference to** *over.* • Mile's new product emphasis is on performance in preference to fashion. *Mile's new product emphasis is on performance over fashion.*

**in proportion to** *for; with.*

**in proximity (to)** *close by; close to; near; nearby.* • The property is in proximity to metropolitan Boston. *The property is near metropolitan Boston.*

**in punishment for (of)** *for.*

**in pursuit of** *exploring; probing; pursuing; searching; seeking.* • One would think they could better spend their time in pursuit of the pressing problems which beset the Redevelopment Authority and the city's development plans. *One would think they could better spend their time pursuing the pressing* *problems which beset the Redevelopment Authority and the city's development plans.*

**input** *clout; pull; say; voice.* • I have a lot of input into what I'll wear on the set. *I have a lot of say about what I'll wear on the set.*

**input** *thoughts; views.* • These style alternatives do not solicit employee input. *These style alternatives do not solicit employee views.*

**(the) . . . in question** *the; that; this;* delete. • Neither Phillips nor any of its subsidiaries has ever sold the chemical in question to Libya. *Neither Phillips nor any of its subsidiaries has ever sold this chemical to Libya.*

**in quick (short) order** *abruptly; apace; briskly; directly; fast; forthwith; hastily; hurriedly; posthaste; presently; promptly; quickly; rapidly; right away; shortly; soon; speedily; straightaway; swiftly; wingedly.* • Surely a motivated work force could whip us back into shape in short order. *Surely a motivated work force could whip us back into shape quickly.*

**inquire (about; of)** *ask.* • I inquired of the doctor why these children have distended stomachs. *I asked the doctor why these children have distended stomachs.*

**in reaction to** *after; because of; by; due to; following; for; from; in; out of; owing to; through; with.*

**in reality** *actually; indeed; in fact; in faith; in truth; really; truly;* delete.

**in recent days (decades; months; weeks; years)** *lately; of late; recent; recently;* delete. • But events have not been kind to the university in recent weeks. *But recent events have not been kind to the university.*

**in recent history (memory; times)** *in days (months; weeks; years); lately; of late; recent; recently;* delete. • It is the largest drop in auto insurance rates in recent memory. *It is the largest drop in auto insurance rates in years.*

**in recorded history** *on record; recorded.* • Though final figures aren't yet in, as of November 1 this has been the hottest year in recorded history. *Though final figures aren't yet in, as of November 1 this has been the hottest year on record.*

**in reference to** *about; as for; as to; concerning; for; in; of; on; over; regarding; respecting; to; toward; with;* delete. • Never make any assumptions or promises in reference to product flaws, but report all instances either to customer service or the appropriate management personnel for corrective action.

*Never make any assumptions or promises about product flaws, but report all instances either to customer service or the appropriate management personnel for corrective action.*

**in regard to** *about; as for; as to; concerning; for; in; of; on; over; regarding; respecting; to; toward; with;* delete. • They questioned me in regard to a 1986 bank robbery. *They questioned me about a 1986 bank robbery.*

**in relation to** *about; as for; as to; concerning; for; in; of; on; over; regarding; respecting; to; toward; with;* delete. • The researchers interviewed the survivors in relation to six areas of postwar life. *The researchers interviewed the survivors regarding six areas of postwar life.*

**in relation (relationship) to** *against; alongside; beside; compared to (with); -(i)er than; less; less than; more; more than; next to; over; than; to; versus; vis-à-vis.* • What has been done is very small in relationship to what needs to be done. *What has been done is very small compared to what needs to be done.*

**in repetition** *again; over.*

**in resistance to** *against; with.*

**in respect of (to)** *about; as for; as to; concerning; for; in; of; on; over; regarding; respecting; to; toward; with;* delete. • Some additional perspective is needed in respect to South Korea. *Some additional perspective is needed on South Korea.*

**in response to** *after; because of; by; due to; following; for; from; in; out of; owing to; through; with.* • The dollar yesterday fell against most major currencies in response to renewed dollar sales by central banks. *The dollar yesterday fell against most major currencies following renewed dollar sales by central banks.*

**in return for** *for.* • Switch traders are willing, in return for a fee, to find buyers for countertraded goods. *Switch traders are willing, for a fee, to find buyers for countertraded goods.*

**(the) ins and (the) outs** *details; features; particulars; specifics.*

**in scale** delete.

**in scope** delete. • Smokeless tobacco is becoming a problem large in scope. *Smokeless tobacco is becoming a large problem.*

**in shape** delete. • The true-size surface is elliptical in shape. *The true-size surface is elliptical.*

**in short supply** *meager; rare; scant; scarce; sparse.*

**inside of** *inside.* • I continued to pack my gear, with pain and anger burning inside of me. *I continued to pack my gear, with pain and anger burning inside me.*

**inside (and) out** *completely; thoroughly.*

**inside the boundaries (limits; parameters) of** *within.*

**in situations when (where)** *if; when; where.* • In situations where market heterogeneity limits opportunity for uniformity, the firm should actively promote global convergence of market segments. *Where market heterogeneity limits opportunity for uniformity, the firm should actively promote global convergence of market segments.*

**in size** delete. • The sides range from 4 to 24 inches in size. *The sides range from 4 to 24 inches.*

**insofar as** *as far as; as much as; so far as; so much as.* • As a historian, Mr. Chaudhuri is useful insofar as he recounts personal experience—for example, his accounts of the Bose brothers. *As a historian, Mr. Chaudhuri is useful so far as he recounts personal experience—for example, his accounts of the Bose brothers.*

**insofar as** *because; considering; for; in that; since.* • Insofar as more than 98 percent of House incumbents were returned to office in the last election, it shouldn't surprise anyone that the members are turning Congress into a family business. *Since more than 98 percent of House incumbents were returned to office in the last election, it shouldn't surprise anyone that the members are turning Congress into a family business.*

**insofar as . . . (goes; is concerned)** *about; as for; as to; concerning; for; in; of; on; over; regarding; respecting; to; toward; with;* delete. • The president's position, insofar as negotiations are concerned, has never changed. *The president's position on negotiations has never changed.*

**in some fashion (manner; way)** *somehow; someway(s).* • He considers it an idea that will be adopted in some fashion to meet the spiraling demands on air travel. *He considers it an idea that will somehow be adopted to meet the spiraling demands on air travel.*

**in spite of** *after all; apart; aside; despite; even with; for all; with all.* • In spite of his malady, he wrote music with great skill and creativity. *Even with his malady, he wrote music with great skill and creativity.*

**in spite of the fact that** *although; but; even though; still; though; yet.* • The number of deaths from asthma has doubled in the past decade in spite of the fact that treatments have improved. *The number of deaths from asthma has doubled in the past decade, yet treatments have improved.* • Some commentators claim that careful writers avoid the adverb *slow* in spite of the fact that it has over four centuries of usage behind it. *Some commentators claim that careful writers avoid the adverb* slow *even though it has over four centuries of usage behind it.*

**instantaneous (instantaneously)** *at once; instant (instantly); straightaway.* • We fell in love with her instantaneously. *We fell in love with her at once.*

**institute** *set up.*

**institution** *building; factory; hospital; institute; jail; office; place; plant; prison; school;* delete.

**institution of higher learning** *college; school; university.*

**in such a fashion (manner; way) as to (so as to)** *so as to; to.* • The light fixture had to be designed in such a manner so as to provide the maximum light to the operating area. *The light fixture had to be designed to provide the maximum light to the operating area.* • Further, we do not authorize any organization to use the Association's name in such a way as to imply that such a relationship exists. *Further, we do not authorize any organization to use the Association's name so as to imply that such a relationship exists.*

**in such a fashion (manner; way) so (so that)** *so; so that.* • Only meter stamped, return address labels may be used on single piece, special fourth-class rate or library rate mail, and these labels must adhere in such a manner so they will not come off in one piece. *Only meter stamped, return address labels may be used on single piece, special fourth-class rate or library rate mail, and these labels must adhere so that they will not come off in one piece.*

**in such a fashion (manner; way) that** *so; so that.* • Export business may be structured in such a way that the buyer bears most of the risks. *Export business may be structured so that the buyer bears most of the risks.* • The first was the "store," designed in such a manner that numbers could be stored in 1,000 "registers," each capable of storing 50 digits. *The first was* *the "store," designed so that numbers could be stored in 1,000 "registers," each capable of storing 50 digits.*

**in such (a; the) . . . fashion (manner; way)** *so -(al)ly;* delete.

**insufficient** *dis-; il-; im-; in-; ir-; lack of; -less(ness); mis-; no; non-; not; not enough; scant; too few; too little; un-.* • There is insufficient reason for joy. *There is not enough reason for joy.*

**(an; the) insufficient amount (of)** *not enough; too little.*

**in sufficient amount** *enough.* • If radon gas enters your lungs in sufficient amounts, it can emit alpha particles that attack tissue and lead to lung cancer. *If enough radon gas enters your lungs, it can emit alpha particles that attack tissue and lead to lung cancer.*

**(an; the) insufficient number (of)** *not enough; too few.* • Within two years, other American cities expect a similar gridlock of hospital beds, largely because of AIDS and an insufficient number of health-care workers. *Within two years, other American cities expect a similar gridlock of hospital beds, largely because of AIDS and too few health-care workers.*

**in sufficient number** *enough.* • I hope you heard from people in sufficient number to alert you to the possibility of a nationwide constituency for extended incarceration of violent felons. *I hope you heard from enough people to alert you to the possibility of a nationwide constituency for extended incarceration of violent felons.*

**in sufficient quantity** *enough.* • Libya doesn't have the industrial capacity to make toxic agents in sufficient quantities for warfare. *Libya doesn't have the industrial capacity to make enough toxic agents for warfare.*

**in summary (summation)** *in brief; in fine; in short; in sum.* • In summary, it is apparent that a country's comparative advantage situation will be vitally affected by the productivity of available factor inputs. *In sum, it is apparent that a country's comparative advantage situation will be vitally affected by the productivity of available factor inputs.*

**in support of** *for; with.* • Radical environmentalists are already demanding that legal and ethical protection be extended to all of nature, and a few of them have demonstrated a willingness to fight, break the law, and even die in support of this conviction. *Radical environmentalists are already demanding that legal and ethical protection be extended to all of nature, and* *a few of them have demonstrated a willingness to fight, break the law, and even die for this conviction.*

**intellectual ability (capacity)** *ability; capacity; intellect; intelligence.* • Tools and other remains left by Neanderthals show no indication that these creatures possessed the intellectual capacity for symbolic thought or language. *Tools and other remains left by Neanderthals show no indication that these creatures possessed the capacity for symbolic thought or language.*

**interdependency** *interdependence.*

**interestingly (enough)** delete. • Interestingly enough, in about 50 percent of the cases involved, the professional offering an opinion believed abuse had occurred. *In about 50 percent of the cases involved, the professional offering an opinion believed abuse had occurred.*

**interlocutor** *speaker; talker.*

**in . . . terms** *-(al)ly;* delete. • They both spoke in optimistic terms. *They both spoke optimistically.*

**in terms of** *about; as; as for; as to; by; concerning; for; in; of; on; regarding; respecting; through; under; with;* delete. • In terms of safety, honesty, and trust, banks consistently score higher than life insurance companies. *In safety, honesty, and trust, banks consistently score higher than life insurance companies.* • How would you say you are different in terms of your personas? *How would you say your personas are different?* • She's more aggressive in terms of what she wants. *She's more aggressive about what she wants.* • Women are looking for help in terms of PMS. *Women are looking for help with PMS.* • Other doctors have criticized IL-2 therapy in terms of its toxicity. *Other doctors have criticized IL-2 therapy for its toxicity.* • The forecast level should be judged in terms of its reasonableness. *The forecast level should be judged on its reasonableness.*

**interpretative** *interpretive.* • Strategically placed U.S. nationals play an important interpretative role between the host country and the U.S. headquarters. *Strategically placed U.S. nationals play an important interpretive role between the host country and the U.S. headquarters.*

**interpret to mean** *interpret as.* • Achieving a desired standard of living must be interpreted to mean finding the pattern of consumption expenditures that yields maximum satisfaction. *Achieving a desired standard of living must be interpreted as finding the pattern of consumption expenditures that yields maximum satisfaction.*

**in that (this) case (circumstance; instance; situation)** *here; now; then; there;* delete. • No ampersand is required in this case because the argument will not be modified. *No ampersand is required now because the argument will not be modified.*

**in that (this) connection** *about (for; in; on; to) that (this);* delete.

**in that (this) day and age** *in that (this) age; in that (this) day; in that (this) time; (just; right) now; nowadays; then; these (those) days; today.* • In this day and age of global violence, I find it interesting that the *Globe Magazine* would publish articles about two international terrorists. *In this age of global violence, I find it interesting that the* Globe Magazine *would publish articles about two international terrorists.*

**in that (this) direction** *toward that (this).* • That means any push in this direction would require guidance from officials of the new administration. *That means any push toward this would require guidance from officials of the new administration.*

**in that (this) fashion (manner; way)** *like this (that); so; thus.* • What can she expect if she continues to behave in this manner? *What can she expect if she continues to behave like this?*

**in that (this) general vicinity** *around (near) here (there); thereabouts (hereabouts).* • There have been a lot of crimes in this general vicinity. *There have been a lot of crimes near here.*

**in (on) that (this) matter** *about (for; in; on; to) that (this);* delete. • Rothko's views on this matter were very well known among his circle of friends. *Rothko's views on this were very well known among his circle of friends.*

**in that (this) regard** *about (for; in; on; to) that (this);* delete. • There will be no change at all in that regard. *There will be no change at all in that.*

**in that (this) respect** *about (for; in; on; to) that (this);* delete.

**in the absence of** *absent; having no; lacking; minus; missing; not having; with no; without.* • In the absence of any other form of security, the shareholders of the contractor might be willing to let the company go out of business in the face of a serious problem. *Absent any other form of security, the shareholders of the contractor might be willing to let the company go out of business in the face of a serious problem.* • In the absence of quality, employees may face an "unclean" environment, which can lead to dissatisfaction for the work force. *Lacking quality, employees may face an "unclean" environment, which can lead to dissatisfaction for the work force.*

**in the act of -ing** *-ing.*

**in the affirmative** *affirmatively; favorably; positively; yes.* • Eight members having voted in the affirmative, the vote carries. *Eight members having voted yes, the vote carries.*

**in the aftermath of** *(just; right) after; (close) behind; ensuing; following; succeeding.* • In the aftermath of the assault-rifle mass murder, Americans should remain rational and not legislate away the right to own any type of firearm. *Following the assault-rifle mass murder, Americans should remain rational and not legislate away the right to own any type of firearm.*

**in the altogether** *naked; nude.*

**in the amount (sum) of** *for; of;* delete. • Enclosed is a check in the amount of $900.00. *Enclosed is a check for $900.00.*

**in the area of** *about; as for; as to; concerning; for; in; of; on; over; regarding; respecting; to; toward; with;* delete. • The secondary gains for the phobic partner may be in the area of fulfilling nurturing needs. *The secondary gains for the phobic partner may be in fulfilling nurturing needs.*

**(something; somewhere) in the area (of)** *about; around; close to; more or less; near; nearly; or so; roughly; some;* delete. • The trial is expected to run in the area of nine months. *The trial is expected to run some nine months.*

**in the assessment of** *assert; believe; claim; consider; contend; feel; hold; judge; maintain; regard; say; think; to; view; with.*

**in (within) the boundaries (limits; parameters) of** *in (within).*

**in the capacity of** *as.*

**in the company of** *alongside; among; beside; during; in; with.* • These children are here in the company of their fathers. *These children are here with their fathers.*

**in the context of** *in.* • In the context of personal financial planning, the application of controls is even more important. *In personal financial planning, the application of controls is even more important.*

**(somewhere) in the course of** *during; for; in; over; throughout; when; while; with.* • There were several suspects that came up in the course of our investigation, but Nancy Douglas was not one of them. *There were several suspects that came up during our investigation, but Nancy Douglas was not one of them.* • In the course of doing these exercises, students are introduced to almost all of their word processing program's features. *When doing these exercises, students are introduced to almost all of their word processing program's features.*

**in the course of events (things; time)** *at length; eventually; in due time; in the end; in time; later; one day; over the months (years); over time; someday; sometime; ultimately; with time; yet.* • Continued observation of such men indicates that this is exactly what happens in many cases, and more evidence of this may show up in the course of time. *Continued observation of such men indicates that this is exactly what happens in many cases, and more evidence of this may show up over time.*

**in the days (decades; months; weeks; years) before (prior to)** *before.* • In the days before LANs, if you wanted a coworker to add to a report you were writing, you copied the file to a disk and delivered it by hand. *Before LANs, if you wanted a coworker to add to a report you were writing, you copied the file to a disk and delivered it by hand.*

**in the direction of (toward)** *at; for; in; on; through; to; toward; with.* • It appears it's headed in the direction of becoming a more conventional school that focuses on finances. *It appears it's headed toward becoming a more conventional school that focuses on finances.*

**in the distant future** *eventual; eventually; future; in many months (years); in time; in two (ten) months (years); later; much later; next month (year); one day; over time; someday; sometime; ultimately; with time; yet;* delete. • In the distant future, the German people may regain unity through self-determination. *In time, the German people may regain unity through self-determination.*

**in the distant past** *before; earlier; formerly; long ago; long since; many months (years) ago; once;* delete.

**in the estimation of** *assert; believe; claim; consider; contend; feel; hold; judge; maintain; regard; say; think; to; view; with.*

**in the eventuality of (that; this)** *if (there were); if . . . should; in case (of); should (there); were (there; . . . to); when;* delete. • In the eventuality that someone decides not to follow a court order, what do you do? *If someone should decide not to follow a court order, what do you do?*

**in the extreme** *extremely; highly; hugely; mightily.* • All three theories seem unlikely in the extreme. *All three theories seem highly unlikely.*

**in the face of** *against; before; confronted by (with); confronting; faced with; facing.* • In the face of those developments, the off-farm work movement was inevitable. *Faced with those developments, the off-farm work movement was inevitable.*

**in the final (last) analysis** *finally; in the end; ultimately;* delete. • In the final analysis, we are still grappling with the inherent problems of being human. *In the end, we are still grappling with the inherent problems of being human.*

**in the first place** *first; first of all;* delete. • We found ourselves troubleshooting the immediate need, not addressing the larger issues that caused the problem in the first place. *We found ourselves troubleshooting the immediate need, not addressing the larger issues that first caused the problem.*

**in the following fashion (manner; way)** *as follows.* • The value of M can be substituted in the equation in the following manner. *The value of* M *can be substituted in the equation as follows.*

**in the foreseeable future** *before long; directly; in a month (week); next month (year); presently; quickly; shortly; soon; this month (year); tomorrow;* delete. • I expect in the foreseeable future we will see them looking inward and opening up to the world. *I expect we will presently see them looking inward and opening up to the world.*

**in the form of** *as;* delete. • I offer these comments in the form of advice, not criticism. *I offer these comments as advice, not criticism.*

**in the function of** *as.*

**in (into) the future** *at length; before long; eventually; in a month (week); in due time; in time; later; next month (year); one day; over time; someday; sometime; ultimately; with time; yet;* delete. • All indications are that these patterns of change will continue into the future. *All indications are that these patterns will continue.*

**in the immediate future** *at once; before long; directly; immediately; in a month (week); momentarily; next month (year); (just; right) now; presently; quickly; shortly; soon; straightaway; this month (year); tomorrow;* delete. • I don't anticipate any layoffs in the immediate future. *I don't anticipate any layoffs immediately.*

**in the immediate past** *a few months (years) ago; lately; not long ago; of late; recent; recently;* delete. • Computer software consulting firms constitute a growth node that will probably continue, but alone it cannot generate the numbers of jobs that have been generated in the immediate past. *Computer software consulting firms constitute a growth node that will probably continue, but alone it cannot generate the number of jobs that have been recently generated.*

**in the interest of (-ing)** *for; so as to; to.* • The secretary took this action in the interest of ensuring an equitable investigation. *The secretary took this action to ensure an equitable investigation.*

**in the interim** *meantime; meanwhile.* • In the interim, law enforcement agencies are bracing for the worst. *Meanwhile, law enforcement agencies are bracing for the worst.*

**in the interval** *meantime; meanwhile.*

**in the judgment of** *assert; believe; claim; consider; contend; feel; hold; judge; maintain; regard; say; think; to; view; with.* • In the judgment of these scientists, it has hurt the effort. *These scientists believe it has hurt the effort.*

**in the least (slightest)** *at all;* delete. • I don't mind in the least. *I don't mind at all.*

**in (over) the long run** *at length; eventually; in the end; in time; later; long-term; one day; over the months (years); over time; someday; sometime; ultimately; with time; yet.* • In the long run, presumably fewer citizens would need Medicaid. *In time, presumably fewer citizens would need Medicaid.*

**in (over) the long term** *at length; eventually; in the end; in time; later; long-term; one day; over the months (years); over time; someday; sometime; ultimately; with time; yet.* • How will the two investments compare over the long term? *How will the two investments compare over time?*

**in the main** *almost all; chiefly; commonly; generally; greatly; in general; largely; mainly; most; mostly; most often; much; nearly all; normally; overall; typically; usually.* • In the main, politicians have become contemptuous of voters. *Generally, politicians have become contemptuous of voters.*

**in the making** *brewing; developing; forming.* • The teams go into action when computers at the National Weather Service foresee a disturbance in the making. *The teams go into action when computers at the National Weather Service foresee a disturbance brewing.*

**in (on) the matter of** *about; as for; as to; concerning; for; in; of; on; over; regarding; respecting; to; toward; with;* delete. • All of these factors assume you have a choice in the matter of where you will hold your meeting. *All of these factors assume you have a choice in where you will hold your meeting.*

**in the meantime** *meantime; meanwhile.* • In the meantime, I will discuss the software potential with our people and see if we can come up with some preliminary conclusions. *Meantime, I will discuss the software potential with our people and see if we can come up with some preliminary conclusions.*

**in the middle of** *amid; among; during; in; in between; inside; through; within.* • Charles said that Britain was in the middle of another building boom and the important question was "whether we can get it right this time." *Charles said that Britain was amid another building boom and the important question was "whether we can get it right this time."*

**in the middle (midst) of -ing** *-ing.* • We are currently in the middle of improving these signs with new panels and brighter lighting. *We are currently improving these signs with new panels and brighter lighting.*

**in the midst of** *amid; among; during; in; in between; inside; through; within.* • Federal and state authorities are in the midst of a criminal investigation of whether an unreported series of leaks and spills was linked to groundwater polluted by more than 55 chemicals. *Federal and state authorities are amid a criminal investigation of whether an unreported series of leaks and spills was linked to groundwater polluted by more than 55 chemicals.*

**in the nature of** *akin to; close to; like; resembling; similar to; such as.* • These days it takes something in the nature of a reception with the Queen Mother to get the Maxwells together. *These days it takes something like a reception with the Queen Mother to get the Maxwells together.*

**(something; somewhere) in the nature (of)** *about; around; close to; more or less; near; nearly; or so; roughly; some;* delete. • The owners anticipate production to be in the nature of 3,000 gallons weekly. *The owners anticipate production to be around 3,000 gallons weekly.*

**in the (very) near future** *before long; directly; in a month (week); next month (year); presently; quickly; shortly; soon; this month (year); tomorrow;* delete. • I will visit my mother's grave site in the near future. *I will visit my mother's grave site next week.*

**in the (very) near past** *a few months (years) ago; before; earlier; formerly; lately; not long ago; of late; once; recent; recently;* delete.

**in (over) the near term** *at first; at present; before long; currently; directly; for now; in (over) a month (week); initially; next month (year); now; presently; short-term; this month (year);* delete. • That, perhaps, best sums up what to expect from AI in the near term. *That, perhaps, best sums up what to expect from AI for now.*

**in the negative** *negatively; no; unfavorably.*

**in the neighborhood (of)** *close by; close to; near; nearby; neighboring.* • "Everything around here shook," said a young woman who works at a restaurant in the neighborhood. *"Everything around here shook," said a young woman who works at a nearby restaurant.*

**(something; somewhere) in the neighborhood (of)** *about; around; close to; more or less; near; nearly; or so; roughly; some;* delete. • We have somewhere in the neighborhood of 6 million illegal aliens in this country. *We have about 6 million illegal aliens in this country.*

**in the next place** *also; and; as well; besides; beyond that (this); further; furthermore; in addition; moreover; more than that (this); next; second; still more; too; what is more.*

**in the normal (ordinary; typical; usual) course of business (events; things)** *as usual; commonly; customarily; normally; ordinarily; typically; usually.* • In the ordinary course of events, they wouldn't go to court over something like this. *Ordinarily, they wouldn't go to court over something like this.*

**in the not-so-distant (not-too-distant) future** *before long; directly; in a month (week); next month (year); presently; quickly; shortly; soon; this month (year); tomorrow;* delete. • We'll be coming out with some new communications products in the not-too-distant future. *We'll be coming out with some new communications products shortly.*

**in the not-so-distant (not-too-distant) past** *a few months (years) ago; before; earlier; formerly; lately; not long ago; of late; once; recent; recently;* delete. • In the not-so-distant past, people could have dropped out of high school and gotten a decent-paying job in manufacturing. *Not long ago, people could have dropped out of high school and gotten a decent-paying job in manufacturing.*

**in the opinion of** *assert; believe; claim; consider; contend; feel; hold; judge; maintain; regard; say; think; to; view; with.* • The Wall Street inside-information scandal could pull in yet another circle of white-collar criminals in the opinion of criminal lawyers and securities specialists. *Criminal lawyers and securities specialists contend the Wall Street inside-information scandal could pull in yet another circle of white-collar criminals.*

**in the opposite direction from (of)** *against.* • Many bicyclists do not observe traffic signals, ride in the opposite direction of motor traffic, and fail to signal when overtaking pedestrians. *Many bicyclists do not observe traffic signals, ride against motor traffic, and fail to signal when overtaking pedestrians.*

**in the overall scope (sphere) of things** *all in all; all told; in all; overall;* delete. • In the overall sphere of things, a vast majority of tax problems never reach the courts, particularly not as criminal prosecutions. *Overall, a vast majority of tax problems never reach the courts, particularly not as criminal prosecutions.*

**in the past** *before; earlier; formerly; once;* delete. • You said, in the past, that you weren't interested in the vice presidency. *Earlier you said that you weren't interested in the vice presidency.*

**in (over) the past few (several) days (decades; months; weeks; years)** *lately; of late; recent; recently.* • Neural networks have generated much interest, not to mention hype, in the past few years. *Neural networks have lately generated much interest, not to mention hype.*

**in the position of** *as.*

**in the presence of** *alongside; among; beside; during; in; with.* • On only one occasion was I in the presence of Jack and Sam at the same time. *On only one occasion was I with Jack and Sam at the same time.*

**in the process of** *in; while.* • In the process of doing so, he threw out some good material. *In doing so, he threw out some good material.* • Answers to these and many other questions had to be resolved in the process of developing and implementing the new system of student assessment. *Answers to these and many other questions had to be resolved while developing and implementing the new system of student assessment.*

**in the process of -ing** *-ing.* • I'm in the process of cleaning the house. *I'm cleaning the house.* • The company is in the process of changing the regulatory framework in most of its states. *The company is changing the regulatory framework in most of its states.* • No publication date has been set for the book, which is in the process of being written. *No publication date has been set for the book, which is being written.*

**in the proximity (of)** *close by; close to; near; nearby.* • Cosmic gamma ray bursts appear to originate in the proximity of neutron stars, but the sources have never been pinned down. *Cosmic gamma ray bursts appear to originate near neutron stars, but the sources have never been pinned down.*

**(something; somewhere) in the range from (of) . . . through (to)** *between . . . and; from . . . to; to;* delete. • According to a recent study by Arthur Andersen & Co., the cost of drilling new wells is in the range of $6 to $8 a barrel. *According to a recent study by Arthur Andersen & Co., the cost of drilling new wells is between $6 and $8 a barrel.*

**(something; somewhere) in the . . . range (of)** *about; around; close to; more or less; near; nearly; or so; roughly; some;* delete. • The price tag on the three-city shuttle was in the range of $200 million. *The price tag on the three-city shuttle was about $200 million.*

**in the realm of** *about; as for; as to; concerning; for; in; of; on; over; regarding; respecting; to; toward; with;* delete. • Furthermore, in the realm of strategic nuclear weapons, he has overseen not reductions but improvements. *Furthermore, in strategic nuclear weapons, he has overseen not reductions but improvements.*

**(something; somewhere) in the realm (of)** *about; around; close to; more or less; near; nearly; or so; roughly; some;* delete. • The company expects to employ somewhere in the realm of 300 people there by 1993. *The company expects to employ around 300 people there by 1993.*

**in (within) the realm of possibility** *conceivable; doable; possible; thinkable.* • She said having a child is still within the realm of possibility. *She said having a child is still possible.*

**in (within) the recent past** *a few months (years) ago; before; earlier; formerly; lately; not long ago; of late; once; recent; recently;* delete. • The belief that we have an open society in which anyone can get ahead is less true than in the recent past. *The belief that we have an open society in which anyone can get ahead is less true than before.*

**(something; somewhere) in the region (of)** *about; around; close to; more or less; near; nearly; or so; roughly; some;* delete. • That's on top of an additional estimated increase in food prices somewhere in the region of 4 percent. *That's on top of an additional estimated increase in food prices of about 4 percent.*

**in the role of** *as.*

**in the same fashion (manner; way) (as; that)** *as (be); like; the same as.* • Though not necessarily displayed on the screen, hard carriage returns are much like other characters you enter in a document; therefore, you delete them in the same way you would other characters. *Though not necessarily displayed on the screen, hard carriage returns are much like other characters you enter in a document; therefore, you delete them as you would other characters.*

**in the second place** *also; and; as well; besides; beyond that (this); further; furthermore; in addition; moreover; more than that (this); next; second; still more; too; what is more.*

**in the sense of** *that is;* delete. • He is in a peculiar—in the sense of unusual—position. *He is in a peculiar—that is, unusual—position.*

**in the sense that** *because; considering; for; in that; since.* • Foreign and domestic marketing are the same in the sense that the purpose is to create and manage profitable exchange relationships. *Foreign and domestic marketing are the same in that the purpose is to create and manage profitable exchange relationships.*

**in (over) the short run** *at first; at present; before long; currently; directly; for now; in (over) a month (week); initially; next month (year); now; presently; short-term; this month (year);* delete. • The tax-cut proposal is the nutritional equivalent of a diet of beer: in the short run, it fills you up and gives you a buzz, but eventually it devastates the body. *The tax-cut proposal is the nutritional equivalent of a diet of beer: at first, it fills you up and gives you a buzz, but eventually it devastates the body.*

**in (over) the short term** *at first; at present; before long; currently; directly; for now; in (over) a month (week); initially; next month (year); now; presently; short-term; this month (year);* delete. • People who can withstand fluctuations over the short term are virtually guaranteed a profit in the stock market. *People who can withstand short-term fluctuations are virtually guaranteed a profit in the stock market.*

**in (on) the subject of** *about; as for; as to; concerning; for; in; of; on; over; regarding; respecting; to; toward; with;* delete. • Both authors have written widely on the subject of behavioral science research and application. *Both authors have written widely on behavioral science research and application.*

**in the support of (-ing)** *for; so as to; to.*

**in the third place** *also; and; as well; besides; beyond that (this); further; furthermore; in addition; moreover; more than that (this); next; still more; third; too; what is more.*

**in the . . . through (to) . . . range** *between . . . and; from . . . to; to.* • Whether they will be willing to pay a base price rumored to be in the $3,000 to $6,000 range is one of the many questions to be answered. *Whether they will be willing to pay a base price rumored to be between $3,000 and $6,000 is one of the many questions to be answered.*

**in the unexpected (unlikely) event of (that)** *if (there were); if . . . should; in case (of); should (there); were (there; . . . to);* delete. • In the unexpected event that those costs exceed $30 million, other joint owners would be obligated. *Should those costs exceed $30 million, other joint owners would be obligated.*

**In the vicinity (of)** *close by; close to; near; nearby.* • It was last seen in the vicinity of the Abbot Street Bridge. *It was last seen near the Abbot Street Bridge.*

**(something; somewhere) in the vicinity (of)** *about; around; close to; more or less; near; nearly; or so; roughly; some;* delete. • On its best day, my corporation earned in the vicinity of $2 million. *On its best day, my corporation earned around $2 million.*

**in the view of** *assert; believe; claim; consider; contend; feel; hold; judge; maintain; regard; say; think; to; view; with.* • In the view of some strategists, he may lose the election unless he can reverse his fortunes on this issue. *Some strategists think he may lose the election unless he can reverse his fortunes on this issue.*

**in the wake of** *(just; right) after; because of; (close) behind; due to; ensuing; following; from; owing to; succeeding.* • In the wake of an office and shopping-center boom comes an employment boom in business custodians. *Following an office and shopping-center boom comes an employment boom in business custodians.*

**in the way of** delete. • This step requires that you research jobs to determine what they call for in the way of education, skills, and aptitudes. *This step requires that you research jobs to determine what education, skills, and aptitudes they call for.* • There is little motivation for long periods of foolishness, and there is much in the way of market discipline to prevent it. *There* *is little motivation for long periods of foolishness, and there is much market discipline to prevent it.* • A sentence such as "It is 93 million miles to the sun" does not generate much in the way of questions; it is too specific. *A sentence such as "It is 93 million miles to the sun" does not generate many questions; it is too specific.*

**in thickness** *thick;* delete. • In their theoretical analysis, Gaylord and Brennan consider a filter consisting of nine layers, each layer a quarter or a half of the electron wavelength in thickness. *In their theoretical analysis, Gaylord and Brennan consider a filter consisting of nine layers, each layer a quarter or a half of the electron wavelength thick.*

**intimately familiar** *familiar; intimate.*

**in (the) time(s) of** *amid; during; in; over; throughout.* • The substantial risk of investment in junk bonds, particularly in times of economic uncertainty, is often disregarded by small investors. *The substantial risk of investment in junk bonds, particularly amid economic uncertainty, is often disregarded by small investors.*

**in . . . tones** *-(al)ly;* delete. • Police officers trooped into every grammar school in the city to talk with kids, explaining in dispassionate tones the use and abuse of crack. *Police officers trooped into every grammar school in the city to talk with kids, explaining dispassionately the use and abuse of crack.*

**in trade (for)** *for.*

**introduce (a; the) new** *introduce.* • In 1983, Apple introduced a new, easier-to-use computer called the Lisa. *In 1983, Apple introduced an easier-to-use computer called the Lisa.*

**inure to the benefit of** *inure to.* • This agreement shall be binding upon and inure to the benefit of the executors, administrators, and assigns of the Author and of the Client. *This agreement shall be binding upon and inure to the executors, administrators, and assigns of the Author and of the Client.*

**in (on; to; with) various (varying) degrees (extents)** *in part; in some way; more or less; partially; partly; rather; some; somehow; someway(s); somewhat; to some degree (extent); various; variously; varying; varyingly;* delete. • Four masters of the art of stretch management rely on varying degrees on a set of nuts-and-bolts techniques. *Four masters of the art of stretch management rely varyingly on a set of nuts-and-bolts techniques.*

**invidious discrimination** *discrimination; invidiousness.* • Few would deny that ferreting out this kind of invidious discrimination is a great if not compelling governmental interest. *Few would deny that ferreting out this kind of invidiousness is a great if not compelling governmental interest.*

**in view of the fact that** *because; considering; for; in that; since; when.* • These results are particularly interesting in view of the fact that Christian Scientists are forbidden to either smoke or drink. *These results are particularly interesting considering Christian Scientists are forbidden to either smoke or drink.*

**in view of the fact that** *whereas.*

**invited guest** *guest.*

**involve** *for; in; mean; of; with;* delete. • Census II involves using several different types of moving averages to identify trends and outliers within a data set. *Census II uses several different types of moving averages to identify trends and outliers within a data set.* • The operation is self-sustaining and has operated with no public-sector funding involved. *The operation is self-sustaining and has operated with no public-sector funding.*

**involved in** *in; of; within;* delete. • The costs involved in refurbishing the building are prohibitive. *The costs of refurbishing the building are prohibitive.*

**in (a; the) ... way** *-(al)ly;* delete. • Each of these variations can be revised in a different way. *Each of these variations can be revised differently.* • Computer systems differ in a significant way from stereos. *Computer systems differ significantly from stereos.* • Every group that has scrutinized this product in an impartial way agrees it is safe. *Every group that has impartially scrutinized this product agrees it is safe.*

**in whatever (whichever) fashion (manner; way)** *despite how; however.* • In whatever way it comes, the decision will be an important one. *Despite how it comes, the decision will be an important one.*

**in what (which) fashion (manner; way)** *how.* • In what fashion does imaging technology offer potential competitive advantage? *How does imaging technology offer potential competitive advantage?*

**in what (which) regard (respect)** *how.* • In what respect was this investment "tax free"? *How was this investment "tax free"?*

**in width** *wide;* delete. • In high-performance hard disks, these tracks are roughly 1 micrometer in width. *In high-performance hard disks, these tracks are roughly 1 micrometer wide.*

**ironical** *ironic.*

**irregardless of** *despite (what); no matter what; regardless of; whatever.*

**irregardless of the fact that** *although; but; even though; still; though; yet.*
• Irregardless of the fact that she was raised by someone else, she is still my daughter. *Even though she was raised by someone else, she is still my daughter.*

**irrelevancy** *irrelevance.*

**irrespective of (what)** *despite (what); no matter what; regardless of; whatever.*
• The product-first approach meant marketing the same product to all customers, irrespective of their profiles. *The product-first approach meant marketing the same product to all customers, regardless of their profiles.*
• Irrespective of the reasons, the voters simply do not want to participate in a collaborative project. *No matter what the reasons, the voters simply do not want to participate in a collaborative project.*

**irrespective of how** *despite how; however; no matter how; regardless of how.*
• The margins are retained irrespective of how many characters are printed per inch. *The margins are retained despite how many characters are printed per inch.*

**irrespective of the fact that** *although; but; even though; still; though; yet.*

**irrespective of when** *despite when; no matter when; regardless of when; whenever.*

**irrespective of where** *despite where; no matter where; regardless of where; wherever.* • A successful company must have the necessary skill sets to meet the needs and wants of its customers irrespective of where they may do business. *A successful company must have the necessary skill sets to meet the needs and wants of its customers wherever they may do business.*

**irrespective of whether . . . (or)** *despite whether; no matter whether; regardless of whether; whether . . . or (not).* • One delegate said his parish would continue to raise money for its diocese irrespective of whether the archdiocesan assessment is met. *One delegate said his parish would continue to raise money for its diocese whether or not the archdiocesan assessment is met.*

**irrespective of which** *despite which; no matter which; regardless of which; whichever.*

**irrespective of who** *despite who; no matter who; regardless of who; whoever.*
• Irrespective of who leads the group, one fact remains. *Whoever leads the group, one fact remains.*

**irrespective of whom** *despite whom; no matter whom; regardless of whom; whomever.*

**... is ... (that; which; who; whom)** delete. • Batch files are files that contain commands that are executed automatically when you turn on your computer or type the batch file's name. *Batch files contain commands that are executed automatically when you turn on your computer or type the batch file's name.* • Domestic corporations are corporations that do business in the state in which they are chartered, and foreign corporations are corporations that do business outside their chartered state. *Domestic corporations do business in the state in which they are chartered, and foreign corporations do business outside their chartered state.*

**is able to** *can.* • Investors are able to buy and sell any quantity of securities. *Investors can buy and sell any quantity of securities.*

**is (was) accustomed to (-ing)** *will (would).* • They are accustomed to talking until late into the night. *They will talk until late into the night.*

**is a consequence of** *arises from; results from; stems from.*

**is a contribution to** *contributes to.* • This is a continuing contribution to a company's profitability. *This continually contributes to a company's profitability.*

**is acquainted with** *knows.*

**is a demonstration of** *demonstrates; shows; proves.*

**is a description of** *describes.* • The attached proposal is a brief description of what I have in mind. *The attached proposal briefly describes what I have in mind.*

**is a deterrent to** *blocks; deters; hinders; impedes; prevents; stops; thwarts.*

**is advantageous for (to)** *aids; benefits; favors; helps.*

**is afraid of (to)** *dreads; fears; frets (about; over); stews (about; over); worries (about; over).*

**is a function of** *depends on; relates to.* • The popularity of fixed-rate versus adjustable-rate mortgages seems to be a function of the level of interest rates. *The popularity of fixed-rate versus adjustable-rate mortgages seems to depend on the level of interest rates.*

**is a hindrance to** *blocks; deters; hinders; impedes; prevents; stops; thwarts.*
• A problem is any organizational issue that could be a hindrance to organizational success. *A problem is any organizational issue that could hinder organizational success.*

**is an acquaintance of** *knows.* • Mr. Branch was an acquaintance of Miss Gregory. *Mr. Branch knew Miss Gregory.*

**is an illustration of** *illustrates.* • I believe that these moves by Texaco are a perfect illustration of the precept that a clear and closer relationship between active ownership and management will increase productivity. *I believe that these moves by Texaco perfectly illustrate the precept that a clear and closer relationship between active ownership and management will increase productivity.*

**is an impediment to** *blocks; deters; hinders; impedes; prevents; stops; thwarts.*

**is an indication (indicator) of** *argues; attests to; bespeaks; betokens; indicates; shows; signals; signifies; suggests; testifies to; witnesses.* • The Roman holiday atmosphere reportedly surrounding the event may be an indicator of the level of civilized intercourse we have attained in this so-called advanced industrial nation. *The Roman holiday atmosphere reportedly surrounding the event may signify the level of civilized intercourse we have attained in this so-called advanced industrial nation.*

**is an obstacle to** *blocks; deters; hinders; impedes; prevents; stops; thwarts.*

**is applicable in (to)** *applies in (to); bears on; concerns; pertains to; relates to.*
• Regardless, the autocratic style is applicable in some situations. *Regardless, the autocratic style applies in some situations.*

**is appreciative of** *appreciates; approves of; cherishes; enjoys; esteems; likes; prizes; treasures; understands; values; welcomes.* • We are especially appreciative of the item which appeared in the paper citing our need for volunteers. *We especially appreciate the item which appeared in the paper citing our need for volunteers.*

**is apprehensive of** *dreads; fears; frets (about; over); stews (about; over); worries (about; over).* • My parents were apprehensive of my going to Iran. *My parents dreaded my going to Iran.*

187

**is appropriate in (to)** *applies in (to); bears on; concerns; pertains to; relates to.*

**is a (the) process that** delete. • Anxiety is a process that alerts people to possible dangers. *Anxiety alerts people to possible dangers.*

**is a reflection of (on; upon)** *reflects (on).* • Could it be that they felt the actions by the school would be a bad reflection on them? *Could it be that they felt the actions by the school would badly reflect on them?*

**is a representation of** *represents.*

**is a result of** *arises from; results from; stems from.*

**is associated to (with)** *correlates to (with); equates with; relates to.* • The development of interest and confidence and infusions of practical, useful applications seem to be associated with success in mathematics. *The development of interest and confidence and infusions of practical, useful applications seem to relate to success in mathematics.*

**is at loggerheads (with)** *clashes with; conflicts with; contradicts; differs from; disagrees with; quarrels with; varies with.* • He ran unsuccessfully for the Florida house and has frequently been at loggerheads with state and federal authorities. *He ran unsuccessfully for the Florida house and has frequently quarreled with state and federal authorities.*

**is at odds over (with)** *clashes with; conflicts with; contradicts; differs from; disagrees with; quarrels with; varies with.* • She said the strong credit figures were at odds with a stream of government reports pointing toward a slowdown and did not reflect the health of the economy. *She said the strong credit figures contradicted a stream of government reports pointing toward a slowdown and did not reflect the health of the economy.*

**is attentive to** *attends to; heeds.*

**is at variance with** *clashes with; conflicts with; contradicts; differs from; disagrees with; quarrels with; varies with.* • Although some of its particulars are at variance with what U.S. officials have heard, most key details tend to coincide. *Although some of its particulars clash with what U.S. officials have heard, most key details tend to coincide.*

**is a variant of** *departs from; deviates from; differs from; diverges from; varies from.* • Endowment insurance policies are a variant of whole life in that, if the insured dies within a specified period, the insurance will be paid to a designated beneficiary. *Endowment insurance policies vary from whole life* *in that, if the insured dies within a specified period, the insurance will be paid to a designated beneficiary.*

**is aware of (that)** *comprehends; knows; realizes; recognizes; sees; understands.* • If you are in the same position as most consumer borrowers, you should be aware that time is not on your side. *If you are in the same position as most consumer borrowers, you should realize that time is not on your side.*

**is based on (upon)** *rests on.* • This policy is based upon three fundamental principles of competitive behavior. *This policy rests on three fundamental principles of competitive behavior.*

**is beneficial to** *aids; benefits; favors; helps.* • Congress needs to make important decisions that will be beneficial to all Americans on a long-range basis. *Congress needs to make important decisions that will benefit all Americans on a long-range basis.*

**is capable of -ing** *can; is able to.* • Obsolescence exists when a person or machine is no longer capable of performing to standards or management's expectations. *Obsolescence exists when a person or machine is no longer able to perform to standards or management's expectations.*

**is characteristic of** *characterizes; depicts; describes; designates; illustrates; pictures; portrays.* • The protein tangles in brain tissue are characteristic of advanced Alzheimer's, and he speculates that A68 may be a precursor of the tangles. *The protein tangles in brain tissue characterize advanced Alzheimer's, and he speculates that A68 may be a precursor of the tangles.*

**is cognizant of (that)** *comprehends; knows; realizes; recognizes; sees; understands.*

**is coherent with** *agrees with; coheres with; concurs with; conforms to (with); corresponds to (with).*

**is comparable to (with)** *compares to (with); contrasts to (with); corresponds to (with); equates with; likens to; relates to; resembles.* • This revolution in medicine is comparable in certain ways to the computer boom, but is more epochal. *This revolution in medicine corresponds in certain ways to the computer boom, but is more epochal.*

**is compatible with** *agrees with; coheres with; concurs with; conforms to (with); corresponds to (with).*

**is competitive with** *competes with.*

**is complementary to** *complements.* • Banking is an obvious area for Nomura's diversification since it is complementary to the firm's securities business. *Banking is an obvious area for Nomura's diversification since it complements the firm's securities business.*

**is compliant with** *complies with.* • Our emphasis is supporting the customers who have been fully compliant with the export regulations. *Our emphasis is supporting the customers who have fully complied with the export regulations.*

**is composed of** *comprises; consists of; contains; includes.* • The informal organization is composed of all the informal groupings of people within a formal organization. *The informal organization consists of all the informal groupings of people within a formal organization.*

**is comprised of** *comprises; consists of; contains; includes.* • The marketing infrastructure is comprised of several elements that change as a country develops its industrial and service sectors. *The marketing infrastructure contains several elements that change as a country develops its industrial and service sectors.*

**is concerned (about)** *brood (on; over); dread; fear; fret (about; over); regret; stew (about; over); worry (about; over).* • Company analysts are concerned about the level of debt that the combined companies would carry if the hostile bid succeeds. *Company analysts worry about the level of debt that the combined companies would carry if the hostile bid succeeds.*

**is concerned with** *concerns; deals with; is about; pertains to; regards; relates to.* • The first two complications are external and are concerned with the environment within which the company competes. *The first two complications are external and concern the environment within which the company competes.*

**is conditional (conditioned) on (upon)** *depends on; hinges on.* • The willingness of VSS to proceed with the transaction is conditioned upon such an agreement. *The willingness of VSS to proceed with the transaction depends on such an agreement.*

**is conducive to** *conduces to.*

**is connected to (with)** *correlates to (with); equates with; relates to.*

**is conscious of (that)** *comprehends; knows; realizes; recognizes; sees; understands.*

**is consistent with** *agrees with; coheres with; concurs with; conforms to (with); corresponds to (with).* • This approach is consistent with earlier rulings requiring actual proof even where overwhelming numerical evidence allows a reasonable assumption of bias. *This approach conforms to earlier rulings requiring actual proof even where overwhelming numerical evidence allows a reasonable assumption of bias.*

**is contemptuous of** *despises; disdains; scorns.*

**is contingent on (upon)** *depends on; hinges on.* • Success is contingent upon careful, continuous, global market research. *Success depends on careful, continuous, global market research.*

**is contributory to** *contributes.* • Patients should also be warned of the cardiovascular and neoplastic liabilities of smoking that along with estrogens may be contributory to these disorders. *Patients should also be warned of the cardiovascular and neoplastic liabilities of smoking that along with estrogens may contribute to these disorders.*

**is conversant with** *knows.* • I wonder whether he knows any of the Asian languages or is conversant with the sources I consulted. *I wonder whether he knows any of the Asian languages or the sources I consulted.*

**is critical of** *complains about; condemns; criticizes.* • It's easy to be critical of others if they don't agree with you. *It's easy to criticize others if they don't agree with you.*

**is dangerous to** *endangers; imperils; jeopardizes.*

**is deficient in** *lacks; wants.* • In perhaps the most troubling of its recent reports, NAEP showed that while few adults in their early 20s are wholly illiterate, most are deficient in necessary skills. *In perhaps the most troubling of its recent reports, NAEP showed that while few adults in their early 20s are wholly illiterate, most lack necessary skills.*

**is defined as** *is; means.* • Management is defined as the process of setting and achieving goals through the execution of five basic management functions that utilize human, financial, and material resources. *Management is the process of setting and achieving goals through the execution of five basic management functions that utilize human, financial, and material resources.*

**is deleterious to** *damages; harms; hurts; impairs; injures; mars; wrongs.*

**is dependent on (upon)** *depends on; hinges on.* • You shouldn't be dependent upon anyone else for your happiness. *You shouldn't depend on anyone else for your happiness.*

**is descriptive of** *characterizes; depicts; describes; designates; illustrates; pictures; portrays.* • The model is descriptive of human behavior across all cultures that we have encountered. *The model describes human behavior across all cultures that we have encountered.*

**is desirous of -ing** *desires to; wants to; wishes to.* • She is desirous of resolving this as soon as possible, so I respectfully request that you have your client consider the proposals. *She wants to resolve this as soon as possible, so I respectfully request that you have your client consider the proposals.*

**is destructive of (to)** *damages; destroys; harms; hurts; impairs; injures; mars; ruins.* • It is a fact that some cats are destructive of property. *It is a fact that some cats destroy property.*

**is detrimental to** *damages; harms; hurts; impairs; injures; mars; wrongs.* • The concern of the EEC is that these powerful drugs would be detrimental to the children. *The concern of the EEC is that these powerful drugs would injure the children.*

**is different from** *departs from; deviates from; differs from; diverges from; varies from.* • If a phrase in the file on the disk is different from a phrase in the document on the screen, the command marks the entire phrase in the document on the screen. *If a phrase in the file on the disk differs from a phrase in the document on the screen, the command marks the entire phrase in the document on the screen.*

**is disposed to** *tends to.*

**is disrespectful of (toward)** *disrespects.*

**is disruptive of** *disrupts.* • Chapter 774 is disruptive of any sense of community because all control over its future has been removed. *Chapter 774 disrupts any sense of community because all control over its future has been removed.*

**is distinguished from** *departs from; deviates from; differs from; diverges from; varies from.*

**is distrustful about (of)** *disbelieves; distrusts; doubts; mistrusts; questions.* • Until students have assimilated these attitudes, they will be distrustful of scientific information. *Until students have assimilated these attitudes, they will distrust scientific information.*

**is doubtful about (of)** *disbelieves; distrusts; doubts; mistrusts; questions.* • Many officials are doubtful about the effectiveness of Shultz's Mideast plan. *Many officials doubt the effectiveness of Shultz's Mideast plan.*

**is dubious about (of)** *disbelieves; distrusts; doubts; mistrusts; questions.* • The A320 and the Concorde are the only commercial aircraft that use exclusively fly-by-wire controls, in part because U.S. aircraft companies are dubious about giving up tried-and-true cables. *The A320 and the Concorde are the only commercial aircraft that use exclusively fly-by-wire controls, in part because U.S. aircraft companies question giving up tried-and-true cables.*

**is duplicative of** *duplicates.* • The Odyssey team's responsibilities are duplicative of the nursing team's. *The Odyssey team's responsibilities duplicate the nursing team's.*

**is emblematic of** *emblemizes; indicates; represents; signifies; stands for; symbolizes; typifies.* • The kind of comprehensive care the Clinic can provide to its cancer patients is emblematic of the Clinic's overall approach to medicine. *The kind of comprehensive care the Clinic can provide to its cancer patients typifies the Clinic's overall approach to medicine.*

**is (the) equal to** *amounts to; duplicates; equals; is; matches; rivals.* • The value of the emperor's palace in the center of Tokyo is equal to the value of the entire state of California. *The value of the emperor's palace in the center of Tokyo equals the value of the entire state of California.*

**is equipped (furnished) with** *comes with.* • The server normally is equipped with a large-capacity hard disk drive that acts as the central file depository for everyone on the network. *The server normally comes with a large-capacity hard disk drive that acts as the central file depository for everyone on the network.*

**is (the) equivalent of (to)** *amounts to; duplicates; equals; is; matches; rivals.* • Ideally, the amount of this fund should be the equivalent of at least three months' income. *Ideally, the amount of this fund should equal at least three months' income.*

**is (a; the) -er (-or) of** *delete.* • She was the originator of the company program. *She originated the company program.* • You should be a helper and encourager of your child's writing efforts. *You should help and encourage your child's writing efforts.*

**is evidence of (that)** *evinces; indicates; proves; reveals; shows; signifies; testifies (to).* • The calls are evidence of the strong temptation in the judicial arena to seize on an array of recent findings on brain chemistry and behavior. *The calls testify to the strong temptation in the judicial arena to seize on an array of recent findings on brain chemistry and behavior.*

**is exploitative of** *abuses; cheats; deceives; exploits; ill-treats; mistreats; misuses; uses; victimizes; wrongs.*

**is faced with** *faces.* • Dynamic high-technology strategy companies are faced with few national competitors. *Dynamic high-technology strategy companies face few national competitors.*

**is familiar with** *knows.* • European participants in the computer industry know Europe extremely well, and they are familiar with the U.S. market. *European participants in the computer industry know Europe extremely well, and they know the U.S. market.*

**is favorable to** *aids; benefits; favors; helps.* • In the five years during which the leveraged buyout has blossomed, the business environment has been particularly favorable to this type of transaction. *In the five years during which the leveraged buyout has blossomed, the business environment has particularly favored this type of transaction.*

**is fearful (about; of; that)** *dreads; fears; frets (about; over); stews (about; over); worries (about; over).* • These leaders tend to be fearful of external forces because they may create a middle class or threaten the existing social structure. *These leaders tend to fret about external forces because they may create a middle class or threaten the existing social structure.*

**is focused on (upon)** *focuses on.* • Although most of the chapters in this volume are focused on incentives for educators, several authors remind us that students are the chief agent of their own learning. *Although most of the chapters in this volume focus on incentives for educators, several authors remind us that students are the chief agent of their own learning.*

**is for certain (sure)** *is certain (sure).* • One thing is for certain: They'll have to deal with the governor when all this is over. *One thing is certain: They'll have to deal with the governor when all this is over.*

**is founded on (upon)** *rests on.*

**is going to** *shall; will.* • We think that is a trend that is going to continue for several years to come. *We think that is a trend that will continue for several years to come.*

**is harmful to** *damages; harms; hurts; impairs; injures; mars; wrongs.* • It will ultimately be harmful to the state's economy in that it will make some products more expensive than anywhere else. *It will ultimately harm the state's* *economy in that it will make some products more expensive than anywhere else.*

**is helpful in (-ing)** *aids in; assists in; helps.* • Intelligent market research will be helpful in settling which product lines to offer. *Intelligent market research will help settle which product lines to offer.*

**is hopeful** *expects; hopes; relies on; trusts.* • I am hopeful that all will go well. *I expect that all will go well.*

**is identical to (with)** *amounts to; duplicates; equals; is; matches; rivals.* • The objective, of course, is to ensure that directors' interests are identical with those of the company and its longer term stockholders. *The objective, of course, is to ensure that directors' interests match those of the company and its longer term stockholders.*

**is illustrative of** *characterizes; depicts; demonstrates; describes; designates; exemplifies; illustrates; pictures; portrays; represents.* • *Some American Feminists* is illustrative of the nearly universal nature of the issues the studio examines. Some American Feminists *exemplifies the nearly universal nature of the issues the studio examines.*

**is imitative of** *imitates.*

**is in accord (accordance) on (with)** *agrees with; coincides with; complies with; concurs with; conforms to (with); corresponds to (with).* • We feel that the activities of our diplomats in Nicaragua were in strict accordance with normal patterns of diplomatic behavior. *We feel that the activities of our diplomats in Nicaragua strictly conformed with normal patterns of diplomatic behavior.*

**is in agreement (on; with)** *agrees (on; with); coincides (with); complies (with); concurs (with); conforms (to; with); corresponds (to; with).* • The client should be in agreement with the goals set. *The client should concur with the goals set.*

**is in attendance (at)** *attends.* • Three presidents were in attendance at the graduation ceremonies. *Three presidents attended the graduation ceremonies.*

**is incapable of -ing** *cannot; is unable to.* • All three companies were incapable of managing their prizes and two of them, Hershey and CBS, eventually discarded their acquisitions in dismay. *All three companies were unable to manage their prizes and two of them, Hershey and CBS, eventually discarded their acquisitions in dismay.*

**is in charge of** *controls; directs; governs; manages.*

**is inclined to** *tends to.*

**is inclined to believe (that)** *asserts; believes; claims; contends; feels; holds; maintains; says; thinks; to.* • I am inclined to believe that we will receive a lot more calls when budgets make clear what cuts and fees public schools will institute. *I believe that we will receive a lot more calls when budgets make clear what cuts and fees public schools will institute.*

**is inclined to think (that)** *asserts; believes; claims; contends; feels; holds; maintains; says; thinks; to.* • I am inclined to think that Windows 95 is in many ways inferior to Windows 3.1. *I think Windows 95 is in many ways inferior to Windows 3.1.*

**is in competition with** *competes with.*

**is in compliance with** *complies with; conforms to (with).* • No register of deeds shall accept a deed for recording unless it is in compliance with the requirements of this section. *No register of deeds shall accept a deed for recording unless it complies with the requirements of this section.*

**is in conflict with** *clashes with; conflicts with; contradicts; differs from; disagrees with; quarrels with; varies with.* • The NTIA petition refers to the information services prohibition in the Modification of Final Judgment as "a cumbersome, unnecessary layer of regulation that is in irreconcilable conflict with the Communications Act." *The NTIA petition refers to the information services prohibition in the Modification of Final Judgment as "a cumbersome, unnecessary layer of regulation that irreconcilably conflicts with the Communications Act."*

**is in conformance to (with)** *agrees with; coincides with; complies with; concurs with; conforms to (with); corresponds to (with).*

**is in conformity to (with)** *agrees with; coincides with; complies with; concurs with; conforms to (with); corresponds to (with).* • As long as they're in conformity with the law, they can do business with whomever they like. *As long as they conform to the law, they can do business with whomever they like.*

**is in contempt of** *defies.*

**is in (marked; sharp) contrast to** *clashes with; conflicts with; contests; contradicts; contrasts with; differs from; disagrees with; disputes; opposes.* • The findings are in contrast to those of the Higher Education Research Institute, which conducts an annual national survey of freshmen. *The findings conflict with those of the Higher Education Research Institute, which conducts an annual national survey of freshmen.*

**is in control of** *controls; directs; governs; manages.* • Risk takers feel that they are in control of their own destiny. *Risk takers feel that they control their own destiny.*

**is in defiance of** *defies.* • They are in defiance of my orders. *They defy my orders.*

**is indicative of** *argues; attests to; bespeaks; betokens; indicates; shows; signals; signifies; suggests; testifies to; witnesses.* • Current sales figures are indicative of a management problem. *Current sales figures indicate a management problem.*

**is in disagreement (about; on; with)** *clashes with; conflicts with; contradicts; differs from; disagrees with; quarrels with; varies with.* • In the most important and urgent political debates of recent years involving science, a major difficulty has been that scientists of equal distinction and accomplishment have been in disagreement. *In the most important and urgent political debates of recent years involving science, a major difficulty has been that scientists of equal distinction and accomplishment have disagreed.*

**is in doubt about (of)** *disbelieves; distrusts; doubts; mistrusts; questions.* • For anyone who is in doubt about whether ministers are ordinary mortals, Mr. Wangerin makes clear that this is the case. *For anyone who doubts whether ministers are ordinary mortals, Mr. Wangerin makes clear that this is the case.*

**is in error** *errs.* • She was in error. *She erred.*

**is in excess of** *exceeds.* • The size of the droplets produced by the unit is in excess of 8 microns. *The size of the droplets produced by the unit exceeds 8 microns.*

**is in existence** *exists.* • More than 1,000 successful AI applications are in existence today. *More than 1,000 successful AI applications exist today.*

**is in favor of** *backs; endorses; favors; prefers; supports.* • We are in favor of reform, but we don't like the way it is being implemented. *We favor reform, but we don't like the way it is being implemented.*

**is in fear for (of)** *dreads; fears (for); frets (about; over); stews (about; over); worries (about; over).* • I was in fear for my life. *I feared for my life.*

197

**is influential in (-ing)** *affects; influences.* • The problem with this generalization is that other factors can be influential in determining how many subordinates a manager has. *The problem with this generalization is that other factors can influence how many subordinates a manager has.*

**is -ing** delete. • What the kids are wanting is to be loved. *What the kids want is to be loved.* • I would like to believe that the trading company concept is deserving of serious treatment by a magazine as exemplary as yours. *I would like to believe that the trading company concept deserves serious treatment by a magazine as exemplary as yours.* • We have gained a much better understanding of what providers are seeking from our networks, and we are looking forward to presenting our plan. *We have gained a much better understanding of what providers seek from our networks, and we look forward to presenting our plan.*

**is in harmony with** *agrees with; coheres with; concurs with; conforms to (with); corresponds to (with).*

**is injurious to** *damages; harms; hurts; impairs; injures; mars; wrongs.*

**is in keeping with** *agrees with; coheres with; concurs with; conforms to (with); corresponds to (with).* • This is in keeping with MicroPro International's focus and marketing. *This conforms to MicroPro International's focus and marketing.*

**is in line with** *agrees with; coheres with; concurs with; conforms to (with); corresponds to (with).* • The figures are in line with recent years, when the number of taxpayers filing early in the season declined each year. *The figures conform with recent years, when the number of taxpayers filing early in the season declined each year.*

**is in need of** *needs.* • Thousands of people are in need of medical attention that private insurance does not offer. *Thousands of people need medical attention that private insurance does not offer.*

**is in opposition to** *conflicts with; contests; disagrees with; disapproves of; disputes; objects to; opposes; protests; resists.* • They are in opposition to the United States. *They oppose the United States.*

**is in possession of** *has; possesses.* • They were in possession of a large quantity of cocaine. *They possessed a large quantity of cocaine.*

**is in receipt of** *receives.* • I am in receipt of your impressive resumé and references. *I received your impressive resumé and references.*

**is insistent on** *demands on; insists on.* • If people are insistent on keeping the Electoral College, why not make it fair? *If people insist on keeping the Electoral College, why not make it fair?*

**is in step with** *agrees with; coheres with; concurs with; conforms to (with); corresponds to (with).*

**is instrumental in (-ing)** *aids in; assists in; helps.* • Far from being the marginal movement they are perceived as being today, 19th-century evangelicals were instrumental in setting the political and social agenda for the century. *Far from being the marginal movement they are perceived as being today, 19th-century evangelicals helped set the political and social agenda for the century.*

**is instrumental in helping** *aids in; assists in; helps.* • He was instrumental in helping them put together a financial plan. *He helped them put together a financial plan.*

**is in support of** *backs; endorses; favors; prefers; supports.* • I myself am in support of women's rights. *I myself support women's rights.*

**is (was) in the habit of (-ing)** *will (would).* • When I was younger, I was in the habit of reading a book a week. *When I was younger, I would read a book a week.*

**is in violation of** *desecrates; infringes on; violates.* • My job is solely to determine whether conduct is in violation of the federal criminal law. *My job is solely to determine whether conduct violates the federal criminal law.*

**is in want of** *wants.*

**is it possible for** *can.* • Is it possible for you to tell us about your relationship with your child? *Can you tell us about your relationship with your child?*

**is knowledgeable about (in; of)** *comprehends; knows; understands.* • We also favor choosing directors who have worked in a company's industry at some point in their careers or are knowledgeable in some collateral industry. *We also favor choosing directors who have worked in a company's industry at some point in their careers or understand some collateral industry.*

**island (completely) surrounded by water** *island.* • White, racist American servicemen had struck again, this time on an island surrounded by water away from all civilization. *White, racist American servicemen had struck again, this time on an island away from all civilization.*

**is mindful of (that)** *comprehends; knows; realizes; recognizes; sees; understands.* • We should be mindful of the benefits of free trade while finding ways to limit it. *We should realize the benefits of free trade while finding ways to limit it.*

**is mistrustful about (of)** *disbelieves; distrusts; doubts; mistrusts; questions.* • The two sides are deeply mistrustful of each other after an estimated 1 million casualties. *The two sides deeply mistrust each other after an estimated 1 million casualties.*

**is needful of** *needs.*

**is of assistance in (-ing)** *aids in (-ing); assists in (-ing); helps.*

**is of benefit to** *aids; benefits; favors; helps.* • He agrees that companies need to take caution when choosing a system, but adds that the technology can be of great benefit to a company. *He agrees that companies need to take caution when choosing a system, but adds that the technology can greatly benefit a company.*

**is of concern to** *bothers; concerns; disturbs; interests; upsets; worries.* • Since these factors vary considerably from one country to another, they are of particular concern to the global company interested in a new foreign market. *Since these factors vary considerably from one country to another, they particularly concern the global company interested in a new foreign market.*

**is offensive to** *insults; offends.* • Halloween represents spiritist forces that are offensive to three of the world's major religions, Judaism, Christianity, and Islam. *Halloween represents spiritist forces that offend three of the world's major religions, Judaism, Christianity, and Islam.*

**is of interest to** *appeals to; attracts; concerns; excites; interests.*

**is of the belief (that)** *asserts; believes; claims; contends; feels; holds; maintains; says; thinks; to.* • The vast majority of physicians are of the belief that Ritalin is a safe drug for children. *To the vast majority of physicians, Ritalin is a safe drug for children.*

**is of the opinion (that)** *asserts; believes; claims; contends; feels; holds; maintains; says; thinks; to.* • I am of the opinion that the Celtics are far better off this year than last. *I believe the Celtics are far better off this year than last.*

**is of the same opinion (as)** *agrees (with); concurs (with).*

**is of the view (that)** *asserts; believes; claims; contends; feels; holds; maintains; says; thinks; to.* • He is of the view that a person between the ages of 30 and 40 is more susceptible to tuberculosis than a person between 60 and 70. *He maintains that a person between the ages of 30 and 40 is more susceptible to tuberculosis than a person between 60 and 70.*

**is one (that; which; who; whom)** *delete.* • A European option is one which can be exercised only at maturity. *A European option can be exercised only at maturity.* • This situation is one that ought not to be forgotten. *This situation ought not to be forgotten.*

**is on (a) par (with)** *equals.* • U.S. factory wages are already at least 20 percent below comparable German wages, on a dollar basis, and virtually on a par with Japanese levels. *U.S. factory wages are already at least 20 percent below comparable German wages, on a dollar basis, and virtually equal Japanese levels.*

**is opposed to** *conflicts with; contests; disagrees with; disapproves of; disputes; objects to; opposes; protests; resists.* • I would not be opposed to doing that. *I would not object to doing that.*

**is outrageous to** *outrages.*

**is persistent in** *perseveres in; persists in.* • Friends must be persistent in helping the griever come out of himself. *Friends must persist in helping the griever come out of himself.*

**is pertinent to** *applies to; bears on; concerns; pertains to; regards; relates to.*

**is predictive of** *forecasts; foretells; predicts; presages; portends.* • It offers a classification system that may be predictive of the outcome. *It offers a classification system that may predict the outcome.*

**is proof of (that)** *evinces; indicates; proves; reveals; shows; signifies; testifies (to).*

**is prone to** *tends to.* • Company managers are prone to underestimate loyalty and their employees' need for it. *Company managers tend to underestimate loyalty and their employees' need for it.*

**is protective against (of)** *defends; guards; insulates; protects; shelters; shields.* • A diet high in complex carbohydrates may be protective against the development of chronic diseases like heart disease and cancer. *A diet high in complex carbohydrates may protect against the development of chronic diseases like heart disease and cancer.*

**is receptive to** *welcomes.* • While lawmakers are generally receptive to his ideas, the feeling is not mutual. *While lawmakers generally welcome his ideas, the feeling is not mutual.*

**is (a; the) recipient of** *receives.* • The University of South Florida was the recipient of a $600,000 grant from a Florida bank to endow a professorship in banking and finance. *The University of South Florida received a $600,000 grant from a Florida bank to endow a professorship in banking and finance.*

**is reflective of** *epitomizes; exemplifies; mirrors; reflects; typifies.* • Films receiving Oscar nominations are reflective of the image that the film industry wants to convey of itself. *Films receiving Oscar nominations mirror the image that the film industry wants to convey of itself.*

**is regretful about (of; that)** *regrets.* • Now I'm regretful that I didn't work harder this week. *Now I regret I didn't work harder this week.*

**is related to** *correlates to (with); equates with; relates to.* • It is generally assumed that a species-wide tendency to favor one hand over the other is related to the development of brain hemispheres with specialized functions. *It is generally assumed that a species-wide tendency to favor one hand over the other relates to the development of brain hemispheres with specialized functions.*

**is relevant to** *applies to; bears on; concerns; pertains to; regards; relates to.*

**is reliant on (upon)** *counts on; depends on; relies on.* • South Korean builders are heavily reliant upon the Mideast market. *South Korean builders rely heavily on the Mideast market.*

**is reminiscent of** *recalls.* • The apparatus is reminiscent of some Asian musical performances emphasizing the gestures used to play instruments. *The apparatus recalls some Asian musical performances emphasizing the gestures used to play instruments.*

**is representative of** *emblemizes; indicates; represents; signifies; stands for; symbolizes; typifies.* • For the reader to assume that this is representative of the norm is unfortunate. *For the reader to assume that this represents the norm is unfortunate.*

**is required to** *has to; must.* • Managers are required to be able to perform certain roles. *Managers must be able to perform certain roles.*

**is resentful of** *resents.*

**is resistant to** *contests; disagrees with; disapproves of; disputes; objects to; opposes; protests; resists.* • In fact, they are resistant to measuring learning and performance in meaningful terms. *In fact, they resist measuring learning and performance in meaningful terms.*

**is respectful of (toward)** *respects.* • The two skaters are friends and respectful of each other. *The two skaters are friends and respect each other.*

**is ruinous to** *damages; destroys; harms; hurts; impairs; injures; mars; ruins.* • The closeups are ruinous to the performances of Aprüe Millo as Aida and Dolora Zajic as Amneris. *The closeups ruin the performances of Aprüe Millo as Aida and Dolora Zajic as Amneris.*

**is scornful of** *despises; disdains; scorns.* • Many scientists are scornful of him because of his claims that fluoride causes everything from cancer to AIDS. *Many scientists scorn him because of his claims that fluoride causes everything from cancer to AIDS.*

**is similar to (with)** *compares to (with); corresponds to (with); equates with; relates to; resembles.* • These commands are similar to English sentences, and most of them make sense to the casual reader. *These commands resemble English sentences, and most of them make sense to the casual reader.*

**is skeptical about (of; that)** *disbelieves; distrusts; doubts; mistrusts; questions.* • Immigration officials often are skeptical of businesses' claims that they didn't know a worker was illegal or that they weren't aware of the new immigration law. *Immigration officials often disbelieve businesses' claims that they didn't know a worker was illegal or that they weren't aware of the new immigration law.*

**is still to be seen** *do not know; is not (now; yet) known; is uncertain; is unclear; is unknown; is unsure.* • They priced it like a Mercedes; whether it's engineered like a Mercedes is still to be seen. *They priced it like a Mercedes; whether it's engineered like a Mercedes is not yet known.*

**issuance** *issue.* • Municipal bonds and municipal notes are debt obligations of states, cities, municipalities, and municipal agencies which generally have maturities, at the time of their issuance, of either one year or more or from six months to three years. *Municipal bonds and municipal notes are debt obligations of states, cities, municipalities, and municipal agencies which generally have maturities, at the time of their issue, of either one year or more or from six months to three years.*

**is subject to** *depends on; hinges on.* • Completion of the transactions is subject to a definitive agreement and the approval of both boards. *Completion of the transactions hinges on a definitive agreement and the approval of both boards.*

**(a; the) . . . issue** delete. • The question of whether a firm's financing decisions affect its value remains an unresolved issue. *The question of whether a firm's financing decisions affect its value remains unresolved.*

**is suggestive of** *argues; attests to; bespeaks; betokens; indicates; shows; signals; signifies; suggests; testifies to; witnesses.* • Any breast mass that is suggestive of malignancy by mammography or on physical examination should be biopsied. *Any breast mass that suggests malignancy by mammography or on physical examination should be biopsied.*

**is suitable to** *applies to; bears on; concerns; pertains to; regards; relates to.*

**is supportive of** *endorses; fosters; nurtures; supports; upholds.* • This report is supportive of our findings. *This report supports our findings.*

**is symbolic (symbolical) of** *emblemizes; indicates; represents; signifies; stands for; symbolizes; typifies.* • The contrast, stark and dramatic, is symbolic of what has happened across California. *The contrast, stark and dramatic, symbolizes what has happened across California.*

**is symptomatic of** *indicates; signals; signifies; symptomizes.* • The small dip is symptomatic of a pause in the housing market in October, as buyers, sellers, and lenders tried to figure out what was occurring in the financial markets. *The small dip indicates a pause in the housing market in October, as buyers, sellers, and lenders tried to figure out what was occurring in the financial markets.*

**is tantamount to** *amounts to; duplicates; equals; is; matches; rivals.*

**is (a) testament to** *affirms; attests to; certifies to; declares; testifies to; verifies.* • An excellent credit card rating is a testament to your success in business. *An excellent credit card rating attests to your success in business.*

**is (a) testimony to** *affirms; attests to; certifies to; declares; testifies to; verifies.* • The high level of business and consumer confidence is testimony to the success of this Fed policy. *The high level of business and consumer confidence testifies to the success of this Fed policy.*

**is trustful of** *trusts.*

**is typical of** *exemplifies; symbolizes; typifies.* • This kind of comment is typical of the Democrat's campaign. *This kind of comment exemplifies the Democrat's campaign.*

**is under the assumption (that)** *assumes; believes; feels; supposes; thinks.* • I am under the assumption that the *Globe* is trying to ameliorate the situation. *I assume the* Globe *is trying to ameliorate the situation.*

**is under the impression (that)** *assumes; believes; feels; supposes; thinks.* • It was fine the first few times, but now he's under the impression I am his grandson. *It was fine the first few times, but now he thinks I am his grandson.*

**is used (for; to)** delete. • Straight lines are used to indicate crest and root lines. *Straight lines indicate crest and root lines.*

**is what** delete. • While consistency is the mainstay of our program, diversity and change are what keep it exciting. *While consistency is the mainstay of our program, diversity and change keep it exciting.*

**is witness to** *affirms; attests to; certifies to; declares; testifies to; verifies.* • Poet Kahlil Gibran's popularity in America is witness to the presence of an essential moral and artistic quality in his work. *Poet Kahlil Gibran's popularity in America testifies to the presence of an essential moral and artistic quality in his work.*

**is (a) witness to** *sees; witnesses.* • He was a witness to the Chinese government's crackdown on students. *He witnessed the Chinese government's crackdown on students.*

**it has been called to (my) attention** *(I) have been told; (I) have learned; (I) understand;* delete.

**it has come to (my) attention** *(I) have been told; (I) have learned; (I) understand;* delete. • It has come to our attention that some people are not aware of how to operate the intercom properly. *We have learned that some people are not aware of how to operate the intercom properly.*

**it is . . . (that; who)** *is; -(al)ly;* delete. • It is our intent to share ideas, thoughts, and methods with GEM users. *Our intent is to share ideas, thoughts, and methods with GEM users.* • It's time for us to rethink what it is we are asking of our employees. *It's time for us to rethink what we are asking of our employees.*

**it is apparent that** *apparently; clearly; evidently; manifestly; obviously; patently; plainly;* delete. • It is apparent that management needs to take into account a wide range of variables when devising international product development policies. *Clearly, management needs to take into account a wide range of variables when devising international product development policies.*

**it is essential that** *must; should.* • It is essential that remaining barriers to women's entrepreneurship be eliminated. *Remaining barriers to women's entrepreneurship must be eliminated.*

**it is evident that** *apparently; clearly; evidently; manifestly; obviously; patently; plainly;* delete. • It is evident that service industries are more exposed to protectionism in international markets than are most other industries. *Clearly, service industries are more exposed to protectionism in international markets than are most other industries.*

**it is (to be) hoped** *I (we) hope; let us hope.* • It is to be hoped that your exposé will help prevent this kind of performance by others. *Let's hope that your exposé will help prevent this kind of performance by others.*

**it is imperative that** *must; should.* • It is imperative that managers and researchers try to assess the value of the information before the research is undertaken. *Managers and researchers should try to assess the value of the information before the research is undertaken.*

**it is important to . . . that** delete. • It is important to emphasize that the incidence of breast cancer has been rising. *The incidence of breast cancer has been rising.*

**it is important to keep in mind** *keep in mind; remember;* delete. • It is important to keep in mind that these applications address only today's problems. *Keep in mind that these applications address only today's problems.*

**it is important to note** *note;* delete. • It is important to note that different stores in a chain may perform differently. *Different stores in a chain may perform differently.*

**it is important to realize (recognize)** *realize (recognize);* delete. • It is important to realize that many Chinese willingly remain in their country despite the violence. *Many Chinese willingly remain in their country despite the violence.*

**it is important to remember** *keep in mind; remember;* delete. • It is important to remember that Social Security reserves are expected to build to about $12 trillion in the next century. *Remember that Social Security reserves are expected to build to about $12 trillion in the next century.*

**it is important to understand** *understand;* delete. • It is important to understand that not all pressures are the result of marketplace changes, nor do they necessarily affect the marketing activity. *Not all pressures are the result of marketplace changes, nor do they necessarily affect the marketing activity.*

**it is interesting to note** *interestingly; note;* delete. • It is interesting to note that an early meaning of the Spanish word *algebrista* was bonesetter or reuniter of broken bones. *Interestingly, an early meaning of the Spanish word* algebrista *was bonesetter or reuniter of broken bones.*

**it is necessary (for; that; to)** *must; need to.* • It is necessary for this causality to be realistic for the model to be useful. *This causality must be realistic for the model to be useful.*

**it is significant to note** *note;* delete. • It is significant to note that this land is owned by the city and leased to Harvard. *This land is owned by the city and leased to Harvard.*

**it is useful (worthwhile) to mention (say; state) (that)** delete. • It is useful to state that most of the modernization in steel production has occurred as part of a general shift toward all-electric steelmaking. *Most of the modernization in steel production has occurred as part of a general shift toward all-electric steelmaking.*

**it is useful (worthwhile) to note (that)** delete. • It is worthwhile to note that in this outline the results specified in step III could refer to any of several results. *In this outline the results specified in step III could refer to any of several results.*

**it must (should) be mentioned (remarked; said; stated) (that)** delete. • It should be remarked, however, that for both methods success is largely dependent on devising an appropriate method for representing the problem. *However, for both methods success is largely dependent on devising an appropriate method for representing the problem.*

**it must (should) be noted** *note;* delete. • It should be noted that people with gastrointestinal disorders share a number of traits. *People with gastrointestinal disorders share a number of traits.*

**it must (should) be pointed out (that)** delete. • It should be pointed out that Boston Technical students have recently received notices of acceptance from institutions such as Princeton, Tufts, Boston College, and the University of California at Berkeley. *Boston Technical students have recently received* *notices of acceptance from institutions such as Princeton, Tufts, Boston College, and the University of California at Berkeley.*

**it must (should) be remembered** *keep in mind; remember;* delete. • It must be remembered that even though this course deals with an easily measurable good, money, you must make personal value judgments concerning how money is best used. *Even though this course deals with an easily measurable good, money, you must make personal value judgments concerning how money is best used.*

**it must (should) be understood** *understand;* delete. • It must be understood that we have a very complex, interrelated economy. *We have a very complex, interrelated economy.*

**it (just) so happens** *by chance; luckily; unluckily.*

**I (we) would appreciate it if** *please.*

# J

**joint agreement** *agreement.*

**joint cooperation** *cooperation.*

**join together** *join.* • All of these can be joined together by soldering, brazing, or welding. *All of these can be joined by soldering, brazing, or welding.*

**judge as** *judge.*

**just about** *about; almost; nearly.*

**just as (more; most) importantly** *just as (more; most) important.* • But perhaps most importantly, they offer trustworthiness. *But perhaps most important, they offer trustworthiness.*

**just as (more; most) significantly** *just as (more; most) significant.* • Most significantly, the product champion must have the drive to get the work done and the decisions made. *Most significant, the product champion must have the drive to get the work done and the decisions made.*

**just exactly** *exactly; just.* • He's just exactly what I'm looking for. *He's just what I'm looking for.*

**just recently** *just; recently.* • We just recently went to England. *We recently went to England.*

**just simply** *just; simply.*

**just the same as** *just like; the same as.* • The DEL command works just the same as the ERASE command. *The DEL command works just like the ERASE command.*

# K

**keep in mind** *remember;* delete. • Keep in mind that few people, if any, match a job perfectly, and few employers look for a perfect fit. *Few people, if any, match a job perfectly, and few employers look for a perfect fit.*

**(a; the) key . . . in (of; to)** *key to.* • Market segmentation is a key aspect to strategic planning at the corporate and business levels. *Market segmentation is a key to strategic planning at the corporate and business levels.* • In contrast, individualism was the key ingredient to the rise of Greece. *In contrast, individualism was key to the rise of Greece.* • Our continued commitment to quality is a key component of our success. *Our continued commitment to quality is a key to our success.*

**kinder (and) gentler** *amiable; compassionate; gentle; humane; kind; tender; tolerant.*

**kind of** delete. • I kind of stumbled onto the job. *I stumbled onto the job.*

**know for a fact** *know.* • We know for a fact that this firm is trying to swindle consumers. *We know that this firm is trying to swindle consumers.*

**known as** *called; named; termed;* delete. • The three most common knowledge representations in expert system shells are known as rules, frames, and semantic networks. *The three most common knowledge representations in expert system shells are rules, frames, and semantic networks.*

# L

**label as** *label.* • The product is labeled as a cosmetic, not a medication. *The product is labeled a cosmetic, not a medication.*

**lackadaisical** *idle; languid; lazy; listless.*

**lack for** *lack.*

**lacking in** *dis-; il-; im-; in-; ir-; lack; -less(ness); mis-; no; non-; not; un-; want; with no; without.* • The defense's case was so often lacking in credibility. *The defense's case was so often incredible.*

**(a; the) lack of** *dis-; few; il-; im-; in-; ir-; -less(ness); mis-; no; non-; not; scant; un-; with no; without.* • This is a result of a lack of cooperation between retailers and financial institutions. *This is a result of noncooperation between retailers and financial institutions.* • Many a computer programming project has failed because of a lack of careful problem analysis and poor program design techniques. *Many a computer programming project has failed because of careless problem analysis and poor program design techniques.* • Jackson concerns me because of his lack of experience in foreign policy and defense. *Jackson concerns me because of his inexperience in foreign policy and defense.*

**(a; the) large (overwhelming; sizable; vast) plurality (of)** *a good (great) deal (of); a good (great) many (of); almost all (of); (nine) in (ten) (of); many (of); most (of); much (of); nearly all (of); (43) of (48) (of); (67) percent (of); three-fourths (two-thirds) (of).* • Large pluralities feel Mr. Bush would do about as well as Mr. Reagan. *Most feel Mr. Bush would do about as well as Mr. Reagan.*

**large-size(d)** *large.*

**last of all** *last.*

**later on** *later.* • I will see you later on. *I will see you later.*

**later on down the line (pike; road; way)** *at length; eventually; from now; in time; later; ultimately.* • Later on down the line, there will have to be a settlement. *In time, there will have to be a settlement.*

**latter part of** *last half of; late.*

**law enforcement officers** *authorities; cops; officers; police.*

**legitimatize** *legitimate; legitimize.* • Unattended operation is being legitimatized by the major hardware and software vendors. *Unattended operation is being legitimized by the major hardware and software vendors.*

**lend out** *lend.*

**(a; the) length of** delete. • While adults typically grew to a length of about 30 feet, the embryos measured only about 1½ feet from head to tail and fit into 7-inch-long eggs. *While adults typically grew to about 30 feet, the embryos measured only about 1½ feet from head to tail and fit into 7-inch-long eggs.*

**lengthy** *long.* • Communists must go through a lengthy selection process and ideological training before being granted membership in the party. *Communists must go through a long selection process and ideological training before being granted membership in the party.*

**less than (enthusiastic)** *dis-; il-; im-; in-; ir-; mis-; non-; un-.* • You can refinance with us even if your credit is less than perfect. *You can refinance with us even if your credit is imperfect.* • This book reveals the sometimes less-than-elegant design of DOS by walking through the source code. *This book reveals the sometimes inelegant design of DOS by walking through the source code.* • The lack of consistent definition and the paucity of carefully designed drug studies of PMS have led to less than satisfactory treatment. *The lack of consistent definition and the paucity of carefully designed drug studies of PMS have led to insatisfactory treatment.*

**(a; the) . . . level (of)** delete. • Each organization must assess its level of willingness to take risks. *Each organization must assess its willingness to take risks.* • When a relationship reaches a certain level of intensity, the church should have some way of recognizing that commitment. *When a relationship reaches a certain intensity, the church should have some way of recognizing that commitment.* • Random access implies that any piece of information can be read with an equal level of difficulty and delay. *Random access implies that any piece of information can be read with equal difficulty and delay.*

**level to the ground** *level; raze.*

**lift up** *lift.*

**lightning (raining; snowing) outside** *lightning (raining; snowing).* • It's raining outside. *It's raining.*

**like . . . also (as well)** *like.* • Like 401(k) plans, 403(b) plans also have various investment alternatives: common stocks, bonds, money-market funds, and so on. *Like 401(k) plans, 403(b) plans have various investment alternatives: common stocks, bonds, money-market funds, and so on.*

**like . . . and others (and so forth; and so on; and such; and the like; et al.; etc.)** *and others (and so forth; and so on; and such; and the like; et al.; etc.); like; such as.* • Sheet sizes are specified by letters like Size A, Size B, and so forth. *Sheet sizes are specified by letters like Size A and Size B.* • It can be printed on any printer, but it will not have formats such as boldfacing, underlining, and so on. *It can be printed on any printer, but it will not have formats such as boldfacing and underlining.*

**like . . . for example (for instance)** *as; for example (for instance); like; such as.* • The drug is good for ailments like insomnia for example. *The drug is good for ailments like insomnia.*

**like-gender individuals (people; persons)** *females; males; men; women.* • The creation of rape crisis centers, centers for battered women, and the like all point to the possibility of women helping like-gender individuals through noncriminal justice channels. *The creation of rape crisis centers, centers for battered women, and the like all point to the possibility of women helping women through noncriminal justice channels.*

**limitation** *limit.* • There is no overall limitation on the percentage of the trust's portfolio securities which may be subject to a hedge position. *There is no overall limit on the percentage of the trust's portfolio securities which may be subject to a hedge position.*

**(very) limited** *bare; few; little; meager; rare; scant; scanty; scarce; short; slight; small; spare; sparse.* • While opportunities for broad-scale consumer advertising may be limited for a while, there are lots of opportunities for commercial communications. *While opportunities for broad-scale consumer advertising may be scarce for a while, there are lots of opportunities for commercial communications.*

**(a; the) limited number of** *a couple; a few; eight (four); little; meager; not many; one or two (two or three); scant; scanty; (only) so many; some; spare;*

*sparse.* • A surgeon can only do a limited number of operations. *A surgeon can only do so many operations.*

**(a; the) limited selection (of)** *a couple; a few; eight (four); little; meager; not many; one or two (two or three); scant; scanty; (only) so many; some; spare; sparse.*

**linkage** *link.* • Particular attention needs to be given to the linkage among the various strategic levels within and across national markets. *Particular attention needs to be given to the link among the various strategic levels within and across national markets.*

**link together** *connect; link.* • It's natural to link the two of them together. *It's natural to link the two of them.*

**liquid refreshment** *drink.*

**literally** delete. • We have a fee maximum on literally every CPT code imaginable. *We have a fee maximum on every CPT code imaginable.*

**little by little** *gradually; slowly.*

**little (small) child** *child.* • How do you tell a little child that his father isn't coming home again? *How do you tell a child that his father isn't coming home again?*

**little (small; tiny) iota** *iota.* • I don't care one little iota less than you do about homelessness in America. *I don't care one iota less than you do about homelessness in America.*

**locality** *area; city; district; locale; place; point; region; site; spot; state; town; zone.* • Today, modern water wells are drilled and in some localities are more than 300 meters deep. *Today, modern water wells are drilled and in some sites are more than 300 meters deep.*

**located** delete. • The school, which is located in an old, poorly cared for building, further added to our misgivings. *The school, which is in an old, poorly cared for building, further added to our misgivings.*

**lodge a complaint (with)** *complain (to).* • He threatened to lodge a complaint with the management if he wasn't reimbursed for his losses. *He threatened to complain to the management if he wasn't reimbursed for his losses.*

**logical reason** *reason.*

**long suit** *forte.*

**look (observe) to see** *check; examine; inspect; look; see.* • Look to see where you have been and where you might go next. *Examine where you have been and where you might go next.*

**lose out on** *lose.*

**lots of** *many; much.*

**loudly bellow (holler; howl; roar; scream; shout; shriek; yell)** *bellow (holler; howl; roar; scream; shout; shriek; yell).* • In the early days of VCRs, movie companies howled loudly at the advent of movie rentals and attempted blocking legislation. *In the early days of VCRs, movie companies howled at the advent of movie rentals and attempted blocking legislation.*

**-(al)ly enough** *-(al)ly;* delete. • Ironically enough, many states have loosened their registration laws in the last decade, but turnout still declines. *Ironically, many states have loosened their registration laws in the last decade, but turnout still declines.*

**-(al)ly speaking** *-(al)ly;* delete. • All four of their parents would be the same, genetically speaking. *All four of their parents would be genetically the same.* • Although there may be small differences between the jobs, they are, relatively speaking, inconsequential. *Although there may be small differences between the jobs, they are relatively inconsequential.* • Personally speaking, I belonged to the Howdy Doody generation. *I belonged to the Howdy Doody generation.*

# M

**made of** delete. • The only data show small vestiges of threads made of cotton. *The only data show small vestiges of cotton threads.*

**made to measure** *custom; customized; custom-made; tailored; tailor-made.*

**made to order** *custom; customized; custom-made; tailored; tailor-made.*

**made up out of** *made of;* delete.

**magnitude** *import; moment; scope; size.* • Nothing is unthinkable when you try to solve a problem of this magnitude. *Nothing is unthinkable when you try to solve a problem of this size.*

**major** delete. • If the vice president comes in third, it's a major disaster. *If the vice president comes in third, it's a disaster.* • Combining these two world-class companies represents a major milestone for the plastics industry. *Combining these two world-class companies represents a milestone for the plastics industry.* • It's going to take a couple of years to shake out, but it won't result in a major calamity. *It's going to take a couple of years to shake out, but it won't result in a calamity.*

**(a; the) majority (of)** *almost all (of); (nine) in (ten) (of); many (of); more (of); most (of); nearly all (of); (43) of (48) (of); (67) percent (of); three-fourths (two-thirds) (of).* • Surveys reveal that the majority of chronic fatigue syndrome victims are between 22 and 45. *Surveys reveal that 60 percent of chronic fatigue syndrome victims are between 22 and 45.*

**(a; the) major part (percentage; portion; proportion) (of)** *a good (great) deal (of); a good (great) many (of); almost all (of); (nine) in (ten) (of); many (of); more (of); most (of); nearly all (of); (43) of (48) (of); (67) percent (of); three-fourths (two-thirds) (of).* • Murdoch could borrow a major portion of the purchase price using Triangle's assets as collateral. *Murdoch could borrow most of the purchase price using Triangle's assets as collateral.*

**make . . . (a; the) . . . (about; of; to)** delete. • Why make that admission to them? *Why admit that to them?* • We made an agreement that she would keep the stereo for me. *We agreed that she would keep the stereo for me.* • The company's management may not see any reason for making a shift from their current approach. *The company's management may not see any reason for shifting from their current approach.* • Make an estimate of what the person might find if the process were revamped to operate as well as is conceivable. *Estimate what the person might find if the process were revamped to operate as well as is conceivable.*

**make . . . acquaintance** meet. • I was very pleased to make your acquaintance. *I was very pleased to meet you.*

**make allowance for** allow for; arrange for; consider; prepare for; provide for.

**make an appearance** appear; arrive; attend; come; show up; visit.

**make an attempt (effort; endeavor)** try. • We are going to make an effort to hold prices or even reduce them. *We are going to try to hold prices or even reduce them.*

**make available** afford; furnish; provide; supply. • Paralleling a business school course of study, our curriculum makes available a stable, inclusive, and continuing transmittal of practices and perspectives to those working managers who want to continue their education in management. *Paralleling a business school course of study, our curriculum affords a stable, inclusive, and continuing transmittal of practices and perspectives to those working managers who want to continue their education in management.*

**make believe** feign; pretend.

**make concession for** allow for; arrange for; consider; prepare for; provide for.

**make contact (with)** call; contact; discover; encounter; find; locate; meet (with); phone; reach; speak (to); talk (to); visit; write. • In Sturgis, we made contact with the Sons of Silence. *In Sturgis, we encountered the Sons of Silence.*

**make conversation** chat; communicate; converse; speak; talk. • It was easy to make conversation with him. *It was easy to talk with him.*

**make (a; the) decision (determination)** conclude; decide; determine; resolve. • I made the decision to keep on good terms with all the candidates. *I decided to keep on good terms with all the candidates.*

**make (a; the) determined decision** *conclude; decide; determine; resolve.* • She made a determined decision to overcome her drug dependency. *She resolved to overcome her drug dependency.*

**make (a; the) distinction** *distinguish.* • For some years, economists have enjoyed making a distinction between "salt water" and "fresh water" approaches to economics. *For some years, economists have enjoyed distinguishing between "salt water" and "fresh water" approaches to economics.*

**make false statements** *lie.* • He did this by using a false Social Security number and making false statements on his application. *He did this by using a false Social Security number and lying on his application.*

**(to) make matters worse** *what is worse; worse still; worse yet.* • Making matters worse, a boom in the herring export market has turned to bust. *Worse yet, a boom in the herring export market has turned to bust.*

**make mention of** *mention.* • You made mention of the fact that S&Ls insure you only up to $100,000. *You mentioned the fact that S&Ls insure you only up to $100,000.*

**make provision for** *allow for; arrange for; consider; prepare for; provide for.* • No family can attempt to establish a budget without making provision for these "unexpected" but forever recurring expenses. *No family can attempt to establish a budget without allowing for these "unexpected" but forever recurring expenses.*

**make (a; the) statement saying (stating)** *comment; remark; say; state.* • I think it's important for us to make a statement saying that this veto should be overridden. *I think it's important for us to state that this veto should be overridden.*

**make up (my) mind** *decide.* • King said he will make up his mind by mid-September on whether to seek the GOP nomination for governor. *King said he will decide by mid-September on whether to seek the GOP nomination for governor.*

**make (my) way** *driving; proceeding; running; walking.* • The vice president is now making his way to the platform. *The vice president is now walking to the platform.*

**many hundreds (thousands)** *hundreds (thousands).* • The abacus shown here has been used in China for many hundreds of years. *The abacus shown here has been used in China for hundreds of years.*

**many times over** *frequently; often; recurrently; regularly; repeatedly.*

**mass exodus** *exodus.* • The mass exodus to Penturbia is the result of a declining quality of life. *The exodus to Penturbia is the result of a declining quality of life.*

**mass extinction** *extinction.* • A comet striking Earth with the power of 300 million Hiroshima-sized atomic bombs may be the cause of mass extinction 11 million years ago. *A comet striking Earth with the power of 300 million Hiroshima-sized atomic bombs may be the cause of extinction 11 million years ago.*

**match exactly** *duplicate; match.* • To find strings that match your case exactly, enter the appropriate characters in uppercase when specifying the string to be searched for. *To find strings that match your case, enter the appropriate characters in uppercase when specifying the string to be searched for.*

**match perfectly** *duplicate; match.* • The fluctuations of the one variable match perfectly the fluctuations of the other variable. *The fluctuations of the one variable duplicate the fluctuations of the other variable.*

**match up** *match.*

**materialize** *develop; evolve; form; happen; occur; result; take place.*

**matter-of-course** *common; customary; habitual; natural; normal; ordinary; regular; routine; typical; usual.*

**matter-of-fact** *businesslike; factual; literal; plain; prosaic; straightforward; unfeeling.*

**maximal** *biggest; greatest; highest; largest; longest; most; top.*

**maximize** *add to; broaden; enlarge; greaten; increase; raise.*

**(a; the) maximum . . . of** *biggest; greatest; highest; largest; longest; most; top.* • It is necessary to get the maximum mileage out of existing and new products as rapidly as possible. *It is necessary to get the most mileage out of existing and new products as rapidly as possible.*

**(a; the) maximum amount (of)** *biggest; greatest; highest; largest; longest; most; top.*

**(a; the) maximum number (of)** *biggest; greatest; highest; largest; longest; most; top.* • Set up your fields for the maximum number of lines. *Set up your fields for the most lines.*

**may or may not** *may; may not.* • Your assessment of Houston's nascent ascent from the urban graveyard may or may not prove to be on the mark, but your classification of its metropolitan area as the nation's fourth largest was not. *Your assessment of Houston's nascent ascent from the urban graveyard may prove to be on the mark, but your classification of its metropolitan area as the nation's fourth largest was not.*

**may (might) perhaps** *may (might).*

**may (might) possibly** *may (might).* • She said Concord Academy might possibly be too difficult. *She said Concord Academy might be too difficult.*

**meaningful** delete. • This slope can represent miles per hour, weight versus length, or a number of other meaningful rates that are important to the analysis of data. *This slope can represent miles per hour, weight versus length, or a number of other rates that are important to the analysis of data.*

**meaningful importance (significance)** *importance (significance); meaning.*

**meaningless gibberish** *gibberish.*

**measured against** *against; alongside; beside; compared to (with); -(i)er than; less; less than; more; more than; next to; over; than; to; versus; vis-à-vis.* • Retrieving data from disks is slow measured against the speed of processing the records once they are in memory. *Retrieving data from disks is slower than the speed of processing the records once they are in memory.*

**measure up to** *meet.* • Because many teachers expect children from the same family to behave in the same manner, it can be particularly difficult for temperamentally different siblings to measure up to their expectations. *Because many teachers expect children from the same family to behave in the same manner, it can be particularly difficult for temperamentally different siblings to meet their expectations.*

**mechanical mechanism** *mechanical; mechanism.* • The final result was the Pascaline, a polished brass box containing a sophisticated, mechanical calculating mechanism composed of gears. *The final result was the Pascaline, a polished brass box containing a sophisticated calculating mechanism composed of gears.*

**meet together** *meet.*

**memorandum** *memo; note.* • This memorandum is for informative purposes only. *This memo is for informative purposes only.*

**mental ability (capacity)** *ability (capacity).*

**mental telepathy** *telepathy.*

**(a; the) -ment of** *-ing.* • The assignment of retirement assets to a money manager may entail a lengthy process of evaluation by the corporate client. *Assigning retirement assets to a money manager may entail a lengthy process of evaluation by the corporate client.* • Meetings do not contribute to the attainment of individual objectives. *Meetings do not contribute to attaining individual objectives.* • The treatment of these items as expenses results in lower rents and more available apartments. *Treating these items as expenses results in lower rents and more available apartments.*

**merge into one (company)** *merge.* • The two departments are being merged into one. *The two departments are being merged.*

**merge together** *merge.* • First, create the files to be merged together. *First, create the files to be merged.*

**mesh together** *mesh.* • Gears are toothed wheels that mesh together to transmit force and motion from one gear to the next. *Gears are toothed wheels that mesh to transmit force and motion from one gear to the next.*

**metaphorically speaking** *as it were; in a sense; in a way; so to speak.*

**methodology** *method.* • When developing estimates of market size, data extrapolation methodologies may be useful. *When developing estimates of market size, data extrapolation methods may be useful.*

**metropolis** *city.*

**(with) might and main** *force; power; strength.*

**might or might not** *might; might not.*

**mingle together** *mingle.* • An invitation-only crowd of some 40 people met at Kate's Mystery Books, though many in the crowd apparently did not want to mingle together. *An invitation-only crowd of some 40 people met at Kate's Mystery Books, though many in the crowd apparently did not want to mingle.*

**minimal** *brief; least; lowest; minor; not much; scant; short; slight; smallest.* • We expect the delay will be minimal. *We expect the delay will be brief.*

**(a; the) minimal number (of)** *a couple (of); a few (of); a handful (of); fewer than half (of); hardly any (of); (one) in (ten) (of); less than half (of); not* *many (of); (9) of (48) (of); one or two (two or three) (of); one-third (one-fifteenth) (of); (12) percent (of); scarcely any (of).* • Smith said a minimal number of people have irreconcilable differences with the roommate they selected. *Smith said hardly any people have irreconcilable differences with the roommate they selected.*

**minimize** *decrease; lower; reduce.*

**(a; the) minimum (of)** *at least; (the) least; little; lowest; minimum; scant; shortest; slightest; smallest; tiniest.* • Most oxyacetylene welding is done manually with a minimum of equipment. *Most oxyacetylene welding is done manually with minimum equipment.*

**(a; the) minority (of)** *a couple (of); a few (of); a handful (of); fewer than half (of); hardly any (of); (one) in (ten) (of); less than half (of); not many (of); (9) of (48) (of); one or two (two or three) (of); one-third (one-fifteenth) (of); (12) percent (of); scarcely any (of).* • A minority of those who are comfortable financially are good givers, but some of the country's wealthiest give dramatically large sums. *Few who are comfortable financially are good givers, but some of the country's wealthiest give dramatically large sums.*

**minutely detail** *detail.* • Given a problem, engineers and computer scientists, accustomed to working with mathematical procedures, would write a program—a list of minutely detailed instructions logically guiding the computer step by step through its assigned task. *Given a problem, engineers and computer scientists, accustomed to working with mathematical procedures, would write a program—a list of detailed instructions logically guiding the computer step by step through its assigned task.*

**mix and mingle** *mingle; mix.*

**mix together** *mix.* • The capability to mix text and graphics together in the same document makes it easy to produce newsletters, instructional materials, and other documents where figures, logos, and/or pictures are needed. *The capability to mix text and graphics in the same document makes it easy to produce newsletters, instructional materials, and other documents where figures, logos, and/or pictures are needed.*

**modern, state-of-the-art** *modern; state-of-the-art.* • Today, with modern, state-of-the-art technologies, breast cancer can be detected at very early stages of development. *Today, with modern technologies, breast cancer can be detected at very early stages of development.*

**(a; the) modicum of** *few; little; some; tiny; trifle.*

**months of age** *months.* • At 14 months of age, these children showed fear and shyness when taken into a room with strangers. *At 14 months, these children showed fear and shyness when taken into a room with strangers.*

**more -(i)er** *-(i)er; more.* • Watching television is more easier than reading. *Watching television is easier than reading.* • Watch "Nightstand," where comedy doesn't get any more better. *Watch "Nightstand," where comedy doesn't get any better.*

**more extended (lengthy; prolonged; protracted)** *longer.* • Even the IRS has been testing itself over a more prolonged period. *Even the IRS has been testing itself over a longer period.*

**more improved** *improved.*

**more inferior** *inferior.*

**more often than not** *almost always; commonly; customarily; generally; most often; nearly always; normally; typically; usually.*

**(the) more . . . of the two** *(the) -(i)er; (the) more.* • Objectivity is certainly the more difficult of the two to sustain. *Objectivity is certainly the more difficult to sustain.*

**more preferable** *preferable.* • We have never said any one group is more preferable to another. *We have never said any one group is preferable to another.*

**more superior** *superior.* • It upsets me to think of her with a man more superior to me. *It upsets me to think of her with a man superior to me.*

**more than exceeded (surpassed)** *exceeded (surpassed).* • From all sides, there is little disagreement that while business more than exceeded its component goals, the schools fell short of theirs. *From all sides, there is little disagreement that while business exceeded its component goals, the schools fell short of theirs.*

**most but not all** *almost all; (nine) in (ten); many; most; nearly all; (43) of (48); . . . percent; three-fourths (two-thirds).* • Most, but not all, accounting programs store the data you enter in a database. *Almost all accounting programs store the data you enter in a database.*

**most -(i)est** *-(i)est; most.* • You missed two of the most simplest questions. *You missed two of the simplest questions.* • This is probably the most happiest moment in my life. *This is probably the happiest moment in my life.*

**most favorite** *favorite; most favored.*

**most important** *above all.* • Most important, the system that files are designated by should be consistent and understood by everyone. *Above all, the system that files are designated by should be consistent and understood by everyone.*

**most important** *central; chief; critical; crucial; foremost; key; leading; main; major; pivotal; principal; seminal.* • The company's most important product, Mechanical Advantage, began shipping in early 1987. *The company's leading product, Mechanical Advantage, began shipping in early 1987.* • Recent studies have shown that for most investors, retiring comfortably is their most important financial goal. *Recent studies have shown that for most investors, retiring comfortably is their foremost financial goal.* • The most important factor in determining the amount of pension plan income you receive is your longevity with one company. *The key factor in determining the amount of pension plan income you receive is your longevity with one company.*

**most . . . one** *most.* • It's fairly obvious that the third approach will get the best results, but it is also the most difficult one to employ. *It's fairly obvious that the third approach will get the best results, but it is also the most difficult to employ.*

**most (of the) time(s)** *almost always; commonly; generally; most often; nearly always; normally; typically; usually.*

**motion picture** *film; movie.*

**motivating force** *drive; energy; force; impetus; motivation; power.* • The primary motivating force behind their behavior is the need to shock others. *The primary motivation behind their behavior is the need to shock others.*

**motivation** *motive.* • There is doubt about the ethical standards of life insurance companies as well as the motivations and practices of the agents selling their products. *There is doubt about the ethical standards of life insurance companies as well as the motives and practices of the agents selling their products.*

**move forward** *advance; continue; go on; move on; proceed; progress.* • We urge all involved to move forward with whatever plans make the most sense for both the city and the college. *We urge all involved to proceed with whatever plans make the most sense for both the city and the college.*

**muchly** *much.*

**multiple** *many; several.* • You are taking in data on multiple levels. *You are taking in data on many levels.*

**(a; the) multiplicity of** *a good (great) many; countless; endless; infinite; many; millions (of); numberless; numerous; thousands (of); untold.* • She suffers from a multiplicity of moods and personalities. *She suffers from many moods and personalities.*

**(a; the) multitude of** *a good (great) many; countless; endless; infinite; many; millions (of); numberless; numerous; thousands (of); untold.* • How do our customers and prospects view us given the multitude of changes in customers' needs and behaviors? *How do our customers and prospects view us given the many changes in customers' needs and behaviors?*

**multitudinous** *a good (great) many; countless; endless; infinite; many; millions (of); numberless; numerous; thousands (of); untold.*

**must necessarily (of necessity)** *inevitably; must; necessarily; of necessity; unavoidably.* • Texts organized around specific topics must of necessity limit their discussion to the features contained in those programs. *Texts organized around specific topics must limit their discussion to the features contained in those programs.*

**mutual agreement (mutually agree)** *agreement (agree).* • The NATO leaders proclaimed mutual agreement about reducing the missile systems. *The NATO leaders proclaimed agreement about reducing the missile systems.*

**mutual ... and (between ... and; both; each other; one another; two)** *and (between ... and; both; each other; one another; two).* • I think all three news directors in town have a mutual respect for one another. *I think all three news directors in town have a respect for one another.* • Both Herzberg's research and the Tarrytown experiment tell us that job enrichment must take place in an atmosphere of mutual trust between labor and management. *Both Herzberg's research and the Tarrytown experiment tell us that job enrichment must take place in an atmosphere of trust between labor and management.* • You can live with many differences of opinion and personal style if you and your partner have mutual respect for each other's abilities. *You can live with many differences of opinion and personal style if you and your partner have respect for each other's abilities.*

**mutual communication** *communication.* • In this way, mutual communication is established, and some type of agreement becomes much more possible. *In this way, communication is established, and some type of agreement becomes much more possible.*

**mutual cooperation** *cooperation.*

**mutual friendship** *friendship.*

**mutual understanding** *understanding.* • Marketing executives and financial managers must strive to develop a mutual understanding of each others' viewpoints. *Marketing executives and financial managers must strive to develop an understanding of each others' viewpoints.*

# N

**name as** *name.* • They would more aptly be named as request and execute entry points. *They would more aptly be named request and execute entry points.*

**. . . nature** delete. • The ashes are a reminder of the transitory nature of life. *The ashes are a reminder of the transitoriness of life.*

**neat and tidy** *clean; neat; orderly; organized; tidy.*

**necessarily have to** *have to.* • It doesn't necessarily have to be a bad place to go. *It doesn't have to be a bad place to go.*

**necessary** *needed; needful; pressing; urgent; vital.* • The symbol is often in a more simple form when all the specifications are not necessary. *The symbol is often in a more simple form when all the specifications are not needed.*

**necessary essential** *essential; necessary.*

**necessary prerequisite** *necessary; prerequisite.*

**necessary requirement** *necessary; requirement.* • Naturally, we are complying with any necessary reporting requirements. *Naturally, we are complying with any reporting requirements.*

**necessary requisite** *necessary; requisite.* • He said he has the "toughness and resolve" to bring government spending under control as a necessary requisite to restoring the public's confidence. *He said he has the "toughness and resolve" to bring government spending under control as a requisite to restoring the public's confidence.*

**necessitate** *demand; exact; must; need; require.* • Your husband's job necessitates a great deal of independence and a lot of latitude in his hours. *Your husband's job demands a great deal of independence and a lot of latitude in his hours.*

**necessity** *need.* • The emphasis on technical expertise is being balanced by a necessity for good interpersonal skills. *The emphasis on technical expertise is being balanced by a need for good interpersonal skills.*

**needless to say** *clearly; naturally; obviously; of course; plainly;* delete.

**need not necessarily (of necessity)** *need not.* • This need not necessarily mean that the regime must fall before it can be studied. *This need not mean that the regime must fall before it can be studied.*

**needs hardly be said** *clearly; naturally; obviously; of course; plainly;* delete.

**need to have** *need.* • We felt in order to support the nugget we needed to have an overall precious metals plan. *We felt in order to support the nugget we needed an overall precious metals plan.*

**negative feelings** *anger; annoyance; disfavor; dislike; displeasure; disregard; distaste; hate; hatred; indifference; resentment.* • I have nothing but negative feelings for her. *I have nothing but hatred for her.*

**neither here nor there** *immaterial; inapt; irrelevant; not pertinent.*

**neither one** *neither.* • Neither one of us wanted to admit it. *Neither of us wanted to admit it.*

**never at any time** *never; not ever; not once.*

**never ever** *never; not ever; not once.* • You never ever make concessions to terrorists. *You never make concessions to terrorists.*

**nevertheless** *anyhow; even so; still; yet.* • There are nagging questions, nevertheless. *Still, there are nagging questions.*

**new and improved** *improved; new.* • The original design goals may not have been much different than to create a new and improved version of an earlier operating system. *The original design goals may not have been much different than to create an improved version of an earlier operating system.*

**new and innovative** *innovative; new.* • The health care industry is marketing many new and innovative products. *The health care industry is marketing many innovative products.*

**(brand) new baby** *baby.*

**new construction** *construction.* • Both firms predict the vacancy rate will fall, if only because of a lack of new construction. *Both firms predict the vacancy rate will fall, if only because of a lack of construction.*

**new creation** *creation.*

**new departure** *departure.* • The environmental community is hopeful that he will represent a new departure in environmental protection. *The environmental community is hopeful that he will represent a departure in environmental protection.*

**new innovation** *innovation.* • There is now ample evidence that the United States is lagging behind Japan in new innovations. *There is now ample evidence that the United States is lagging behind Japan in innovations.*

**new introduction** *introduction.*

**new (high) record** *record.* • This computer, introduced in 1981, set a new record for sales and quickly became the standard around which most other manufacturers designed their machines. *This computer, introduced in 1981, set a record for sales and quickly became the standard around which most other manufacturers designed their machines.*

**new recruit** *recruit.*

**next of all** *also; and; as well; besides; further; furthermore; moreover; next; second; still more; too.*

**no basis in fact** *baseless; groundless; unfounded.*

**no better (than)** *best.* • This last point is perhaps no better illustrated than by the recent acquisition of Applied Data Research by Computer Associates. *This last point is perhaps best illustrated by the recent acquisition of Applied Data Research by Computer Associates.*

**no longer in existence** *dead; defunct; extinct.*

**no longer with us** *dead; fired.*

**no matter (what)** *despite (what); whatever.* • No matter what the period to maturity, they are accepted for payment of taxes due at face or par value. *Whatever the period to maturity, they are accepted for payment of taxes due at face or par value.*

**no matter how** *despite how; however.* • She was determined, no matter how long it took, to find out the truth. *She was determined, however long it took, to find out the truth.*

**no matter when** *despite when; whenever.* • No matter when you use them, voice-mail messages are usually a lot briefer and more efficient than the give-and-take of ordinary conversation. *Despite when you use them, voice-mail messages are usually a lot briefer and more efficient than the give-and-take of ordinary conversation.*

**no matter where** *despite where; wherever.* • From the state's point of view, the collider will be a boon no matter where it is located. *From the state's point of view, the collider will be a boon wherever it is located.*

**no matter whether . . . (or)** *despite whether; whether . . . or (not).*

**no matter which** *despite which; whichever.* • No matter which way I decide, I will be blamed for making the wrong decision. *Whichever way I decide, I will be blamed for making the wrong decision.*

**no matter who** *despite who; whoever.* • It is still a good idea and should be adopted, no matter who wins the presidency. *It is still a good idea and should be adopted, whoever wins the presidency.*

**no matter whom** *despite whom; whomever.* • No matter whom the voters choose, investors will be contemplating the first change of presidents since 1980, with all the questions about future economic policies that implies. *Whomever the voters choose, investors will be contemplating the first change of presidents since 1980, with all the questions about future economic policies that implies.*

**no more (and) no less** *exactly; just; precisely.*

**no more than** *but; merely; only.*

**nonetheless** *anyhow; even so; still; yet.*

**noontime** *noon.* • The meeting on the 29th will be held at noontime in room 901. *The meeting on the 29th will be held at noon in room 901.*

**not anything** *nothing.* • There's not anything wrong with this housing code. *There's nothing wrong with this housing code.*

**not anywhere** *nowhere.* • But this total is not anywhere near the level of demand. *But this total is nowhere near the level of demand.*

**not a one** *none; no one.*

**not . . . at any time** *never; not ever; not once.* • My mother was not in a coma at any time; her last few weeks were the only period of very serious pain. *My mother was never in a coma; her last few weeks were the only period of very serious pain.*

**notation** *memo; note.* • Read the entire chapter carefully and methodically, underlining key points and making marginal notations as you go. *Read the entire chapter carefully and methodically, underlining key points and making marginal notes as you go.*

**note how (that)** delete. • Note how in this case, the pathname is not preceded by a slash. *In this case, the pathname is not preceded by a slash.*

**(does) not ever** *never.* • This routine is called only when a known internal command is executed, so it does not ever attempt to mediate command line switches for program calls. *This routine is called only when a known internal command is executed, so it never attempts to mediate command line switches for program calls.*

**not hardly (scarcely)** *hardly (scarcely).*

**notice how (that)** delete. • Notice how the message line indicates how many characters were saved on the disk. *The message line indicates how many characters were saved on the disk.*

**not in favor of** *disagree (with); oppose.*

**not in the least** *not at all.*

**notwithstanding** *after all; apart; aside; despite; even with; for all; with all.* • These misfortunes notwithstanding, the numbers of gorillas are believed to be growing. *These misfortunes aside, the numbers of gorillas are believed to be growing.*

**notwithstanding the fact that** *although; but; even though; still; though; yet.* • Of what relevance to usage (notwithstanding the fact that the topic is interesting) is an entry on eponyms? *Of what relevance to usage (even though the topic is interesting) is an entry on eponyms?*

**null and void** *invalid; not binding; null; void; worthless.*

**number-one** *central; chief; foremost; key; leading; main; major.* • That slow start-up is often the number-one reason why many financial analysts consider biotechnology companies to be a gamble. *That slow start-up is often the main reason why many financial analysts consider biotechnology companies to be a gamble.*

**numerical** *numeric.*

**numerous** *countless; endless; many; untold.* • There were numerous women in his life. *There were untold women in his life.*

O

**observe** *see.*

**obtain (a; the) . . . (for; of; to)** delete. • Using the first number less than 3.257 and the first number greater than 3.257, it is possible to obtain an approximation for log 3.257 by using linear interpolation. *Using the first number less than 3.257 and the first number greater than 3.257, it is possible to approximate log 3.257 by using linear interpolation.*

**obviate the necessity (need) for (of; to)** *obviate (-ing).* • Of course, an awareness of this uncertainty doesn't obviate the need to make decisions based on your best guess about what the future holds. *Of course, an awareness of this uncertainty doesn't obviate making decisions based on your best guess about what the future holds.*

**occasionally** *at times; now and again; now and then; sometimes.* • Getting to the actual command you want to execute occasionally means you must select a series of commands from the displayed submenus. *Getting to the actual command you want to execute sometimes means you must select a series of commands from the displayed submenus.*

**occur again** *recur.* • No resident should place items having any value in these bins without being aware that a theft may occur again. *No resident should place items having any value in these bins without being aware that a theft may recur.*

**of (a; the) . . .** delete. • I'd like to ask a question of the senator. *I'd like to ask the senator a question.* • The article failed to mention that a two-year-old investigation concluded that any irregularities were minor and of no significance. *The article failed to mention that a two-year-old investigation concluded that any irregularities were minor and insignificant.* • Both of these options draw the reader's attention to data of importance. *Both of these options draw the reader's attention to important data.*

**(a; the) . . . of** *-ing.* • For most American families, this means an analysis of the costs of operating and financing their automobiles. *For most American* *families, this means analyzing the costs of operating and financing their automobiles.* • Even more important is a knowledge of the costs of consumption in terms of the alternative consumption opportunities that are given up because of the particular choices made. *Even more important is knowing the costs of consumption in terms of the alternative consumption opportunities that are given up because of the particular choices made.*

**of all** delete. • A cyclical pattern is the most difficult of all to predict. *A cyclical pattern is the most difficult to predict.*

**of between . . . and** *between . . . and; of . . . to.* • The benefit is phased out for investors with incomes of between $200,000 and $250,000. *The benefit is phased out for investors with incomes between $200,000 and $250,000.*

**of (a; the) . . . character** delete. • A license may be revoked if a meter is used in operating any scheme or enterprise of an unlawful character, for nonuse during any consecutive 12 months, or for any failure of the licensee to comply with the regulations governing the use of postage meters. *A license may be revoked if a meter is used in operating any scheme or unlawful enterprise, for nonuse during any consecutive 12 months, or for any failure of the licensee to comply with the regulations governing the use of postage meters.*

**of (a) different opinion** *at odds.*

**of . . . dimensions (magnitude; proportions; size)** delete. • It was a success of monumental dimensions. *It was a monumental success.*

**offer (a; the) . . . (at; of; to)** delete. • In this column, we offer a brief look at five organizations that have found methods of reducing the burden. *In this column, we briefly look at five organizations that have found methods of reducing the burden.* • This author offers an examination of the research findings on age and performance. *This author examines the research findings on age and performance.*

**official business** *business.*

**off of** *from; off.* • She lived one block off of campus. *She lived one block off campus.*

**of from . . . to** *from . . . to; of . . . to.*

**of (a; the) . . . importance (that; to)** *important; -(al)ly important;* delete. • Information service issues are of vital importance to the telecommunications industry as well as to the general public. *Information service issues are vital to the telecommunications industry as well as to the general public.*

• Since increased involvement is generally associated with increased management and financial costs, not all foreign markets are of equal importance. *Since increased involvement is generally associated with increased management and financial costs, not all foreign markets are equally important.*

**of (a; the) . . . nature** delete. • First-level management deals with day-to-day operations of a repetitive nature. *First-level management deals with repetitive day-to-day operations.* • This type of analysis is of recent origin and is primarily of a conceptual rather than analytical nature. *This type of analysis is of recent origin and is primarily conceptual rather than analytical.*

**of (to) no avail** *unsuccessful.*

**of one form (kind; sort; type) or another** *in some way; some form (kind; sort; type) of; somehow; someway(s);* delete. • About 15 percent of all U.S. and Soviet missions involving nuclear reactors have suffered failures of one sort or another. *About 15 percent of all U.S. and Soviet missions involving nuclear reactors have suffered some sort of failure.*

**of . . . own accord (free will)** *gladly; readily; willingly.*

**of (a; the) . . . persuasion** delete. • A physician of liberal persuasion agonized over the senator's fall from grace. *A liberal physician agonized over the senator's fall from grace.*

**of such** *so.* • The personal balance sheet is of such simplicity that anyone who can add and subtract can also develop the entries. *The personal balance sheet is so simple that anyone who can add and subtract can also develop the entries.*

**oftentimes (ofttimes)** *often.* • Oftentimes, bacteria is present in food when you buy it. *Bacteria is often present in food when you buy it.*

**of that (this) kind (sort; type)** *like that (this).* • For an accident of this kind, you can't help blaming yourself. *For an accident like this, you can't help blaming yourself.*

**of that (this) nature** *like that (this).* • The Boston Juvenile Court deals with cases of this nature. *The Boston Juvenile Court deals with cases like this.*

**of that (this) year** *(1995);* delete. • In July of this year, the 3-month Treasury stood at 6.73 percent. *In July, the 3-month Treasury stood at 6.73 percent.*

**of the (them; these)** delete. • Each of the binomial random variables tends toward *v.* *Each binomial random variable tends toward* v.

**of the fact that** *that;* delete. • She was jealous of the fact that I could do these things. *She was jealous that I could do these things.*

**of the first magnitude** *best; central; chief; finest; foremost; key; leading; main; major; most important; principal; superior.*

**of the first (highest) order** *best; central; chief; finest; first-class; foremost; great; key; leading; main; major; most important; principal; superior.* • She called it a tragedy of the first order. *She called it a major tragedy.*

**of the same opinion** *at one.*

**of (a; the) . . . variety** delete. • Snow of the heavy variety is now falling. *Heavy snow is now falling.*

**(a; the) . . . of which** *whose.* • It is one of the few gifts the value of which can be juggled successfully to get greater leverage. *It is one of the few gifts whose value can be juggled successfully to get greater leverage.*

**old adage** *adage.* • As the old adage says, "Patriotism is the last refuge of a scoundrel." *As the adage says, "Patriotism is the last refuge of a scoundrel."*

**old cliché** *cliché.* • Must you always rely on such old clichés? *Must you always rely on such clichés?*

**old maxim** *maxim.* • Your analysis of that proposal vividly demonstrates an old maxim: For every complex problem, there is an answer that is absolutely obvious, absolutely simple, and absolutely wrong. *Your analysis of that proposal vividly demonstrates a maxim: For every complex problem, there is an answer that is absolutely obvious, absolutely simple, and absolutely wrong.*

**old proverb** *proverb.* • He referred to the old proverb: If I give you a fish, you will eat for a day; if I teach you to fish, you will eat for a lifetime. *He referred to the proverb: If I give you a fish, you will eat for a day; if I teach you to fish, you will eat for a lifetime.*

**old relic** *relic.*

**old saw** *saw.* • The essence of marginal utility boils down to the old saw that pearls don't cost a lot because men have to dive for them, but rather men dive for them because they command a high price. *The essence of marginal utility boils down to the saw that pearls don't cost a lot because men have to dive for them, but rather men dive for them because they command a high price.*

**old saying** *saying.* • The old saying "a picture is worth a thousand words" appropriately applies to computer graphics. *The saying "a picture is worth a thousand words" appropriately applies to computer graphics.*

**on a (the) . . . basis** *-(al)ly; delete.* • The exercises must be done for 20 to 25 minutes on a continuous basis. *The exercises must be done continuously for 20 to 25 minutes.* • Every exchange has a clearinghouse that transfers funds from losers to winners on a daily basis. *Every exchange has a clearinghouse that transfers funds daily from losers to winners.* • Our sole interest in the report is to be sure that each application is evaluated on a fair basis. *Our sole interest in the report is to be sure that each application is evaluated fairly.*

**on account of** *after; because of; by; due to; following; for; from; in; out of; owing to; through; with.* • There are millions of women in this country who have been discriminated against on account of their sex. *There are millions of women in this country who have been discriminated against because of their sex.*

**on account of the fact that** *because; considering; for; in that; since.* • Brown suggests that this might be on account of the fact that it posed little challenge to the homosocial order. *Brown suggests that this might be because it posed little challenge to the homosocial order.*

**on a couple of (a few) occasions** *a few times; once or twice; twice; two or three times.* • On a couple of occasions, the entire system shut down. *Once or twice, the entire system shut down.*

**on a (the) . . . note** *-(al)ly; delete.* • On a disconcerting note, 18 percent of the children surveyed said they had been approached to buy or use drugs. *Disconcertingly, 18 percent of the children surveyed said they had been approached to buy or use drugs.* • The market began the week on a cautious note. *The market began the week cautiously.*

**on a number of (any number of; frequent; many; numerous; several) occasions** *frequently; many times; numerous times; often; regularly; repeatedly; several times.* • They have done that on a number of occasions. *They have often done that.*

**on a regular basis** *bimonthly; biweekly; daily; hourly; monthly; regularly; weekly; yearly; delete.* • Does it mean we should all start taking aspirin on a regular basis? *Does it mean we should all start taking aspirin regularly?*

**on a (the) . . . scale (scope)** -*(al)ly*; delete. • We can do projects on a much larger scale today. *We can do much larger projects today.*

**on a (the) . . . scene** -*(al)ly*; delete. • On the national scene, here's what's happening. *Here's what's happening nationally.*

**on (an; the) average** *commonly; customarily; generally; normally; often; ordinarily; typically.*

**on . . . behalf (of)** *for.* • Nobody is authorized to speak on my behalf. *Nobody is authorized to speak for me.*

**once (and) for all** *conclusively; decisively; finally;* delete. • Analysts expect their questions about Raytheon's nondefense subsidiaries to be answered once and for all when Phillips' successor makes known his intentions. *Analysts expect their questions about Raytheon's nondefense subsidiaries to be finally answered when Phillips' successor makes known his intentions.*

**once in a (great) while** *at times; now and again; now and then; on occasion; sometimes.*

**on certain (some) occasions** *at times; now and again; now and then; occasionally; sometimes.* • On some occasions, the treatment may retard progression of the disease. *Sometimes, the treatment may retard progression of the disease.*

**once . . . then** *once.* • Once this analysis is done, then special attention may be paid to various short pieces of code that consume the most time. *Once this analysis is done, special attention may be paid to various short pieces of code that consume the most time.*

**on (the) condition (of; that)** *as long as; if; provided; so long as.* • The Maynard computer maker will offer a generous financial support package to 700 employees on condition that they agree to leave the company. *The Maynard computer maker will offer a generous financial support package to 700 employees provided they agree to leave the company.*

**on -day** -*day.* • All that the police know is the bank was robbed sometime on Monday morning. *All that the police know is the bank was robbed sometime Monday morning.*

**on each (every) occasion** *all; always; consistently; constantly; each; each time; for (in) each; for (in) every; every time; invariably; unfailingly;* delete.

**one and all** *all; everyone.*

**one and only** *one; only; sole.* • Is that the one and only time you have engaged in group counseling? *Is that the only time you have engaged in group counseling?*

**one and the same** *identical; one; the same.* • We do not believe that computers and communications are going to converge and become one and the same business. *We do not believe that computers and communications are going to converge and become the same business.*

**on earlier (former; previous; prior) occasions** *before; earlier; formerly; previously.* • I asked Governor Cuomo for his support, as I have on prior occasions. *I asked Governor Cuomo for his support, as I have before.*

**one best (most)** *best (most).* • Each alternative needs to be evaluated to determine which one best achieves the objective. *Each alternative needs to be evaluated to determine which best achieves the objective.*

**one-half (one-third)** *half (third).* • The data is derived from the first one-third of the observations. *The data is derived from the first third of the observations.*

**one-half (seven-eighths) of an inch** *one-half (seven-eighths) inch.* • Alternate pages are offset from the left margin by an additional one-half of an inch. *Alternate pages are offset from the left margin by an additional one-half inch.*

**one more time** *again; once more; re-.* • If you position the highlight over the first or last choice on the menu and then press the arrow key one more time, the highlight wraps around to the other end of the menu. *If you position the highlight over the first or last choice on the menu and then press the arrow key again, the highlight wraps around to the other end of the menu.*

**(the) one of** *delete.* • In the United States, such a gesture is merely one of politeness. *In the United States, such a gesture is merely politeness.* • The strategy then shifts from one of consolidation to one of integration. *The strategy then shifts from consolidation to integration.*

**one-of-a-kind** *matchless; novel; peerless; singular; special; unequaled; unique; unmatched; unrivaled.* • "Learn C Now" is a one-of-a-kind course that's designed to make beginning programmers productive quickly. *"Learn C Now" is a unique course that's designed to make beginning programmers productive quickly.*

**one single** *one; (a) single.* • Not one single college president has ever attempted to lay off a single high-paid administrator. *Not one college president has ever attempted to lay off a single high-paid administrator.*

**one (two) time(s)** *once (twice).* • We visited them two times in two days. *We visited them twice in two days.*

**(in) one way or another** *anyhow; anyway; by some means; however; in any way; in some way; in whatever way; somehow; somehow or another; some-way(s).* • He seemed deranged in one way or another. *He seemed deranged somehow.*

**(in) one way or the other** *at all; either way; in the least; in the slightest;* delete. • It didn't change my religious beliefs one way or the other. *It didn't change my religious beliefs in the least.*

**on (the) grounds that** *because; considering; for; in that; since.* • Democratic leaders oppose the tax cut on grounds that it benefits mainly the rich. *Democratic leaders oppose the tax cut since it benefits mainly the rich.*

**on ... grounds** *about; -(al)ly; on;* delete. • The proposed increase in rapid transit fares may be justified on economic grounds. *The proposed increase in rapid transit fares may be economically justified.*

**on its (the) face (of it; of things)** *apparently; appear (to); outwardly; seem (to); seemingly; superficially.* • On the face of it, no term fits the Parisian beau monde of the late 18th century better than the one invented 200 years later by Tom Wolfe. *No term seems to fit the Parisian beau monde of the late 18th century better than the one invented 200 years later by Tom Wolfe.*

**on its (the) face (of it; of things) ... appear (seem)** *appear (seem).* • On the face of it, this would appear to be a simple evaluation to make. *This would appear to be a simple evaluation to make.*

**on (a; the) ... level** *-(al)ly;* delete. • On a personal level, I cannot stand how he behaves. *Personally, I cannot stand how he behaves.* • I feel it's not possible to have a relationship with a man on a spiritual and emotional level. *I feel it's not possible to have a spiritual and emotional relationship with a man.* • In the past year, the media has gotten to know her, at least on a superficial level. *In the past year, the media has gotten to know her, at least superficially.*

**on more than one occasion** *a few times; frequently; many times; more than once; often; several times.* • I've been asked that question on more than one occasion. *I've been asked that question more than once.*

**on no consideration** *never; not ever; not once.*

**on no occasion** *never; not ever; not once.*

**on (the) one hand . . . on the other (hand)** delete. • Another way of looking at the basic strategic tradeoffs that Bell Operating Companies are facing is to look at the relationship between their competitiveness on one hand and the need to avoid conflict with various players on the other. *Another way of looking at the basic strategic tradeoffs that Bell Operating Companies are facing is to look at the relationship between their competitiveness and the need to avoid conflict with various players.*

**on one (two; three) occasion(s)** *a few times; once; once or twice; one time; several times; three times; twice; two times.* • On only one occasion in the three years of our negotiations were the Angels and Dick unable to come to a satisfactory agreement. *Only once in the three years of our negotiations were the Angels and Dick unable to come to a satisfactory agreement.*

**on . . . part** *among; by; for; from; of; -'s;* delete. • To beat them will take a great effort on our part. *To beat them will take a great effort by us.* • I think it's foolhardy on your part. *I think it's foolhardy of you.* • The shorter work hours logged by women had more to do with their heavy concentration in retail trade and service-oriented industries than a reluctance on their part to work longer hours. *The shorter work hours logged by women had more to do with their heavy concentration in retail trade and service-oriented industries than their reluctance to work longer hours.* • It was the first time I felt a real commitment on his part. *It was the first time I felt a real commitment from him.*

**on . . . terms** delete. • We are no longer on speaking terms with each other. *We are no longer speaking with each other.*

**on that (this) (particular) occasion** *at present; at that (this) time; currently; (just; right) now; presently; then; today; (just) yet;* delete.

**on the basis of** *after; based on; because of; by; due to; following; for; from; in; on; owing to; through; with.* • The Money Study segmented the U.S. adult population into five groups on the basis of financial attitudes. *The Money Study segmented, by financial attitudes, the U.S. adult population into five groups.* • Employees do not act on the basis of what management thinks, or what management thinks they think; they act on their own opinions. *Employees do not act on what management thinks, or what management thinks they think; they act on their own opinions.* • Its managers should be selected on the basis of their ability to further the company's goals and maximize its earnings. *Its managers should be selected for their ability to further the company's goals and maximize its earnings.*

**on the basis of the fact that** *because; considering; for; in that; since.*

**on the bottom of** *below; beneath; under; underneath.*

**on the contrary** *but; conversely; however; instead; not so; rather; still; whereas; yet.*

**on the decline** *abating; declining; decreasing; waning.*

**on the decrease** *abating; declining; decreasing; waning.*

**on the increase** *booming; flourishing; growing; increasing; rising.* • The Department of Revenue recently released a report on the state's economic indicators that showed personal savings are on the increase. *The Department of Revenue recently released a report on the state's economic indicators that showed personal savings are increasing.*

**on the inside of** *inside.* • An undercut could also be a recessed neck on the inside of a cylindrical hole. *An undercut could also be a recessed neck inside a cylindrical hole.*

**on (upon) the heels of** *(just; right) after; (close) behind; ensuing; following; succeeding.* • On the heels of an FBI investigation, a federal grand jury has indicted five people on charges they defrauded ComFed Savings Bank. *Following an FBI investigation, a federal grand jury has indicted five people on charges they defrauded ComFed Savings Bank.*

**on the occasion of** *if (there were); if . . . should; in case (of); should (there); were (there; . . . to); when;* delete. • The machinists' union has agreements that members of other unions will not do their work on the occasion of a strike. *The machinists' union has agreements that members of other unions will not do their work if there were a strike.*

**(something; somewhere) on the order (of)** *about; around; close to; more or less; near; nearly; or so; roughly; some;* delete. • Typically, the ratio of injury to mortality is something on the order of three or four to one. *Typically, the ratio of injury to mortality is some three or four to one.* • I counted something on the order of 50 interruptions for applause. *I counted 50 or so interruptions for applause.*

**on the order of** *akin to; close to; like; resembling; similar to; such as.* • What you won't see in Chatham is anything on the order of the commercial changes going on in other Cape towns. *What you won't see in Chatham is anything resembling the commercial changes going on in other Cape towns.*

**on the other hand** *but; by (in) contrast; conversely; however; whereas; yet;* delete. • A parallel device, on the other hand, sends or receives information in packets all at once over many data lines. *A parallel device, in contrast, sends or receives information in packets all at once over many data lines.*

**on the outside of** *outside.* • The fan blades are on the outside of the engine like a propeller, and all the air that passes inside the engine goes through the combustion chamber as in the earliest jets. *The fan blades are outside the engine like a propeller, and all the air that passes inside the engine goes through the combustion chamber as in the earliest jets.*

**on the part of** *among; by; for; from; of; -'s;* delete. • Though deliberate discrimination on the part of the Japanese is often charged, it isn't necessary to prove a discriminatory intent. *Though deliberate discrimination by the Japanese is often charged, it isn't necessary to prove a discriminatory intent.* • The effective teaching of language arts requires a commitment to excellence on the part of the classroom teacher. *The effective teaching of language arts requires a commitment to excellence from the classroom teacher.* • His apt observations point out the need for greater awareness on the part of the public of the architecture that surrounds them. *His apt observations point out the need for greater public awareness of the architecture that surrounds them.*

**on the rise** *booming; flourishing; growing; increasing; rising.* • Interest rates are on the rise in the United States, Europe, and Japan. *Interest rates are rising in the United States, Europe, and Japan.*

**on the side of** *for; with.* • The second factor working on the side of savings is the president and his wife. *The second factor working for savings is the president and his wife.*

**on the . . . side** *among; in; -(al)ly;* delete. • How would you assess the progress that she has made on the artistic side? *How would you assess the artistic progress that she has made?* • There will be some job losses on the manufacturing side, but some employees will be transferred. *There will be some job losses in manufacturing, but some employees will be transferred.*

**on the surface (of it; of things)** *apparently; appear (to); outwardly; seem (to); seemingly; superficially.*

**on the surface (of it; of things) . . . appear (seem)** *appear (seem).* • On the surface, a firm may appear to be sound—its balance sheet contains an impressive amount of current assets. *A firm may appear to be sound—its balance sheet contains an impressive amount of current assets.*

242

**on the surface of** *on.*

**on the threshold of** *about to; approaching; close to; near; nearly; verging on.*
• We are on the threshold of real educational quality and achievement. *We are verging on real educational quality and achievement.*

**on the verge of** *about to; approaching; close to; near; nearly; verging on.* • Is he or is he not on the verge of producing chemical weapons? *Is he or is he not about to produce chemical weapons?*

**on the whole** *all told; in all; overall.*

**on (upon) the whole** *almost all; chiefly; commonly; generally; greatly; in general; largely; mainly; most; mostly; most often; much; nearly all; normally; overall; typically; usually.* • On the whole, Boston's registered nurses were more likely to describe themselves as satisfied with their earnings than their counterparts in other cities. *Overall, Boston's registered nurses were more likely to describe themselves as satisfied with their earnings than their counterparts in other cities.*

**on top of (that; this)** *also; and; as well; besides; beyond that (this); even; further; furthermore; moreover; more than that (this); still more; then; too; what is more.* • On top of that, interest rates went up to 18 percent or more. *What's more, interest rates went up to 18 percent or more.*

**on (the) understanding (of; that)** *as long as; if; provided; so long as.*

**open to doubt** *arguable; debatable; disputable; doubtful; dubious; in doubt; in question; moot; questionable.*

**open to question** *arguable; debatable; disputable; doubtful; dubious; in doubt; in question; moot; questionable; uncertain; unclear; undecided; unknown; unsettled; unsure.* • His clout on Capitol Hill remains open to question. *His clout on Capitol Hill remains in doubt.*

**open up** *open.* • When you use the Note command, a window opens up. *When you use the Note command, a window opens.*

**(a; the) . . . operation** *delete.* • With the measurement of quality and quantity, process control is a fairly automatic operation. *With the measurement of quality and quantity, process control is fairly automatic.*

**operational** *active; live; running; working.*

**operative** *active; at work; effective; in action; in effect; in force; in play; working.*

**optimal (optimum)** *best.* • As organizations begin to move their R&D back and forth to various countries, it will be the responsibility of the company's tax advisors to provide counseling on the optimal tax structure for a variety of arrangements. *As organizations begin to move their R&D back and forth to various countries, it will be the responsibility of the company's tax advisors to provide counseling on the best tax structure for a variety of arrangements.*

**or anything** delete.

**or else** *or.* • Two pathnames must be specified, or else the first letter parameter will be incorrectly interpreted as a pathname. *Two pathnames must be specified, or the first letter parameter will be incorrectly interpreted as a pathname.*

**orientate(d)** *orient(ed).* • I didn't have a family-orientated family. *I didn't have a family-oriented family.*

**oriented** delete. • Some depressed people become more activity oriented. *Some depressed people become more active.*

**original coiner (originally coined)** *coiner (coined).* • Usually the identity of the original coiner of a new word is lost in the mists of history. *Usually the identity of the coiner of a new word is lost in the mists of history.*

**original creator (originally created)** *creator (created).* • An impressive number of neologisms can be traced to their original creators. *An impressive number of neologisms can be traced to their creators.*

**original founder (originally founded)** *founder (founded).*

**original inventor (originally invented)** *inventor (invented).* • The courts determined the patents were invalid on the grounds that Atanasoff was the original inventor. *The courts determined the patents were invalid on the grounds that Atanasoff was the inventor.*

**original source** *source.*

**originate** *arise; begin; start.*

**originate from** *come from; date from.*

**origination** *origin.*

**or something** delete.

**or thereabouts** *or so.*

**or whatever** delete.

**other people (persons)** *others.* • Elizabeth Taylor, among other people, has written about this topic. *Elizabeth Taylor, among others, has written about this topic.*

**other similar** *similar.* • In addition, the order permits the companies to provide electronic mail, voice messaging, and other similar services. *In addition, the order permits the companies to provide electronic mail, voice messaging, and similar services.*

**other than** *besides.*

**other than . . . also (as well)** *besides; beyond; other than.*

**other than to** *but to.*

**otherwise** *other.* • In many competitions, athletic and otherwise, the Finns and Swedes excel. *In many competitions, athletic and other, the Finns and Swedes excel.*

**out in** *in.* • I have several relatives out in the Springfield area. *I have several relatives in the Springfield area.*

**out loud** *aloud.*

**out of** *in; of.* • Three out of every four parents never visit their child's school. *Three of every four parents never visit their child's school.*

**(just) out of curiosity** delete. • Just out of curiosity, is Alexander Haig on the Minnesota ballot? *Is Alexander Haig on the Minnesota ballot?*

**out of favor** *deprecate; disapprove; disfavor; dislike; disparage.* • But he goes on to say, the time to buy them is when they are out of favor. *But he goes on to say, the time to buy them is when they are disfavored.*

**out of fear (of; that) . . . can (could; may; might; shall; should; will; would)** *lest.* • No one would be so foolish as to sell one's house out of fear that it might someday burn to the ground. *No one would be so foolish as to sell one's house lest it someday burn to the ground.*

**out of focus** *blurred; indistinct.*

**out of the ordinary** *curious; different; exceptional; extraordinary; irregular; novel; odd; rare; singular; strange; uncommon; unusual.* • Will you give me a call if anything out of the ordinary happens? *Will you give me a call if anything curious happens?*

**out of the question** *impossible; inconceivable; undoable; unthinkable.* • Returning to college was out of the question, so with nothing to do, she signed up for oil painting lessons. *Returning to college was unthinkable, so with nothing to do, she signed up for oil painting lessons.*

**out of the realm of possibility** *impossible; inconceivable; undoable; unthinkable.* • It is not out of the realm of possibility that Exxon could be facing a billion dollars or more in punitive damages. *It is not impossible that Exxon could be facing a billion dollars or more in punitive damages.*

**outside of** *outside.* • Chase Manhattan and Bank of America are following a similar strategy, with less emphasis on domestic markets outside of the United States. *Chase Manhattan and Bank of America are following a similar strategy, with less emphasis on domestic markets outside the United States.*

**over again** *again; afresh; anew; once more; over; re-.* • They asked me to do it over again. *They asked me to do it over.*

**overall look (view)** *overview.* • The introduction gives the readers an overall view of your business and what you want to achieve. *The introduction gives the readers an overview of your business and what you want to achieve.*

**over and above** *besides; beyond; more than; over.* • Anesthesia doesn't add to the risk over and above that of the surgery itself and the extent of the medical problem the patient already has. *Anesthesia doesn't add to the risk more than that of the surgery itself and the extent of the medical problem the patient already has.*

**over and done with** *complete; done; ended; finished; over; past.* • I just want this to be over and done with. *I just want this to be over.*

**over and over (again)** *frequently; often; recurrently; regularly; repeatedly.* • Professor Sommers refers over and over to a "bag of virtues." *Professor Sommers refers often to a "bag of virtues."*

**overly** *over-.* • We thought he was overly enthusiastic about winning. *We thought he was overenthusiastic about winning.*

**over the course (duration; length) of** *during; for; in; over; throughout; when; while; with.* • Over the duration of the project, we expect there will be some disruption due to noise, dirt, and dust. *During the project, we expect there will be some disruption due to noise, dirt, and dust.*

**over the fact that** *because; for; in that; since; that;* delete. • I am concerned over the fact that they made us work so hard. *I am concerned that they made us work so hard.*

**over the long haul** *at length; eventually; in the end; in time; later; long-term; one day; over the months (years); over time; someday; sometime; ultimately; with time; yet.* • Over the long haul, I still believe that housing is a good investment. *I still believe that housing is a good long-term investment.*

**over the short haul** *at first; at present; before long; currently; directly; for now; in (over) a month (week); initially; next month (year); (just; right) now; presently; quickly; shortly; short-term; soon; straightaway; this month (year); tomorrow;* delete. • Industry analysts say they expect the new rules to have little impact, at least over the short haul. *Industry analysts say they expect the new rules to have little impact, at least initially.*

**(an; the) overwhelming (vast) consensus (of opinion)** *consensus.*

**(an; the) overwhelming (vast) preponderance (of)** *a good (great) deal (of); a good (great) many (of); almost all (of); (nine) in (ten) (of); many (of); most (of); much (of); nearly all (of); (43) of (48) (of); (67) percent (of); three-fourths (two-thirds) (of);* delete. • A recent poll showed that a vast preponderance of city councilors oppose the relocation. *A recent poll showed that almost all city councilors oppose the relocation.*

**over with** *complete; done; ended; finished; over; past.*

**owing to the fact that** *because; considering; for; in that; since.* • However, owing to the fact that NRDC is a well-thought-of organization, capable of good quality research, we're clearly going to go through their report carefully. *However, since NRDC is a well-thought-of organization, capable of good quality research, we're clearly going to go through their report carefully.*

# P

**pack together** *pack.* • Recent advances have made it possible to pack thousands, even millions, of transistors together on a single silicon chip. *Recent advances have made it possible to pack thousands, even millions, of transistors on a single silicon chip.*

**(a) pair of twins** *twins.* • Such a proximity is literalized in the documentation of the plight of Viet and Duc, a pair of twins joined at the abdomen and sharing a leg. *Such a proximity is literalized in the documentation of the plight of Viet and Duc, twins joined at the abdomen and sharing a leg.*

**parameter** *boundary; limit.*

**par for the course** *normal; typical; usual.*

**part and parcel** *part.* • This generalized tendency to place conflicts in the outside world is part and parcel of a well-known mechanism of the mind called projection. *This generalized tendency to place conflicts in the outside world is part of a well-known mechanism of the mind called projection.*

**partially** *partly.* • My difficulty with her is partially due to a clash of personalities. *My difficulty with her is partly due to a clash of personalities.*

**particular** delete. • We would hope that you have already found a new church home that you can serve and that can meet your needs at this particular time in your life. *We would hope that you have already found a new church home that you can serve and that can meet your needs at this time in your life.*

**pass away (on)** *die.*

**passing craze (fad; fancy)** *craze (fad; fancy).*

**passing phase** *phase.*

**pass judgment (sentence) on (upon)** *judge (sentence).* • Passing judgment on one's potential earnings is even more painful than passing judgment on a former colleague. *Judging one's potential earnings is even more painful than judging a former colleague.*

**past (previous; prior) accomplishment** *accomplishment.* • It is startling that he supposes some imagined past accomplishment of his should exempt him from paying rent. *It is startling that he supposes some imagined accomplishment of his should exempt him from paying rent.*

**past (previous; prior) achievement** *achievement.*

**past (previous; prior) experience** *experience.* • A shortage of workers for jobs requiring little skill is forcing some employers to hire people without considering their references, past experience, or education. *A shortage of workers for jobs requiring little skill is forcing some employers to hire people without considering their references, experience, or education.*

**past (previous; prior) history** *history.* • Even though forecasts deal with the future, past history is not irrelevant. *Even though forecasts deal with the future, history is not irrelevant.*

**past (previous; prior) performance** *performance.* • Normally, one judges the ability to succeed based on past performance. *Normally, one judges the ability to succeed based on performance.*

**past (previous; prior) practice** *practice.* • But in keeping with past practice for such flights, the Pentagon is expected to announce a three-hour launch-window early this week. *But in keeping with practice for such flights, the Pentagon is expected to announce a three-hour launch-window early this week.*

**past (previous; prior) precedent** *precedent.* • Based on past precedent, Mr. Indelicato would likely serve between 12 and 18 months in prison. *Based on precedent, Mr. Indelicato would likely serve between 12 and 18 months in prison.*

**past (previous; prior) record** *record.* • Both the summer's drought and the fire's extent surpassed all previous records in the park. *Both the summer's drought and the fire's extent surpassed all records in the park.*

**patchwork quilt** *patchquilt; patchwork.* • The question then becomes how to organize this patchwork quilt of topics. *The question then becomes how to organize this patchwork of topics.*

**pathetical** *pathetic.*

**pathological** *pathologic.* • Even though this response is accompanied by redness, warmth, and pain, it is not naturally a pathological process. *Even though this response is accompanied by redness, warmth, and pain, it is not naturally a pathologic process.*

**pay attention to** *attend to; consider; hearken to; heed; listen to; mind; note; notice; observe; regard; see; tend to; watch; witness.* • We need to pay attention to the image we're projecting. *We need to consider the image we're projecting.*

**pay a visit to** *visit.* • Pay a visit to your nearest McDonald's. *Visit your nearest McDonald's.*

**pay heed to** *attend to; consider; hearken to; heed; listen to; mind; note; notice; observe; regard; see; tend to; watch; witness.* • Many Americans have paid heed to the results of research and changed their ways of living remarkably. *Many Americans have heeded the results of research and changed their ways of living remarkably.*

**peace and quiet** *peace; quiet.* • South Korea's four major parties declared a one-month political truce yesterday to assure peace and quiet during this month's Summer Olympics. *South Korea's four major parties declared a one-month political truce yesterday to assure peace during this month's Summer Olympics.*

**penetrate into** *penetrate.*

**per** *a.* • According to this study, the average executive spends 11 weeks per year reading memos. *According to this study, the average executive spends 11 weeks a year reading memos.*

**percentage point (unit)** *percent; point (unit).* • The U.S. Labor Department reported that the September unemployment rate fell 0.2 percentage points, to 5.4 percent. *The U.S. Labor Department reported that the September unemployment rate fell 0.2 points, to 5.4 percent.*

**per each (every)** *per.* • NYNEX will deliver your message for just ten cents per each message. *NYNEX will deliver your message for just ten cents per message.*

**perfect (perfectly) match** *duplicate; exact; identical; match; (the) same.* • Spreadsheets and television may seem unlikely partners, but if what's going on at the Tulsa, Oklahoma, offices of United Video is anything to go by, they are a perfect match. *Spreadsheets and television may seem unlikely* *partners, but if what's going on at the Tulsa, Oklahoma, offices of United Video is anything to go by, they are a match.*

**perform (a; the) . . . of** *do;* delete. • He performed an extensive analysis of the financing patterns of U.S. corporations. *He extensively analyzed the financing patterns of U.S. corporations.* • Then perform a comparison of the two disks. *Then compare the two disks.*

**perhaps . . . may (might)** *may (might); perhaps.* • Perhaps you may want to reread our introductions and note places where we have traded in our role as guides for one as "tour directors." *You may want to reread our introductions and note places where we have traded in our role as guides for one as "tour directors."*

**periodical** *periodic.*

**(a; the) period (time) of** delete. • After the shock comes a period of doubt and resignation. *After the shock comes doubt and resignation.*

**permit . . . to** *let.*

**(a; the) . . . person** delete. • You do not need to be a gourmet cook or model housecleaner to be a worthwhile person. *You do not need to be a gourmet cook or model housecleaner to be worthwhile.*

**personal belief (opinion; point of view; view; viewpoint)** *belief (opinion; point of view; view; viewpoint).* • My personal opinion is that he should be publicly scolded for his actions. *My opinion is that he should be publicly scolded for his actions.*

**personal bias** *bias.* • Some experts do inject personal bias into the process. *Some experts do inject bias into the process.*

**personal charm** *charm.*

**personal feeling** *feeling.* • What are your personal feelings about this? *What are your feelings about this?*

**personal friend (friendship)** *friend (friendship).* • She is a personal friend of mine. *She is a friend of mine.*

**personal rapport** *rapport.* • Account managers are advised to develop a personal rapport with their clients. *Account managers are advised to develop a rapport with their clients.*

**pertain (pertaining) to** *about; as for; as to; concerning; for; in; of; on; over; regarding; to; toward; with.* • An assets management system can answer these what-if budget questions pertaining to equipment. *An assets management system can answer these what-if budget questions about equipment.*

**pharmacological** *pharmacologic.*

**phone up** *phone.*

**physiological** *physiologic.* • It is believed that anxiety is expressed through physiological processes rather than symbolically through coping mechanisms. *It is believed that anxiety is expressed through physiologic processes rather than symbolically through coping mechanisms.*

**pick and choose** *choose; cull; pick; select.* • Its organization into independent topics that you can pick and choose from allows you to use it in a one-semester course. *Its organization into independent topics that you can pick from allows you to use it in a one-semester course.*

**pick up the phone (telephone) and call** *call; phone.* • Buying or selling ownership in a corporation is simply a matter of picking up the phone and calling a stockbroker, who can, within minutes, buy or sell stock listed on a stock exchange. *Buying or selling ownership in a corporation is simply a matter of calling a stockbroker, who can, within minutes, buy or sell stock listed on a stock exchange.*

**place (put) (a) . . . (in; into; on; under; upon)** delete. • In determining the relative quality of municipal securities, many investors place great reliance on the rating provided by the two major rating agencies. *In determining the relative quality of municipal securities, many investors greatly rely on the rating provided by the two major rating agencies.* • The Act only covers the actual cost of cleaning up pollution damage, and does not put a limit on compensation claims from third parties. *The Act only covers the actual cost of cleaning up pollution damage, and does not limit compensation claims from third parties.*

**place (put) a burden on (upon)** *burden; encumber; hamper; hinder; oppress; overtax; strain; tax; weigh down.* • The result can be the gradual accumulation of policies and practices that, like a bad diet, overload the organs and place burdens on the members struggling to keep it alive. *The result can be the gradual accumulation of policies and practices that, like a bad diet, overload the organs and burden the members struggling to keep it alive.*

**place (put) a premium on (upon)** *appreciate; cherish; esteem; prize; respect; treasure; value.* • Like our staff members, who place a premium on their intellectual and professional independence, our clients made it clear that they consider it essential to be able to work with us without concern about any conflicting interests. *Like our staff members, who prize their intellectual and professional independence, our clients made it clear that they consider it essential to be able to work with us without concern about any conflicting interests.*

**place (put) a priority on (upon)** *esteem; favor; prefer; prize; treasure; value.*

**place (put) a strain on (upon)** *burden; encumber; hamper; hinder; oppress; overtax; strain; tax; weigh down.* • Hot weather puts a strain on the heart and can lead to exhaustion, heart failure, and stroke. *Hot weather overtaxes the heart and can lead to exhaustion, heart failure, and stroke.*

**place (put) a value on (upon)** *appreciate; cherish; esteem; prize; respect; treasure; value.*

**place (put) credence in** *accept; believe; credit.* • A physical model of health and illness was emphasized that didn't place credence in the idea that our thinking and health were related. *A physical model of health and illness was emphasized that didn't accept the idea that our thinking and health were related.*

**place (put) . . . in danger** *endanger; imperil; jeopardize.* • I would prefer a plan that doesn't put people in danger. *I would prefer a plan that doesn't endanger people.*

**place (put) . . . in jeopardy** *endanger; imperil; jeopardize.* • The opposition Liberal Party, two weeks away from a crucial general election, has strengthened its position among voters and placed the U.S.-Canada trade agreement in serious jeopardy. *The opposition Liberal Party, two weeks away from a crucial general election, has strengthened its position among voters and seriously endangered the U.S.-Canada trade agreement.*

**place (put) . . . in (into) peril** *endanger; imperil; jeopardize.* • To do otherwise would invite serious trouble and even place our nation in great peril. *To do otherwise would invite serious trouble and even greatly imperil our nation.*

**place (put) into question** *challenge; contradict; dispute; doubt; question.*

**place of business (employment; work)** *business; company; firm; job; office; work; workplace.* • The defendant indicated that he intended to call two witnesses to testify to having overheard Janice yelling at the defendant at his place of employment, a restaurant where the witnesses also worked. *The defendant indicated that he intended to call two witnesses to testify to* *having overheard Janice yelling at the defendant at his workplace, a restaurant where the witnesses also worked.*

**place (put) restrictions on (upon)** *bind; compel; force; obligate; restrict.*

**place (put) stress on (upon)** *strain; stress.* • Fasting places great stress on your body. *Fasting greatly stresses your body.*

**place (put) under obligation** *bind; compel; force; obligate; restrict.*

**plain and simple** *clear; obvious; plain; simple.* • Associating tobacco with the pastoral joy of watching a baseball game or a golf or tennis tournament is plainly and simply false advertising. *Associating tobacco with the pastoral joy of watching a baseball game or a golf or tennis tournament is clearly false advertising.*

**plan ahead** *plan.* • If people would plan ahead, they wouldn't be confronted by these crisis situations. *If people would plan, they wouldn't be confronted by these crisis situations.*

**plan in advance** *plan.* • Plan carefully in advance so that you know exactly when to start and stop the tape. *Plan carefully so that you know exactly when to start and stop the tape.*

**plan of action (attack; battle)** *action; course; direction; intention; method; move; plan; policy; procedure; route; scheme; strategy.* • Environmentalists say their failure to agree on a plan of battle raises doubts about whether they are up to the challenge. *Environmentalists say their failure to agree on a strategy raises doubts about whether they are up to the challenge.*

**plan out** *plan.* • It pays in the long run to plan out your career. *It pays in the long run to plan your career.*

**plans and specifications** *plans; specifications.* • A contractor entered into a written agreement to construct a building according to plans and specifications prepared by the architect. *A contractor entered into a written agreement to construct a building according to plans prepared by the architect.*

**plummet down** *down; plummet.* • I can provide a litany of cases where competition has brought prices plummeting down. *I can provide a litany of cases where competition has brought prices plummeting.*

**plunge down** *down; plunge.*

**(a; the) plurality (of)** *almost all (of); (nine) in (ten) (of); many (of); more (of); most (of); nearly all (of); (43) of (48) (of); (67) percent (of); three-fourths* *(two-thirds) (of).* • The poll also found that 89 percent of Americans would not want to be president, and a plurality would not want their children to be. *The poll also found that 89 percent of Americans would not want to be president, and 60 percent would not want their children to be.*

**(3:00) P.M. . . . afternoon (evening; night)** *afternoon (evening; night); (3:00) P.M.* • It was 2 P.M. in the afternoon before we got to see her. *It was 2 P.M. before we got to see her.*

**poetical** *poetic.*

**point of departure** *starting point.*

**point of view** *attitude; belief; opinion; position; posture; stand; standpoint; vantage; view; viewpoint.* • In the United States, there is an increase in sympathy for the Palestinian point of view. *In the United States, there is an increase in sympathy for the Palestinian viewpoint.*

**point to the conclusion** *indicate; show; signal; signify; suggest.*

**polish up** *polish.*

**polite euphemism** *euphemism.* • Even its fans call it "difficult" and "uningratiating," polite euphemisms for off the wall, a very appropriate pun to describe this museum-proof collection of dirt piles, rusted girders and "conceptual" creations. *Even its fans call it "difficult" and "uningratiating," euphemisms for off the wall, a very appropriate pun to describe this museum-proof collection of dirt piles, rusted girders and "conceptual" creations.*

**popular consensus** *consensus.* • The opportunity to conduct a rigorous drug trial can only come early in a drug's life, before a popular consensus develops. *The opportunity to conduct a rigorous drug trial can only come early in a drug's life, before a consensus develops.*

**position** *job.*

**(a; the) . . . position** delete. • In the mid-1980s, they began a succession of investments in Telerate, which had a monopoly position in the distribution of quotations on U.S. government securities. *In the mid-1980s, they began a succession of investments in Telerate, which had a monopoly in the distribution of quotations on U.S. government securities.*

**positive assurance** *assurance.* • Through the end of last week, we received positive assurances the vote would go through, which makes this doubly frustrating. *Through the end of last week, we received assurances the vote would go through, which makes this doubly frustrating.*

**positive feelings** *affection; attraction; confidence; esteem; faith; favor; fondness; hope; interest; liking; love; regard; tenderness; trust.* • I'm anticipating this launch with positive feelings. *I'm anticipating this launch with confidence.*

**possess (a; the) . . . (about; for; of; on; over)** *have; own;* delete. • If teachers do not possess a firm understanding of both science content and science curriculum goals, even the best of assessments will not be sufficient to guide their classroom instruction. *If teachers do not firmly understand both science content and science curriculum goals, even the best of assessments will not be sufficient to guide their classroom instruction.*

**possibly may (might)** *may (might).* • Swaggart possibly may decide to start his own church. *Swaggart may decide to start his own church.*

**posterior to** *after; behind; following; later.*

**potentiality** *potential.* • All these tools have the same power sources, materials, and styling, and most important, each has identical market potentiality. *All these tools have the same power sources, materials, and styling, and most important, each has identical market potential.*

**pouring (down) rain** *pouring.* • It'll probably be pouring down rain at the lake. *It'll probably be pouring at the lake.*

**predicate on (upon)** *base on.*

**predict ahead of time (beforehand; in advance)** *predict.* • I'm not privy to the secret of how to predict ahead of time who will succeed. *I'm not privy to the secret of how to predict who will succeed.*

**predict . . . future** *forecast; foretell; predict.* • No one, not the fund manager, not the investor, can predict the future course of financial markets. *No one, not the fund manager, not the investor, can predict the course of financial markets.*

**predominant (predominantly)** *almost all; chief; chiefly; generally; in general; largely; main; mainly; most; mostly; most often; nearly all.* • The social structure of this country is predominantly white. *The social structure of this country is largely white.*

**prefer . . . as opposed to (instead of; rather than)** *prefer . . . over; prefer . . . to.* • Most people in any way connected to tourism speak English and prefer to do so rather than deal with a foreigner's French. *Most people in any way connected to tourism speak English and prefer doing so to dealing with a foreigner's French.* • Nurses who prefer listening and comprehension as opposed to verbalization generally experience the most productive and satisfying interactions. *Nurses who prefer listening and comprehension over verbalization generally experience the most productive and satisfying interactions.*

**preliminary draft** *draft.* • He gave me the preliminary draft of their report to review. *He gave me the draft of their report to review.*

**preliminary to** *before.*

**premises** *building; house; office; store.*

**preparation (prepare) . . . ahead of time (before; beforehand; in advance)** *preparation (prepare) . . . for.* • We did not prepare these people for this ahead of time. *We did not prepare these people for this.*

**prepare (for) . . . ahead of time (before; beforehand; in advance)** *prepare (for).* • Try to anticipate problems and prepare for them in advance. *Try to anticipate problems and prepare for them.*

**preplan** *plan.* • In short programs, much of the cognitive input or preplanning takes place on the trainees' own time, thus keeping the seminar to the shortest possible number of hours. *In short programs, much of the cognitive input or planning takes place on the trainees' own time, thus keeping the seminar to the shortest possible number of hours.*

**present (a; the) . . . (of; on; to)** *(v)* delete. • We present a summary of the key trends that are important to monitor in the future. *We summarize the key trends that are important to monitor in the future.* • Increased competition, shrinking profit margins, and escalating costs are presenting challenges to management. *Increased competition, shrinking profit margins, and escalating costs are challenging management.*

**present everywhere** *all over; everywhere; omnipresent; ubiquitous; widespread.* • Talk about sex is present everywhere. *Talk about sex is ubiquitous.*

**present incumbent** *incumbent.*

**presently** *quickly; shortly; soon.*

**presently** *(just; right) now; today; (just) yet;* delete. • No one is presently available to answer your call. *No one is available just yet to answer your call.*

**present with** *give.* • The disabled people met with James O'Leary, MBTA general manager, and presented him with a list of 19 demands. *The disabled people met with James O'Leary, MBTA general manager, and gave him a list of 19 demands.*

**pressurize** *pressure.*

**pretty** delete. • It's pretty awesome to think of a single gene abnormality that can accelerate the age for a heart attack by 50 years. *It's awesome to think of a single gene abnormality that can accelerate the age for a heart attack by 50 years.*

**preventative** *preventive.* • The idea of preventative training seems to be a necessity in any educational program. *The idea of preventive training seems to be a necessity in any educational program.*

**previous (previously)** *ago; before; earlier;* delete. • We are no closer to resolution than we were three years previously. *We are no closer to resolution than we were three years ago.*

**previous to** *before.* • Previous to yesterday, there was no reason to sound an alarm. *Before yesterday, there was no reason to sound an alarm.*

**primary (primarily)** *almost all; chief; chiefly; largely; main; mainly; most; mostly; most often; nearly all.* • The assumption is that foreign customers are primarily interested in product availability. *The assumption is that foreign customers are mainly interested in product availability.*

**principal (principally)** *almost all; chief; chiefly; largely; main; mainly; most; mostly; most often; nearly all.*

**prior approval (consent)** *approval (consent).* • This Software is licensed only to you, the Licensee, and may not be transferred to anyone without the prior written consent of Microsoft. *This Software is licensed only to you, the Licensee, and may not be transferred to anyone without the written consent of Microsoft.*

**prioritize** *arrange; list; order; rank; rate.* • By prioritizing your objectives, devising your plan, and controlling your expenditures, you should be able to build your net worth over the course of your career. *By ranking your objectives, devising your plan, and controlling your expenditures, you should be able to build your net worth over the course of your career.*

**prior to** *before.* • Prior to the sixteenth century, unknown quantities were represented by words. *Before the sixteenth century, unknown quantities were represented by words.*

**prior to that (the; this) time (of)** *before; before now (then).* • We will not pay for transportation expenses incurred prior to that time. *We will not pay for transportation expenses incurred before then.*

**probability** *chance; likelihood; prospect.* • Others may be less familiar with the model or unfamiliar with the program, thus increasing the probability of mistakes. *Others may be less familiar with the model or unfamiliar with the program, thus increasing the likelihood of mistakes.*

**problematical** *problematic.* • Since the U.K. banking industry was both mature and increasingly competitive, the clear differentiation of services was becoming problematical. *Since the U.K. banking industry was both mature and increasingly competitive, the clear differentiation of services was becoming problematic.*

**(a; the) . . . procedure** delete. • Autocorrelation analysis is a useful procedure for identifying the existence and shape of a trend. *Autocorrelation analysis is useful for identifying the existence and shape of a trend.*

**proceed** *go; move; run; walk.*

**(then) . . . proceed (to)** *later; next; then;* delete. • He took my number, which he proceeded to lose. *He took my number, which he later lost.* • When you are ill, you don't read the medical encyclopedia, diagnose your case, and then proceed to doctor yourself. *When you are ill, you don't read the medical encyclopedia, diagnose your case, and then doctor yourself.*

**proceed ahead (forward; on; onward)** *advance; continue; go on; move on; proceed; progress.* • We ran into a brick wall on getting the kind of commitment from a big player that we felt was necessary to proceed ahead. *We ran into a brick wall on getting the kind of commitment from a big player that we felt was necessary to proceed.*

**(a; the) . . . process** delete. • It's been a gradual process. *It's been gradual.* • The assessment process involves rigorously examining the methods used. *Assessment involves rigorously examining the methods used.* • Getting into the honesty business, in short, can be an expensive and arduous process. *Getting into the honesty business, in short, can be expensive and arduous.* • Doctors should not dismiss complaints of incontinence as an inevitable part of the aging process. *Doctors should not dismiss complaints of incontinence as an inevitable part of aging.*

**procure** *get.*

**produce (a; the) . . . (of; to)** delete. • The model is an analytic framework that produces estimates of future sales. *The model is an analytic framework that estimates future sales.*

**proffer** *give; offer.* • An interesting response to the pricing dilemma has been proffered by several traditional broker-distributed fund sponsors. *An interesting response to the pricing dilemma has been offered by several traditional broker-distributed fund sponsors.*

**profitability (profitableness)** *profits.* • The strategy for achieving higher profitability was simple: Organize our businesses around the customer, not the product. *The strategy for achieving higher profits was simple: Organize our businesses around the customer, not the product.*

**progress ahead (forward; on; onward)** *advance; continue; go on; move on; proceed; progress.*

**project out** *project.* • The movement of endolymph in the cochlea results in displacement of tiny hairs projecting out from specialized sensory cells. *The movement of endolymph in the cochlea results in displacement of tiny hairs projecting from specialized sensory cells.*

**protestation** *protest.* • Despite Solomon's protestation, the five-member board is expected to consider changing its rules, which also prohibit CPAs from taking commissions. *Despite Solomon's protest, the five-member board is expected to consider changing its rules, which also prohibit CPAs from taking commissions.*

**protrude out** *protrude.*

**proven** *(v) proved.* • The exact number of data points has not yet been proven. *The exact number of data points has not yet been proved.*

**proven fact** *fact; proof.* • That's a proven fact. *That's a fact.*

**prove of benefit to** *benefit.*

**provide (a; the) . . . (for; of; to)** delete. • This book provides a review of those techniques. *This book reviews those techniques.* • Nurses check with other members of the health team when they are unable to provide answers to questions. *Nurses check with other members of the health team when they are unable to answer questions.* • The size of the resulting MSE provides an indication of whether additional information is needed. *The size of the resulting MSE indicates whether additional information is needed.*

**provided (providing) (that)** *if.* • You can use the same filename more than once provided that the files are stored in different directories. *You can use the same filename more than once if the files are stored in different directories.*

**provide . . . with** *give.* • It provides us with a starting point for our analysis. *It gives us a starting point for our analysis.*

**proximity** *closeness; nearness.* • Its proximity to the edge of the street and the limits of one's field of vision restrict how much of it one can see. *Its nearness to the edge of the street and the limits of one's field of vision restrict how much of it one can see.*

**psychiatrical** *psychiatric.*

**psychical** *psychic.*

**psychoanalytical** *psychoanalytic.*

**psychobiological** *psychobiologic.*

**psychometrical** *psychometric.*

**psychopathological** *psychopathologic.*

**psychophysiological** *psychophysiologic.*

**purchase** *buy.* • Why would a sensitive, intelligent woman purchase a handgun? *Why would a sensitive, intelligent woman buy a handgun?*

**pure and simple** *pure; simple.*

**pure (and) unadulterated** *pure; simple; unadulterated.* • This movie is pure, unadulterated blasphemy. *This movie is pure blasphemy.*

**pursuant to** *by; following; under.* • Licenses issued pursuant to this Article shall be issued for terms not exceeding one year. *Licenses issued under this Article shall be issued for terms not exceeding one year.*

**put a halt to** *cease; close; complete; conclude; end; finish; halt; settle; stop.* • Before things get out of hand again this year, let's try to put a halt to it now. *Before things get out of hand again this year, let's try to halt it now.*

**put an end to** *cease; close; complete; conclude; end; finish; halt; settle; stop.* • In the last century, liberals fought to put an end to the cruel traffic in human flesh known as slavery. *In the last century, liberals fought to end the cruel traffic in human flesh known as slavery.*

**(to) put (it) another way** *namely; that is; to wit.*

**put a stop to** *cease; close; complete; conclude; end; finish; halt; settle; stop.* • I want you to put a stop to all of this nonsense. *I want you to stop all of this nonsense.*

**put . . . finger on (upon)** *identify.*

**put forth** *advance; exert; give; offer; present; propose; submit; suggest.* • Their employees, free to put forth their best efforts, thrive in this environment. *Their employees, free to give their best efforts, thrive in this environment.*

**put forward** *advance; give; offer; present; propose; submit; suggest.*

**put in alphabetical order** *alphabetize.* • Suppose we have a list of words that we want to put in alphabetical order. *Suppose we have a list of words that we want to alphabetize.*

**put in an appearance** *appear; arrive; attend; come; show up; visit.*

**put into effect** *effect; make; perform; produce.* • Quaker Fabrics Corp. said it would put into effect cost-cutting measures that specifically exclude personnel reductions. *Quaker Fabrics Corp. said it would effect cost-cutting measures that specifically exclude personnel reductions.*

**put on an act** *feign; pretend.*

**put together** *assemble; build; construct; create; devise; fashion; form; mold; set up; shape.* • Thus far, KKR has put together four of the largest leveraged buyouts in history. *Thus far, KKR has fashioned four of the largest leveraged buyouts in history.*

**put to sleep** *destroy; kill.*

**put two and two together** *conclude; deduce; draw; infer; reason.*

**put up with** *abide; bear; endure; stand; suffer; tolerate.*

**puzzlement** *puzzle.*

# Q

**qualified expert** *expert.*

**question mark** *enigma; mystery; puzzle; question; unknown.* • For scientists trying to forecast how the world will react to the burgeoning burden of greenhouse gases, clouds pose a vexing question mark. *For scientists trying to forecast how the world will react to the burgeoning burden of greenhouse gases, clouds pose a vexing question.*

**(a; the) question to answer** *question.* • The question to answer is what value should be used for the beginning periods in the series. *The question is what value should be used for the beginning periods in the series.*

**quickly expedite** *expedite.*

**quixotical** *quixotic.*

# R

**radiate out** *radiate.* • Tracks run in concentric circles around the disk, and sectors radiate out from the center in pie-shaped wedges. *Tracks run in concentric circles around the disk, and sectors radiate from the center in pie-shaped wedges.*

**raise doubts about (on)** *challenge; contradict; dispute; doubt; question.*

**raise objections about (on; to)** *challenge; complain about; criticize; demur; deprecate; differ in; disagree with; disapprove of; dispute; find fault with; object to; oppose; protest; question; resent.* • Government employees raised objections to the bill, saying they were worried about getting jobs after leaving government. *Government employees objected to the bill, saying they were worried about getting jobs after leaving government.*

**raise opposition about (on; to)** *challenge; complain about; criticize; demur; deprecate; differ in; disagree with; disapprove of; dispute; find fault with; object to; oppose; protest; question; resent.* • One longs to get a wider view of the times and the people she presents, particularly the women of the period who were raising strong opposition to male authority. *One longs to get a wider view of the times and the people she presents, particularly the women of the period who were strongly deprecating male authority.*

**raise questions about (on)** *challenge; contradict; dispute; doubt; question.* • Congressional critics have raised questions about the plane's future, particularly as cost estimates have increased. *Congressional critics have questioned the plane's future, particularly as cost estimates have increased.*

**raise up** *raise.*

**range anywhere (somewhere) from . . . to** *range from . . . to.* • Estimates of sales growth in the industry this year range anywhere from 12 to 50 percent. *Estimates of sales growth in the industry this year range from 12 to 50 percent.*

**range from . . . all the way to (all the way up to; up to)** *range from . . . to.*
• The cost ranges from $500 up to $10,000. *The cost ranges from $500 to $10,000.*

**range from a low of . . . to a high of** *range from . . . to.* • The 1987 rates range from a low of 14.8 percent at St. Vincent's Hospital to a high of 35.8 percent at St. Joseph's Hospital. *The 1987 rates range from 14.8 percent at St. Vincent's Hospital to 35.8 percent at St. Joseph's Hospital.*

**rant and rave** *rant; rave.*

**rapidity** *quickness; speed.*

**rarely (seldom) ever** *rarely (seldom).*

**rationale** *reason; thinking.* • The primary rationale is that it is a necessary condition for an otherwise attractive business deal. *The primary reason is that it is a necessary condition for an otherwise attractive business deal.*

**rational reason** *reason.* • There's no rational reason for astrology to work. *There's no reason for astrology to work.*

**raze to the ground** *level; raze.*

**reach (a; the) . . . (of)** delete. • The dividends question is part of the union's proxy fight with the company that is expected to reach a culmination at next week's annual meeting. *The dividends question is part of the union's proxy fight with the company that is expected to culminate at next week's annual meeting.* • We tried to reach an accommodation with both parties. *We tried to accommodate both parties.*

**reach (an; the) accord** *agree; compromise; concur; decide; resolve; settle.* • An attorney representing Eastern said the airline wants to reach an accord with the American Society of Travel Agents. *An attorney representing Eastern said the airline wants to settle with the American Society of Travel Agents.*

**reach (an; the) agreement** *agree; compromise; concur; decide; resolve; settle.* • Both he and Chandler said the two sides had reached a tentative agreement on an educational trust fund demanded by the union. *Both he and Chandler said the two sides had tentatively agreed on an educational trust fund demanded by the union.*

**reach (an; the) agreement** *agree; compromise; concur; decide; resolve; settle.*

**reach (a; the) conclusion** *conclude; decide; deduce; determine; infer; judge; reason; resolve; settle.* • The Japanese did not reach that conclusion by engaging in abstract reasoning but by observing England's industrial relations. *The Japanese did not deduce that by engaging in abstract reasoning but by observing England's industrial relations.*

**reach (a; the) decision (on; upon)** *conclude; decide; deduce; determine; infer; judge; reason; resolve; settle.* • He said the committee also is weighing the issue of who was responsible for the overstatement and probably will reach a decision within a few weeks. *He said the committee also is weighing the issue of who was responsible for the overstatement and probably will decide within a few weeks.*

**reach (a; the) determination (on; upon)** *conclude; decide; deduce; determine; infer; judge; reason; resolve; settle.*

**reach (an; the) estimate (estimation) (of)** *approximate; assess; estimate; evaluate; rate.*

**reach (an; the) opinion** *conclude; decide; deduce; determine; infer; judge; reason; resolve; settle.*

**reach (a; the) resolution (about; on);** *agree; conclude; decide; determine; resolve; settle.*

**reach (a; the) settlement** *agree; conclude; decide; resolve; settle.* • One union source said that the Justice Department and the union leadership were not likely to reach an out-of-court settlement before the start of the racketeering trial. *One union source said that the Justice Department and the union leadership were not likely to settle out of court before the start of the racketeering trial.*

**reach (an; the) understanding** *agree; compromise; concur; decide; resolve; settle.*

**read where** *read (that).*

**real (really)** delete. • We know the governor has really serious budget problems this year. *We know the governor has serious budget problems this year.*

**(a; the) real fact** *fact; truth.*

**real live** delete. • This is a real live medical problem. *This is a medical problem.*

**really (and) truly** *actually; indeed; in fact; in faith; in reality; in truth; really; truly;* delete. • They really truly did have a very unique product. *They truly did have a very unique product.*

**reason being is** *reason is.*

**(the) reason (why) . . . is because** *because; reason is (that).* • The reason the business failed was because it was undercapitalized. *The business failed because it was undercapitalized.* • Another reason why the example fails as a good strategic goal is because it violates the rule of accountability. *Another reason the example fails as a good strategic goal is it violates the rule of accountability.*

**reason (why) . . . is due to (the fact that)** *because of; due to; reason is (that).* • The reason the flooding is so bad this year is due to torrential rains and soil erosion. *The flooding is so bad this year because of torrential rains and soil erosion.*

**reason (why) . . . is that** *because.* • The reason we're so successful is that the projects we work with are good ones and we're good at working with community groups. *We're so successful because the projects we work with are good ones and we're good at working with community groups.*

**reason why** *reason.* • It's one of the reasons why we have so much misconduct, so much scandal, in government. *It's one of the reasons we have so much misconduct, so much scandal, in government.*

**rebound back** *rebound.*

**recall back** *recall.*

**receive back** *receive.* • People express doubt that they will receive back as much in benefits as they paid in Social Security taxes. *People express doubt that they will receive as much in benefits as they paid in Social Security taxes.*

**recoil back** *recoil.*

**record-breaking (high)** *record.* • The Cape is burdened with a record-breaking number of houses for sale. *The Cape is burdened with a record number of houses for sale.* • As record-breaking temperatures continue to assault the nation, people may find themselves snarling where they used to smile and being grouchy when they used to grin. *As record temperatures continue to assault the nation, people may find themselves snarling where they used to smile and being grouchy when they used to grin.*

**record-high** *record.* • Young adults are returning home to live with their parents in record-high numbers. *Young adults are returning home to live with their parents in record numbers.*

**record-setting** *record.* • That should mean a blessed end to record-setting heat and a host of problems that arose from or probably interacted with it. *That should mean a blessed end to record heat and a host of problems that arose from or probably interacted with it.*

**record-size** *record.* • It appears we've had a record-size turnout at the polls. *It appears we've had a record turnout at the polls.*

**rectify** *correct; fix; improve.* • Why can't they rectify the conditions at Danvers State Hospital? *Why can't they improve the conditions at Danvers State Hospital?*

**recur again (and again)** *recur.* • The lapse has already been corrected within our systems to ensure that the problem will not recur again. *The lapse has already been corrected within our systems to ensure that the problem will not recur.*

**reduce by (to) half** *halve.*

**reduce down** *reduce.* • Reduce the number of paid sick days from 20 down to some lower number. *Reduce the number of paid sick days from 20 to some lower number.*

**refer back** *refer.* • The reader may find it helpful to refer back to this diagram after we have completed our discussion. *The reader may find it helpful to refer to this diagram after we have completed our discussion.*

**refer to as** *call; name; term;* delete. • Unconscious attempts to manage anxiety are referred to as defense mechanisms. *Unconscious attempts to manage anxiety are termed defense mechanisms.*

**reflect back** *reflect.* • Reflecting back on my years at BB&N, I tried to understand why neither the school nor the parents were willing to give this case the publicity it deserved. *Reflecting on my years at BB&N, I tried to understand why neither the school nor the parents were willing to give this case the publicity it deserved.*

**regard (regarding)** *about; as for; as to; for; in; of; on; over; to; toward; with.* • New Jersey has no law regarding traffic circles. *New Jersey has no law on traffic circles.*

**regard as being** *regard as.*

**regardless of (what)** *despite (what); no matter what; whatever.* • Regardless of what women may accomplish one on one, the most effective agent for change is the company itself. *No matter what women may accomplish one on one, the most effective agent for change is the company itself.*

**regardless of how** *despite how; however; no matter how.* • All lines and lettering must be absolutely black regardless of how fine the lines may be. *All lines and lettering must be absolutely black despite how fine the lines may be.*

**regardless of the fact that** *although; but; even though; still; though; yet.* • Because the aquarium is a private enterprise—regardless of the fact that it is nonprofit—such a transfer is not supposed to take place. *Because the aquarium is a private enterprise—although it is nonprofit—such a transfer is not supposed to take place.*

**regardless of when** *despite when; no matter when; whenever.* • Both proposals would cover all capital assets regardless of when taxpayers bought them. *Both proposals would cover all capital assets despite when taxpayers bought them.*

**regardless of where** *despite where; no matter where; wherever.* • Visible soft hyphens appear on the screen and print out regardless of where they fall in the document. *Visible soft hyphens appear on the screen and print out wherever they fall in the document.*

**regardless of whether . . . (or)** *despite whether; no matter whether; whether . . . or (not).* • Men's masculinity, looks, and concern about their appearance were rated the same regardless of whether lunch was a salad and coffee or a five-course extravaganza. *Men's masculinity, looks, and concern about their appearance were rated the same whether lunch was a salad and coffee or a five-course extravaganza.* • Regardless of whether the reason is internal or external, it has an important bearing on the market-presence alternatives investigated. *Whether the reason is internal or external, it has an important bearing on the market-presence alternatives investigated.*

**regardless of which** *despite which; no matter which; whichever.* • Regardless of which happens, you can change the result. *Whichever happens, you can change the result.*

**regardless of who** *despite who; no matter who; whoever.* • Regardless of who we may be, we all have the right to economic opportunity. *Whoever we may be, we all have the right to economic opportunity.*

**regardless of whom** *despite whom; no matter whom; whomever.* • Regardless of whom these books are meant for, I think they should be designed and developed to look and feel more accessible. *Whomever these books are meant for, I think they should be designed and developed to look and feel more accessible.*

**regular -(al)ly** *-(al)ly.* • We attend the regular monthly meeting of the BCS. *We attend the monthly meeting of the BCS.*

**regular routine** *routine.* • Hiring, training, and record-keeping are part of the regular routine for running any business. *Hiring, training, and record-keeping are part of the routine for running any business.*

**reiterate** *iterate; repeat.* • Baker also reiterated his insistence that Bush would not debate before September 22. *Baker also repeated his insistence that Bush would not debate before September 22.*

**reiterate again (and again)** *iterate; reiterate; repeat.*

**reject as untrue** *disbelieve.*

**relate (to)** *say; tell.* • One executive related to us that in Chile he had almost single-handedly stopped a strike. *One executive told us that in Chile he had almost single-handedly stopped a strike.*

**relate back** *relate.* • This involves the activation of cognitive processes in your brain in which you think about the meaning of the words, weigh ideas, correlate new ideas with your experiences, and relate the ideas back to former material. *This involves the activation of cognitive processes in your brain in which you think about the meaning of the words, weigh ideas, correlate new ideas with your experiences, and relate the ideas to former material.*

**-related** *delete.* • This division provides telemarketing-related and other direct marketing services for clients in four areas. *This division provides telemarketing and other direct marketing services for clients in four areas.*

**relate (relating) to** *about; as for; as to; concerning; for; in; of; on; over; regarding; to; toward; with.* • We may add to the basic rental price any taxes or other governmental assessments relating to the use or operation of the postage meter or scale. *We may add to the basic rental price any taxes or other governmental assessments on the use or operation of the postage meter or scale.*

**relationship** *bond; connection; link; relation; tie.* • The photograph had no relationship to any of the elements of the story. *The photograph had no relation to any of the elements of the story.*

**relatively** *-(i)er; less; more.* • Lawyer Dukakis repeatedly has expressed disdain for the merger and acquisition business; oil man Bush seems to harbor relatively few such concerns. *Lawyer Dukakis repeatedly has expressed disdain for the merger and acquisition business; oil man Bush seems to harbor fewer such concerns.*

**relatively . . . as (when) compared to (with)** *compared to (with).* • Housing is relatively inexpensive and affordable when compared to Boston and other higher-priced nearby housing markets. *Housing is inexpensive and affordable compared to Boston and other higher-priced nearby housing markets.*

**relatively . . . compared (contrasted) to (with)** *compared (contrasted) to (with).* • Shrinkage remains relatively low compared to mass retailing standards. *Shrinkage remains low compared to mass retailing standards.*

**relatively -(i)er than (less than; more than)** *-(i)er than (less than; more than);* delete. • This country is in relatively better shape than other major industrialized nations. *This country is in better shape than other major industrialized nations.* • Its real estate portfolio grew relatively faster than anybody else's. *Its real estate portfolio grew faster than anybody else's.*

**relatively . . . in comparison (in contrast) to (with)** *compared (contrasted) to (with).* • Solving the legal problems of partnerships is relatively simple in comparison to solving the problems of other types of ownership. *Solving the legal problems of partnerships is simple compared to solving the problems of other types of ownership.*

**relative to** *about; concerning; for; on; regarding.* • We want to talk to him relative to his wife's death. *We want to talk to him about his wife's death.*

**relative to** *against; alongside; beside; compared to (with); -(i)er than; less; less than; more; more than; next to; over; than; to; versus; vis-à-vis.* • Relative to other societies, Brazil and the United States place considerable emphasis on youth. *Brazil and the United States place considerably more emphasis on youth than other societies.*

**relevancy** *relevance.* • Define the term *system,* and explain its relevancy to the study of mass communication. *Define the term* system, *and explain its relevance to the study of mass communication.*

**relic of the past** *relic.* • But for most people today, CPM is an all-but-forgotten relic of the past which is just a few years old. *But for most people today, CPM is an all-but-forgotten relic which is just a few years old.*

**remainder** *remains; rest.* • No economic indicators are due for the remainder of the week. *No economic indicators are due for the rest of the week.*

**remains to be seen** *do not know; is not (now; yet) known; is uncertain; is unclear; is unknown; is unsure.* • It remains to be seen if he can sustain a housing partnership. *It's not yet known if he can sustain a housing partnership.*

**remand back** *remand.*

**remember again** *remember.* • Remember again, ten dollars times thirty million is three hundred million dollars. *Remember, ten dollars times thirty million is three hundred million dollars.*

**remember back** *remember.* • One of the easiest ways to understand this operator is to remember back to elementary school mathematics. *One of the easiest ways to understand this operator is to remember elementary school mathematics.*

**reminisce about the past** *reminisce.*

**remit back** *remit.*

**remittance** *cash; fee; money; pay; payment; wage.*

**remunerate** *pay.*

**remuneration** *cash; fee; money; pay; payment; reward; wage.*

**render** *act; do; give; make.* • The biggest question remaining about the use of phenethanolamines is whether the drugs will contaminate meat and render it unsafe for human consumption. *The biggest question remaining about the use of phenethanolamines is whether the drugs will contaminate meat and make it unsafe for human consumption.*

**render assistance to** *help.*

**reoccur (reoccurrence)** *recur (recurrence).* • This behavior tends to reoccur every year. *This behavior tends to recur every year.* • It is even more important that more be done to protect them from the occurrence and reoccurrence of that which precipitates these disorders: sexual abuse. *It is even more important that more be done to protect them from the occurrence and recurrence of that which precipitates these disorders: sexual abuse.*

**repay back** *repay.*

**repeat again (and again)** *repeat.* • All of this is based on predictable behaviors that are repeated again and again in rather exact ways. *All of this is based on predictable behaviors that are repeated in rather exact ways.*

**repeat back** *repeat.*

**repeat occurrence** *recurrence.* • What should he do so as not to have a repeat occurrence of this? *What should he do so as not to have a recurrence of this?*

**repeat over (and over)** *repeat.* • A loop is a sequence of commands, the last of which refers the program back to the first so that the commands repeat over and over until stopped. *A loop is a sequence of commands, the last of which refers the program back to the first so that the commands repeat until stopped.*

**reply back** *reply.* • I sent her a letter and then waited two weeks for a reply back. *I sent her a letter and then waited two weeks for a reply.*

**report back** *report.* • The Insurance Division will report back to the high court within 30 days on whether to rehabilitate them in some ways or declare them insolvent. *The Insurance Division will report to the high court within 30 days on whether to rehabilitate them in some ways or declare them insolvent.*

**represents** *is.* • These numbers represent the washer's inside diameter, outside diameter, and thickness. *These numbers are the washer's inside diameter, outside diameter, and thickness.* • We believe that our offer represents a fair price and is in the best interest of Pennwalt's shareholders. *We believe that our offer is a fair price and is in the best interest of Pennwalt's shareholders.*

**require** *need.*

**requirement** *need.*

**requisite** *need.*

**reside** *dwell; live.* • I am now residing in New York City. *I am now living in New York City.*

**residence** *home; house.*

**residual trace** *trace.* • Her appearance is scarcely marred by residual traces of three massive strokes suffered when she was three-months pregnant. *Her appearance is scarcely marred by traces of three massive strokes suffered when she was three-months pregnant.*

**resiliency** *resilience.*

**respective (respectively)** delete. • Microsoft hereby limits the duration of any implied warranty (-ies) on the disk or such hardware to the respective periods stated above. *Microsoft hereby limits the duration of any implied warranty (-ies) on the disk or such hardware to the periods stated above.*

**respond back** *respond.* • I was disappointed the governor could not have responded back to me personally. *I was disappointed the governor could not have responded to me personally.*

**respond in the affirmative** *agree; say yes.* • We hope he will respond in the affirmative. *We hope he will say yes.*

**respond in the negative** *disagree; say no.*

**restore back** *restore.* • If something happens to the files on the disk that you back up, you can use the backup copies to restore files back onto it. *If something happens to the files on the disk that you back up, you can use the backup copies to restore files onto it.*

**rest up** *rest.*

**resultant** *(n) effect; result.*

**resultant effect** *effect; result.* • Concern exists over the antiandrogenic activity of cimetidine and its resultant effect on feminization of male rats. *Concern exists over the antiandrogenic activity of cimetidine and its effect on feminization of male rats.*

**resume again** *resume.*

**retain . . . position as** *remain.*

**retreat back** *retreat.* • Having conquered consumer electronics, the Japanese firms are attacking in industrial electronics, and the American firms are once again in the process of retreating back to defense electronics to get those higher returns on investment. *Having conquered consumer electronics, the Japanese firms are attacking in industrial electronics, and the American firms are once again in the process of retreating to defense electronics to get those higher returns on investment.*

**return back** *return.* • In the 1980s, we're returning back to the cultural norm of marriage and family. *In the 1980s, we're returning to the cultural norm of marriage and family.*

**reuse again** *reuse.* • If you want to create more than one graph for a model so that you can reuse them again, what must you do? *If you want to create more than one graph for a model so that you can reuse them, what must you do?*

**revert back** *revert.* • Some companies that encounter operational problems during an advanced stage may revert back to a previous stage. *Some companies that encounter operational problems during an advanced stage may revert to a previous stage.*

**root cause** *cause; reason; root; source.* • White-collar crimes, not poor economic conditions or deregulation, are the root cause of the S&L crisis. *White-collar crimes, not poor economic conditions or deregulation, are the root of the S&L crisis.*

**rough sketch** *sketch.* • A rough sketch is made to indicate the type of illustration required and the method of reproduction to be used. *A sketch is made to indicate the type of illustration required and the method of reproduction to be used.*

**routine procedure** *routine.* • There is a routine procedure that we follow. *There is a routine that we follow.*

**rules and regulations** *regulations; rules.* • Rules and regulations regarding the use of the library have been posted throughout the building. *Rules regarding the use of the library have been posted throughout the building.*

**run of the mill** *average; common; everyday; mediocre; ordinary; typical; usual.*

# S

**sad to relate (say)** *sadly.* • Sad to relate, some bicyclists have become a menace to pedestrian and motor vehicle traffic. *Sadly, some bicyclists have become a menace to pedestrian and motor vehicle traffic.*

**satirical** *satiric.* • My neighbor often makes satirical remarks about the fanaticism with which people mow and rake their lawns. *My neighbor often makes satiric remarks about the fanaticism with which people mow and rake their lawns.*

**save and except** *except; save.*

**say, for example (for instance)** *for example (for instance); say.* • Say, for example, you use a 12 percent home equity loan to finance $10,000 of an automobile purchase. *Say you use a 12 percent home equity loan to finance $10,000 of an automobile purchase.*

**scatter in all (every) direction(s)** *scatter.*

**scream and yell** *scream; yell.*

**secondarily** *second.*

**secondly** *second.* • First, be correct in your vocabulary or word choices; secondly, use standard grammar in your speeches. *First, be correct in your vocabulary or word choices; second, use standard grammar in your speeches.*

**second of all** *second.*

**seeing (as; as how; that)** *because; considering; for; in that; since.* • Seeing as how I don't have any stamps, I'm going to deliver this myself. *Since I don't have any stamps, I'm going to deliver this myself.*

**seek out** *seek.* • In most cases, we actively seek out foreign investment. *In most cases, we actively seek foreign investment.*

**seesaw back and forth (up and down)** *seesaw.* • The Hang Seng index seesawed back and forth last week as student demonstrations fueled speculation. *The*

*Hang Seng index seesawed last week as student demonstrations fueled speculation.*

**see where** *see (that).*

**select out** *choose; pick out; select.* • The other approach, selecting out for doctors' treatment those at particularly high risk, is already well established, but it has limitations. *The other approach, selecting for doctors' treatment those at particularly high risk, is already well established, but it has limitations.*

**(my)self** *(I; me).* • Richard and myself are going to lunch. *Richard and I are going to lunch.* • Very large people like yourself can eat tiny amounts of food and not lose an ounce. *Very large people like you can eat tiny amounts of food and not lose an ounce.* • Let's hope someone comes along, like myself, to take his place. *Let's hope someone comes along, like me, to take his place.* • We feel Mr. Roedler's comments do an injustice to collectors like ourselves who currently pay $1,500 to $2,000 for radios of this type. *We feel Mr. Roedler's comments do an injustice to collectors like us who currently pay $1,500 to $2,000 for radios of this type.* • Neither the mayor nor myself desires to comment on the status of the matter. *Neither the mayor nor I desire to comment on the status of the matter.*

**selfsame** *same.*

**seminal fluid** *semen.*

**(a) sense of** delete. • Our sense of foreboding grew as the afternoon wore on. *Our foreboding grew as the afternoon wore on.* • I felt a sense of helplessness when he beat me. *I felt helpless when he beat me.*

**(five; many; several) separate** *(five; many; several); separate.* • The report cites 171 separate studies, most of them conducted during the past decade, as references. *The report cites 171 studies, most of them conducted during the past decade, as references.*

**separate and apart** *apart; separate.* • We agreed that these issues ought to be separate and apart from the treaty. *We agreed that these issues ought to be separate from the treaty.*

**separate and autonomous** *autonomous; separate.*

**separate and discrete** *discrete; separate.* • We found that 58 percent of respondent worksites had a separate and discrete unit that supports end-user computing. *We found that 58 percent of respondent worksites had a discrete unit that supports end-user computing.*

**separate and distinct** *distinct; separate.* • Each of us has four separate and distinct vocabularies: a written, a spoken, a heard, and a visual vocabulary. *Each of us has four distinct vocabularies: a written, a spoken, a heard, and a visual vocabulary.*

**separate and independent** *independent; separate.* • Uncoupling is complete when the partners have defined themselves and are defined by others as separate and independent of each other. *Uncoupling is complete when the partners have defined themselves and are defined by others as independent of each other.*

**separate and individual** *individual; separate.* • A Covered Person will be fully insured for benefits under the Policy while taking an airline trip only when the fare has been charged separately and individually to the Basic or Additional Cardmember's enrolled account. *A Covered Person will be fully insured for benefits under the Policy while taking an airline trip only when the fare has been charged separately to the Basic or Additional Cardmember's enrolled account.*

**separate apart** *separate.*

**separate entity** *entity; separate.* • The artificial separation of these three dimensions is confusing when they are seen as three separate entities. *The artificial separation of these three dimensions is confusing when they are seen as three entities.*

**separate individual** *individual; separate.* • The children were never seen and treated as separate individuals. *The children were never seen and treated as individuals.*

**separate out** *separate.* • If length permits, we should separate out user input from other functions. *If length permits, we should separate user input from other functions.*

**seriously addicted** *addicted.* • I was never seriously addicted to heroin. *I was never addicted to heroin.*

**serve up** *serve.* • Can I serve you up some quiche? *Can I serve you some quiche?*

**seventy-five (75) percent (of)** *three-fourths; three-quarters.*

**shaken up** *shaken.*

**share (a; the) common** *share.* • Group action is possible in your meeting, even when everyone does not share a common understanding of the subject. *Group action is possible in your meeting, even when everyone does not share an understanding of the subject.*

**share . . . in common (with)** *share.* • U.S. research on global change shares something in common with the legendary horseman who roamed the hills of Washington Irving's Sleepy Hollow: They both appear to lack heads. *U.S. research on global change shares something with the legendary horseman who roamed the hills of Washington Irving's Sleepy Hollow: They both appear to lack heads.*

**share together** *share.* • If there is one commitment that defines him, it is the commitment that we share together. *If there is one commitment that defines him, it is the commitment that we share.*

**short and sweet** *brief; concise; pithy; short; succinct; terse.*

**short and to the point** *brief; concise; pithy; short; succinct; terse; to the point.*

**should . . . then** *should.* • Should the Department of Public Utilities concur that the blame for these plant outages rests with Boston Edison, then the company's stockholders—not the customers—must absorb the costs. *Should the Department of Public Utilities concur that the blame for these plant outages rests with Boston Edison, the company's stockholders—not the customers—must absorb the costs.*

**show (a; the) . . . (of; to)** delete. • Figure 14.3 shows a comparison of dimensions in millimeters with those in inches. *Figure 14.3 compares dimensions in millimeters with those in inches.* • The respondents preferred to retain but not retrain obsolete older employees and showed a tendency to withhold promotions from older workers. *The respondents preferred to retain but not retrain obsolete older employees and tended to withhold promotions from older workers.*

**shown at (in)** *at (in).* • Each of the sequences shown at the right is an arithmetic sequence. *Each of the sequences at the right is an arithmetic sequence.*

**shuttle back and forth between . . . and** *shuttle between . . . and.* • He shuttles back and forth between his home in New Hampshire and his office in Washington. *He shuttles between his home in New Hampshire and his office in Washington.*

**sick and tired** *annoyed; disgusted; sick; tired.*

**side by side (with)** *alongside; among; beside; next to; with.*

**significance** *import; moment.*

**significant (substantial)** *ample; big; grand; great; heavy; huge; immense; large; many; most; much; vast.* • The region began the decade with a significant surplus of power. *The region began the decade with a large surplus of power.*

**(a; the) significant (substantial) amount (of)** *a good (great) deal (of); a good (great) many (of); almost all (of); considerable; many (of); most (of); much (of); nearly all (of); vast.* • This difficulty is a major stumbling block, costing end users significant amounts of time and money. *This difficulty is a major stumbling block, costing end users much time and money.*

**(a; the) significant (substantial) degree (of)** *a good (great) deal (of); considerable; great; much (of); vast.*

**(a; the) significant (substantial) element (of)** *a good (great) deal (of); a good (great) many (of); considerable; great; many (of); much (of); vast.*

**(a; the) significant (substantial) fraction (of)** *a good (great) deal (of); a good (great) many (of); almost all (of); (nine) in (ten) (of); many (of); most (of); much (of); nearly all (of); (43) of (48) (of); (67) percent (of); three-fourths (two-thirds) (of).* • A significant fraction of leading U.S. weapons production specialists met last weekend to discuss the proposal, with predictable results. *Six of ten leading U.S. weapons production specialists met last weekend to discuss the proposal, with predictable results.*

**significant importance** *consequence; importance; significance.* • Finally, and of significant importance, he was sensitive to our concerns for minimizing the disruption to our lives inherent to most renovation projects. *Finally, and of significance, he was sensitive to our concerns for minimizing the disruption to our lives inherent to most renovation projects.*

**significantly (substantially)** *a good (great) deal; amply; far; greatly; largely; mostly; much; vastly.* • Two of the thirteen had slightly higher earnings; only three did substantially better. *Two of the thirteen had slightly higher earnings; only three did far better.*

**(a; the) significant (substantial) majority (of)** *a good (great) deal (of); a good (great) many (of); almost all (of); (nine) in (ten) (of); many (of); most (of); much (of); nearly all (of); (43) of (48) (of); (67) percent (of); three-fourths* *(two-thirds) (of)*. • A substantial majority think certain reforms would improve the present primary system. *Many think certain reforms would improve the present primary system.*

**(a; the) significant (substantial) minority (of)** *almost half (of); fewer than half (of); (one) in (three) (of); less than half (of); nearly half (of); (20) of (48) (of); one-third (one-fifth) (of); (20) percent (of).* • A significant minority of agents said that they would not sell the type of insurance our researchers requested in the amount they wanted to buy. *Eighteen of fifty agents said that they would not sell the type of insurance our researchers requested in the amount they wanted to buy.*

**(a; the) significant (substantial) number (of)** *a good (great) many (of); almost all (of); countless; dozens (of); hundreds (of); many (of); millions (of); most (of); nearly all (of); numerous; scores (of); six hundred (twelve hundred) (of); thousands (of).* • We did this because we received a substantial number of reports that the election was unfair. *We did this because we received hundreds of reports that the election was unfair.*

**(a; the) significant (substantial) part (of)** *a good (great) deal (of); a good (great) many (of); almost all (of); (nine) in (ten) (of); many (of); most (of); much (of); nearly all (of); (43) of (48) (of); (67) percent (of); three-fourths (two-thirds) (of).* • Businessland Inc. says mice represent a substantial part of its computer accessories sales. *Businessland Inc. says mice represent 8 percent of its computer accessories sales.*

**(a; the) significant (substantial) percentage (of)** *a good (great) deal (of); a good (great) many (of); almost all (of); (nine) in (ten) (of); many (of); most (of); much (of); nearly all (of); (43) of (48) (of); (67) percent (of); three-fourths (two-thirds) (of).* • The drug can cause serious kidney damage and other side effects, and a substantial percentage of patients cannot absorb it. *The drug can cause serious kidney damage and other side effects, and many patients cannot absorb it.*

**(a; the) significant (substantial) portion (of)** *a good (great) deal (of); a good (great) many (of); almost all (of); (nine) in (ten) (of); many (of); most (of); much (of); nearly all (of); (43) of (48) (of); (67) percent (of); three-fourths (two-thirds) (of).* • The company said that a significant portion of the cuts will be achieved through early retirement. *The company said that most of the cuts will be achieved through early retirement.*

**(a; the) significant (substantial) proportion (of)** *a good (great) deal (of); a good (great) many (of); almost all (of); (nine) in (ten) (of); many (of); most (of);*

*much (of); nearly all (of); (43) of (48) (of); (67) percent (of); three-fourths (two-thirds) (of).* • West German and British firms also account for a significant proportion of U.S. patents. *West German and British firms also account for many U.S. patents.*

**(a; the) significant (substantial) quantity (of)** *a good (great) deal (of); a good (great) many (of); almost all (of); dozens (of); hundreds (of); many (of); millions (of); most (of); nearly all (of); scores (of); six hundred (twelve hundred) (of); thousands (of).*

**simple (and) fundamental** *fundamental; simple.* • We welcome the opportunity to present the following two descriptions of barriers and gateways to communication, in the thought that they may help to bring the problem down to earth and show what it means in terms of simple fundamentals. *We welcome the opportunity to present the following two descriptions of barriers and gateways to communication, in the thought that they may help to bring the problem down to earth and show what it means in terms of fundamentals.*

**simply and solely** *simply; solely.* • She was fired simply and solely on account of her sex. *She was fired solely on account of her sex.*

**simultaneously** *as one; at once; collectively; concurrently; jointly; together.* • A collaborative work group is several people working on the same document simultaneously. *A collaborative work group is several people working on the same document at once.*

**simultaneously . . . while** *while.* • A dissemination system must simultaneously develop the capability of people at several levels through staff development and ongoing support while it works to create a context in schools, districts, and states. *A dissemination system must develop the capability of people at several levels through staff development and ongoing support while it works to create a context in schools, districts, and states.*

**simultaneous (simultaneously) with** *with.* • The selection of the media to be used for advertising campaigns needs to be done simultaneously with the development of message, theme, concepts, and copy. *The selection of the media to be used for advertising campaigns needs to be done with the development of message, theme, concepts, and copy.*

**(ever) since that time** *since; since then.* • Since that time, a lot has changed in my life. *A lot has since changed in my life.*

**(ever) since then** *since.* • Since then several states have passed laws against the misuse of sickle cell screening. *Several states have since passed laws against the misuse of sickle cell screening.*

**since . . . then** *since.* • Since the objective of unattended operation is quality, then the primary benefit is consistent, high-quality service. *Since the objective of unattended operation is quality, the primary benefit is consistent, high-quality service.*

**single best (biggest; fastest; greatest; largest; most)** *best (biggest; fastest; greatest; largest; most).* • Our single biggest concern is the capacity issue. *Our biggest concern is the capacity issue.* • The BSA does give its prestigious annual Harleston Parker Award for the single best new building in the Boston area. *The BSA does give its prestigious annual Harleston Parker Award for the best new building in the Boston area.*

**sink down** *sink.*

**(a; the) -sion (-tion) of (that; to)** *-ing.* • Determination of consumer's needs requires greater attention. *Determining consumer's needs requires greater attention.* • Their subordinates are nonmanagement workers—the group on which management depends for the execution of their plans. *Their subordinates are nonmanagement workers—the group on which management depends for executing their plans.* • Self-improvement and career planning both begin with an identification of your skills. *Self-improvement and career planning both begin with identifying your skills.*

**situated** *delete.* • Many of the hospital incinerators are situated in heavily populated areas. *Many of the hospital incinerators are in heavily populated areas.*

**(a; the) . . . situation** *delete.* • We are in a crisis situation. *We are in a crisis.* • If he doesn't do something, it could be an embarrassing situation for him. *If he doesn't do something, it could be embarrassing for him.*

**skilled craftsman (craftswoman)** *craftsman (craftswoman).* • High wages ensure skilled craftsmen will work on public projects, saving money in the long run on repairing shoddy work. *High wages ensure craftsmen will work on public projects, saving money in the long run on repairing shoddy work.*

**skirt around** *skirt.*

**slight trace** *trace.*

**(a; the) small (tiny) amount (degree; part; percentage; portion; proportion; quantity) (of)** *a couple (of); a few (of); a handful (of); fewer than half (of); hardly any (of); (one) in (ten) (of); less than half (of); not many (of); (9) of (48) (of); one or two (two or three) (of); one-third (one-fifteenth) (of); (12) percent (of); scarcely any (of).* • Only a small percentage of the state's bridges will be repaired. *Only one-fourth of the state's bridges will be repaired.*

**(a; the) smaller (tinier) amount (degree; part; percentage; portion; proportion; quantity) (of)** *less (of).* • Americans are spending a smaller percentage of their incomes on food than ever before. *Americans are spending less of their incomes on food than ever before.*

**(a; the) smaller (tinier) number (of)** *fewer.* • The instructor would back off, slow down, and give students a chance to follow and absorb the development of a smaller number of scientific ideas. *The instructor would back off, slow down, and give students a chance to follow and absorb the development of fewer scientific ideas.*

**(a; the) small (tiny) fraction (of)** *a couple (of); a few (of); a handful (of); fewer than half (of); hardly any (of); (one) in (ten) (of); less than half (of); not many (of); (9) of (48) (of); one or two (two or three) (of); one-third (one-fifteenth) (of); (12) percent (of); scarcely any (of).* • His deputy sold only a small fraction of his stock, not one-third as reported. *His deputy sold only one-twelfth of his stock, not one-third as reported.*

**(a; the) small (tiny) minority (of)** *a couple (of); a few (of); a handful (of); fewer than half (of); hardly any (of); (one) in (ten) (of); less than half (of); not many (of); (9) of (48) (of); one or two (two or three) (of); one-third (one-fifteenth) (of); (12) percent (of); scarcely any (of).* • A small minority may be troubled or are troublemakers. *A few may be troubled or are troublemakers.*

**(a; the) small (tiny) number (of)** *a couple; a few; eight (four); hardly any; not many; one or two (two or three); scarcely any.* • Many observers believe that by the turn of the century only a small number of giant financial supermarkets will cover the range of financial services. *Many observers believe that by the turn of the century only eight giant financial supermarkets will cover the range of financial services.*

**small (tiny) particle** *particle.* • With the high speeds and small spaces involved, even a small particle can cause the readwrite head to crash. *With the high speeds and small spaces involved, even a particle can cause the readwrite head to crash.*

**small (tiny) peccadillo** *peccadillo.*

**small-size(d)** *small.*

**so as to** *to.* • Salespeople often make their estimates low so as to keep their sales quotas down and make them easier to attain. *Salespeople often make their estimates low to keep their sales quotas down and make them easier to attain.*

**sociological** *sociologic.*

**so consequently** *consequently; hence; so; then; therefore; thus.*

**some but not all** *a few; several; some.* • Some studies, but not all, found cancerous tumors in rats and mice fed dye chemicals. *Some studies found cancerous tumors in rats and mice fed dye chemicals.*

**some day (time) in the future** *at length; eventually; in due time; in the end; in time; later; one day; over the months (years); over time; someday; sometime; ultimately; with time; yet.* • Some time in the future, the problems could precipitate a crisis—a run on the dollar, a decline in living standards—the price the United States must pay for its profligacy. *Eventually, the problems could precipitate a crisis—a run on the dollar, a decline in living standards— the price the United States must pay for its profligacy.*

**somehow or other** *in some way; somehow; someway(s).* • Somehow or other, people get used to a system, even if it takes a little time. *Somehow, people get used to a system, even if it takes a little time.*

**someplace (somewhere) else** *elsewhere.* • The meeting should run no more than two or three hours and provide obvious benefits for being there instead of somewhere else. *The meeting should run no more than two or three hours and provide obvious benefits for being there instead of elsewhere.*

**something like** *or so; some.* • Pensions and Social Security may provide, on average, something like 60 percent of the household's prior working income. *Pensions and Social Security may provide, on average, some 60 percent of the household's prior working income.*

**somewhere along the line (the way)** *at some point; at some time.* • Somewhere along the way, people got the idea that biotechnology is a magic solution to the food problem. *At some point, people got the idea that biotechnology is a magic solution to the food problem.*

**somewhere around (round)** *or so; some.*

**sooner or later** *eventually; ultimately; yet.*

**sort of** delete. • I'm sort of curious to find out what your thoughts are. *I'm curious to find out what your thoughts are.*

**so therefore** *hence; so; then; therefore; thus.*

**space consuming** *big; bulky; huge; large; massive.* • Second best are fire-resistant, locked files, which are expensive, heavy, and space consuming. *Second best are fire-resistant, locked files, which are expensive, heavy, and bulky.*

**speaking of** *about; as for; as to; for; in; of; on; over; to; toward; with.*

**speciality** *specialty.*

**specifically prescribe** *prescribe; specific.* • Verbal and unsigned instructions should be handled in a specifically prescribed manner. *Verbal and unsigned instructions should be handled in a prescribed manner.*

**springtime** *spring.*

**stall for time** *stall.*

**stand in (marked; sharp) contrast to** *clash with; conflict with; contest; contradict; contrast with; differ from; disagree with; dispute; oppose.* • That view stands in sharp contrast to those expressed by legislators and state business leaders. *That view sharply differs from those expressed by legislators and state business leaders.*

**stand in need of** *need; require.* • The country stands in need of a strong gesture in support of both science and education. *The country needs a strong gesture in support of both science and education.*

**stand in opposition to** *conflict with; contest; disagree with; disapprove of; dispute; object to; oppose; protest; resist.*

**stand in support of** *back; endorse; favor; prefer; support.* • With only 8 of the 1,176 voting delegates refusing to stand in support of the election, it appears Lee may have won the mandate he has been seeking. *With only 8 of the 1,176 voting delegates refusing to support the election, it appears Lee may have won the mandate he has been seeking.*

**stand in the way of** *block; frustrate; hinder; impede; interfere with; obstruct; prevent; thwart.* • The public health threat posed by AIDS is so great that we must find ways to overcome social and cultural taboos that stand in the way of improved AIDS prevention. *The public health threat posed by AIDS is so great that we must find ways to overcome social and cultural taboos that thwart improved AIDS prevention.*

**start off (out)** *start.* • Lotus 1-2-3 assumes that you would prefer to start off by typing information into the worksheet. *Lotus 1-2-3 assumes that you would prefer to start by typing information into the worksheet.*

**(a; the) . . . state of** delete. • All cultural dimensions of a society and individuals are in a constant state of flux. *All cultural dimensions of a society and individuals are in constant flux.*

**stereotypical** *stereotypic.* • These theorists believe women have been taught and conditioned in stereotypical role behavior that predisposes them to the development of agoraphobia. *These theorists believe women have been taught and conditioned in stereotypic role behavior that predisposes them to the development of agoraphobia.*

**stick-to-itiveness** *determination; perseverance; persistence; resolve; tenacity.* • Loyalty, empathy, diligence, and stick-to-itiveness are highly regarded, whether in a co-worker or a friend. *Loyalty, empathy, diligence, and resolve are highly regarded, whether in a co-worker or a friend.*

**still and all** *even so; still; yet.*

**still continue (endure; last; persevere; persist; prevail; remain; survive)** *continue (endure; last; persevere; persist; prevail; remain; survive); still.* • The department has set up an internal review process to deal with some of these cases, but problems still persist. *The department has set up an internal review process to deal with some of these cases, but problems persist.* • Unfortunately, that attitude still prevails today. *Unfortunately, that attitude prevails today.*

**still in existence** *current; extant; surviving.*

**stoical** *stoic.*

**straight horizontal (vertical)** *horizontal (vertical).*

**strange to relate (say)** *oddly; strangely.* • Strange to say, that interest does not seem to be more than a few hundred years old. *Strangely, that interest does not seem to be more than a few hundred years old.*

**strangle to death** *strangle.*

**stressed out** *stressed.*

**strong point (suit)** *forte.*

**study up** *study.*

**subject (topic) area (field; matter)** *area; field; subject; theme; topic.* • Each new title is arranged by subject area. *Each new title is arranged by subject.*

**subsequently** *after; afterward; later; since (then); then.* • He resigned his positions in 1963 and was subsequently jailed. *He resigned his positions in 1963 and was later jailed.* • I have subsequently learned the manner in which Mr. Satoh was chosen for the position. *I have since learned the manner in which Mr. Satoh was chosen for the position.*

**subsequent to (that; this)** *after; afterward; later; since (then); then.* • Subsequent to that, I had surgery to remove half of my stomach. *Afterward, I had surgery to remove half of my stomach.*

**subsequent to the time (of; that; when)** *after; following.* • The stock can be transferred any time subsequent to the time that a person actually receives it. *The stock can be transferred any time after a person actually receives it.*

**substantiality** *substance.* • Jackson has exhibited a remarkable degree of substantiality and common sense. *Jackson has exhibited a remarkable degree of substance and common sense.*

**substantiate** *back up; confirm; prove; support; verify.* • Recent studies clearly substantiate the health and economic advantage of car safety seat belts. *Recent studies clearly confirm the health and economic advantage of car safety seat belts.*

**substantive** *ample; big; grand; great; heavy; huge; immense; large; many; most; much; vast.* • The recent improvement in the economic well-being of most nations occurred without substantive change in the physical bulk or weight of gross national product. *The recent improvement in the economic well-being of most nations occurred without much change in the physical bulk or weight of gross national product.*

**succumb to (the) illness (injuries)** *die.* • Shortly after Harold's return, his father succumbed to the illness. *Shortly after Harold's return, his father died.*

**such as . . . and others (and so forth; and so on; and such; and the like; et al.; etc.; or whatever)** *and others (and so forth; and so on; and such; and the like; et al.; etc.; or whatever); like; such as.* • In addition to individuals, you may select a topic that informs your audience about groups of people such as skinheads, the Mafia, Motown musicians, and others. *In addition to individuals, you may select a topic that informs your audience about groups of people such as skinheads, the Mafia, and Motown musicians.* • You can explore the results of various approaches such as gross margin, markup over cost, and so on. *You can explore the results of various approaches such as gross margin and markup over cost.*

**such as . . . for example (for instance)** *as; for example (for instance); like; such as.* • One of the book's main themes is the "fact" that women were responsible for all the important contributions to the advancement of civilization (such as the development of agriculture, for instance), often despite the arrogance and stupidity of men. *One of the book's main themes is the "fact" that women were responsible for all the important contributions to the advancement of civilization (such as the development of agriculture), often despite the arrogance and stupidity of men.*

**such as (your)self** *like (you).* • It's very rare that we have an opportunity to talk to someone such as yourself. *It's very rare that we have an opportunity to talk to someone like you.*

**such is the case** *so it is.* • Such is the case with an individual who is considered a high potential in a semiconductor firm. *So it is with an individual who is considered a high potential in a semiconductor firm.*

**suddenly and without warning** *suddenly; without warning.* • Survivors said the pier in Butterworth, 180 miles northwest of Kuala Lumpur, collapsed suddenly and without warning yesterday. *Survivors said the pier in Butterworth, 180 miles northwest of Kuala Lumpur, collapsed suddenly yesterday.*

**sufficient (sufficiently)** *due (duly); enough.* • Bright ideas alone are not sufficient. *Bright ideas alone are not enough.* • Since responsibility is assigned not to individuals but to the group, members may not devote sufficient time and effort to the task. *Since responsibility is assigned not to individuals but to the group, members may not devote due time and effort to the task.*

**(a; the) sufficient amount (of)** *due; enough.* • It's time we include a sufficient amount of money in the state budget for snow removal. *It's time we include enough money in the state budget for snow removal.*

**sufficient (sufficiently) enough** *duly; enough.* • There may be an economy of scale if the outcome is sufficiently rigorous enough to warrant the state's participation. *There may be an economy of scale if the outcome is sufficiently rigorous to warrant the state's participation.*

**symmetrical** *symmetric.* • If one of the functions is symmetrical, then reflection is unnecessary. *If one of the functions is symmetric, then reflection is unnecessary.*

**symptomatize** *symptomize.*

**systematical** *systematic.*

# T

**tailor-made** *custom; tailored.* • The event seemed tailor-made to give the vice president the upper hand. *The event seemed tailored to give the vice president the upper hand.*

**take account for (of)** *allow for; consider; provide for; reckon with; regard; weigh.* • But HMO officials say that current reimbursements fail to take account for medical inflation. *But HMO officials say that current reimbursements fail to allow for medical inflation.*

**take action (to)** *act;* delete. • If we are to save the right whales, we will have to take action. *If we are to save the right whales, we will have to act.*

**take . . . action (on; to)** *act -(al)ly;* delete. • The operator has to determine the cause of the deviation and then take corrective action. *The operator has to determine the cause of the deviation and then correct it.* • He issued a statement calling on the NRC to take immediate action to correct deficiencies identified in the report. *He issued a statement calling on the NRC to act immediately to correct deficiencies identified in the report.*

**take advantage of** *abuse; cheat; deceive; exploit; ill-treat; mistreat; misuse; use; victimize; wrong.* • He took advantage of her good nature. *He exploited her good nature.*

**take advantage of** *benefit from; gain; profit by; reap.* • There are several easy ways to take advantage of Fidelity's expertise in retirement planning. *There are several easy ways to profit by Fidelity's expertise in retirement planning.*

**take aim** *aim.*

**take a . . . look (at)** *consider; look; regard; view.* • We need to examine each, but let's first take a brief look at the foundations of management theory. *We need to examine each, but let's first briefly look at the foundations of management theory.*

**take a measure of** *approximate; estimate.* • The balance sheet yields financial data that can be used in various ratio calculations to take a measure of the company's financial health. *The balance sheet yields financial data that can be used in various ratio calculations to estimate the company's financial health.*

**take a stand against (in opposition to)** *contest; contradict; contrast with; differ from; disagree with; dispute; oppose; resist.*

**take a stand for (in favor of; in support of)** *back; endorse; favor; prefer; support.* • Delegates at the annual meeting of the American Medical Association took a strong stand in favor of abortion rights this week. *Delegates at the annual meeting of the American Medical Association strongly backed abortion rights this week.*

**take a (the) . . . view (of)** *consider; look; regard; view.* • Financial institutions can no longer take a passive view of product development. *Financial institutions can no longer regard product development passively.*

**take delivery of (on)** *receive.*

**take enjoyment in** *admire; delight in; enjoy; rejoice in; relish; savor.*

**take exception to** *challenge; complain about; criticize; demur; differ in; disagree with; dispute; find fault with; object to; oppose; protest; question; resent.* • I take exception to the statement: "Angiography is not only expensive but also painful and risky." *I disagree with the statement: "Angiography is not only expensive but also painful and risky."*

**take (a) hold of** *grasp; seize; take.*

**take into account** *allow for; consider; provide for; reckon with; regard; weigh.* • It fails to take into account the impact of the U.S. federal budget deficit on U.S. competitiveness. *It fails to regard the impact of the U.S. federal budget deficit on U.S. competitiveness.*

**take into consideration** *allow for; consider; provide for; reckon with; regard; weigh.* • His prior offenses, even though they were in a different state, can be taken into consideration by the court. *His prior offenses, even though they were in a different state, can be weighed by the court.*

**take into custody** *arrest; capture; catch; seize.*

**take issue (with)** *attack; challenge; contradict; demur; differ (with); disagree (with); dispute; object (to); oppose; question.* • He also takes issue with the state plan to pay. *He also opposes the state plan to pay.*

**take measures (to)** *act (to); delete.*

**taken by surprise** *startled; surprised.* • Everyone I talked to today was taken by surprise by his announcement. *Everyone I talked to today was surprised by his announcement.*

**take note (of)** *attend to; consider; hearken to; heed; listen to; mind; note; notice; observe; regard; see; tend to; watch; witness.* • The United States should take note of the percentage of technical graduates and lawyers in Japan's population. *The United States should note the percentage of technical graduates and lawyers in Japan's population.*

**take notice (of)** *attend to; consider; hearken; heed; listen to; mind; note; notice; observe; regard; see; tend to; watch; witness.* • Clouds in the extremely dry stratosphere were rarely sighted—mostly because they form near the poles only during winter and early spring, when darkness eclipses the sky and few spectators are around to take notice. *Clouds in the extremely dry stratosphere were rarely sighted—mostly because they form near the poles only during winter and early spring, when darkness eclipses the sky and few spectators are around to watch.*

**take offense (at)** *disagree with; dislike; object to; resent.* • I take offense at the *Globe*'s editorial ("Scorsese and the stone-casters") and will no longer sit by and watch the Christian-bashing continue. *I resent the* Globe's *editorial ("Scorsese and the stone-casters") and will no longer sit by and watch the Christian-bashing continue.*

**take pity on (upon)** *pity; sympathize (with).*

**take place** *happen; occur.*

**take pleasure in** *admire; delight in; enjoy; rejoice in; relish (in); savor.*

**take precedence over** *antecede; come before; forego; go before; precede.* • Criminals' rights take precedence over the victims'. *Criminals' rights come before the victims'.*

**take priority over** *antecede; come before; forego; go before; precede.* • He says that in women's shoes, fashion always takes priority over comfort. *He says that in women's shoes, fashion always precedes comfort.*

**take satisfaction in** *admire; delight in; enjoy; rejoice in; relish (in); savor.*

**take the position (that)** *assert; believe; claim; consider; contend; feel; hold; judge; maintain; regard; say; think; to; view.* • He takes the position that, as a meeting leader, you will be more effective if you view yourself "as the servant of the group rather than as its master." *He maintains that, as a* *meeting leader, you will be more effective if you view yourself "as the servant of the group rather than as its master."*

**take the view (that)** *assert; believe; claim; consider; contend; feel; hold; judge; maintain; regard; say; think; to; view.*

**take the wrong way** *misinterpret; misunderstand.*

**take to task** *admonish; chide; criticize; rebuke; reprimand; reproach; reprove; scold.* • He took the project's tenant leaders to task for their selection of an architectural consultant for the remodeling job. *He admonished the project's tenant leaders for their selection of an architectural consultant for the remodeling job.*

**take umbrage at (with)** *disagree with; dislike; object to; resent.* • Some people, such as the NRA, took umbrage with the message of the show. *Some people, such as the NRA, disliked the message of the show.*

**take under advisement** *consider; contemplate; reflect on; review; think about; weigh.* • Pillsbury's board is taking the franchisee group's protest under advisement. *Pillsbury's board is reviewing the franchisee group's protest.*

**take under consideration** *consider; contemplate; reflect on; review; think about; weigh.* • About 1 in 50 products is taken under consideration. *About 1 in 50 products is considered.*

**tell the difference** *discriminate; distinguish; tell apart.* • The reality is that science and technology have made it almost impossible to tell the difference between telecommunications and computers. *The reality is that science and technology have made it almost impossible to distinguish between telecommunications and computers.*

**temperature** *fever.*

**temporary reprieve** *reprieve.*

**temporary stopgap** *stopgap.*

**(my) tendency is to** *(I) tend to.* • Our tendency is to get up a little later each morning and go to sleep a little later each night. *We tend to get up a little later each morning and go to sleep a little later each night.*

**tense up** *tense.*

**term as** *term.*

**terminate** *cancel; cease; conclude; end; finish; halt; stop.* • Having no plan at all would be better than terminating one. *Having no plan at all would be better than canceling one.*

**test out** *test.* • At this point, you might want to test out our map by trying the following experiment. *At this point, you might want to test our map by trying the following experiment.*

**that (this) being the case** *consequently; hence; so; then; therefore; thus.* • That being the case, the only apparent remedy is for owners of family firms to begin early in earmarking shares of the business for their children. *The only apparent remedy, then, is for owners of family firms to begin early in earmarking shares of the business for their children.*

**that (the; this) business of** *that (this);* delete. • We've got to get over this business of seeing everything in cartoon terms. *We've got to get over seeing everything in cartoon terms.*

**that (this) fact** *that (this).* • The world beyond visual range is a haze of anxiety, and the most sophisticated radar sets in the world do not change that fact. *The world beyond visual range is a haze of anxiety, and the most sophisticated radar sets in the world do not change that.*

**that (which) happens (occurs; takes place) when** *when.* • What about the inevitable disappointment that happens when a child doesn't win a trophy? *What about the inevitable disappointment when a child doesn't win a trophy?*

**that is** delete. • This relates to the cost that is incurred by start-up firms. *This relates to the cost incurred by start-up firms.*

**that is (this is; which is) as much as to say** *namely; that is; to wit.*

**that is (which is) to say (that)** *namely; that is; to wit.* • That is to say, the person named by the testator in his will will normally be appointed by the court, despite lack of great intelligence or experience. *That is, the person named by the testator in his will will normally be appointed by the court, despite lack of great intelligence or experience.*

**that (this) kind (sort; type) of stuff (thing)** *it; that (this);* delete. • If there's a lot of that kind of thing, I will try to figure out whether things will stay depressed forever. *If there's a lot of that, I will try to figure out whether things will stay depressed forever.*

**that (this) juncture (moment; period; point; stage) in time** *(just; right) now; that (this) time; then.* • Not until that moment in time did I understand what being homeless meant. *Not until then did I understand what being homeless meant.*

**that (those) of -'s.** • Toronto's population is close to 3 million, which is slightly larger than that of Boston. *Toronto's population is close to 3 million, which is slightly larger than Boston's.* • As the more aggrieved party, the victim's rights must take precedence over those of the perpetrator. *As the more aggrieved party, the victim's rights must take precedence over the perpetrator's.*

**that (these; this; those) of** delete. • Another exercise is that of completing the views when some or all of them have missing lines. *Another exercise is completing the views when some or all of them have missing lines.*

**(of) that (these; this; those)** delete. • For those calculators that do not have a 10x key, the antilogarithm can be found by using the INV or 2nd key. *For calculators that do not have a 10x key, the antilogarithm can be found by using the INV or 2nd key.* • Those options with the word *patch* in their titles are especially complicated. *Options with the word* patch *in their titles are especially complicated.*

**that (this) time around (round)** *that (this) time; then (now).* • Such an outcome has a far higher probability this time around. *Such an outcome has a far higher probability now.*

**the above** *that; the; this.* • Please call me if you have any questions concerning the above. *Please call me if you have any questions concerning this.*

**the above-mentioned** *that (those); the; this (these).*

**the act of** delete. • The act of making sketches and writing statements about the problem helps to get the designer off dead center. *Making sketches and writing statements about the problem helps to get the designer off dead center.*

**the aforementioned** *that (those); the; this (these).* • Each of the aforementioned techniques can be used to solve a specific employee problem in the workplace. *Each of these techniques can be used to solve a specific employee problem in the workplace.*

**the aforesaid** *that (those); the; this (these).*

**the age of** delete. • It predicts a tightening labor market will force the hiring of more people between the ages of 35 and 45. *It predicts a tightening labor market will force the hiring of more people between 35 and 45.*

**the area of (the . . . area)** delete. • The main interest for me is the history area. *The main interest for me is history.* • These teams should be granted broad functions, with key roles being played by representatives from the engineering, manufacturing, marketing, and finance areas. *These teams should be granted broad functions, with key roles being played by representatives from engineering, manufacturing, marketing, and finance.*

**the (this) author (writer)** *I; me; my; our; us; we.* • Every word processing manual the authors have seen assumes you know what a hanging indent, widow, and running header are. *Every word processing manual we have seen assumes you know what a hanging indent, widow, and running header are.*

**the better part (of)** *almost all; most; nearly all.* • Manufacturers Hanover Corp. spent the better part of 175 years reaching the top of American banking alongside the Citicorps and Chase Manhattans. *Manufacturers Hanover Corp. spent most of 175 years reaching the top of American banking alongside the Citicorps and Chase Manhattans.*

**the biggest (greatest; highest; largest) amount (degree; extent; number; part; percentage; portion; proportion; quantity) (of)** *(the) most.* • The concept of calories has been well embedded in the minds of people throughout the largest portion of the twentieth century. *The concept of calories has been well embedded in the minds of people throughout most of the twentieth century.*

**the both (of)** *both.* • I saw the both of them on a talk show today. *I saw both of them on a talk show today.*

**the (great) bulk (of)** *almost all; most; nearly all.* • Unfortunately for the start-ups, though, a few major players have secured the bulk of the orders. *Unfortunately for the startups, though, a few major players have secured most of the orders.*

**the case** *right; so; true;* delete. • I think that's probably the case. *I think that's probably true.* • Such companies are often durable goods manufacturers, but this is not always the case. *Such companies are often durable goods manufacturers, but this is not always so.*

**the character of** delete. • He played the character of a picaro. *He played a picaro.*

**the city (town) of** delete. • In the city of Chicago, there are a lot of counseling centers. *In Chicago, there are a lot of counseling centers.*

**the color** delete. • I noticed the predominance of the color green in their costumes. *I noticed the predominance of green in their costumes.*

**the . . . company** delete. • In 1986, the Hitachi company displaced General Electric as the firm receiving the most U.S. patents. *In 1986, Hitachi displaced General Electric as the firm receiving the most U.S. patents.*

**the concept of** delete. • The following example illustrates the concept of correlation. *The following example illustrates correlation.*

**the condition of** delete. • British companies do not hesitate to go to the market with a share issue when the condition of the balance sheet warrants it. *British companies do not hesitate to go to the market with a share issue when the balance sheet warrants it.* • The condition of his health has deteriorated. *His health has deteriorated.*

**the continent of (the . . . continent)** delete. • Despite droughts, floods, wars, and low oil and commodity prices, the African continent as a whole is better off now than a year ago. *Despite droughts, floods, wars, and low oil and commodity prices, Africa as a whole is better off now than a year ago.*

**the country of** delete.

**the decade (period; period of time; span of time; time; years) between . . . and** *between . . . and; from . . . through (to); to.*

**the decade (period; period of time; span of time; time; years) (from) . . . through (till; to; until)** *between . . . and; from . . . through (to); to.* • The United Nations General Assembly recently declared the decade from 1990–2000 to be the International Decade of Natural Disaster Reduction. *The United Nations General Assembly recently declared 1990–2000 to be the International Decade of Natural Disaster Reduction.*

**the degree of** *how much; the;* delete. • The closer the value of $r$ to either extreme, the greater the degree of association. *The closer the value of r to either extreme, the greater the association.* • I am concerned with the degree of difficulty they're having getting the product out. *I am concerned with how much difficulty they're having getting the product out.*

**the degree to which** *how; how far; how much; how often.* • The GOP's principal concern is the degree to which the law would regulate child-care facilities nationwide. *The GOP's principal concern is how much the law would regulate child-care facilities nationwide.*

**the equal (equivalent) of** *equal (equivalent) to; like.* • The loss of 1 high-value customer was the equivalent of losing the business of 36 small-value customers. *The loss of 1 high-value customer was equivalent to losing the business of 36 small-value customers.*

**the existence of** delete. • The existence of even one extra, undocumented Write statement in a module may change what appears on a user's terminal. *Even one extra, undocumented Write statement in a module may change what appears on a user's terminal.*

**the extent of** *how much; the;* delete. • Most people know something about Social Security, but few know the extent of the monthly benefits they will eventually receive when they retire. *Most people know something about Social Security, but few know the monthly benefits they will eventually receive when they retire.* • Despite early campaign rhetoric, the extent of actual change a new treasurer would attempt is of course unknown. *Despite early campaign rhetoric, how much actual change a new treasurer would attempt is of course unknown.*

**the extent to which** *how; how far; how much; how often.* • The extent to which these facilitating and reconciling capabilities are needed, and how they are developed and structured, depends on the company's involvement in exporting or foreign marketing. *How much these facilitating and reconciling capabilities are needed, and how they are developed and structured, depends on the company's involvement in exporting or foreign marketing.* • Eastern cannot predict the extent to which its operations and financial results will continue to be affected by the negative public perception generated by the investigations. *Eastern cannot predict how its operations and financial results will continue to be affected by the negative public perception generated by the investigations.*

**the fact that** *that.* • This ignores the fact that increased use of kilowatts has significantly decreased our use of oil. *This ignores that increased use of kilowatts has significantly decreased our use of oil.*

**the fact is (that)** *actually; indeed; in fact; in faith; in truth; really; truly;* delete. • The fact is we have to deal with the public every day. *We have to deal with the public every day.* • The fact is that Mrs. Eddy doesn't advocate any kind of a positive thinking or "think good, feel good" philosophy. *Indeed, Mrs. Eddy doesn't advocate any kind of a positive thinking or "think good, feel good" philosophy.*

**the (simple) fact of the matter is (that)** *actually; indeed; in fact; in faith; in reality; in truth; really; truly;* delete. • The fact of the matter is you cannot copyright an idea. *You cannot copyright an idea.*

**the fact remains (that)** delete. • The fact remains we have the overwhelming support of the Christian and Jewish religions. *We have the overwhelming support of the Christian and Jewish religions.*

**(what is) the fashion (manner; way) (in which; that)** *how.* • What do you think about the fashion in which this testing program was introduced into the plant? *What do you think about how this testing program was introduced into the plant?* • More important than the sample's size is the manner in which the sample is taken. *More important than the sample's size is how the sample is taken.*

**the feeling of** delete.

**the field of** delete. • This process became known as Boolean algebra and is widely used in the fields of computing and philosophy. *This process became known as Boolean algebra and is widely used in computing and philosophy.*

**the foregoing** *that (those); the; this (these).* • On top of the foregoing, the recent legislation on extending mandatory retirement further heightens the concern about job performance in the later years. *On top of this, the recent legislation on extending mandatory retirement further heightens the concern about job performance in the later years.*

**the forenamed** *that (those); the; this (these).*

**the function of** delete. • The function of settling disputes requires the exercise of tact and concern for resolution of conflicts. *Settling disputes requires the exercise of tact and concern for resolution of conflicts.*

**the heart of the matter** *center; core; crux; essence; gist; heart; pith; substance; sum.*

**the history of** delete. • For the first time in the history of this century, the death penalty is extended beyond the borders of a single country, in spite of the laws of other countries. *For the first time in this century, the death penalty is extended beyond the borders of a single country, in spite of the laws of other countries.*

**the hows and (the) whys** *aims; causes; goals; motives; purposes; reasons.* • Our association has attempted to encourage proactive lending in low-income communities by working with the Fed to educate banks about the hows and whys of these investment opportunities. *Our association has attempted to encourage proactive lending in low-income communities by working with the Fed to educate banks about the aims of these investment opportunities.*

**the idea of** delete. • A large number of today's teens have actually thought about the idea of suicide. *A large number of today's teens have actually thought about suicide.*

**the interesting thing is (that)** *interestingly;* delete. • The interesting thing is that he never realized what he had done. *He never realized what he had done.*

**the issue of** delete. • We shall first consider the issue of plotting the historical series we want to analyze. *We shall first consider plotting the historical series we want to analyze.*

**theistical** *theistic.*

**the language of (the . . . language)** delete. • Twelve of his novels have been translated into the Russian language. *Twelve of his novels have been translated into Russian.*

**the last time** *last.* • A fifth bit acts as a flag indicating whether the file has been modified since the last time it was backed up. *A fifth bit acts as a flag indicating whether the file has been modified since it was last backed up.*

**the length of time** *how long; the time.* • The purpose of a network is to show all activities needed to complete a project and to enable the planner to calculate the length of time a project will take from start to finish. *The purpose of a network is to show all activities needed to complete a project and to enable the planner to calculate the time a project will take from start to finish.*

**the lion's share** *almost all; most; nearly all.*

**the long and (the) short** *center; core; crux; essence; gist; heart; pith; substance; sum.*

**the manifestation of** delete. • Looking first at managers, one once again sees the manifestation of the tendency toward caution with age. *Looking first at managers, one once again sees the tendency toward caution with age.*

**(what is) the manner (means; mechanism; method; procedure; process; technique) by which** *how.* • What is the means by which a nation can increase investment? *How can a nation increase investment?* • The manner by which the man ultimately inflicts himself on his companion is, of course, immaterial. *How the man ultimately inflicts himself on his companion is, of course, immaterial.* • We will now examine the process by which natural and global marketing activities are controlled. *We will now examine how natural and global marketing activities are controlled.*

**the medium of** delete.

**the method of** delete.

**the month of** delete. • Between the months of July and September, only three more ventured-financed firms went public. *Between July and September, only three more ventured-financed firms went public.*

**the more (most)** *more (most).* • Testing can answer which of these two models is the more appropriate. *Testing can answer which of these two models is more appropriate.*

**then and only then** *only then; then.* • I suggest that then and only then will people such as Mr. Becker realize that there really is no free lunch. *I suggest that only then will people such as Mr. Becker realize that there really is no free lunch.*

**then at that (this) juncture (juncture in time; moment; moment in time; period; period of time; point; point in time; stage; stage in time; time)** *then.*

**the nature of** *like;* delete. • Disagreement on the viability of standardization strategies also reflects varying interpretations on the nature of the environment facing the international company. *Disagreement on the viability of standardization strategies also reflects varying interpretations of the environment facing the international company.*

**the notion of** delete. • While not necessarily new, the notion of live-work developments is seeing a revival. *While not necessarily new, live-work developments are seeing a revival.*

**then subsequently** *then.* • Then subsequently he left Digital and started his own business. *Then he left Digital and started his own business.*

**theocratical** *theocratic.*

**the . . . of** *-'s.* • I needed the help of my mother to care for my child. *I needed my mother's help to care for my child.* • The task of the analyst is to find the coefficients *a* and *b* in Equation 2-2. *The analyst's task is to find the coefficients* a *and* b *in Equation 2-2.* • The failure to recognize expenses of this type can affect the profitability of a product. *The failure to recognize expenses of this type can affect a product's profitability.*

**theological** *theologic.*

**the one (that)** delete. • The one that seems to be the most popular is the use of the pull-down Mac menus for function keys. *The most popular seems to be the use of the pull-down Mac menus for function keys.*

**the one best** *the best.* • The emphasis of scientific management was to try to find the one best way by examining the way work was done, the sequence of steps, and the skills of the workers. *The emphasis of scientific management was to try to find the best way by examining the way work was done, the sequence of steps, and the skills of the workers.*

**(of) the opposite sex** *female; male; man; woman.* • He is abandoning his hemline indicator because it tended to offend too many investors of the opposite sex. *He is abandoning his hemline indicator because it tended to offend too many female investors.*

**theoretical** *theoretic.*

**the other way around (round)** *the opposite; the reverse.*

**the passage of time** *time.* • Meanwhile, the passage of time has made it increasingly apparent that last year's stock market crash was not the immediate precursor of a corresponding plunge for the economy. *Meanwhile, time has made it increasingly apparent that last year's stock market crash was not the immediate precursor of a corresponding plunge for the economy.*

**the practice of** delete. • Japan shares the United States' concern about the practice of using aid funds for export promotion. *Japan shares the United States' concern about using aid funds for export promotion.*

**the presence of** delete. • Mammography uses an X-ray technique to detect the presence of lesions, such as tumors, within the breast. *Mammography uses an X-ray technique to detect lesions, such as tumors, within the breast.*

**(of) the present** . . . *here; this;* delete. • In the present chapter, we introduce capital structure theories. *In this chapter, we introduce capital structure theories.*

**the present author (writer)** *I.*

**the present day** *(just; right) now; nowadays; the present; these days; today.* • Ever since MIT economist Rudiger Dornbusch first firmly broached the suggestion, the financial world has been absorbed in the resemblance between 1968 and the present day in macroeconomic terms. *Ever since MIT economist Rudiger Dornbusch first firmly broached the suggestion, the financial world has been absorbed in the resemblance between 1968 and today in macroeconomic terms.*

**the present-day** *nowaday's; the present's; today's.* • Discoveries, innovations, surprises, and complexities of the present-day South multiply beyond what it seemed possible for him to cover. *Discoveries, innovations, surprises, and complexities of today's South multiply beyond what it seemed possible for him to cover.*

**the principle of** delete.

**the problem of** delete. • Of all the approaches that can be taken to address the problem of fraud, the most important may be a demonstrated intolerance for the problem. *Of all the approaches that can be taken to address fraud, the most important may be a demonstrated intolerance for the problem.*

**the procedure of** delete. • Let's now look at the procedure of how teams are eliminated. *Let's now look at how teams are eliminated.*

**the process of** delete. • The process of selecting the proper school for your child can be hugely exciting. *Selecting the proper school for your child can be hugely exciting.*

**the purpose of . . . is to** delete. • The purpose of this view is to allow you to work on the outline's organization. *This view allows you to work on the outline's organization.*

**the question of** delete. • Corporate dividend policy deals with the question of how much of the firm's earnings should be paid to its stockholders in cash dividends. *Corporate dividend policy deals with how much of the firm's earnings should be paid to its stockholders in cash dividends.*

**therapeutical** *therapeutic.*

**the (this) reader** *I; me; my; you;* delete. • This book is meant to help the reader learn how to program in C. *This book is meant to help you learn how to program in C.* • This reader was dismayed by his cynical and narrow view of the public sector. *I was dismayed by his cynical and narrow view of the public sector.*

**thereafter** *later; next; then.*

**the reality of** delete. • Patients facing an ileostomy, colostomy, or urostomy must come to terms with the reality of the disease. *Patients facing an ileostomy, colostomy, or urostomy must come to terms with the disease.*

**the realm of** delete. • Brainstorming has broadened its appeal to the business world and has found widespread acceptance in the realm of business meetings. *Brainstorming has broadened its appeal to the business world and has found widespread acceptance in business meetings.*

**there exists . . . (that; who)** *exists;* delete. • This is true for current products where there exists a sales history. *This is true for current products where a sales history exists.* • There exist two kinds of photoreceptors in the retina. *Two kinds of photoreceptors exist in the retina.* • This means that either party has the right to terminate the relationship, whether or not there exists just cause for doing so. *This means that either party has the right to terminate the relationship, whether or not just cause for doing so exists.*

**therefore** *hence; so; then; thus.* • The front view is more descriptive than the top view; therefore, the front view should be dimensioned. *The front view is more descriptive than the top view, so the front view should be dimensioned.*

**the region of** delete.

**therein** *there.*

**there is . . . (that; who)** *is;* delete. • There are fifteen people in the group. *Fifteen people are in the group.* • There are millions of people who feel the way you do. *Millions of people feel the way you do.* • For every discovery that scientists make about Egyptian antiquity, there are hundreds that remain unsolved. *For every discovery that scientists make about Egyptian antiquity, hundreds remain unsolved.*

**thereupon** *later; next; then.*

**the role of** delete. • The role of research and development is crucial to the future of a nation's economic growth and to the future of an industry and an individual business. *Research and development is crucial to the future of a nation's economic growth and to the future of an industry and an individual business.*

**the same (thing) as** *equal to; like.* • Asserting that the deficit numbers "have no clothes" is not the same thing as saying that all is fine in the nation's economic affairs. *Asserting that the deficit numbers "have no clothes" is not like saying that all is fine in the nation's economic affairs.*

**the same exact** *just (the); the exact; the same.* • These are high-grade municipal bonds, the same exact ones that the banks buy. *These are high-grade municipal bonds, the same ones that the banks buy.*

**the same thing** *as much; the same.* • Looking back, I find I did the same thing. *Looking back, I find I did the same.* • Other rivals have discovered the same thing. *Other rivals have discovered as much.*

**the same way** *as; like.* • Normally when you make a printout, it looks the same way it does when displayed on the screen. *Normally when you make a printout, it looks as it does when displayed on the screen.*

**the scale of** delete.

**the scope of** delete. • The scope of the loss of control over one's body can only be understood through a personal experience. *The loss of control over one's body can only be understood through a personal experience.*

**the single best (biggest; greatest; largest; most)** *the best (biggest; greatest; largest; most).* • The single most important issue for women is equal pay for equal work. *The most important issue for women is equal pay for equal work.*

**the situation (with)** *right; so; the case; true;* delete. • This is often the situation with inexperienced managers, but it can be remedied with management training. *This is often so with inexperienced managers, but it can be remedied with management training.*

**the space of** delete. • Within the space of a few minutes, he was dead. *Within a few minutes, he was dead.*

**the state of** delete. • The state of Massachusetts is considering a similar law. *Massachusetts is considering a similar law.*

**the state of (the . . . state)** *the;* delete. • Consumers were more confident about the state of the economy in December than during the same month last year. *Consumers were more confident about the economy in December than during the same month last year.* • Many priests feel celibacy is no greater than the married state. *Many priests feel celibacy is no greater than marriage.*

**the sum of** *all*; delete.

**the time will come when** *at length; eventually; in due time; in the end; in time; later; one day; over the months (years); over time; someday; sometime; ultimately; with time; yet.* • The time will come when you will appreciate all I've done for you. *One day you will appreciate all I've done for you.*

**the topic of** delete. • He spoke on the topic of probate lawyers and fiduciaries at the recent ABA convention in Toronto. *He spoke on probate lawyers and fiduciaries at the recent ABA convention in Toronto.*

**the total (of)** *all*; delete.

**the totality of** *all*; delete. • If you look at the totality of votes cast, Jackson is very well off. *If you look at all the votes cast, Jackson is very well off.*

**the truth is (that)** *actually; indeed; in fact; in faith; in truth; really; truly;* delete.

**the truth of the matter is (that)** *actually; indeed; in fact; in faith; in reality; in truth; really; truly;* delete. • The truth of the matter is that glasnost and communism are incompatible. *In truth, glasnost and communism are incompatible.*

**the . . . use of** *using;* delete. • Would the use of these exacerbate the situation? *Would using these exacerbate the situation?* • This construction is performed with the use of a compass and a straightedge. *This construction is performed with a compass and a straightedge.*

**the way** *as.* • Look carefully at the results, and try to determine why they behave the way they do. *Look carefully at the results, and try to determine why they behave as they do.*

**the why and (the) wherefore (of)** *aim; cause; goal; motive; purpose; reason.* • We're going to be talking about the whys and the wherefores of his lead. *We're going to be talking about the reasons for his lead.*

**the year (of)** delete. • Nearly 2,500 years ago, in the year 500 B.C., the first object which could project an image was made in ancient China. *Nearly, 2,500 years ago, in 500 B.C., the first object which could project an image was made in ancient China.*

**(a; the) . . . thing** delete. • Censorship is a very dangerous thing. *Censorship is very dangerous.* • It's a very difficult thing. *It's very difficult.*

**thinking in (my) mind** *thinking.* • What were you thinking in your mind when you bought the two guns and the knife? *What were you thinking when you bought the two guns and the knife?*

**think to myself** *think.* • As they were yelling at me, I thought to myself, "These can't be my parents." *As they were yelling at me, I thought, "These can't be my parents."*

**thirdly** *third.*

**third of all** *third.*

**this coming** *next; this.* • This coming Wednesday we are having our town fair. *This Wednesday we are having our town fair.*

**those individuals (people; persons)** *people (persons); those.* • Only those people authorized to have access to information are allowed to see it. *Only people authorized to have access to information are allowed to see it.*

**through and through** *all through; completely; entirely; thoroughly; throughout; totally; wholly.*

**throughout . . . entire (whole)** *entire (whole); throughout.* • He was in trouble throughout his entire life. *He was in trouble his entire life.*

**throughout the length and breadth (of)** *all through; completely; entirely; thoroughly; throughout; totally; wholly.*

**through (throughout) the course (duration; length) of** *during; for; in; over; throughout; when; while; with.* • This report is our opportunity to share the insights we have gained throughout the course of the study. *This report is our opportunity to share the insights we have gained throughout the study.*

**through the medium of** *by; from; in; on; over; through; with.* • My basic interest is the lucid communication of ideas through the medium of print. *My basic interest is the lucid communication of ideas through print.*

**through the use of** *by; in; through; with.* • Verbal reasoning is the ability to think, comprehend, and communicate effectively through the use of words. *Verbal reasoning is the ability to think, comprehend, and communicate effectively with words.*

**through whatever (whichever) manner (means)** *despite how; however.*

**through what (which) means (mechanism)** *how.*

**throw into a rage** *enrage.*

**throw into doubt** *challenge; contradict; dispute; doubt; question.*

**throw into jeopardy** *endanger; imperil; jeopardize.* • The sale was thrown into jeopardy Friday when an FTC request for more information for antitrust appraisal pushed the transaction into 1989. *The sale was jeopardized Friday when an FTC request for more information for antitrust appraisal pushed the transaction into 1989.*

**throw into question** *challenge; contradict; dispute; doubt; question.*

**thusly** *thus.*

**till (until) after** *before; till (until).* • Do not delete the first code until after you have made the adjustments. *Do not delete the first code until you have made the adjustments.*

**till (until) the juncture (juncture in time; moment; moment in time; period; period in time; point; point in time; stage; stage in time; time) (that; when)** *till (until).* • Until the time that deposit interest rates were set free to seek levels dictated by the financial markets, the thrift business was uncomplicated. *Until deposit interest rates were set free to seek levels dictated by the financial markets, the thrift business was uncomplicated.*

**till (until) . . . then** *till (until).* • Until we realize that all addictive chemical substances are fair game in the war on drugs, then the war cannot be won, much less fought. *Until we realize that all addictive chemical substances are fair game in the war on drugs, the war cannot be won, much less fought.*

**till (until) the recent past** *till (until) lately; till (until) of late; till (until) recently; delete.* • Until the recent past, such courses were taken, often as electives, by advanced undergraduates who already had a certain degree of sophistication. *Until recently, such courses were taken, often as electives, by advanced undergraduates who already had a certain degree of sophistication.*

**time after time** *frequently; often; recurrently; regularly; repeatedly.* • Time after time, the Democrats have turned to the idea of raising taxes. *The Democrats have regularly turned to the idea of raising taxes.*

**time and (time) again** *frequently; often; recurrently; regularly; repeatedly.* • This has been demonstrated time and time again in their subsequent on-the-job experiences. *This has been repeatedly demonstrated in their subsequent on-the-job experiences.*

**(a; the) time frame (of)** *age; eon; epoch; era; interval; period; time; delete.* • Outpacing both, however, were the regional banks, which moved up 29 percent over the same time frame. *Outpacing both, however, were the* *regional banks, which moved up 29 percent over the same period.* • Some automotive assemblers can make every car to order, at a reasonable price and in a reasonable time frame. *Some automotive assemblers can make every car to order, at a reasonable price and in a reasonable time.*

**(a; the) time horizon (of)** *age; eon; epoch; era; interval; period; time;* delete. • Estimates are then made of the values of these factors over an appropriate time horizon. *Estimates are then made of the values of these factors over an appropriate time.*

**(a; the) time interval (of)** *interval; period; time.* • Float is the time interval between the time a check is written and the time it is finally taken from the check writer's account. *Float is the interval between the time a check is written and the time it is finally taken from the check writer's account.*

**time of day** *time.*

**(a; the) time period (of)** *age; eon; epoch; era; interval; period; time;* delete. • The Greek material is similar to stone tools from Hungary and Bulgaria dated to about the same time period. *The Greek material is similar to stone tools from Hungary and Bulgaria dated to about the same age.*

**(five) times over** *(five)fold.* • He was able to increase the conviction of drug traffickers five times over. *He was able to increase the conviction of drug traffickers fivefold.*

**(a; the) time span (of)** *age; eon; epoch; era; interval; period; time;* delete. • Over the same time span, the savings rate rose from 4.1 to 5.4 percent. *Over the same period, the savings rate rose from 4.1 to 5.4 percent.*

**time was when** *formerly; long ago; once.*

**tiny (little) bit** *bit; fragment; hint; piece; shred; speck; trace.* • I think Kroger management is just a tiny bit more relaxed than they were yesterday. *I think Kroger management is just a bit more relaxed than they were yesterday.*

**tiny little** *little; tiny.*

**(in order) to accomplish (achieve) that (this) aim (end; goal; objective)** *to that (this) end; toward that (this) end.* • To accomplish this goal, two special task forces were established. *To this end, two special task forces were established.* • In order to achieve that objective, Congress in 1985 authorized the Peace Corps to double its volunteers to 10,000. *Toward that end, Congress in 1985 authorized the Peace Corps to double its volunteers to 10,000.*

311

**to a certain (limited; some) degree** *in a sense; in part; less often; less so; more or less; partially; partly; rather; some; somewhat;* delete. • This depends to a limited degree on whether the company follows a global or a national strategy focus. *This partly depends on whether the company follows a global or a national strategy focus.* • You can intimidate umpires to a certain degree. *You can intimidate umpires somewhat.*

**to a certain (limited; some) extent** *in a sense; in part; less so; more or less; partially; partly; rather; some; somewhat;* delete. • These are two factors that women can control to some extent. *These are two factors that women can somewhat control.* • In Germany, and to some extent in Japan, our products are now priced competitively. *In Germany, and less so in Japan, our products are now priced competitively.*

**to a degree** *in part; more or less; partially; partly; rather; some; somewhat;* delete. • Any choice would have been controversial to a degree. *Any choice would have been somewhat controversial.*

**to a (the) . . . degree** *-(al)ly;* delete. • We have reduced our nuclear weaponry to a significant degree. *We have significantly reduced our nuclear weaponry.* • To a surprising degree, we find the outlook hopeful. *We find the outlook surprisingly hopeful.*

**to a (the) . . . extent** *-(al)ly;* delete. • It's a change that's already been worked out to a considerable extent at the local level. *It's a change that's already been considerably worked out at the local level.*

**to a great (large) degree** *almost all; chiefly; commonly; generally; greatly; in general; largely; mainly; most; mostly; most often; much; nearly all; normally; overall; typically; usually; well.* • Because the state will pay for the bulk of building and running the school, it will naturally be involved in the project to a large degree. *Because the state will pay for the bulk of building and running the school, it will naturally be much involved in the project.* • In Malaysia, imports are controlled to a great degree by a handful of European commission houses. *In Malaysia, imports are mostly controlled by a handful of European commission houses.*

**to a greater (larger) degree (extent)** *more; more often; more so.* • The risks of radiation are understood to a much greater degree than many other risks we take for granted. *The risks of radiation are understood much more than many other risks we take for granted.* • Black males suffer from debilitating health problems to a greater degree than males in other ethnic and racial groups. *More black males suffer from debilitating health problems than males in other ethnic and racial groups.*

**to a greater or lesser degree (extent)** *in part; in some way; more or less; partially; partly; rather; some; somehow; someway(s); somewhat; to some degree (extent); various; variously; varying; varyingly;* delete. • When people leave an organization, their departure results in a disruption that affects the remaining people to a greater or lesser degree. *When people leave an organization, their departure results in a disruption that variously affects the remaining people.*

**to a great (large) extent** *almost all; chiefly; commonly; generally; greatly; in general; largely; mainly; most; mostly; most often; much; nearly all; normally; overall; typically; usually; well.* • To a large extent, the success of any business venture depends on planning. *The success of any business venture chiefly depends on planning.*

**to a lesser (lower; smaller) degree (extent)** *less; less often; less so.* • Some have been dramatically affected by this pilgrimage; others to a lesser degree. *Some have been dramatically affected by this pilgrimage; others less so.* • It is only in Iowa and, to a lesser extent, in New Hampshire, that candidates meet so many rural Americans. *It is only in Iowa and, less often, in New Hampshire that candidates meet so many rural Americans.*

**to all appearances** *apparently; appear (to); outwardly; seem (to); seemingly; superficially.*

**to all appearances . . . appear (seem)** *appear (seem).*

**to all intents and purposes** *effectively; essentially; in effect; in essence; practically; virtually.*

**to all practical purposes** *effectively; essentially; in effect; in essence; practically; virtually.*

**to a major or minor degree (extent)** *in part; in some way; more or less; partially; partly; rather; some; somehow; someway(s); somewhat; to some degree (extent); various; variously; varying; varyingly;* delete. • All of us are involved in the writing of the shows to a major or minor degree. *All of us are somehow involved in the writing of the shows.*

**to an extent** *in part; more or less; partially; partly; rather; some; somewhat;* delete.

**to an increasing degree (extent)** *increasingly; more and more.*

313

**to a (the) point of** *to.* • The business is very close to the point of breaking even. *The business is very close to breaking even.*

**to a (the) point (stage) that (when; where)** *so (that); so far (that); so much (that); so that; to; to when; to where;* delete. • It got to the point where I didn't leave the house at all for fear of missing her phone call. *It got so that I didn't leave the house at all for fear of missing her phone call.* • Because of the mathematics involved, forecasting intimidates some managers to the point that they accept projections at face value. *Because of the mathematics involved, forecasting so intimidates some managers that they accept projections at face value.* • Her Parkinson's disease has progressed to a point where she is now semipsychotic. *Her Parkinson's disease has progressed to where she is now semipsychotic.*

**to be** *-(al)ly; to;* delete. • To be frank, I think their products are inferior to ours. *Frankly, I think their products are inferior to ours.* • To be successful, you must work furiously. *To succeed, you must work furiously.* • If tobacco were to be declared illegal, I would feel comfortable in predicting a black market in nicotine smuggling. *If tobacco were declared illegal, I would feel comfortable in predicting a black market in nicotine smuggling.*

**to begin (start) with** *first.* • To begin with, I never thought so many people would respond to such an intimate question. *First, I never thought so many people would respond to such an intimate question.*

**to be sure** *certainly; of course; surely.*

**to do** delete. • Saving money can be difficult to do. *Saving money can be difficult.* • I have to decide if I should retrace Sherman's route to the South as I originally planned to do. *I have to decide if I should retrace Sherman's route to the South as I originally planned.*

**to find (a) fault in (with)** *blame; criticize; fault.*

**together as a team (unit)** *as a team (unit); together.* • Here, in one location, specialists work together as a team to fulfill all aspects of a patient's needs. *Here, in one location, specialists work together to fulfill all aspects of a patient's needs.*

**together . . . in combination** *in combination; together.* • They can even be used together in combination. *They can even be used in combination.*

**together . . . in groups** *in groups; together.* • Although people around the world live together in groups and create their own cultures, in few cases does the intensity of human interaction approach the level found in prisons. *Although people around the world live in groups and create their own cultures, in few cases does the intensity of human interaction approach the level found in prisons.*

**together with** *along with; and; as well as; combined with; coupled with; joined with; paired with; with.* • Morgan proposed construction of a system of five reservoirs together with substantial channel improvements. *Morgan proposed construction of a system of five reservoirs coupled with substantial channel improvements.*

**to make (a; the) ... (about; of; on; with)** *to; to -(al)ly.* • I need to make a correction about something I said yesterday. *I need to correct something I said yesterday.* • I wanted to make a comment on his appearance. *I wanted to comment on his appearance.* • We will give the audience a chance to make inquiries about this. *We will give the audience a chance to inquire about this.* • I will do everything possible to make a thorough evaluation of your application. *I will do everything possible to thoroughly evaluate your application.* • I am eager to make a deal. *I am eager to deal.*

**to one degree (extent) or another** *in part; in some way; more or less; partially; partly; rather; some; somehow; someway(s); somewhat; to some degree (extent); various; variously; varying; varyingly;* delete. • Competition is present in nearly all of our markets to one extent or another. *Competition is present to some extent in nearly all of our markets.*

**to such a degree** *so; so far; so much; so well; such.* • Never have so many crucial issues confronting a president depended to such a degree on science and technology. *Never have so many crucial issues confronting a president depended so much on science and technology.* • The writings of Thoreau retain importance and vitality to such a degree that a century later they have had significant influence on the greatest leaders of our time. *The writings of Thoreau retain such importance and vitality that a century later they have had significant influence on the greatest leaders of our time.*

**to such an extent** *so; so far; so much; so well; such.* • He believes Americans are deluged to such an extent with health messages that they exist in a state of heightened health consciousness all the time. *He believes Americans are so deluged with health messages that they exist in a state of heightened health consciousness all the time.* • Young Sioux boys literally lived with their favorite horse and came to know it to such an extent that they commonly talked with their animals. *Young Sioux boys literally lived with their* *favorite horse and came to know it so well that they commonly talked with their animals.*

**to summarize (sum up)** *in brief; in fine; in short; in sum.*

**to take this opportunity** delete. • I'd like to take this opportunity to commend these women for their courage in sharing their stories. *I'd like to commend these women for their courage in sharing their stories.*

**total (totally)** delete. • He went totally bankrupt. *He went bankrupt.* • This person totally destroyed my career. *This person destroyed my career.* • I'm the total antithesis of my mother. *I'm the antithesis of my mother.*

**total up** *add; sum; total.* • When you total up the outside and inside executives, you get an overwhelming preponderance of board members with a managerial mindset. *When you total the outside and inside executives, you get an overwhelming preponderance of board members with a managerial mindset.*

**to tell (you) the truth** *actually; candidly; frankly; honestly; truthfully;* delete. • She was a very sweet, kind woman, but to tell you the truth, a few of us worried about her. *She was a very sweet, kind woman, but frankly a few of us worried about her.*

**to that (this) degree (extent)** *so; so far; so much; such.* • I didn't realize women could lose hair to that extent. *I didn't realize women could lose so much hair.*

**(something) to that (the; this) effect (that)** *affirming; claiming; conveying; declaring; professing; purporting; saying; suggesting.* • A call to its former office in Dallas resulted in a telephone company answer to the effect that "service has been disconnected." *A call to its former office in Dallas resulted in a telephone company answer declaring "service has been disconnected."* • He has never met him, and he produced witnesses to that effect. *He has never met him, and he produced witnesses professing that.*

**to the contrary** *but; conversely; however; instead; no; not so; rather.* • To the contrary, we found there's a strong tendency for counties that have high radon levels to have low lung-cancer rates. *Instead, we found there's a strong tendency for counties that have high radon levels to have low lung-cancer rates.*

**. . . to the contrary** *after all; apart; aside; despite; even with; for all; with all.* • Appearances to the contrary, he insists he doesn't plan to run for office. *Despite appearances, he insists he doesn't plan to run for office.*

**to the degree (that; to which)** *as far as; as much as; so far as; so much as.* • To the degree that Divi Hotels can do so, it has purchased distressed properties at discount prices and has then renovated them. *So far as Divi Hotels can do so, it has purchased distressed properties at discount prices and has then renovated them.* • Volume markdowns did not occur to the degree they did last year. *Volume markdowns did not occur as much as they did last year.*

**to the degree (extent) of** *up to.* • In the event of either a partial or total loss, the person is self-insured to the extent of one-third of the damage. *In the event of either a partial or total loss, the person is self-insured up to one-third of the damage.*

**to the extent (that; to which)** *as far as; as much as; so far as; so much as.* • To the extent that the distribution of income and wealth goes to the heart of a country's political ethic, the United States has grown unfair. *So far as the distribution of income and wealth goes to the heart of a country's political ethic, the United States has grown unfair.* • I help out here and there, but maybe not to the extent that she'd like me to. *I help out here and there, but maybe not as much as she'd like me to.*

**to the greatest (largest) degree (extent)** *as far as; as much as; so far as; so much as.* • NYNEX asked the judge to expedite consideration of the request to the greatest extent possible by ordering the DOJ to submit its response within 14 days under special procedures. *NYNEX asked the judge to expedite consideration of the request as much as possible by ordering the DOJ to submit its response within 14 days under special procedures.*

**to the point** *apt; pertinent; relevant.*

**to the purpose** *apt; pertinent; relevant.*

**to the tune of** delete. • It's the lagniappe that members of Congress collect (to the tune of $9.8 million in 1987) in return for talking to special interest groups with money to spend on them. *It's the lagniappe that members of Congress collect ($9.8 million in 1987) in return for talking to special interest groups with money to spend on them.*

**toward the direction of** *toward.*

**toward the east (north; south; west)** *eastward (northward; southward; westward).*

**to what degree** *how; how far; how much; how often.* • Privacy provisions in current law leave ambiguous to what degree such information can be shared.

*Privacy provisions in current law leave ambiguous how much such information can be shared.* • To what degree are you conscious of the theme as you write? *How conscious of the theme are you as you write?*

**to whatever degree (extent)** *however.*

**to what extent** *how; how far; how much; how often.* • What I would like to know is to what extent this is the result of reduced parental involvement in the child's upbringing. *What I would like to know is how much this is the result of reduced parental involvement in the child's upbringing.* • To what extent they carried that admiration, only they know. *How far they carried that admiration, only they know.*

**to what length** *how far; how much.* • We are shown to what lengths some will go to further their objectives. *We are shown how far some will go to further their objectives.*

**trace amount** *trace.* • He found trace amounts of chemicals in unrinsed containers, probably from the glue used to keep felt on the balls. *He found traces of chemicals in unrinsed containers, probably from the glue used to keep felt on the balls.*

**trace back** *trace.* • From dinosaurs to dogs, all land vertebrates trace their ancestry back to the water. *From dinosaurs to dogs, all land vertebrates trace their ancestry to the water.*

**track record** *record.* • He built the company into a fine organization with an excellent track record, until the last three or four years. *He built the company into a fine organization with an excellent record, until the last three or four years.*

**tragical** *tragic.*

**trained expert** *expert.*

**transvestitism** *transvestism.*

**trivial details (facts; ideas; information; matters; things)** *trivia.* • While withholding such seemingly trivial information as the astronauts' in-orbit menus might appear ridiculous, even that might provide some clues as to the timing of the launch. *While withholding such seeming trivia as the astronauts' in-orbit menus might appear ridiculous, even that might provide some clues as to the timing of the launch.*

**(a; the) true fact** *a fact; factual; the truth; true; truthful.* • That's a true fact. *That's a fact.*

**true to fact** *fact; factual; the truth; true; truthful.*

**turn and turn about** *by turns.*

**twelve midnight** *midnight.*

**twelve noon** *noon.*

**twenty-five (25) percent (of)** *one-fourth (of); one-quarter (of).*

**two twins** *twins.*

**type (of)** delete. • It was a small, compact type of car. *It was a small, compact car.* • It's not a premeditated type of act. *It's not a premeditated act.* • Dungeons and Dragons is a very seductive type of game. *Dungeons and Dragons is a very seductive game.* • I'm basically a creative type person. *I'm basically a creative person.*

# U

**unaccustomed to** *not used to; unused to.* • Adults and children who are unaccustomed to caffeine are more likely to be affected than the habitual consumer. *Adults and children who are not used to caffeine are more likely to be affected than the habitual consumer.*

**unbeknown (unbeknownst)** *unknown.* • Condominium loans were the favored product, but unbeknownst to the bank, the market for condos had already peaked. *Condominium loans were the favored product, but unknown to the bank, the market for condos had already peaked.*

**unconfirmed (unfounded; unsubstantiated) rumor** *rumor.* • The Committee on Standards suspended him for two terms and permanently marred his academic record on the basis of innuendo and unfounded rumor. *The Committee on Standards suspended him for two terms and permanently marred his academic record on the basis of innuendo and rumor.*

**under any circumstances (conditions)** *altogether; at all; completely; entirely; ever; fully; never; no matter what; not ever; utterly; whatever; wholly.* • I will not see him under any circumstances. *I will not see him at all.*

**under certain (some) circumstances (conditions)** *at times; every so often; for (in; with) some (of us; people); from time to time; now and again; now and then; occasionally; once in a while; on occasion; some; sometimes;* delete. • Why does fiber, which fights constipation, also cause constipation under some circumstances? *Why does fiber, which fights constipation, also at times cause constipation?*

**underneath** *below; beneath; under.* • Here was a perfect chance to demonstrate that the Square had not completely ossified underneath a layer of brick and limestone. *Here was a perfect chance to demonstrate that the Square had not completely ossified beneath a layer of brick and limestone.*

**under no circumstances (conditions)** *in no way; never; not; not ever; not once.* • Under no circumstances is it to be used or considered as an offer to sell, or a solicitation of any offer to buy, any security. *Never is it to be used* *or considered as an offer to sell, or a solicitation of any offer to buy, any security.*

**under obligation** *bind; compel; force; obligate; oblige; require; restrict.* • The lessee usually has the option to buy the auto at the end of the lease for the assumed residual value but is not under obligation to do so. *The lessee usually has the option to buy the auto at the end of the lease for the assumed residual value but is not obligated to do so.*

**under the weather** *ill; sick; unwell.*

**unfair and inequitable** *inequitable; unfair.*

**unfortunately** *sadly;* delete.

**unite into one** *unite.*

**unite together** *unite.*

**universal panacea** *panacea.*

**unless and (or) until** *till; unless; until.*

**unless . . . then** *unless.* • Unless we're prepared to say the Japanese are just smarter than we are, then we're looking at motivation and role models and parents encouraging kids to keep their options open. *Unless we're prepared to say the Japanese are just smarter than we are, we're looking at motivation and role models and parents encouraging kids to keep their options open.*

**unnecessarily** *needlessly.* • The Japanese countered that moving part of the wing production would unnecessarily drive up the costs. *The Japanese countered that moving part of the wing production would needlessly drive up the costs.*

**unnecessary** *unneeded.*

**unproven** *unproved.* • In the context of Western medicine, acupuncture is still unproven. *In the context of Western medicine, acupuncture is still unproved.*

**unsubstantiated** *baseless; groundless; unfounded.*

**until and (or) unless** *till; unless; until.*

**until such point (time) as** *until.* • Instead of a 50-percent pay raise, they should have a 50-percent pay cut until such time as they rule with honesty, integrity, and compassion. *Instead of a 50-percent pay raise, they should have a 50-percent pay cut until they rule with honesty, integrity, and compassion.*

• Discussions will continue until such point as I have something to show on paper. *Discussions will continue until I have something to show on paper.*

**(an; the) untold number (of)** *countless; endless; infinite; millions (of); myriad; numberless; untold.* • If state government fails to actively support one of the world's most promising industries, it will be letting an untold number of jobs and revenue dollars slip through its fingers. *If state government fails to actively support one of the world's most promising industries, it will be letting untold jobs and revenue dollars slip through its fingers.*

**up in the air** *unanswered; uncertain; unclear; undecided; unresolved; unsettled; unsure.* • Plans for an interview with Castro himself remain up in the air, according to a CBS News spokesperson. *Plans for an interview with Castro himself remain uncertain, according to a CBS News spokesperson.*

**upon** *on.* • Do you wish something of the sort had happened when the senate was called upon to ratify ABM? *Do you wish something of the sort had happened when the senate was called on to ratify ABM?*

**up till (until)** *till (until).* • I was a model up until the age of 19. *I was a model until the age of 19.*

**up till (until) that (this) juncture (juncture in time; moment; moment in time; period; period in time; point; point in time; stage; stage in time; time)** *so far; thus far; till (until) now (then); to date; up to now (then); (as) yet.* • Up until this point, he hasn't been able to show what he stands for. *Until now, he hasn't been able to show what he stands for.* • Up until this time, we have had one personnel director who took care of everybody. *To date, we have had one personnel director who took care of everybody.*

**up to a maximum of** *up to.* • If set to Yes, text wraps around the box (up to a maximum of 20 boxes per page). *If set to Yes, text wraps around the box (up to 20 boxes per page).*

**up to and including** *through.* • Every WordStar Professional command, feature, and function up to and including Release 5 is listed and described in detail. *Every WordStar Professional command, feature, and function through Release 5 is listed and described in detail.*

**up to a point** *rather; somewhat.*

**up to the current (present) (time)** *so far; thus far; till now; to date; until now; up to now; (as) yet.*

**up to that (this) juncture (juncture in time; moment; moment in time; period; period in time; point; point in time; stage; stage in time; time)** *so far; thus far; till now (then); to date; until now (then); up to now (then); (as) yet.* • Up to this point, we have discussed these motivation theories relating to the needs of the individual. *Until now, we have discussed these motivation theories relating to the needs of the individual.*

**upward(s) of** *more than; over.* • In 1984, Peru had upwards of 40,000 acres of coca plants; today, it has 600,000 acres. *In 1984, Peru had more than 40,000 acres of coca plants; today, it has 600,000 acres.*

**usage** *use.* • We project that ATM usage will increase to nearly 60 percent by 1995. *We project that ATM use will increase to nearly 60 percent by 1995.*

**usually but not always** *almost always; most often; nearly always; often; usually.*

**utility** *use; usefulness.* • This has resulted in the much needed return to utility of our long-idled bridge. *This has resulted in the much needed return to use of our long-idled bridge.*

**utilization** *use.* • Utilization of existing schools in a region could be optimized to reduce variances caused by local population fluctuations. *Use of existing schools in a region could be optimized to reduce variances caused by local population fluctuations.*

**utilize** *employ; use.* • If utilizing the master antenna system is impossible, we will devise a plan for running the cable within the building. *If using the master antenna system is impossible, we will devise a plan for running the cable within the building.*

# V

**(a) valuable asset** *(an) asset; valuable.* • The wasting of this valuable national asset, through neglect and privation, makes no sense. *The wasting of this national asset, through neglect and privation, makes no sense.*

**vantage point** *vantage.* • That it should do so is hardly surprising when one considers the unique vantage point from which he is able to view the historical scene. *That it should do so is hardly surprising when one considers the unique vantage from which he is able to view the historical scene.*

**various and sundry** *assorted; diverse; sundry; varied; various; varying;* delete. • There was a huge group of kids there of various and sundry ages. *There was a huge group of kids there of various ages.*

**various different** *assorted; countless; different; diverse; extensive; many; numerous; scores of; sundry; varied; various; varying.* • Couples have various different ways of splitting their money. *Couples have various ways of splitting their money.*

**verbalization** *speech; talk.*

**verbalize** *speak; talk; write.* • Request that those who call you regularly put their thoughts in writing instead of verbalizing on the phone. *Request that those who call you regularly put their thoughts in writing instead of talking on the phone.*

**very** delete. • It's a very tragic story. *It's a tragic story.* • The driving conditions are very treacherous. *The driving conditions are treacherous.* • I thought her performance was very memorable. *I thought her performance was memorable.*

**very much -ed (-en)** *much -ed (-en).* • I was very much concerned about that. *I was much concerned about that.* • Their efficacy as classroom texts would be very much improved if their pedagogical features were more plentiful. *Their efficacy as classroom texts would be much improved if their pedagogical features were more plentiful.*

**vestigial remnant** *remnant; vestige.* • We Americans have only a vestigial remnant of several basic industries—consumer electronics, photography, toymaking, and office equipment to name a few. *We Americans have only a remnant of several basic industries—consumer electronics, photography, toymaking, and office equipment to name a few.*

**viable** delete. • Having an affair is not a viable solution. *Having an affair is not a solution.*

**violent explosion** *explosion.*

**(a; the) vital . . . in (of; to)** *vital in (to).* • We have been very pleased with their performance and have found them to be a vital part of our operation. *We have been very pleased with their performance and have found them to be vital to our operation.*

**vital necessity** *necessity; vital.*

**vocalize** *express; say; state; tell; voice.*

**voice . . . (about; for; of; to)** delete. • They voiced doubt that trees will prove to be a bigger source of hydrocarbons than cars in most cities. *They doubted that trees will prove to be a bigger source of hydrocarbons than cars in most cities.* • He voiced strong support for the international effort to make ISDN the universally accepted worldwide network of the future. *He strongly supported the international effort to make ISDN the universally accepted worldwide network of the future.*

**voice concern (about)** *agonize (about; over); brood (on; over); dread; fear; fret (about; over); regret; stew (about; over); worry (about; over).* • U.S. officials have voiced concern about possible Chinese sales of newly developed short-range M-9 missiles elsewhere in the Middle East. *U.S. officials have worried about possible Chinese sales of newly developed short-range M-9 missiles elsewhere in the Middle East.*

**voice opposition to** *contest; criticize; disagree with; disapprove of; dispute; object to; oppose; protest.* • Congress in 1986 passed the Montgomery Amendment after several governors voiced opposition to the Reagan administration's Central American policy. *Congress in 1986 passed the Montgomery Amendment after several governors objected to the Reagan administration's Central American policy.*

**voice skepticism (about)** *disbelieve; distrust; doubt; mistrust; question.*

**voice sorrow (about)** *bemoan; deplore; grieve; lament; moan; mourn; regret.*

**wage (a; the)** ... delete. • The report notes that the state has been waging a battle against drugs for several years. *The report notes that the state has been battling against drugs for several years.*

**wait around** *wait.* • The key customers are not going to wait around while those issues get resolved. *The key customers are not going to wait while those issues get resolved.*

**want to have** *want.* • We don't want to have the drug in our formulary unless it has a superior patient care advantage. *We don't want the drug in our formulary unless it has a superior patient care advantage.*

**warn in advance** *warn.*

**(the) way (in which)** *how;* delete. • This overview should give you a feel for the way these programs work and the way you can use them. *This overview should give you a feel for how these programs work and how you can use them.* • That's the way people can reduce their blood pressure. *That's how people can reduce their blood pressure.*

**ways and means** *means; methods; ways.*

**weather conditions** *weather.* • The adverse weather conditions on Saturday postponed the running of the race until a day later. *The adverse weather on Saturday postponed the running of the race until a day later.*

**weld together** *weld.* • They manufactured their samples by welding together two single-crystal gold films. *They manufactured their samples by welding two single-crystal gold films.*

**(all) well and fine (good)** *all right; fine; good; great; nice; pleasant; pleasing; welcome; well.* • Variety and customization are well and good, but they are low on most consumers' lists of priorities. *Variety and customization are nice, but they are low on most consumers' lists of priorities.*

**were it not for** *but for; except for.*

**what appears (seems) to be** *apparent; seeming.* • Manchester police also said a bottle of nonprescription pills was found in the room along with what appeared to be a suicide note. *Manchester police also said a bottle of nonprescription pills was found in the room along with an apparent suicide note.*

**what . . . for** *why.* • What did you do that for? *Why did you do that?*

**what . . . happens (occurs; results; takes place) is (that)** delete. • What happens with motherhood is you rarely repeat the problems of your own mother. *With motherhood you rarely repeat the problems of your own mother.* • What happens, again and again, is that people with good intentions falter. *Again and again, people with good intentions falter.*

**what have you** *whatnot.*

**what in God's (heaven's) name** *whatever; what ever.* • What in God's name does it have to do with the subject of business? *Whatever does it have to do with the subject of business?*

**what in the world (on earth)** *whatever; what ever.* • What on earth are you talking about? *Whatever are you talking about?*

**what is . . . (is that)** *-(al)ly;* delete. • What we need is a way to go directly to the partition block. *We need a way to go directly to the partition block.* • What we hope to do is increase our inventory and decrease our costs. *We hope to increase our inventory and decrease our costs.* • What we have described is a typical, hierarchical, central-processor-based, on-line architecture. *We have described a typical, hierarchical, central-processor-based, on-line architecture.* • What is not so clear or commonly accepted is the scope and nature of these obligations. *Not so clear or commonly accepted is the scope and nature of these obligations.*

**what is called (known as; named; referred to as; termed)** delete. • Many municipal and rural developments are located within what is referred to as the flood plain. *Many municipal and rural developments are located within the flood plain.*

**what is the time frame (time horizon; time period; time span) in which (of)** *when.* • What was the time frame in which you had your relationship with President Kennedy? *When did you have your relationship with President Kennedy?*

**what is the likelihood (probability) (of)** *how likely (probable).* • What is the likelihood of that? *How likely is that?*

**what (whatever; which; whichever) one(s)** *what (whatever; which; whichever).* • Which one would be accomplished better or faster with the help of a computer? *Which would be accomplished better or faster with the help of a computer?* • Whichever one you select, it will be an improvement on the one you now have. *Whichever you select, it will be an improvement on the one you now have.*

**whatsoever** *at all; whatever.* • As far as I'm concerned, twins have no ESP ability whatsoever. *As far as I'm concerned, twins have no ESP ability whatever.*

**what with** *with.* • What with the constant change in today's world, financial plans must be continually updated. *With the constant change in today's world, financial plans must be continually updated.*

**when all is said and done** *all in all; all things considered; all told; altogether; in all; on the whole; overall.* • When all is said and done, Mr. Marshall emerges as a monster by anyone's standards. *All in all, Mr. Marshall emerges as a monster by anyone's standards.*

**when and as** *as; when.* • Late payments are subject to a late-payment charge of 1½ percent per month, and the advertisers agree to pay any such late-payment penalty when and as billed by the publisher. *Late payments are subject to a late-payment charge of 1½ percent per month, and the advertisers agree to pay any such late-payment penalty when billed by the publisher.*

**when and (or) if** *if; when.* • So when and if the discount rate is charged, it could well be interpreted on Wall Street as nothing more than a "catch-up" move. *So if the discount rate is charged, it could well be interpreted on Wall Street as nothing more than a "catch-up" move.*

**when and (or) whether** *if; when; whether.*

**when, as, and if** *if; when.*

**when compared to (with)** *against; alongside; beside; compared to (with); -(i)er than; less; less than; more; more than; next to; over; than; to; versus; vis-à-vis.* • There is a 23 percent higher suicide rate of Vietnam veterans when compared to other persons in the same age group. *There is a 23 percent higher suicide rate of Vietnam veterans compared to other persons in the same age group.* • IBM is expected to price the line aggressively, when compared to the competition. *IBM is expected to price the line more aggressively than the competition.*

**when (a; the) . . . done (finished; over; through)** *after.*

**when it (you) comes (gets) right down to it** *all in all; all things considered; all told; altogether; in all; on the whole; overall.*

**when it comes to** *about; as for; as to; concerning; for; in; of; on; over; regarding; respecting; to; toward; when; with;* delete. • She's very shy when it comes to performing in front of an audience. *She's very shy about performing in front of an audience.* • Employers, employees, and society are often in conflict when it comes to dealing with five key issues facing them today in the workplace. *Employers, employees, and society are often in conflict over dealing with five key issues facing them today in the workplace.*

**when measured against** *against; alongside; beside; compared to (with); -(i)er than; less; less than; more; more than; next to; over; than; to; versus; vis-à-vis.* • The size of the Pennwalt takeover offer isn't large when measured against the multibillion-dollar bidding wars that have reshaped 1988 as the year of unprecedented megadeals. *The size of the Pennwalt takeover offer isn't large alongside the multibillion-dollar bidding wars that have reshaped 1988 as the year of unprecedented megadeals.*

**whensoever** *whenever.*

**when . . . then** *when.* • When the detector no longer sounds, then you know you have reached safety. *When the detector no longer sounds, you know you have reached safety.*

**whereabouts** *where.*

**where . . . at** *where.* • We don't really know where we are at. *We don't really know where we are.*

**wherefore** *why.*

**where . . . is concerned** *about; as for; as to; concerning; for; in; of; on; over; regarding; respecting; to; toward; with;* delete. • Bank customers are often less venturesome where their money is concerned. *Bank customers are often less venturesome with their money.* • Keep in mind that bigger isn't necessarily better where information is concerned. *Regarding information, keep in mind that bigger isn't necessarily better.* • It's beginning to show signs of weakness where demand is concerned, but that's true everywhere. *It's beginning to show signs of weakness in demand, but that's true everywhere.*

**wheresoever** *wherever.*

**where . . . to** *where.*

**whereupon** *whereon.*

**wherewithal** *assets; cash; funds; means; money; supplies.* • He added that the Minnesotan also has the wherewithal to shore up finances during bad times. *He added that the Minnesotan also has the cash to shore up finances during bad times.*

**whether** *if.* • A patent can be granted only after the PTO examiners have searched existing patents to determine whether the invention has been previously patented. *A patent can be granted only after the PTO examiners have searched existing patents to determine if the invention has been previously patented.*

**whether and (or) when** *if; when; whether.*

**whether or not** *if; whether.* • With so many choices, the question is not whether or not to buy a server but what to implement as a server. *With so many choices, the question is not whether to buy a server but what to implement as a server.*

**which is** delete. • There's a certain enzyme which is lacking in their systems. *There's a certain enzyme lacking in their systems.* • Tandy Corp., which is probably the largest U.S. distributor of small business systems, also sells personal computers in its stores. *Tandy Corp., probably the largest U.S. distributor of small business systems, also sells personal computers in its stores.* • The Moscow Papyrus dealt with solving practical problems which are related to geometry, food preparation, and grain allowance. *The Moscow Papyrus dealt with solving practical problems related to geometry, food preparation, and grain allowance.*

**whichsoever** *whichever.*

**while at the same time** *as; at the same time; while.* • So the objective of the game within the Administration was to finesse the longer-term implications of SDI while at the same time manipulating the shorter-term impact of the program in such a way as either to advance arms control or to stop it in its tracks. *So the objective of the game within the Administration was to finesse the longer-term implications of SDI while manipulating the shorter-term impact of the program in such a way as either to advance arms control or to stop it in its tracks.* • Women's colleges are offering women innovative programs, while at the same time they are opening doors for minorities.

*Women's colleges are offering women innovative programs, as they are opening doors for minorities.*

**while concurrently** *as; while.* • Researchers joined development projects for one month and participated in interface design while concurrently interviewing other project participants and employees. *Researchers joined development projects for one month and participated in interface design while interviewing other project participants and employees.*

**while simultaneously** *as; while.* • While getting signatures, volunteers were simultaneously assessing the degree of support for my candidacy. *While getting signatures, volunteers were assessing the degree of support for my candidacy.*

**who in the world (on earth)** *who ever.* • Who in the world is that? *Who ever is that?*

**who is** delete. • The groups can vary from project associates to laymen who are unfamiliar with the project and its objectives. *The groups can vary from project associates to laymen unfamiliar with the project and its objectives.*

**whole (wholly)** delete. • Never in my whole life have I ever seen such a thing. *Never in my life have I ever seen such a thing.* • There's a whole plethora of new technologies emerging. *There's a plethora of new technologies emerging.*

**whomsoever** *whomever.*

**whosoever** *whoever.*

**why in the world (on earth)** *why ever.* • Why in the world would liberals oppose the idea? *Why would liberals ever oppose the idea?*

**(many) widely varying** *assorted; broad; countless; different; diverse; extensive; many; numerous; scores of; sundry; varied; various; varying.* • If a distributor bases its application programs on the Unix operating system, it can choose among many widely varying computers. *If a distributor bases its application programs on the Unix operating system, it can choose among various computers.*

**widow (widower) of the late** *widow (widower).*

**widow woman** *widow.*

**window of opportunity** *chance; opportunity.* • Interviews with government scientists and physicians suggest a critical window of opportunity was missed. *Interviews with government scientists and physicians suggest a critical opportunity was missed.*

**wintertime** *winter.* • In the wintertime, however, the sun's weaker rays generate less heat energy near the Earth's surface. *In the winter, however, the sun's weaker rays generate less heat energy near the Earth's surface.*

**-wise** delete. • He has a lot of sense, businesswise. *He has a lot of business sense.* • I don't know that that would be very effective, costwise. *I don't know that that would be very cost effective.*

**with a (the) thought of (to) (-ing)** *for (-ing); so as to; to.* • We assume that they wish to examine their consumption patterns with a thought to increase their savings rate. *We assume that they wish to examine their consumption patterns so as to increase their savings rate.*

**with a (the) view of (to) (-ing)** *for (-ing); so as to; to.* • All categories of terms have been reviewed and in some areas an entirely new approach has been adopted with a view to making the book more useful for the reader. *All categories of terms have been reviewed and in some areas an entirely new approach has been adopted so as to make the book more useful for the reader.*

**with few (rare) exception(s)** *almost all; almost every; most; nearly all; nearly every.* • With few exceptions, federal and state policies are not aimed at upgrading the technology of existing firms. *Almost all federal and state policies are not aimed at upgrading the technology of existing firms.*

**with increasing frequency** *increasingly; more and more.* • Women are dating younger men with increasing frequency. *More and more women are dating younger men.*

**without a (any) question (shadow) of a doubt** *certainly; doubtless; no doubt; surely; without (a; any) doubt.*

**without basis in fact** *baseless; groundless; unfounded.*

**without (a; any) doubt** *certainly; doubtless; no doubt; surely.*

**without equal** *matchless; novel; peerless; singular; special; unequaled; unique; unmatched; unrivaled.*

**without exception** *all; always; consistently; constantly; every; everybody; everyone; every time; invariably; unfailingly;* delete. • Without exception, consumers should be aware that caveat emptor is an understatement in this field. *Consumers should always be aware that caveat emptor is an understatement in this field.*

**without foundation** *baseless; groundless; unfounded.* • Most allegations of men abusing their children are totally without foundation. *Most allegations of men abusing their children are totally unfounded.*

**without number** *countless; endless; infinite; millions (of); myriad; numberless; untold.*

**without peer** *matchless; novel; peerless; singular; special; unequaled; unique; unmatched; unrivaled.* • He is the entrepreneur extraordinaire; he is without peer. *He is the entrepreneur extraordinaire; he is peerless.*

**without (a) question** *certainly; doubtless; no doubt; surely.*

**with reference to** *about; as for; as to; concerning; for; in; of; on; over; regarding; respecting; to; toward; with; delete.* • With reference to the stereo, I think she should have put it in storage. *Concerning the stereo, I think she should have put it in storage.* • With reference to your article on the World Bank, the Bank has no plans to issue commodity bonds or to make commodity-indexed loans. *As for your article on the World Bank, the Bank has no plans to issue commodity bonds or to make commodity-indexed loans.*

**with regard to** *about; as for; as to; concerning; for; in; of; on; over; regarding; respecting; to; toward; with; delete.* • The evidence is mixed with regard to the existence of an optimal capital structure. *The evidence is mixed on the existence of an optimal capital structure.* • With regard to the first rationalization, how can a manager know how far is too far? *As to the first rationalization, how can a manager know how far is too far?*

**with relation to** *about; as for; as to; concerning; for; in; of; on; over; regarding; respecting; to; toward; with; delete.* • There are conflicting reports with relation to the altitude of the Iranian airliner. *There are conflicting reports about the altitude of the Iranian airliner.*

**with respect to** *about; as for; as to; concerning; for; in; of; on; over; regarding; respecting; to; toward; with; delete.* • Something very interesting was said with respect to gender differences. *Something very interesting was said about gender differences.* • Each Licensee hereunder shall have the following rights with respect to the Licensed Software. *Each Licensee hereunder shall have the following rights concerning the Licensed Software.* • The floodway within communities that have adopted flood-plain regulations is usually subject to strong restrictions with respect to building. *The floodway within communities that have adopted flood-plain regulations is usually subject to strong building restrictions.*

**with the exception of (that)** *apart from; aside from; barring; besides; but for; except; except for; excepting; excluding; other than; outside of.* • With the exception of their paper, these studies found a link between financial structure and industry class. *Except for their paper, these studies found a link between financial structure and industry class.* • Overall, bears and other stuffed animals, with the exception of dinosaurs, are out. *Overall, bears and other stuffed animals, other than dinosaurs, are out.*

**with the exclusion of (that)** *apart from; aside from; barring; besides; but for; except; except for; excepting; excluding; other than; outside of.*

**with the intent of -ing (to)** *for (-ing); so as to; to.* • The Intra-Arterial Cardiac Support System 8000 is being designed with the intent to expand the use of nonsurgical cardiac support systems by providing significantly greater support to the heart than is possible with clinically available nonsurgical systems. *The Intra-Arterial Cardiac Support System 8000 is being designed to expand the use of nonsurgical cardiac support systems by providing significantly greater support to the heart than is possible with clinically available nonsurgical systems.*

**with the passage of time** *at length; eventually; in due time; in the end; in time; later; one day; over the months (years); over time; someday; sometime; ultimately; with time; yet.* • The distinctions that now exist between stationary and mobile communications will disappear with the passage of time. *The distinctions that now exist between stationary and mobile communications will ultimately disappear.* • He did not improve with the passage of time. *He did not improve over time.*

**with the purpose of -ing** *for (-ing); so as to; to.* • The writer wrote the article with the purpose of teaching American businesspeople about Japanese gifts. *The writer wrote the article to teach American businesspeople about Japanese gifts.*

**with the result (that)** *so (that).*

**worthy of attention** *considerable; newsworthy; noteworthy.* • To give the media pride of place reinforces the impression that any event is worthy of attention only to the extent that a cameraman is blocking our view. *To give the media pride of place reinforces the impression that any event is noteworthy only to the extent that a cameraman is blocking our view.*

**worthy of blame** *blamable; blameworthy.*

**worthy of commendation** *admirable; commendable; praiseworthy.* • The fact that her article presents the Palestinian as well as the Israeli viewpoint is worthy of commendation. *The fact that her article presents the Palestinian as well as the Israeli viewpoint is commendable.*

**worthy of (my) consideration** *considerable; newsworthy; noteworthy.* • As a critical reader, you will be able to recognize ideas that are accurate, logical, and worthy of consideration. *As a critical reader, you will be able to recognize ideas that are accurate, logical, and considerable.*

**worthy of gratitude (thanks)** *thankworthy.*

**worthy of note** *considerable; newsworthy; noteworthy; outstanding.* • One change worthy of note has been made in the condominium form. *One noteworthy change has been made in the condominium form.*

**worthy of praise** *admirable; commendable; praiseworthy.*

**worthy of trust** *honest; trustworthy.*

**would appear (guess; hope; imagine; seem; submit; suggest; suspect; think)** *appear (guess; hope; imagine; seem; submit; suggest; suspect; think).* • I would suspect that the greatest gains would be from teaching the existing users to make even better use of current machines. *I suspect that the greatest gains would be from teaching the existing users to make even better use of current machines.* • I would hope that's what he meant. *I hope that's what he meant.* • I would submit that a number of shaky S&Ls could be salvaged over the next few years. *I submit that a number of shaky S&Ls could be salvaged over the next few years.*

**written communication (correspondence)** *correspondence; letter; memo; note; report.* • Written correspondence is answered within a week, and phone calls are returned within 24 hours. *Letters are answered within a week, and phone calls are returned within 24 hours.*

# X Y Z

**x-ray photograph** *x-ray.*

**year in (and) year out** *annually; always; ceaselessly; consistently; constantly; endlessly; eternally; everlastingly; every year; forever; invariably; never ending; perpetually; routinely; unfailingly; yearly.* • Eighty percent of what retailers are ordering are classic lines whose demand is stable year in and year out. *Eighty percent of what retailers are ordering are classic lines whose demand is always stable.*

**years (old)** delete. • The study began in 1981–82 with a statewide survey of a sample of women 45 to 55 years old. *The study began in 1981–82 with a statewide survey of a sample of women 45 to 55.*

**years of age** delete. • I have committed my life to public service since I was 29 years of age. *I have committed my life to public service since I was 29.*

**yell and scream** *scream; yell.* • My wife and I yell and scream at each other about a lot of things, and we have a very healthy marriage. *My wife and I yell at each other about a lot of things, and we have a very healthy marriage.*

**you know?** delete.

**you know what I mean?** delete.

**you know what I'm saying?** delete.

**young child (infant)** *child (infant); young.*

**zero in on** *focus on; pinpoint.* • It zeroes in on the problem of how expectations are formed—and changed. *It pinpoints the problem of how expectations are formed—and changed.*

**zoological** *zoologic.*

**zoological garden** *zoo.*

# About the Author

Robert Hartwell Fiske, who writes "Not only will *The Writer's Digest Dictionary of Concise Writing* help you write and speak more clearly, it will help you understand humankind more keenly," is the owner of Vocabula Communications Company, a writing and editing service in Andover, Massachusetts. Founded in 1986, Vocabula offers business and technical writing, copyediting, developmental editing, copywriting, keystroke testing, literary criticism and the like. Among Vocabula's many clients are Houghton Mifflin Company, Prentice Hall, The Benjamin/Cummings Publishing Company and The NETWORK, Inc.

# More Great Books for Writers!

**The 30-Minute Writer**—Write short, snappy articles that make editors sit up and take notice. Full-time freelancer Connie Emerson reveals the many types of quickly written articles you can sell—from miniprofiles and one-pagers to personal essays. You'll also learn how to match your work to the market as you explore methods for expanding from short articles to columns, and even books! *#10489/$14.99/256 pages/paperback*

**Writer's Encyclopedia, Third Edition**—Rediscover this popular writer's reference—now with information about electronic resources, plus more than 100 new entries. You'll find facts, figures, definitions and examples designed to answer questions about every discipline connected with writing and help you convey a professional image. *#10464/$22.99/560 pages/62 b&w illus.*

**Discovering the Writer Within: 40 Days to More Imaginative Writing**—Uncover the creative individual inside who will, with encouragement, turn secret thoughts and special moments into enduring words. You'll learn how to find something exciting in unremarkable places; write punchy first sentences for imaginary stories; give a voice to inanimate objects and much more! *#10472/$14.99/192 pages/paperback*

**The Writer's Digest Sourcebook for Building Believable Characters**—Create unforgettable characters as you "attend" a roundtable where six novelists reveal their approaches to characterization. You'll probe your characters' backgrounds, beliefs and desires with a fill-in-the-blanks questionnaire. And a thesaurus of characteristics will help you develop the many other features no character should be without. *#10463/$17.99/288 pages*

**How to Write Attention-Grabbing Query & Cover Letters**—Use the secrets Wood reveals to write queries perfectly tailored, too good to turn down! In this guidebook, you will discover why boldness beats blandness in queries every time, ten basics you *must* have in your article queries, ten query blunders that can destroy publication chances and much more. *#10462/$17.99/208 pages*

**Writing to Sell**—You'll discover high-quality writing and marketing counsel in this classic writing guide from well-known agent Scott Meredith. His timeless advice will guide you along the professional writing path as you get help with creating characters, plotting a novel, placing your work, formatting a manuscript, deciphering a publishing contract—even combating a slump! *#10476/$17.99/240 pages*

**How to Write Fast (While Writing Well)**—Discover what makes a story and what it takes to research and write one. Then, learn step by step how to cut wasted time and effort by planning interviews for maximum results, beating writer's block with effective plotting, getting the most information from traditional library research and online computer databases and much more! Plus, a complete chapter loaded with tricks and tips for faster writing. *#10473/$15.99/208 pages/paperback*

**The Writer's Digest Handbook of Magazine Article Writing**—This handbook is a valuable guide to every type of magazine article writing, featuring more than 35 chapters of writing and marketing instruction. Practical instructions are included to guide you through the development, proposal and manuscript preparation process. *#10171/$12.99/248 pages/paperback*

**1996 Novel & Short Story Writer's Market**—Get published with over 1,900 markets, contests, conferences, writers' colonies and other opportunities for fiction writers. Plus get loads of advice in the form of articles and interviews from some of the biggest names in writing. *#10441/$22.99/624 pages*

**The Writer's Ultimate Research Guide**—Save research time and frustration with the help of this guide. 352 information-packed pages will point you straight to the information you need to create better, more accurate fiction and nonfiction. With hundreds of listings of books and databases, each entry reveals how current the information is, what the content and organization is like and much more! *#10447/$19.99/352 pages*

**Make Your Words Work**—Loaded with samples and laced with exercises, this guide will help you clean up your prose, refine your style, strengthen your descriptive powers, bring music to your words and much more! *#10399/$14.99/304 pages/paperback*

**How to Write Like an Expert About Anything**—Find out how to use new technology and traditional research methods to get the information you need; envision new markets and write proposals that sell; find and interview experts on any topic and much more! *#10449/$17.99/224 pages*

**Freeing Your Creativity: A Writer's Guide**—Discover how to escape the traps that stifle your creativity. You'll tackle techniques for banishing fears and nourishing ideas so you can get your juices flowing again. *#10430/$14.99/176 pages/paperback*

**Writing the Blockbuster Novel**—Let a top-flight agent show you how to weave the essential elements of a blockbuster into your own novels with memorable characters, exotic settings, clashing conflicts and more! *#10393/$18.99/224 pages*

**1996 Writer's Market**—Celebrating 75 years of helping writers realize their dreams, this newest edition contains information on 4,000 writing opportunities. You'll find all the facts vital to the success of your writing career, including an up-to-date listing of buyers of books, articles and stories, listings of contests and awards, plus articles and interviews with top professionals. *#10432/$27.99/1008 pages*

**Getting the Words Right: How to Rewrite, Edit, & Revise**—Reduction, rearrangement, rewording and rechecking—the four Rs of powerful writing. This book provides concrete instruction with dozens of exercises and pages of samples to help you improve your writing through effective revision. *#10172/$14.99/218 pages/paperback*

**The Wordwatcher's Guide to Good Writing and Grammar**—Avoid embarrassing grammar mistakes with this handy volume. Freeman gives hundreds of examples to clarify word usage, meaning, spelling and pronunciation. *#10197/$16.99/320 pages/paperback*

**The Writer's Digest Guide to Manuscript Formats**—Don't take chances with your hard work! Learn how to prepare and submit books, poems, scripts, stories and more with the professional look editors expect from a good writer. *#10025/$19.99/200 pages*

**Write Tight: How to Keep Your Prose Sharp, Focused and Concise**—Discover how to say exactly what you want with grace and power, using not only the right word, but also the right number of words. Specific instructions and helpful exercises explain and demonstrate the process for you. *#10360/$16.99/192 pages*

**Writing for Money**—Discover where to look for writing opportunities—and how to make them pay off. You'll learn how to write for magazines, newspapers, radio and TV, newsletters, greeting cards and a dozen other hungry markets! *#10425/$17.99/256 pages*

**How to Write a Book Proposal**—Don't sabotage your great ideas with a so-so proposal. This guide includes a complete sample proposal, a nine-point Idea Test to check the salability of your book ideas, plus hot tips to make your proposal a success! *#10173/$12.99/136 pages/paperback*

**The 29 Most Common Writing Mistakes And How to Avoid Them**—Weak comparisons, too many adjectives, excessive self-expression—with clarity and good humor, Delton shows how to correct these and 26 other common writing mistakes to help you get published! *#10221/$10.99/96 pages/paperback*

**The Writer's Digest Handbook of Short Story Writing, Volume II**—Orson Scott Card, Dwight V. Swain, Kit Reed and other noted authors bring you sound advice and timeless techniques for every aspect of the writing process. *#10239/$12.99/252 pages/paperback*

**The Complete Guide to Writing Fiction**—This concise guide will help you develop the skills you need to write and sell long and short fiction. You'll get a complete rundown on outlining, narrative writing details, description, pacing and action. *#10158/$18.95/312 pages*

**30 Steps to Becoming a Writer and Getting Published**—This informational and inspirational guide helps you get started as a writer, develops your skills and style and gets your work ready for submission. *#10367/$16.99/176 pages*

**The Writer's Digest Guide to Good Writing**—In one book, you'll find the best in writing instruction gleaned from the past 75 years of *Writer's Digest* magazine! Successful authors like Vonnegut, Steinbeck, Oates, Michener and over a dozen others share their secrets on writing technique, idea generation, inspiration and getting published. *#10391/$18.99/352 pages*